by Jim Dietz

Those Who Flew

Aviation History of Thayer County Nebraska

Including

The Bruning Army Air Field
&
The First Modern Hot Air Balloon

Compiled by Virginia Priefert

TURNER PUBLISHING COMPANY
Paducah, Kentucky

The PX at Bruning Army Air Field. (Photo from Lorraine Doggett)

The PX - Coffee Shop and Soda Fountain. (Photo from Lorraine Doggett)

The Bruning Army Air Field Infirmary. Photo from Byron Behm.

Bruning Army Air Field Chapel. Picture from Tom Aamren.

Barracks — note the three coal stoves for heating.

TURNER PUBLISHING COMPANY
412 Broadway • P.O. Box 3101
Paducah, KY 42002-3101
270-443-0121

Copyright © 2002 Thayer County Historical Society
Publishing Rights: Turner Publishing Company
This book or any part thereof may not be reproduced
without the written consent of the Thayer County
Historical Society and Turner Publishing Company.

Turner Publishing Company's
Publishing Consultant: C.T. Spear

Library of Congress Catalog Control No. 2002106863
ISBN 978-1-63026-941-8

Printed in the United States of America. Additional
copies may be purchased directly from the publisher.
Limited Edition.

CONTENTS

Publisher's Message 5
Ballooning 10
Marv's Spruce Goose 56
Bruning Army Air Field 59
50 Mission Crush 126
Fighter Group 141
Air Field Plane Crashes 184
Naper 28 209
BAAF Marker Dedication 239
BAAF Personal Stories 249
Those Who Flew — Local Flyers 293
Effects of WWII on Homefront 336
Army Air Fields In Nebraska 351
Index 366

BIBLIOGRAPHY AND CONTRIBUTORS

Wonderful Contributors:
Jackie Williamson
Dorothy Skrivanek
Dorothy and James Bunker
Dewaine Ericson
Hollie Wilkes

Dick Downey
Pat Gentry
Dale Hueske
Larry and Vi Carpenter
Craig Fuller
Byron Behm

Books

Modern Aviation Library
"Final Report — One Man Hot Air Balloon…"
Pre-Astronauts — Craig Ryan
Hot Air Balloons — Christine Kalakuka and Brent Stockwell
"Aviation History" Magazine Sept. 2000
Tucson to Grotagglie — 449th Heavy Bomber Group
449th Bomb Group — Book III
Maximum Effort — 449th HB Group
Of Men and Wings — 449th HB Group
456th Bomb Group — 456th HB Group
"Air Force Combat Units of WWII"
"The Way it Was" Memories of Arthur Todd Rice
"Battle Stars" 464th Sqd. History of 507th Fighter Group
Nebraska History Summer/Fall 1995 "Nebraska Army Air Fields"
The Internet

Those Who Flew

Aviation History of Thayer County Nebraska
Including The Bruning Army Air Field
&
The First Modern Hot Air Balloon

Thayer County Historical Society Museum
Belvidere, Nebraska

Board Members of the
Thayer County Historical Society:

Jackie Williamson, Pres.
Virginia Priefert, Sec.
Lois Struve, Deshler
James Kenner, Hebron
Marsha Welch, Hubbell
Lois Ream, Alexandria

Steve Delay, Vice Pres.
Marilyn Russell, Treas.
Mary Bruning, Bruning
LaDonna Avers, Hebron
Nancy Baden, Alexandria
Daryl Ream, Alexandria

Publisher's Message

Dave Turner, Founder - Turner Publishing Company

It is a pleasure to present the history of flight in Thayer County, Nebraska, a twentieth century phenomenon with many unique historical events in what the world might imagine an unlikely place. Including aviators, balloonists, and Bruning Army Air Field, this is the story of those who flew.

The fine citizens who conceived this publication have brought it to birth as a sacrificial labor of love, providing a source of inspiration to all who will enjoy it. They and their generous benefactors have previously demonstrated their dedication to preserving Thayer County history by establishing the museum in Belvidere, Nebraska, and maintaining the ongoing work of the Thayer County Historical Society.

We are indebted to those who submitted photographs, stories, documents, news clippings, and other materials. Thayer County's strategic role in World War II, the losses of those whose land became the sites of the air field and gunnery, human interest stories and related fatalities make the book a compelling read.

The untiring contribution of Virginia Priefert, secretary of Thayer County Historical Society, who often burned the midnight oil, can not be overstated. Other key players in the project were Jackie Williamson, president; Steve Delay, vice president; Marilyn Russell, treasurer; LaDonna Avers, Mary Bruning, Bob Dill, Dewaine Erickson, Dale Harmon, Dale Hueske, Nancy Boeckman Kirk, Jacque Rocole, Lucile Thomas, and Kent Williamson.

As evidenced in over 900 titles of military, law enforcement, fire department, county, community, organization, association, and church histories and pictorials; as well as a host of other topics, Turner Publishing Company has become the leader in producing books similar to *Those Who Flew*, preserving stories of those who were there. Turner Publishing Company and C. T. Spear, a Nebraska native and consultant for this project, are committed to documenting history accurately in archival quality. With great honor, we add Thayer County, Nebraska's aviation, ballooning, and Bruning Army Air Field to our index of topics and catalog of titles as we present this volume, *Those Who Flew*.

Dave Turner

Dave Turner, Founder
Turner Publishing Company

About the Cover

"Euphoria"

"Euphoria" is owned by Rich Jaworski of Blair, Nebraska. It is the fourth red and white balloon Dr. Jaworski has owned named "Euphoria." In 1976, he flew his first "Euphoria" in Bruning, Nebraska at the Bicentennial German Volksfest. It was retired in the spring of 1977 with 200 hours of flight service as the fabric did not pass the required annual strength test. He had purchased it in 1972 for $4,200.

His fourth and present "Euphoria" was purchased in 1995 and after 360 hours of flight service the fabric is still as good as new because of better materials as technology progress. It is guaranteed for 500 hours but will probably last 1000 hours based on inspections of other balloons made of the Aerostar Diamond Weave fabric. This balloon lists for $25,000 in 2001.

"Lucky"

Lucky is Dr. Jaworsky's purple gorilla mascot. He has flown around the world as evidenced by pictures and mail received by his owner in Blair, Nebraska. He hitchhikes with other balloonists to go to other balloon events. Once he was gone for a whole year, but came back just as happy and silent as usual. He never tells!

"MAXIMUM EFFORT"

Lt. Colonel Hollie Wilkes (retired) and his wife, Exie, of Biloxi, Mississippi, commissioned the artist, Jim Dietz, to paint a picture commemorating the 50th anniversary of the 15th Air Force in WWII. This painting, which shows some of B-24 planes of the 449th Heavy Bomber Group returning after a bombing raid in Italy, is entitled "Maximum Effort."

In the painting, the B-24 named "Paper Doll" is in the foreground with her exhausted crew wearing their orange heat vests and dragging their flight bags. The pilot, Garrison, drags on a cigarette while the other officers are debriefed and queried about what planes were seen shot down with the number and position of the parachutes seen. Only if two men reported the same number would that report become official.

In the foreground, a jeep with "449th B.G." and "15th A.F." stenciled on the bumper waits to take the men to their quarters while the ground crew surveys the damage done to the number 3 engine. Hollie is represented as the Crew Chief standing on the wing of the plane with his hands on his hips. The ground crew must make the repairs through the night so that the plane is ready to go out on a raid the following morning.

On the muddy runway a second B-24, "Reluctant Liz" is taxiing into position. In the sky are 3 more planes. There is a space between the third and fourth plane representing a missing plane.

All the planes in the picture commemorate the seven B-24s which were shot down on April 4th, 1944 -- which has come to be known as 4-4-44. Five of those planes were from the 719th squadron. All were original planes flown off the Bruning Army Air Field in Nebraska.

Lt. Col. Wilkes and his wife, Exie, who was a McDowell and a native of Hebron, Nebraska, have donated a copy of this famous painting to the Thayer County Historical Society Museum in Belvidere, Nebraska. The Wilkes also gave a few extras to be sold to raise money for the State Historical Marker sponsored by the Thayer County Historical Society. Col. Wilkes has also donated to the Museum copies of the early attempts made by the artist Dietz to capture the mood, story and detail used to immortalize this moment in history. Mr. Wilkes paid Mr. Dietz $10,000.00 for this masterful painting. The original hangs in the Pentagon.

"Reluctant Liz" was so named because the pilot wanted his wife, Liz, to see what it was to go up in a B-24. He persuaded her to go although she was very reluctant to do this as she realized the consequences that would have to be paid if they were caught. Dressed in a smaller man's uniform, Liz waited until the guard went to the north end of the field and then ran to the plane hoping no one noticed this soldier was wearing high heels.

Liz had been staying with a farm couple near Bruning, and the farmer's wife was in her garden when the B-24 zoomed past her and she could see Liz waving to her. The excited farm wife told her husband she had seen Liz in the plane. Her husband said that it just couldn't be and the farmer's wife was later told not to report seeing this incident which "didn't happen." The plane carried the name "Reluctant Liz" because of Liz's reluctance to ride in it.

Those Who Flew
Bruning Army Air Field

"Maximum Effort"
by Jim Dietz

Jim Dietz was paid $10,000 for his masterful prize winning painting entitled "Maximum Effort." He made several attempts, however, before getting the final painting. Here are some of his rejected attempts:

Those Who Flew
Bruning Army Air Field
"Maximum Effort" Evolution

Lt. Col. (Ret.) Hollie Wilkes was in charge of maintenance of the 449th Bomb Group. He received a field commission after they arrived in Italy, from Bruning.

Hollie commissioned the famous military artist, Jim Dietz, to paint this picture that hangs in the Pentagon.

In the picture, Hollie stands on the wing of the plane with his hands on his hips as he determines if the crew from Maintenance should repair or replace the #2 engine.

Ballooning in Thayer County Nebraska

**Including:
Early Smoke Jumpers
Albert Santos-Dumont
"Ed" Paul Yost, Father of Hot Air Balloon
Story of First Hot Air Balloon
Picture of First Hot Air Balloon
Jim Winkler, Raven Ind.
Joe Kittinger, Balloon Record Holder
Outhaus Balloon Club
Story by Peg Hart, Organizer
Erection Granite Balloon Marker
Balloon Marker Dedication**

Ballooning in Thayer County
"Smoke Jumpers"

Annual County Woodman's Picnic
Hebron, NE   Aug. 22, 1907

At the Annual County Woodman's Picnic this hot air balloon ascension was featured on Aug. 22, 1907. The *Hebron Journal* reported that the ascension was very successful and the parachutist jumped from the balloon and landed before a nice crowd of people. The paper said this year's crowd wasn't as large as it had been in other years.

Those Who Flew
Chapter 1
Ballooning
"Smoke Jumpers"

Professor S. B. Hendricks will make a balloon ascension in Hebron on the 4th of July in 1898 according to the July 1, 1898 issue of the Hebron Journal. He is at work in the Gallant building making his balloon. It will require 692 yards of single width muslin or 346 yards of double width muslin. There are 20 sections sewed together with linen thread.

In another article it states that Prof. S. B. Hendricks gave a trial trip on Monday evening ascending 2000 feet directly over the city and made a parachute drop, alighting directly in front of A. C. Ring's house on second street. It was a quiet evening and everything was favorable for a successful ascent. The exhibition was thoroughly enjoyed by the people. He will make another ascent on the 4th of July for the public.

"Smoke Jumper" balloons were popular in Thayer County through the 1920's. The earliest picture that the Thayer County Museum in Belvidere, Nebraska has of one was taken at the Annual County Woodsman Picnic in Hebron, Nebraska on August 22, 1907. The **_Hebron Journal_** newspaper reported that the crowd of people for this annual picnic was smaller than had been on other years.

"The Largest Balloon in the West" appeared at the Woodman picnic in Hebron on August 19, 1910 with Prof. Daredevil Green appearing at 4:00. On August 26th the 14th annual MWA and RNA Lodge picnic had two successful balloon flights in Hebron. The empty area just west of the Courthouse was often used for these flights.

"Ed" Yost, the father of the modern day Hot Air balloon, said that "Smoke Jumper" balloons were made of cotton material, then rubbed with soot to make them hold air. According to Ed, the hotel people dreaded having Smoke Jumper balloonists stay in their hotel, as the balloonists would frequently tear up the bed sheets to patch their balloons. These balloons required a large fire. Many early balloonists thought the smoke made the balloon rise, not realizing it was the heat. When the smoke and hot air collected in the balloon, the balloon would rise. The balloonists, who nearly always called themselves "Professor," would go up in the tethered balloon and then jump out with their parachute before the amazed audience.

Chester Herald - Aug. 1910

Albert Santos-Dumont, born in Brazil and educated in France, used his wealth to develop and promote aviation. He pioneered lighter-than-air, and later, heavier-than-air machines. In 1903 he flew his airship seven miles from a Paris suburb, around the Eiffel Tower and back. For this he received world-wide acclaim.

Those Who Flew
Ballooning
Santos-Dumont

Alberto Santos-Dumont was an aviation pioneer in both lighter-than-air and heavier-than-air machines. He was born in Brazil in 1873 and was educated and lived in France. His parents were very wealthy coffee plantation owners and he spent his time and money developing a cigar shaped rubber airship, which was often referred to as "the rubber cow." This gas-tight covering was filled with hydrogen gas. It had its own motive power and could be steered by a crew-member riding a keel structure outside the hull.

In 1903 he flew his airship 7 miles from the Paris suburb around the Eiffel Tower and back again. For this he received worldwide acclaim. In <u>The Complete Book of Airships, Dirigibles Blimps and Balloons</u> by Don Dwiggens, he states that Santos-Dumont found he could make a fast buck by featuring his "Rubber Cow" at circuses and Carnivals. Ed Yost who has visited Santos-Dumont's home in Brazil felt Santos-Dumont didn't need any fast bucks as he was a very wealthy man in his own right. Santos-Dumont died in 1932 and his hometown in Brazil is very proud of him.

**Santos-Dumont's
"Rubber Cow"
circled Eiffel Tower in
Paris.
Came to Chester, NE
on Burlington Railroad
August 13, 1910.**

**But it didn't fly
as it was rained out.**

The First Modern Hot Air, Balloon
By Virginia Priefert

Information on the First Balloon is taken from
Final Report
One Man Hot Air Balloon System Development
For Office of Naval Research
Report No. 19631 November 1963
Prepared by P. E. Yost, Program Manager
Raven Industries, Inc. Box 916
Sioux Falls, South Dakota

Prepared for the Dedication of Yost Marker, Bruning Air Field, Bruning, Nebraska, 19 May 2001, donated to Thayer County Historical Society Museum book #37 of 150 printed. The Thayer County Historical Society is indebted to Jim Winkler of Raven Industries for permission to use this copyrighted information.

In December 2000, Mr. James Potter, of the Nebraska State Historical Society who is in charge of marking the historical sites in Nebraska sent a letter stating the State Historical Society had given permission to the Outhaus Balloon Association to put a marker near the State Historical Society marker near the Bruning Air Base on Highway 4. He gave us the name of Peg Hart of Campbell, Nebraska, who was in charge and requested that the Thayer County Historical Society help and cooperate with the project.

As Bruning Air Base Historians, having put together a book about the Bruning Air Base, it was unbelievable that such a historic event had passed us by. To make it worse, in 1985 I spent all winter gathering information for a little booklet which was called *"Those With Wings"* which tells of the aviation history of Thayer County in Nebraska. We knew that after the base had been closed as an Army Air Field in 1945, the State of Nebraska kept it open as a State Air Field for another 20 years, but that didn't seem too noteworthy.

BUT it was during those years that ballooning history was made at the Bruning Base and only a few were aware of it. It seems Mr. Paul "Ed" Yost was given a grant from General Mills to experiment with high altitude balloons. I understood this was a $40,000 grant in the 1950's. He was the Senior Engineer with the High Altitude Division. In his work he often flew over the Bruning Air Field on his way to Texas. They wanted to test the helium balloons which they were making for altitude and distance as well as other experimental things.

They realized that if they released balloons from Sioux Falls, South Dakota, where they were located, that their balloons, following the westerly wind currants, would end up in the Great Lakes where they could not retrieve them. If they came down in latitude and launched them south of South Dakota -- like from the Bruning Air Base, the balloons would come

The First Hot Air Balloon (continued)

down somewhere in Ohio. As the Bruning Air Base was away from any obstructions, buildings, power lines and curious people and reporters, they launched 2 helium filled high altitude balloons from the Base.

As a result of this work with General Mills, Mr. Yost received an order from the Office of Naval Research to develop a balloon which would fill the following requirements:
1. It must carry one man.
2. It must have fuel supply to last 3 hours.
3. It must be capable of going to 10,000 feet.
4. It must be reusable.
5. It must be launched with a minimum of personnel.
6. Its size and weight must be kept to a minimum.

To develop this balloon, he started Raven Industries in Sioux Falls, SD. He realized the following:
1. They must develop the balloon envelope, as it is called.
2. It must have a heating system.
3. It must have flight instrumentation.
4. It must have a gondola for the man to sit in.
5. It must have a ground inflamer.

The Balloon:
1. They first considered plastic for the balloon material but life expectancy was inadequate.
2. Then aluminum coating, but thought that made it too much of a target for radar detection.
3. Woven fabrics such as nylon, dacron and orlon were tried, but the price was prohibitive.
4. A laminating firm, Chase--Foster, suggested a fabric they called "FLARE CLOTH." It had the tensile weight of 40 lbs. an inch. It was porous, so they lined it with a coating of Mylarplastic and it worked. One thousand five hundred yards of the material was ordered. They had the fabric.

The Shape: The Balloon had been designed to have a shape which minimizes the stresses horizontally around the equator of the envelope. Since this new balloon would utilize heated air, a new shape was desired. They manufactured a polyethylene balloon having a diameter of 39 feet and volume of 27,000 feet, gore length of 61.6 feet with surplus fabric around the equator.

They took this new shaped balloon to the fair ground in Minnesota and inflated it with a Herman-Nelson aircraft heater and it obtained a gross lift of 450 pounds. The excess material just assumed a natural shape. Now they had the desired material and the desired shape.

The First Modern Hot Air Balloon (continued)

Heating System:
What kind of fuel would they use? It had to be
1. Inexpensive
2. Available on a universal basis
3. Have high heat value per pound of feet.
4. Easy to handle and convert to heat
   Gasoline, kerosene and propane were all tested. Although propane required a special tank, it was decided to be the best.

Instruments:
The two instruments required were an altimeter and a rate of climb indicator.
The crown of the balloon was fixed with a release tie-off Squib. Mr. Yost got a patent on this Squib. When landing the top of the balloon is popped off so the hot air can escape and the balloon will come down.
A release was fixed electrically and 2 "D" flashlight batteries provided the power to activate the release.

Gondola:
At this time this was of little concern. A piece of half-inch plyboard served as the seat. The balloon was then moored and tested in Minnesota. They tested the temperature of the balloon at all areas of the balloon.

On October 22, 1960 they were ready to test the balloon in free flight. For this they again selected the Bruning Air Base as it was free from obstructions, buildings and curious people.

Four Raven employees made the trip to Bruning.
Two Herman Nelson Aircraft heaters were used to heat the balloon initially. A slight breeze seemed to keep the balloon from obtaining enough heat. After 5 minutes the balloon was still not airborne. The crew walked downwind with the balloon and after 50 feet, buoyancy was achieved.

Ed Yost flew for 25 minutes and covered three miles. The group was jubilant. The first free flight of a controlled balloon was successful. There were 4 changes, which had to be made:

1. The balloon should be reinforced at the equator so handling lines could be attached.

2. The apex at the top of the balloon was only 9 feet and Mr. Yost was dragged trying to get it down. The apex was increased to 13 feet.

3. The propane burner was designed so that the vaporized propane was transmitted from the top portion of the fuel tank into the burner. The fuel would not evaporate rapidly enough to provide adequate heat and the refrigeration effect further aggravated this phenomenon. Mr. Yost had

The First Hot Air Balloon (continued)

to keep shaking the fuel tanks to make them vaporize. This was corrected by having the fuel under pressure enter a jacket which surrounded the burner flame thus heating it.

The corrections were made. Two improved balloons were built and after 65 hours of experimentation the final product was presented to the Navy. It had met all the requirements, but the Navy didn't buy it. Raven Industries then developed a better basket gondola and sold their first balloon for sporting purposes. Since that time hot air ballooning has become a national past time.

Peg Hart of Campbell, Nebraska, was instrumental in getting a marker to be put up at the Bruning base to commemorate this historic event. She has written the details of this accomplishment.

22 October 1960

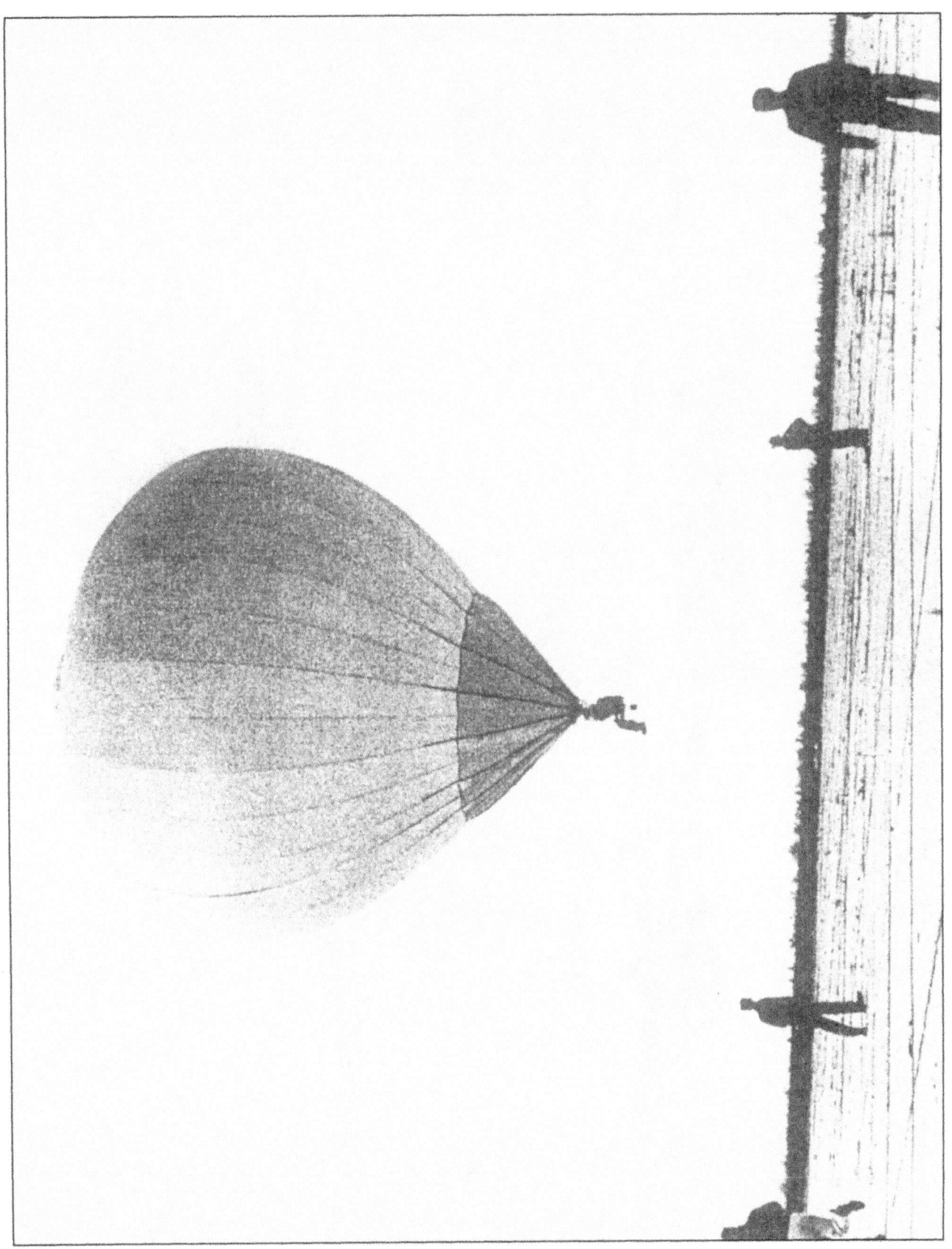

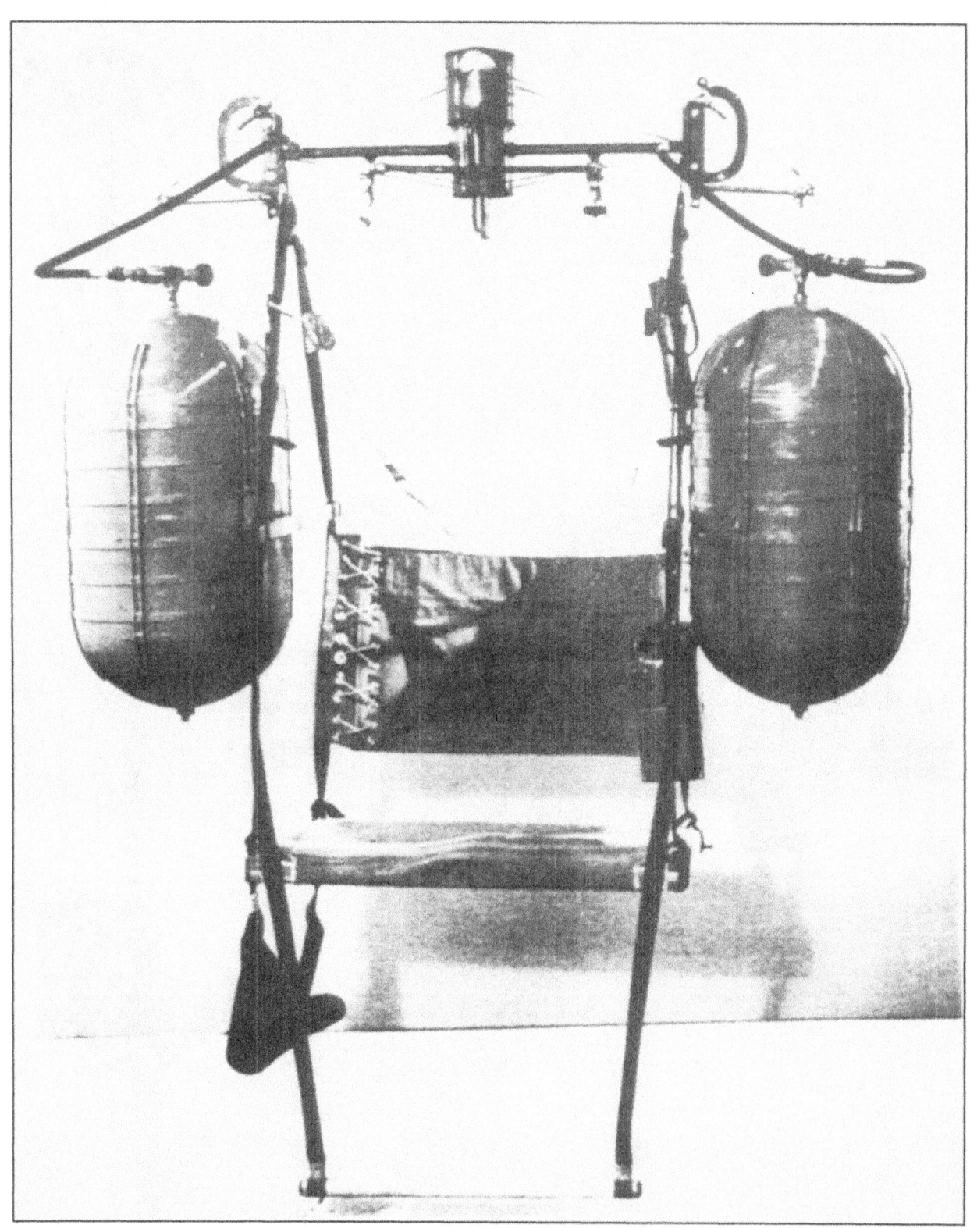

The Balloon Marker
by Peggy Hart
Campbell, Nebraska

On September 16, 2000, the "Outhaus Balloon Club were together in Cozad, Nebraska, for a fun fly-in. That evening, Peggy Hart, Bev Kennedy and Kevin Lehmann were looking through a coffee table book on ballooning, "The Joy of Ballooning" written by George Denniston, when Peggy noticed that Ed Yost had made the "First Flight of a Modern Hot Air Balloon" from Bruning, Nebraska on October 22, 1960.

This would make October 22, 2000, the 40th anniversary of the flight. The three started discussing the fact that there should be some recognition of this fact. Since Bev is very much into 'Historical Markers' she suggested that maybe we would qualify for a marker at the site in Bruning. Peggy was nominated to get on the internet and check into how we go about getting a historical marker. Since it was so close to Albuquerque Fiesta, which Ken & Bev Kennedy, Chet & Peggy Hart and Gary & Cathy Luenenborg attend, the marker was put on hold until we got back.

However, while in Albuquerque the 6 of us discussed the prospect of putting this together. The following are the steps that we made: Contacted Ed & Suzi Yost to get his approval for recognition of his first flight with a marker. End of October, started corresponding with the State Historical Society and Mr. James Potter, Historian. After receiving approval from the Historical Society, Peggy had to receive permission from the State Department of Roads and the Thayer County Historical Society. (The latter is where Peggy connected with Virginia Priefert who was so very helpful with the project.) The next step was to raise money in a short period of time. (It had been requested by Mr. Yost to have the marker dedicated by May 22, 2001, which would be the 40 years, 6 months anniversary).

On November 22, 2000, Peggy went to the internet and the balloon reflector to enlist everyone's help with financing this project. We set up an account with a local bank and contributions from balloonists in the United States, Canada and England started coming in. By the end of April we had received more than our projected goal! During this time of collecting the funds the "Outhaus Balloon Club" had many meetings planning the dedication week-end, etc. Those putting this together were: Peggy & Chet Hart, Bev & Ken Kennedy, Cathy & Gary Luenenborg, Karen & Kevin Lehmann and Kathy & Tom McCoy.

The Balloon Marker
by Peggy Hart
Campbell, Nebraska

One of the biggest contributors to our cause were Christine Kalakuka and Brent Stockwell, a husband and wife balloon team from California who are very close friends of Ed & Suzi Yost. They have written and published several books on ballooning and were instrumental in helping us get the text written for the marker. Our next step was ordering the marker.

During our many meetings Ken Kennedy suggested the possibility of getting a granite marker instead of the usual state marker. After getting approval from the State, Peggy contacted Ken Vogel of Price 171, Funeral Home in Hebron, Nebraska. He was very helpful in helping us decide which type of stone, engraving, etc. After ordering the stone the planning for the dedication was started.

The date of May 19, 2001. was chosen for the dedication with balloon flights scheduled for the 18th in Hebron and the l9th & 20th for Bruning. We also scheduled a brunch at the Bruning Opera House for the 19th before the dedication of the marker and followed by a tour of the, Thayer County Historical Museum. We had balloonists from 16 states attend the dedication with balloon flights from Hebron on Friday and Bruning on Saturday morning.

"Sleepy Hollow" is the name of Peg and Chet's balloon.
Chet is getting it ready to take Kent Williamson for a ride.

Jackie Williamson photo

Balloon Marker

The Balloon Marker was designed and arranged for by Peg Hart of Campbell, Nebraska. The Price Funeral Home, under the direction of Ken Vogel, provided the stone. It was a Keystone Blue granite from Elberton, Georgia. It weighed 3500 pounds at a total cost of $3,975 and was installed on May 17, 2001.

It was put in place by The Bell Monument Co. of Beloit, Kansas with the fifth generation of Bell monument workers, Jim Bell in charge. Mike Spicher and Travis Long assisted him.

Mike Spicher and Travis Long mixing cement for the base of the marker. Jim Bell is by the truck.

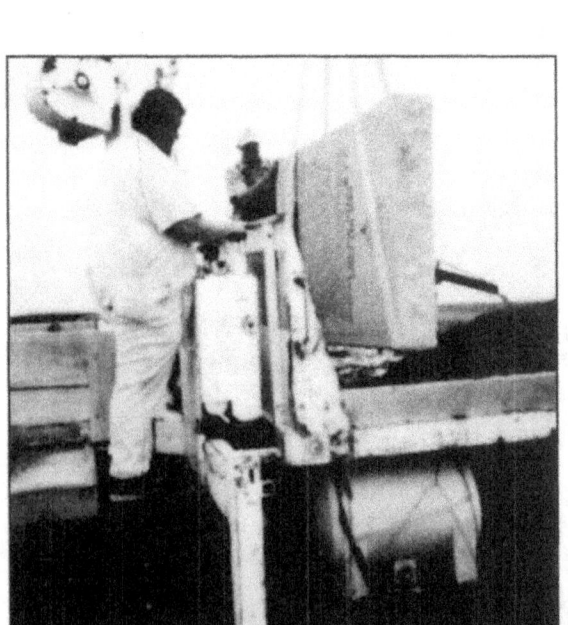

Jim Bell lifting the granite monument off the truck. Mike Spicher is helping to guide it.

Those Who Flew
Putting up the Balloon Marker

3500 pounds of granite. It didn't break.

Airborne like the balloons it commemorates.

Getting in place.

Ken Vogel of Hebron

The First Modern Hot Air Balloon

The First Free Flight Balloon Ascension
At the Bruning Air Base
October 22, 1960
Picture taken by Jim Winkler of Raven Industries
Sioux Falls, South Dakota

Those Who Flew
Ed Yost, Father of the Modern Hot-Air Balloon
Taken from Christine Kalakuka and Brent Stockwell's presentation

Paul E. (Ed) Yost

Paul E. (Ed) Yost invented the First Modern Hot Air Balloon and made the first free flight from Bruning, Nebraska on October 22, 1960. He had created a propane heater and a nylon envelope. The gross weight of the balloon, including Yost and fuel was 404 pounds. He was in the air 25 minutes and landed 3 miles from his take off point.

He had been interested in Aeronautics for years. In 1935, he watched Stevens and Anderson depart in South Dakota to set an altitude record of 72,395. Born in Bristol, Iowa in 1919, he graduated from the Boeing School of Aeronautics in Oakland, CA in 1940 and learned meteorology at the University of Minnesota. In 1949 Yost was the Senior Engineer and tracking Pilot for the High Altitude Research Division of General Mills. In '52 they sent a 3.2 million cubic foot balloon carrying U.S. lanky instruments into the stratosphere to study cosmic rays, as part of a scientific project that spanned many years.

After making the first free flight at Bruning, Nebraska, his next flight was made November 12, 1960, from the Stratobowl in South Dakota. He had made the necessary changes of increasing the burner power, reinforcing the envelope at the equator for handling lines, and increasing the apex hole from 9 to 13 feet. He made a flight of 39 miles in 1 hour and 50 minutes.

CROSSING THE CHANNEL: In 1963, Ed Yost made the first hot-air balloon crossing of the English channel with crew member Don Piccard.

CROSSING THE ATLANTIC: On October 6, 1976, Yost attempted to cross the Atlantic in a hot air balloon. After flying 107 hours 39 minutes and covering 2,740 miles, the balloon touched down in the Atlantic 200 miles east of the Azores.

Montgolfier Brothers in Paris had developed a Hot Air Balloon 175 years before, but their straw and wool burning system with the buttoned paper and linen envelopes were very limited. Now with these modern materials of nylon for the envelope and the propane burner for heater, the duration and lifting capacity appeared to far exceed any expectations for free flight.

Raven Industries sold their first sport balloon in November 1961 and the new sport of ballooning was born.

Those Who Flew
Ed Yost (continued)
written by Christine Kalakuka and Brent Stockwell

PATENTS HELD BY ED YOST

2,871,597 Dropping Mechanism
2,924,408 Mechanical Balloon Load Releasing Device
2,937,825 Balloon and Load Bearing Attachment
2,932,469 Balloon System
2,950,882 Balloon Gondola
2,990,147 Balloon Wad Attachment fitting

3,006,584 Balloon Load Lowering Mechanism
3,096,048 Heated Gas Generator for Balloons
3,109,612 Taped Plastic Balloon with J.A. Winker
3,109,611 Balloon Seam Structure and Method of Sealing Balloon Material
3,116,037 Balloon Body Structure for Towed Balloon
3,128,969 Cartridge Inflated Balloon
3,131,889 Balloon Structure with Release Mechanism
3,112,900 Towed Balloon Lift Control
3,170,658 Rapid Controlled Balloon Inflation Mechanism
3,168,266 Method and Apparatus for Supporting Air-borne Loads
3,229,932 Maneuvering Valve for Hot Air Balloon
3,312,427 Balloon Structure with Launching Cells
3,642,400 Illumination Flare/Balloon "Briteye"
3,670,440 Inflatable Display
4,432,513 Improved Gas-Proof Fastening System for a Non-Rigid Airship

SOME HONORS AND AWARDS

- Wingfoot Lighter-than-Air Society *Achievement Award,* 1963, for the first successful crossing of the English Channel by balloon.

- Balloon Federation of America *Award of Appreciation,* 1970, for serving as Clerk of the Course, first United States National Hot Air Balloon Championship, Indianola, Iowa.

- Balloon Federation of America *Shields-Trauger Award,* 1973, for advancing the science of aerostation and ballooning safety.

- Balloon Federation of America *Award of Appreciation,* 1973, for serving as Clerk of the Course of the First World Hot Air Balloon Championship, Albuquerque, New Mexico.

- *Diplôme Paul Tissandier,* 1975, (France), for pioneering work in hot air-balloon development and for the English Channel crossing by hot air balloon.

- *Montgolfier Diplôme,* 1976, Fédération Aéronautique International, (France) for the *Silver Fox* flight from Milbridge, Maine, to San Miguel Island, Azores.

- Coupe Château de Balleroy, 1977, (France), for contribution to the sport of Ballooning, particularly the flight of *Silver Fox.*

- Wingfoot Lighter-Than-Air Society *Achievement Award,* 1977, for pioneering work in designing, building, and flying lighter-than-air aircraft, and for the flight of *Silver Fox* helium balloon, October 5 through 10, 1976.

- National Aeronautic Association *Certificate of Honor,* 1993, for lifetime contributions to aviation worldwide.

- National Aeronautic Association *Elder Statesman Award,* 1994, one of its highest honors.

- First living inductee, Fédération Aéronautique International *Hall of Fame,* 1995.

- In June 1999, Yost will receive the prestigious Aero club of New England's *Godfrey L. Cabot Award* for unique, significant, and unparalleled contributions to advance and foster aviation and space flight.

Those Who Flew

Joe Kittinger
Man, Legend and Myth

Joe Kittinger Jr. was among the dignitaries who came to Thayer County to pay tribute to Ed Yost, The Father of Hot-Air ballooning, and to attend the Balloon Marker dedication on May 18, 19, and 20th 2001. He was the main speaker at that banquet. Non-balloonists soon learned that he is a ballooning legend. After record breaking flights in the balloons EXCELSOR I and II on August 16, 1960, Joe launched the balloon EXCELSOR III to a height of 102,500 feet, higher than any balloon before. For this he is called the Pre-astronaut as he went into outer space testing man's ability to survive re-entry to the earth's atmosphere from outer-space and thus made way for future astronauts.

He jumped out of his gondola, setting a record for the highest parachute jump to date. He set the longest free fall record falling for 4 minutes and 36 seconds. He not only broke the sound barrier but he is the only human ever to attain 714-mph falling speed.

A high powered telescope was bolted to his gondola for a flight on Dec. 13, 1962. His passenger, an astronomer, studied the stars from this height of 81,500 feet for over 13 hours.

He volunteered for the Air Forces Aero commanders and logged over 1000 hours in combat flight over Southeast Asia in the '60's and '70's, shot down a Soviet MIG but was shot down himself and spent 11 months in solitaire as a POW in the "Hanoi Hilton". While there, he kept his sanity by designing the logistics in his mind to make a balloon trip around the world.

He holds 15 meritorious awards for solo transatlantic balloon flights, 12 civilian decorations and 17 military decorations of distinction. Vietnam Service medals with 7 service stars, and 3 Distinguished Flying Crosses.

Not only has he accomplished these actual feats, he has acquired the title of being the red-headed mystery man of the Roswell, NM UFOology. He is truly a man of legend and of myth.

Those Who Flew
The First Modern Hot Air Balloon Marker Dedication

Joe Kittinger

File picture

Picture by Jacque Rocole

Joe Kittinger was a speaker at the First Hot Air Balloon Marker Dedication held in the Opera House in Bruning on May 19, 2001. He is a retired Colonel in the United States Air Force and is noted for making a 19-mile parachute jump, for being a Vietnam POW and the first solo balloonist to cross the Atlantic Ocean in the helium balloon called "Rosie O'Grady". He was featured on the cover of "LIFE" magazine on the August 29, 1960, issue as he plummeted towards the earth for 16 miles before his chute opened.

On Saturday morning he was in "Lifesaver" one of the three balloons which drifted over the Bruning Air Base where Mr. Yost had made the first Hot Air balloon landing 40 years and 6 months before. Jacque Rocole was honored to visit with both Mr. Kittinger and his wife and featured him in a front page story in ***The Hebron Journal***.

Balloonists came from California to Connecticut to this important celebration. The 3,500 pound Keystone Blue Granite Marker came from a quarry near Elberton, Georgia at a cost of $3,975.00.

"Euphoria"
Owned by Rich Jaworski
The first Euphoria flew at Bruning's "Volksfest" — 1976.

"George's Money"
Purchased by Gene Davenport of Belvidere in 1988.
It was an AX-7 made by the "Balloon Works" in North Carolina purchased in Grand Junction, CO. Gene gave rides and performed at many local activities.

"Up, Up and Away"
"Sleepy Hollow" Chet and Peg Hart's balloon leaving the Hebron Airport
May 18, 2001. Photo by Burdette "Stub" Priefert.

"Sleepy Hollow" had a hole burned in it,
but it flew fine anyway.
Top photo by Stub Priefert, bottom photo by Jackie Williamson.

Photos by Judy Kassebaum.

Balloons at the Bruning Ball Park, May 19, 2001. Pictures taken by Mary Bruning.

"Mr. Twister" and "Cloud 9" going towards Hebron.

Ken Kennedy of Broken Bow, NE, a self-employed machinist, designed and made the balloons shown here. "Whoosh" the checkerboard balloon is made of silicone-impregnated nylon and weighs only 135 pounds. "Ytivarg" has flown in nearly every Dawn Patrol in Albuquerque, NM. (Although Ytivarg is claimed to be a science by some, balloonists are known for spelling words backwards.)

Dawn Patrol
"Sleepy Hollow" owned by Chet and Peg Hart of Campbell, NE, "Mrs. Twister" owned by Cathy and Gary Luenenbotg of Omaha and "Terpsnickery" owned by Bev and Ken Kennedy of Broken Bow, NE.

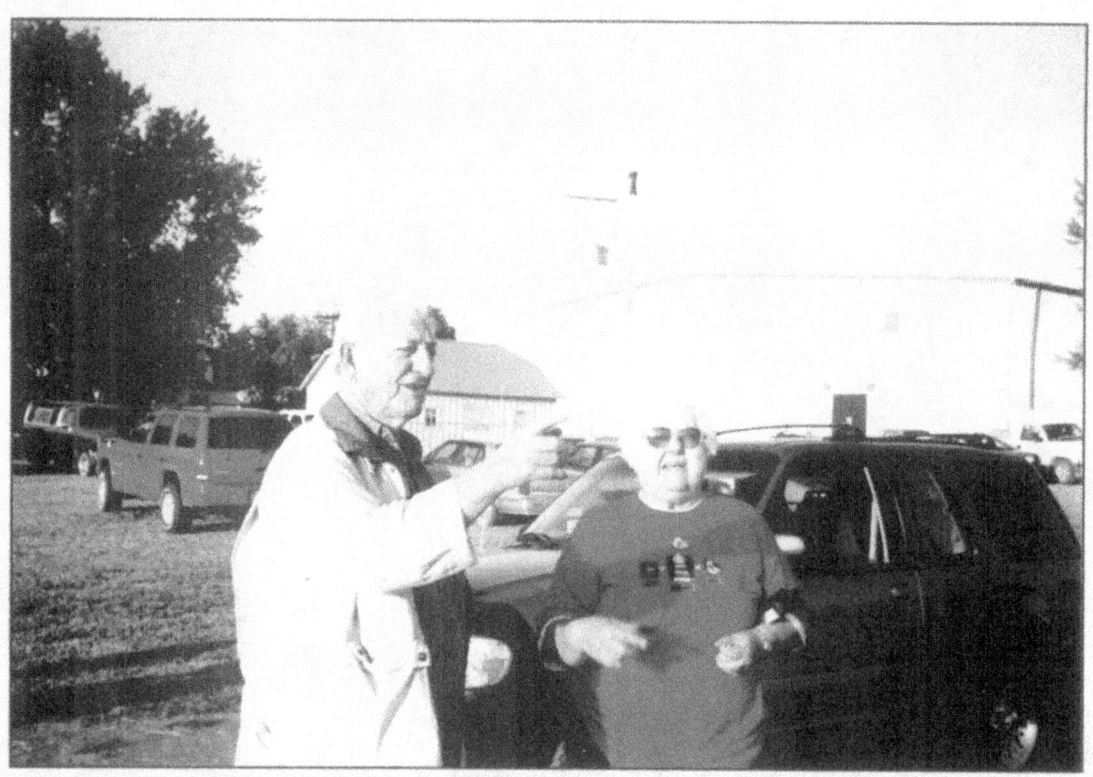

"Ed" Yost shared his breakfast of unshelled peanuts with Virginia Priefert as he explained ballooning on May 19th, 2001 at Bruning Ball Park.
Picture by Stub Priefert.

Bev and Ken Kennedy and crew ready to go.
Picture by Jackie Williamson.

Photos by Ray Mieth.

Balloons with two shadows over field of soybean stubble.
Taken by Jacque Rocole.

The "First Modern Hot Air Balloon" Historical Marker is located near the State Historical Society's Bruning Army Air Field Marker on Nebraska Highway 4, seven miles east of U.S. Highway 81 which is southwest of the original BAAF.

Mr. Yost, Peg Hart, Ken Vogel, and Jim Winkler.

Mr. and Mrs. Yost.

Golfing on the Hebron Golf Course.
Photo by Jacque Rocole of the Hebron Journal.
Allen Schlenker, pilot, with Joe Kittinger help golfers.

Balloons that came for the "First Modern Hot Air Balloon Marker Dedication." Picture taken by Jacque Rocole, May 18, 2001 from Hebron Golf course. The frame of the old Hebron Drive-In Theatre is on the left.

Ballooning In Thayer County NE

Jim Winkler
Ballooning Consultant

Jim Winkler was a co-designer of the first modern hot air balloon at Raven Industries in South Dakota and took the picture of the First Balloon Ascension taken on the Bruning Air Base on October 22, 1960. Mr. Winkler donated a beautiful copy of this First Balloon Ascension, along with an easel to display it, to the Thayer County Museum when the Balloon Marker was dedicated at the Bruning Air Base on May 19, 2001.

Mr. Winkler of the Rekin Co. in Sioux Falls, South Dakota is a balloon consultant. He has had a lifetime career in ballooning from 1947 to his retirement in 1991. He was a co-designer of the first modern hot air balloon.

He helped on the Nazco project in Peru, South America. The Nazco culture is classified into three ages--the early, middle and late classic 250-750 AD. Geoglyphs are large drawings on the earth which can be only recognized from the air. There are fish, birds, monkeys, spiders and plants spread on the ground 12 to 800 miles long. As these pictures can only be recognized from the air, Mr. Winkler demonstrated the possibility of "prehistoric" balloon flight in Peru.

Mr. Winkler received the Shield-Trauger Award in 1978, This is the highest award that the BFA (Balloon Federation of America) bestows. He is an honorary member of the "Lighter than Air Society".

Mr. Winkler has flown in 14 states and 9 countries. Some of the interesting places he has flown have been at the Winter Olympics in 1980 at Lake Placid, NY; Gran Festival, Aerostatigo, Mexico City in 1982; International Hot Air Festival, Johannesburg, South Africa in 1986; Corawindra Bicentennial Festival in Australia in 1988 and First Open Championship in USSR, Rylsk, Russia in 1991.

His balloon is called "My Blue Heaven".

Those Who Flew
The First Modern Hot Air Balloon
Famous Balloonists at the Balloon Marker Dedication
May 19, 2001

"Ed" Yost, father of the First Modern Hot Air Balloon
Joe Kittinger, balloon record holder
Jim Winkler, Co-designer at Raven Industries.

Picture by Jacque Rocole

When Ed Yost visited the Thayer County Museum, he was surprised to learn that Albertos Dumont's famous balloon visited the county in 1910. Years from now, balloonists will be surprised to learn that Yost, Kittinger and Winkler visited our county in 2001.

Authors of many Ballooning Books, Christine Kalakuka and Brent Stockwell of Oakland, CA and Craig Ryan, the author of **_Pre-Astronauts_** were also here.

Those Who Flew The Balloon Marker

The Balloon Marker Celebration

Mr. Yost asked Mr. Jim Winkler to bring a large picture of the first Balloon ascension, which took place at the Bruning Air Base on Oct. 22, 1960, and present it to the Thayer County Museum. Mr. Winkler also brought an easel to place it on.

On Friday evening, May 19, 2001, five balloons took off from the Hebron Airport. On Saturday morning 9 balloons took off from the Bruning ball field in the town of Bruning. The winds took three of these balloons over the Bruning Air Base where the elated balloonists sat down on the historical place where the first balloon had flown 40 years before.

The balloonists who flew at the Hebron Airport on Friday evening were **"Sleepy Hollow"**, owned by Peg and Chet Hart of Campbell, NE; **"Terpsnickery"** which is owned by Bev and Ken Kennedy from Broken Bow, NE; Gary and Kathy Luenenborg in **"Mr. Twister"** from Omaha, NE. Mr. Allen Yost who owns **"Spectrum"** rode with the Luenenborgs but did not fly; Duane Waack of Sioux Falls, SD flew in **"Cloud 9"**; and Allen Schlenker who works with Arrowstar from Sioux Falls, SD flew **"Lifesaver"**. From California, Brent Stockwell flew in "Quetzal."

Glen Moyer, Publication Chairperson of BFA (Balloon Federation of America) and **"Ballooning"** wrote:

"... While the Montgolfier brothers invented the hot air balloon, today's aerostat is far removed from their straw-burning smoke belching ships of two centuries ago. Our roots are more closely aligned with BRUNING, NEBRASKA than Paris, France."

Montgolfier brothers
April 4, 1783

Alberto Santos-Dumont sails over the streets of Paris, France.

HOT AIR BALLOONISTS

75 people are expected
They are staying in Hebron, Geneva, Belleville and Fairbury

Schedule:

All flights are determined by weather

Fri. May 18 -- 2 balloons fly Hebron Airport at 6:30 PM

Sat. May 19-- 7:00 AM -- 15 or more balloons expect to fly from Bruning School Ball Park

11:00 -- Lunch at Bruning Opera House

Public invited IF you make reservation with

KATE & NELLIE SUE

Followed by Program at Opera House

Talk by Ed Yost, inventor, with pictures of

First Modern Hot Air Balloon

Flight at Bruning Air Field on Oct. 22, -1960

2:00 PM Dedication and unveiling of Balloon marker at **BRUNING ARMY AIR FIELD MARKER**

On Highway 4

3:00 PM Tour Thayer County Museum at Belvidere

See Bruning AAF Exhibit -- Cookies & Coffee

Free time until

6:30 PM Another flight of many balloons from Bruning School Grounds

Sunday 7:00 AM Flight of some balloons from Bruning School Grounds

Breakfast of rolls & coffee by Bruning Auxiliary served on School grounds

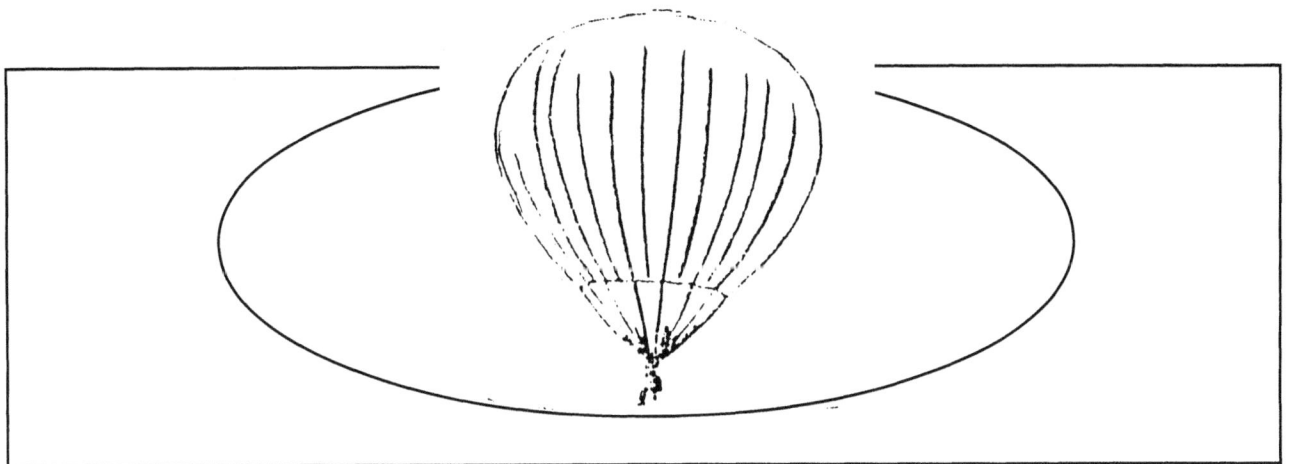

FIRST FREE FLIGHT
A MODERN HOT-AIR BALLOON

ON OCTOBER 22, 1960, PAUL E. 'ED' YOST MADE THE FIRST FREE FLIGHT OF A MODERN HOT-AIR BALLOON FROM THE FORMER BRUNING ARMY AIR FIELD. THE FLIGHT LASTED 25 MINUTES AND COVERED 3 MILES.
HUMANS FIRST FLEW IN 1783 IN A HOT-AIR BALLOON CONCEIVED AND BUILT BY THE MONTGOLFIER BROTHERS IN FRANCE, 120 YEARS BEFORE AN AIRPLANE FLEW.
THE HOT-AIR BALLOON LANGUISHED UNTIL 1956 WHEN ED YOST RECEIVED A CONTRACT FROM THE OFFICE OF RESEARCH TO DEVELOP A PRACTICAL HOT-AIR BALLOON. YOST DESIGNED THE SHAPE OF THE ENVELOPE, PIONEERED THE USE OF NYLON, AND DEVELOPED PROPANE HEATERS THAT MADE CONTROLLED AND SUSTAINED FLIGHT POSSIBLE.

WHILE WORKING ON SCIENTIFIC BALLOON PROJECTS YOST MADE MANY AIRPLANE FLIGHTS FROM RAVEN INDUSTRIES IN SIOUX FALLS, SOUTH DAKOTA TO TEXAS, FLYING DIRECTLY OVER BRUNING ARMY AIR FIELD. AFTER LAUNCHING 2 LARGE HELIUM SCIENTIFIC BALLOONS FROM BRUNING, YOST IT WOULD BE A GOOD LOCATION FROM WHICH TO TEST FLY THE NEW HOT-AIR BALLOON BECAUSE THERE WAS OPEN SPACE WITH FEW OBSTRUCTIONS.

ED YOST'S MODERN HOT-AIR BALLOON FIRST FLOWN IN BRUNING, TRANSFORMED BALLOONING FROM AN ELITE ACTIVITY TO A SPORT OPEN TO THOUSANDS OF BALLOONISTS WORLDWIDE.

OUTHAUS BALLOON CLUB   NEBRASKA STATE HISTORICAL SOCIETY

Hot Air Balloon Flights

Flying balloons in Nebraska and Iowa since 1972.
Commercial flights for all the special events in your life.

"Euphoria", Nebraska's Big Red balloon, piloted by Dr. Richard Jawarski of Blair, went aloft as scheduled Saturday evening at Bruning's Volksfest despite what the balloonists called "marginal winds" at 10-12 mph. Ideal wind for a balloon ascension is 5 mph.," he said. The huge 60' by 50' nylon bag was filled with the aid of local men who helped hold the "mouth" open while powerful fans put air into the bag. Later propane burners heated the 56,500 cu. ft. of hot air. The balloon gradually tilted into a vertical position, the pilot jumped aboard, the ropes were released and he rose rapidly aloft. The balloonist sailed northwest, across Highway 81 and landed in a field belonging to Arnold Heinrichs, about a four-mile flight. (Taken from the July 22, 1976 Thayer County Banner-Argus).

Those Who Flew
Marvin's Flying Boat
or
The Spruce Goose

Marvin Lewis' Flying Boat or Model of the Spruce Goose

The giant model — weighing 50 pounds with a wingspan of 12 feet 8 inches — was completed and flown after Marvin Lewis' death by the Boulder, Colo. Aeromodeling Society.

HK-1 Hercules- in Hebron, NE

When Marvin Lewis first laid eyes on the Spruce Goose displayed along side the Queen Mary in Long Beach, California in 1989, it was love at first sight. The Spruce Goose was the largest aircraft ever built. It had 8 engines and was designed by Howard Hughes to carry 750 troops at one time during WWII. The plane flew less than a minute and it flew only once. Sometimes called "the flying lumber yard", it was made of birch plywood, spruce and balsa.

At that time, Marvin and his wife, Eileen, had a bar and restaurant in Nederland, CO called "MARVIN'S GARDEN". After visiting the Spruce Goose in Long Beach, Marvin returned home with a plastic model of the plane. He and his daughter ruined Eileen's blender by mixing plaster of Paris in it to fill the

Those Who Flew
Marvin's Flying Boat
or
The Spruce Goose

plastic model to make a solid model of the plane. He then carefully sawed the solid model in increments of about a half inch and carefully made a blue print of each section about 10 times larger than the plastic model.

Patrons of "MARVIN'S GARDEN" got used to seeing a model of the Spruce Goose develop on the pool table in the bar. Eileen asked him to do his gluing outside as the smell bothered the restaurant customers. Members of the Boulder Aeromodeling Society would stop for lunch and check the progress.

Marvin got acquainted with the staff people at the Hughes Museum and Chuck Junker, Hughes's crew chief on the original Goose's 1947 flight, gave Marv a commemorative test flight jacket. When the plane was to be disassembled to be taken to Oregon, Marvin Lewis and his sons were invited to sit in the cockpit where Howard Hughes once sat. This was a thrill of a lifetime for this admirer.

Eileen Lewis modeling the Jacket actually worn by Junker
when the first Spruce Goose flew.

Those Who Flew
Marvin's Flying Boat
or
The Spruce Goose

The song "Dream" was played. It was a tense and emotional time. Fingernails were chewed and tears flowed not only from Marvin's family, but from many of the people who came to see if this dream could fly. All hoped for the best.

Top picture is Marvin's Flying boat.
Bottom is the actual Spruce Goose.

Then on the third try, it took off across the water and up into the air. A cheer rose from the crowd. Marvin's family jumped for glee. It got up 40 feet in the air, but then it stalled out as there was not adequate control. It plunged virtually undamaged into the Boulder reservoir. In size comparison to the actual Spruce Goose, it flew longer and better. But the important thing was, it had flown. The family wore Tee shirts with Marv's and his Flying Boat's picture on it with the words **"A man and his dream."** Marvin Lewis's dream had been fulfilled.

THE BAAFLER

Bruning Army Air Field History

Prepared by the

Thayer County Historical Society

BRUNING ARMY AIR FIELD, BRUNING, NEBRASKA

THE BRUNING BANNER

THE READING HABIT OF NORTHERN THAYER COUNTY

BRUNING, THAYER COUNTY, NEBRASKA, THURSDAY, SEPTEMBER 3, 1942 — NUMBER 21

BRUNING GETS GOV'T AIR FIELD

Work on Bruning's Satellite Air Field Getting Underway

Offices Being Set Up and Work Well Underway; Many Laborers Wanted

Bruning air base activity began in earnest Monday, when Mr. Glantz and his crew of 25 engineering inspectors arrived to headquarter here. Mr. Glantz has set up his office at the T. H. Wilken residence until quarters are provided at the air field being built east of town.

Wednesday, G. H. Lowe arrived and has set up an office in the former Fairmont creamery building. He has the contract for the dirt moving and has announced that he wants men immediately for common and skilled labor and tractor operators.

Peter Keiwit & Sons and George Condon & Co. of Omaha have the contract for the frame buildings and sewerage disposal at the air base. This crew has not arrived, but a representative was here the first of the week to make arrangements to run the payroll through the Bruning bank.

The well drillers are already at work at the location, and expect to put down two wells.

Condemnation proceedings were begun in federal court by U. S. Attorney Votava this week to secure the land for the Bruning satellite air field. Definite information is still unavailable as to the exact size of the base.

T. H. Wilken is acting as "housing man" here. Local folks — town or country — who have rooms to rent, or can serve meals, should notify him at once as to how many they can care for. Also if they can accommodate trailer houses on their property.

Air Field Labor Needed

WESTERN UNION

Fairmont, Nebr., 7:07 p.m., Oct. 6

The Bruning Banner, Bruning, Nebr.

It is requested that you bring to the attention of the people the urgent need for labor at the Air Field Projects being converted at Fairmont, Bruning and Harvard, Nebr., to be able to complete these jobs on time. In order to be of service to the Country it is necessary that all available be received.

Major Burgwin, Area Engineer.

Part of State Network Of "Satellite Bases"

Rapidly on its way toward being the center of a defense area, the village of Bruning hummed with excitement this week as officials were informed that the town had been selected as a headquarters for an army air base to be located six miles directly east of the city limits.

Bruning as a "boom town" was the topic of street conversations, telephone calls, and over-the-back-fence discussions. With definite information yet limited, rumors reached the fantastic stage, and the Banner, through several news channels, has attempted to glean from reports a fairly accurate picture of plans for the base.

Original plans for the air field, not an emergency landing field, stipulated that it would cover 2,000 acres, taking in all of sections 3 and 10, the south half of section 4, north half of section 9 and the north half of the southeast quarter of section 9, all in Highland precinct. It is reported, however, that these plans have lately undergone an alteration which will increase the size of the field. Though it will be located in the same place, it is possible, according to these recent developments, that it will extend beyond the original northern boundary, into Fillmore county.

In charge of the preliminary surveying for the field has been

BRUNING AIR BASE NEARS COMPLETION

The Bruning Satellite Air Base is nearing completion, and finds men leaving as certain work ends. The runways will be finished in less than a week, it is reported, and the buildings are practically ready for occupancy. A concrete water tower over 100 feet high is fast nearing the finishing stage. Soldiers are expected to arrive any day — their material and equipment now coming in here daily.

Major Bert Burgwin, of the Army Engineers Corps. It is understood that the surveys include plans for three runways approximately 9,000 feet in length, and barracks for a sizeable contingent of men. Wyatt Hedrich of Fort Worth, Texas, is architect-engineer for the project.

It is anticipated that the farm land and growing crops will be appraised soon in preparation for government purchase, although it was not learned when notice would be given for farm homes to be evacuated. Farms included in the area surveyed are those of Marie Carey, Paul Weber Estate, Henry Holtegrew, Warner place, R. H. Marks, Mrs. Lizzie Heston, Frank Vostroz, and parts of the Schweer, Steck and Culp farms.

Plans for the field assumed a more realistic appearance early this week when it was reported the Lincoln Telephone and Telegraph company received an order to install a PBX cable from Bruning to the field, with a switchboard accommodating fifty telephones. Officials of the Burlington railroad visited the village Tuesday, looking over the rail set-up here in their consideration of laying new and heavier tracks in order to become a supply line for the construction of the base. It is reported that the government would have the railroad complete such an enlargement in thirty days, so that the increased shipments of government supplies could be accommodated at that time.

The Bruning air base will be part of a network of such army air fields over the state. Other towns named as cites for the fields, christened "satellite bases," are McCook, Fairmont and Harvard. Work on the McCook base, which must be finished December 1, has already begun, and a staff of fifty army men and architects' assistants are aready located at Fairmont.

The fields are called "satellite bases" because they are built around larger air corps tactical units to provide protection. additional flying facilities.

DEPARTMENT OF THE AIR FORCE
HEADQUARTERS UNITED STATES AIR FORCE
BOLLING AFB, D.C. 20332

30 January 1985

Virginia Priefert
Co-Curator
Thayer County Historical Society
Thayer County Museum
Belvidere, NE 68315

Dear Mrs. Priefert

This is in response to your request for information concerning Bruning Army Air Field in Bruning, Nebraska, during World War II.

Our microfilm holdings include histories of Bruning Field from October 1942 to December 1944. A sample is attached. Due to the length of these materials of over 860 pages, we are unable to reproduce the histories in their entirety. However, you may want to purchase the material on 16mm microfilm from the United States Air Force Historical Research Center (USAFHRC/CC), at Maxwell Air Force Base, AL, 36112-6678, where the Air Force maintains its official historical document collection. A brochure is enclosed describing the Center and its resources.

Thank you for your interest in Air Force history. We welcome the opportunity to be of assistance.

Sincerely

ROGER A. JERNIGAN, MSgt, USAF   2 Atch
Historian   1. Microfilm Extract
NCOIC, Reference Services Branch   and Index
Office of Air Force History   2. Brochure

Permission for the Thayer County Historical Society to reproduce this history and the history contained on microfilm from the Maxwell AFB was granted via telephone from retired Major Les Jackson, a volunteer with the United States Air Force Historical Research Cenenter on June 5, 1996. Telephone # 202-767-0412. No further information has been declassified since this history. V.R.P.

THE BRUNING AIR BASE
BRUNING, NEBRASKA

CHAPTER I

THE BEGINNING

The flat plains of Nebraska would be a perfect place to have airfields as they were not well populated; they were far from either coast--in case of invasion; the flat terrain made it easy for pilots to see; and they couldn't be sabotaged easily. Fairmont, Harvard and Bruning Airfields were all built about the same time and they were all built in a generic nature using basic materials such as wood, tar paper covering, asbestos & cement.

As early as July 1942, the war department sent out surveyors to look at the area 6 miles east of Bruning. It was rumored that there was to be an Army Air Base Training Camp located there.

The official word came when land owners received their notice on September 12, 1942, that they had to move out within 10 days--sell their farms, homes, barns, chicken houses, machine sheds, and all other buildings. These buildings had to be moved or they would be destroyed or burned. Growing crops such as hay, corn, sorghums, windbreaks of trees and orchards had to be left.

The people who received these notices were people who had planned this would be their home for generations to come. Some had been homesteaded by their parents and grandparents. They had never heard of Eminent Domain. They were shocked when they received these notices. Some of the farmers fought diligently to keep their farms and refused to move until they were forced out.

These were picturesque well-kept farms, the pride of German and English immigrants such as the Robert Marks family who had a model farm with well kept buildings. Farming was done at first with horses, but when the tractor was invented and developed the Marks family realized that an oil filter was necessary on tractors to farm in the Nebraska dust. Howard Marks and his father had developed and patented the **AERO PURE OIL FILTER** and sold it under the name of **AERO**. It was made of cast aluminum and stuffed with cotton waste which would be taken out and burned when saturated with oil, dust and sludge. New cotton waste would then be inserted. Nearly every farmer around who owned an International FARMALL F-20 tractor came to the Marks to purchase a filter. They were also put on automobiles or any combustible engine. It was a business with good prospects. The Marks had a store on their farm where these filters and cotton waste could be purchased.

What a shock to these farmers to learn that their land was going to be purchased and developed into an Air Base. It was traumatic--all their homes, all their farm buildings, all their work, all their crops, all their hopes were to be sold. Mr. Marks was never the same. It crushed his spirit.

Airbase Beginning (continued)

Others were thrilled to hear the Air Base was coming. It meant excitement, jobs, prosperity--a new life for Thayer, Fillmore, and Jefferson Counties. What a thrill--an Army Air Base in our own community. The government was going to spend millions of dollars here!

A declaration of intent to buy 1,480 acres of land, which included crops and damages, in Fillmore and Thayer Counties was filed in Federal Court by Secretary of War, Harry L. Stimson. $73,000 was judged as compensation for the 12 tracts of land involved. According to the **BRUNING BANNER** in December of 1942, the land and compensation were as follows

			total	per acre
Tract 1,	40 acres	Wanda Rippe, Ohiowa	$1,600	($40.00)
Tract 2,	80 acres	Marie Kerrie, Ohiowa	$3,965	(49.56)
Tract 3,	80 acres	Geneva Cemetery Assoc.	$3,363	(41.51)
Tract 4,	160 acres	Henry W. Holtgrewe Nebraska City, NE.	$7,675	(47.96)
Tract 5,	160 acres	Olga Steck Duncan Lexington, NE	$8,934	(55.80)
Tract 6,	240 acres	Chris Schweer, Ohiowa	$9,694	(40.39)
Tract 7,	300 acres	John Culp, deceased Alexandria, NE	$13,730	(45.77)
Tract 8,	260 acres	Mr. & Mrs. Robert Marks Ohiowa, NE.	$15,580	(59.92)
Tract 9,	40 acres	Mr. and Mrs. Eugene Shane Alexandria, NE	$1,604	(40.10)
Tract 10,	40 acres	Loren J. Huston, deceased	$1,832	(45.80)
Tract 11,	40 acres	Lena Wedeking, Hebron	$1,825	(45.63
Tract 12,	40 acres* *(80 acres?)	Mr. and Mrs. F. F. Garrison Ohiowa, NE	$3,598	

The average price paid was $49.32 per acre.

In October 1, 1942 the BRUNING BANNER states: "Five families are forced to move out and reside elsewhere. George Ortgies has moved to Bruning, where he has purchased the Ulm estate property in the west part of town. This forced the Norman Collison's to move and they purchased the Keil property adjoining on the west.

Richard Vostrez and Frank Garrison are moving to other farms. James Rut is moving to Ohiowa. R. H. Marks is moving temporarily to Ohiowa. Mr. Marks has lived on his farm since boyhood--58 years. (moved there in 1894) He has stored his machinery with neighbors.

Emil Schweer has to make some change, as part of his buildings are on the area taken over.

Rural School No. 16, known as the Excelsior School, is about in the center of the area and will naturally be eliminated." Virginia Williamson was the teacher there and had only 2 students in the little one-room school house.

The Bruning Army Air Field

ADDITIONAL LAND TAKEN FOR BRUNING GUNNERY BASE
NOVEMBER 25, 1943 **BRUNING BANNER:**

An additional 2,122 acres of land in Thayer County has been added to the Bruning Army Air Base for use as a gunnery range. Petition in condemnation and an order for immediate possession were filed Wednesday in Federal Court.

Named as respondents in the action were the following Thayer County land owners: **Roy Marsh, Parks and McClure, J. B. Headrick, John Marsh, Mutual Benefit Insurance Co., Daryl Easley, A. L Polage, E.T. Stacup, Wagner Estate, Wagner Brothers, Reinhardt Tjaden and M. C. Brinegar**

Newspaper Accounts

Before the air base was under military control, Wayne Thompson, the editor of THE BRUNING BANNER, gave a lot of information regarding the building of the Air Base. The first notice was in bold headlines:

"STATE NETWORK OF 'SATELLITE BASES'
BRUNING GETS GOV'T AIR FIELD
September 3, 1942

Rapidly on its way toward being the center of a defense area, the village of Bruning hummed with excitement this week as officials were informed that the town had been selected as a headquarters for an Army Air Base to be located six miles directly east of the city limits.

Bruning as a "Boomtown" was the topic of street conversations, telephone calls, and over-the-fence discussions. With definite information yet limited rumors reached the fantastic stage, and the Banner, through several news channels, has attempted to glean from reports a fairly accurate picture of plans for the base.

Original plans for the air field, not an emergency landing field, stipulated that it would cover 2,000 acres, taking in all of sections 3 and 10, the south half of section 4, north half of section 9 and the north half of the Southeast quarter of section 9, all in the HIGHLAND PRECINCT. It is reported, however, that these plans have lately undergone an alteration which will increase the size of the field. Though it will be located in the same place, it is possible, according to these recent developments, that it will extend beyond the original northern boundary, into Fillmore County.

In charge of the preliminary surveying for the field has been Major Bert Burgwin, of the Army Engineers Corps. It is understood that the surveys include plans for three runways approximately 9,000 feet in length and barracks for a sizable contingent of men. Wyatt Hedrich of Fort Worth, Texas is architect-engineer for the project.

The Bruning Army Air Field

It is anticipated that the farm land and growing crops will be appraised soon in preparation for government purchase although it was not learned when notice would be given for farm homes to be evacuated. Farms included in the area surveyed are those of Marie Carey, Paul Weber Estate, Henry Holtegrew, Warner Place, R.H. Marks, Mrs. Lizzie Heston, Frank Vostrez and parts of the Schweer, Steck and Culp Farms.

Plans for the field assumed a realistic appearance early this week when it was reported that the Lincoln Telephone and Telegraph Company received an order to install a PBX cable from Bruning to the field, with a switchboard accommodating fifty telephones. Officials of the Burlington Railroad visited the village Tuesday, looking over the rail set up here in their consideration of laying new and heavier tracks in order to become a supply line for the construction of the base. It is reported that the government would have the railroad complete such an enlargement in thirty days, so that the increased shipments of government supplies could be accommodated at that time.

The Bruning Air Base will be part of a network of such army air fields over the state. Other towns named as sites for the fields, christened 'Satellite Bases,' are McCook, Fairmont and Harvard. Work on the McCook base which must be finished December 1, has already begun and a staff of fifty army men and architects' assistants are already located at Fairmont.

The fields are called 'Satellite Bases' because they are built around larger air corps tactical units to provide protection, additional flying facilities, and accommodations for the dispersal of planes.

Some activity will probably be noted before long on Highway 81, which some time ago was designated as a military highway.

Lincoln State Journal
September 10, 1942

"Plans are being drawn up for three "war projects" to be built in the vicinities of Fairmont, Bruning and Harvard, Neb. in the immediate future, Major W. H. Burgwin at the Kansas City district engineer's corps, announced Tuesday night while in McCook, Captain William E. Grubb of the Army Engineers Corps announced that construction of an army air base nine miles north of that city would begin immediately."

Major Burgwin, who already is area engineer for the three southern Nebraska projects has set up offices in Fairmont, did not disclose the nature of the projects.

THE JOURNAL learned earlier Tuesday, however, that more than half a dozen sites in Nebraska had been chosen by the Army as locations for "satellite" air bases to form a far-flung aerial protective network.

The Bruning Army Air Field

So far, according to information received by the BANNER, no appraisal has yet been made on the land to be used. Farmers in the tract are making arrangement to leave at once. Owners will have first chance to buy their buildings.

The exact size of the Bruning Air Field has not been revealed, but last reports indicated it would cover about 1600 acres and would cost about $2,000,000. It will have three paved runways, each from 7,000 to 9,000 feet long, as well as barracks, hangars, water plans and other buildings, it is reported."

DAYKIN HERALD

"The new military airfield six miles west of Daykin is a beehive of activity. Work on runways is proceeding day and night. Several large machines are working under special lights.

Latest reports are that the airfield is to be completed about February 1. Workmen were on the scene last Friday, Sept. 18, building several portable offices-temporary buildings on skids so they can be moved any place--for contractors offices. These were being built three-fourths mile west of the R. H. Marks--Henry Holtgrewe corner, seven miles west of the R.H.Marks--Daykin.

A quarter of a mile south of the offices' sites, machinery was on the ground to sink wells for a water system. Northward, a street was staked out. A new road is also planned from this point to the northwest, leading toward the Ohiowa road and avoiding the bluffs and uneven ground to the west.

It was learned there are to be about 40 barracks, one hangar and about 40 more buildings making over 80 in all. Five families were given ten days notice by the government to move from their farm homes, the time expiring Sept. 22."

BRUNING BANNER

Bruning is gradually filling up with trailer houses, and many homes in town and country are accommodating workmen.

General offices of Kiwit, Condon, and Cunningham Construction Co., contractors in charge of the construction of the buildings at the three major satellite air bases in this area--Bruning, Fairmont and Harvard--were opened at Sutton Monday, according to the SUTTON NEWS. The office personnel totals about fifty.

Haymond Scott Construction Company, having the contract for utilities and plumbing in the three bases, have opened a general office at Sutton. The Miller Electric Co., engineers in charge of all electric writing and installation on the three sites are also officiating at Sutton.

The Labor Union has also set up an office at Sutton, according to the NEWS The United Brotherhood of Carpenters and Joiners have opened headquarters for the issuing of cards, under the supervision of Harry Beaver of Hastings.

The Bruning Army Air Field

"The fact that the war will affect every person in the nation is made plain in a statement by Rear Admiral Woodward at Cincinnati. He said Americans would very soon be placed in three classes. These will be fighters, material producers and women, children and the aged. The later class will be absolutely essential to the maintenance of homes and institutions. He added: "The final test for any individual in any group will be the answer to the question "Are you doing your utmost for American victory? The outcome of the war will depend on the answer, he said."

"That will mean total war--every American and every resource of the nation, publicly or individually controlled, taking part in the struggle.

Total war in its grimmest sense comes to a government of the people and the test of such government will depend on how general is the response to the call. It is for that America is preparing--for that fighter Air Bases are being installed in so many places--for that we fight, we sacrifice and we offer our lives on the altar of human freedom."

BRUNING BANNER
Wayne Thompson, Editor

"Bruning Air Base activity began in earnest Monday (Sept. 14, 1942) when Mr. Glantz set up his office at the T. H. Wilken residence until quarters are provided at the air base being built east of town.

Wednesday, G. H. Lowe arrived and has set up an office in the former Fairmont Creamery Building. He has the contract for the dirt moving and has announced that he wants men immediately for common and skilled labor and tractor operators.

Peter Kiewit and Sons and George Condon and Co. of Omaha have the contract for the frame buildings and sewerage disposal at the air base. This crew has not arrived, but a representative was here the first of the week to make arrangements to run the payroll through the Bruning Bank.

The well drillers are already at work at the location and expect to put down two wells.

Condemnation proceedings were begun in Federal Court by US Attorney Votava this week to secure the land for the Bruning Satellite Air Field. Definite information is still unavailable as to the exact size of the base.

T.H. Wilken is acting "housing man" here. Local folks--town and country--who have rooms to rent, or can serve meals, should notify him at once as to how many they can care for. Also if they can accommodate trailer houses on their property.

Actual construction of the Bruning Satellite Air Base began Monday (Sept. 21, 1942) when G. H. Lowe's crew started the dirt moving on the site. Much heavy machinery has been moving to the scene and more workmen are going in every day. In addition, considerable local labor is being signed up.

The Bruning Army Air Field

G. H. Lowe of Bruning, contractor in charge of the dirt moving here, informed the BANNER that their employees were not required to join any union."

THE BRUNING BANNER October 1, 1942 states: "Recent developments on the Bruning satellite Air Field was announced the first of the week by the war department that Stephen-Brown Company and Poole Contracting Company of Kansas City, Mo. had been awarded the contract for the construction of concrete paving and incidental work--cost to be between $1,000,000 and $5,000,000.

The construction of roads, drainage and fencing is to cost between $50,000 and $100,000. The G. H. Lowe Company, who has been here from the start, is doing this work. Most of the buildings on the site have not been moved--being used temporarily for offices and storage space. Lights have been installed and work progresses 24 hours a day."

A **WESTERN UNION** telegram was received by the **BRUNING BANNER** and printed in large print:
"It is requested that you bring to the attention of the people the urgent need for labor at the Air Field. Projects being converted at Fairmont, Bruning and Harvard, Nebraska, to be able to complete these jobs on time. In order to be of service to the county it is necessary that all available be received.
    (signed) Major Burgwin, Area Engineer"

The October issues of the **BRUNING BANNER** states "the pouring of concrete for the runways at the Bruning Satellite Air Base commenced the first of the month and has been gaining momentum ever since as more material, equipment and help arrived on the scene. Grading the runways varies from 300 to 500 feet wide. Three runways are being built in the shape of a triangle--one about 9,000 feet long and the other two some 6,000 feet long. The concrete will be run to a depth of 12 inches.

Carpenters are now busily engaged in construction of the various buildings on the site. This work will progress more rapidly as the flow of material increases.

The United States Employment Service is anxiously looking for laborers to work on the satellite air bases in this area. It is brought out that farmers, who might be interested in working for a few weeks, can work on these projects without any danger of being frozen to their job. Should they, after two weeks' work desire to be released to harvest their crops, the contractor will gladly release them. Common labor wages are 60c per hour for the first 40 hours and time and a half for overtime on the 70 hour a week basis. Lt. Zingler of the Army Air Base at Topeka, Kansas is in town today interviewing applicants for work the Bruning Air Field Post Exchange."

Not a lot is known about what happened on the plains which were now to be the Bruning Air Base. Not too much was printed after this because it was all "TOP SECRET." Picture taking was absolutely forbidden. After all, the nation was at war, everything was under censorship; and this was to be a military air base, vital to our nations security.

The Bruning Army Air Field

Eligibility List For War Housing Here

A step to assist builders of privately-financed war housing in Bruning, Nebr., to determine the eligibility of war workers to occupy such housing was made effective on July 12, it was announced by Charles J. Horan, Acting Regional Representative of the National Housing Agency.

This action applies to all privately-financed war housing for which priority applications were made after February 10, 1943. Use of this housing is limited to essential in-migrant civilian war workers, Mr. Horan explained. The builder can accept war worker tenants he believes to be eligible, filling out forms (NHA 60-8) citing proof of eligiblity and sending those forms to the Regional Representative.

Builders of war housing for which application for priority assistance was made prior of Feb. 10, 1943, are not obligated to house only "in-migrant" war workers, nor are they obligated to follow the procedure outlined above. These builders have the right under their priorities, to house war workers who are not necessarily in-migrants. However in view of the critical housing shortage, the NHA has requested their cooperation by applying voluntarily the same criteria of eligibility and the same method of selection which apply to war housing receiving priority assistance after Feb. 10, 1943. If they have not voluntarily used the Compliance Report (NHA 60-8) or rented to a war worker with a Referral Card, these builders also are requested to fill out a Special Occupancy Report (Form NHA 60-9) when a dwelling has been rented and return it to the Regional Representative as a notification that the house is no longer available.

To expediate further the choice of tenants, Mr. Horan announced a list of firms and industries at Bruning, prepared by his office and the regional office of the War Manpower Commission, whose workers are eligible for war housing accommodations. These workers, if they are not in-migrants, are only eligible for privately-financed housing on which application for priority assistance was made prior of Feb. 10, 1943, he explained.

Information relative to the names of firms and industries which appear on the locality list may be obtained from the State Office of the Federal Housing Ad-

Bruning Allotted 120 FHA Dwellings

Omaha. (From the Office of War Information)—New housing programs for five Nebraska communities -- Grand Island, Sidney, Harvard, Bruning and Fairmont -- have been approved by the National Housing Agency in Washington, according to an announcement received Monday.

Details of the programs, made public by Willard F. Day, regional NHA representative in Kansas City, include:

(1) Grand Island—200 family dwelling units, for employes of the Cornhusker Ordnance Plant and the Army Air Base. These are in addition to the 640 dormitory units approved some time ago, and 282 private family units approved in March.

(2) Sidney—790 dwelling units of which 150 will be for single women and 640 for families, for employes of the Sioux Ordnance Depot.

(3) Harvard—400 dwelling units of which 140 will be for single women and 260 for families, for employes of the Army Air Base.

(4) Bruning—120 additional family dwellings for employes of the Army Air Base.

(5) Fairmont—120 family dwelling units, for employes of the Army Air Base.

These units are to be constructed by the Federal Public Housing Authority with federal funds. All the programs have been referred to the FPHA regional office in Kansas City.

Government To Build 120 Housing Units In Bruning

The Federal Public Housing program to construct 120 family dwelling units with federal funds for civilian war workers at Bruning is taking form.

A twenty-acre tract in the southeast part of town has been acquired from Rhine Tjaden on which these units will be built. Surveyors are already at work on the project.

According to information, there will be 30 buildings, each comprising four family units. They will vary in size—some units to contain more rooms than others, according to need.

On this site, the government will also take care of the building of streets and alleys, light and power lines and laying water mains. A sewerage disposal unit for these dwellings will also be included in the project.

The Banner will be able to give further information when actual work gets underway.

Housing Project For Civilian Air Field Workers

Omaha. (From Office of War Information)—A program for the construction or conversion of 60 housing units, to provide needed quarters for persons moving into the vicinity of Bruning, Nebraska to accept jobs as essential civilian employes of the Army Air Base there, has been approved by the National Housing Agency in Washington, according to word received May 12th.

Willard F. Day, regional NHA representative at Kansas City, pointed out that while the housing is intended primarily for the town of Bruning, the towns of Hebron and Ohiowa also may construct new houses or convert existing houses under this quota.

Of the 51 new dwelling units, 26 are to be rented from $31 up to $40, and 25 from $40 to $50. Rent for the 15 units to be converted from existing structures will range from $31 up to $40. All will be constructed by private industry and with private funds.

Contract Let July 20 For Bruning Housing Project

Sealed bids will be received until July 20 by the Public Housing Authority for providing all labor, materials and equipment and performing all work necessary for and incidental to the construction and completion of War Housing Project No. NEB-25064, located at Bruning, Nebr., it has been announced.

This project, to be constructed on a 19.72-acre tract acquired from R. Tjaden in the southeast part of town, consists of 25 dwelling unit buildings containing 120 dwelling units, one community building and one field construction office.

Construction of the entire project consists of: Excavating and grading, site improvement, utilities (sewer, gas and water), overhead electrical distribution, construction of all buildings, field construction office and lawns. The entire work for the project is to be completed with 120 calendar days (except dawns and road surfacing operations).

These housing units are to be constructed by the Federal Housing Authority and are to be occupied by in-migrant civilian war workers at the Bruning army air field.

The Bruning Army Air Field

Fairbury Is the Next to Vie For Housing at Bruning's Briar Park

(Fairbury Journal)

Several towns in the vicinity of the former Bruning Air Base, northwest of Fairbury about 20 miles, are trying to get the material which has been declared "surplus" from that base to use to put in buildings to relieve the housing shortage.

It is understood that an act of Congress has been signed by the President which would permit this to be done. Under this new act it is expected that the government will furnish public housing to towns without cost to be rented exclusively to returned veterans. It is presumed that under this new law the city would be required to furnish a location and proper connections with light, water, sewer and gas, on a term basis of three or five years.

Lincoln, Beatrice and Fairbury are in line for some of this surplus material.

C. B. Willard, secretary of the Chamber of Commerce of Beatrice, has gone to Chicago to represent Beatrice, to see if they can get 50 housing units from the Bruning base.

Russell A. Davis, secretary of the Chamber of Commerce of Fairbury, was in consultation with Mr. Willard and it is our understanding that they have worked together. There are 121 units at Bruning and Fairbury stands in line to get its share of these units if we can meet the conditions of the act of Congress, which no one knows anything about yet but will in a few days.

The Beatrice secretary will represent Fairbury in presenting arguments to help secure these units to relieve the housing shortage.

* * *

FHA approval of the transfer of 50 Bruning government housing units to Beatrice is expected within ten days, Chamber Secretary Ben Willard said after conferring with FHA officials in Chicago.—Lincoln Journal.

Traer, Iowa, In Line For Housing Units

Accommodations for 21 families has been allocated to Traer, Iowa, from Bruning's housing project, according to a letter received by The Banner this week from the newspaper publisher there.

The writer asked many questions in regard to the construction and condition of the housing units, and stated their allotment would be converted into three-family apartments. Traer is about 100 miles miles northeast of Des Moines.

On Tuesday, the town sent two representatives here by plane to make arrangements for the transfer.

20 Brair Park Dwellings Moved To Minnesota

The federal public housing authority last week authorized the moving of 20 dwellings from Bruning's housing project to Fergus Falls, Minn., where they will house veterans' families. Previously, 21 units were allocated to Traer, Iowa.

The Great Western Construction Co., of Omaha, have been authorized to do the dismantling work at the local project for the various transfers and have been at work here for the past two weeks.

The contract calls for removal of buildings, including masonry, with grounds smoothed off and put back in original condition. The streets and sidewalks will remain.

Bruning Is Allocated Ten Housing Units

That the Village of Bruning would be allocated ten housing units at Brair Park, was the decision handed to Trustees Fred H. Bruning and John Henkel when they conferred with housing officials in Chicago last week. Arrangements are also being made for the local Legion post to obtain the administration building at the site.

Village Seeks To Get Part Of Briar Park

Working To Acquire 24 Units; Also Main Office Building For Legion Post

Following a special order issued by the Surplus Property Administration that local governments may acquire government housing for a period of five years, Mayor Fred H. Bruning has been notified by the Federal Housing Authority that it is entirely probable that the Village of Bruning may take over Section E at Briar Park.

Section E comprises 24 units and is located in the southwest portion of the existing project. As to rentals, it is suggested that the rents be adjusted in accordance with the income of veterans who would have preference under the ruling. The units may be rented furnished, and are of one- two- and three-bedroom sizes.

Arrangements are also underway to acquire the main office building to be used by the local American Legion Post.

A program is being prepared by the National Housing Agency to make such projects available. When all the red tape is cleared through the various channels, the Village will make every effort to speed up the transfer and relieve the housing shortage here.

The Bruning Army Air Field

Instructions To Citizens On Blackouts

1. Stay in your house if possible.
2. Keep your radio turned on low during the test period.
3. Do not, under any circumstances, get into the streets, but if unavoidably caught on the street don't hurry, push or crowd. Be calm and cool.
4. At the warning signal of the siren all traffic must cease. Park your car and extinguish all lights at once. Remain nearby. You may remain seated therein but do not smoke, light matches or flashlights or use any lights whatever. You may double park when so directed by the police.
5. No smoking, lighting of matches or flashlights is permitted on sidewalks, in doorways, in alleys or any open places.
6. At the All Clear signal of the siren you may resume your activities but please do not hurry. Traffic will be congested and the danger of accidents caused by too much hurry will be present.
7. All lights in homes, stores, public buildings, apartments, etc., must be blacked out until the All Clear Signal of the siren.
8. Emergency vehicles, such as fire department trucks, ambulances, police cars, doctors' cars, and special emergency cars, if absolutely necessary, will be authorized to travel but should be equipped with approved blackout devices. Special lighting, only for use during this test blackout, may be allowed by certain necessary industries which would not be allowed during a real blackout. (This is so as to not slow up necessary defense production.) In the event of a fire alarm, the fire department will proceed as usual and street lights may be turned on during their run to such fire. Emergency and official vehicles will proceed cautiously so as not to endanger persons or property.
9. Merchants should have a member of their organization at their places of business to extinguish all lights and to guard such establishments. All signs and window lights must be extinguished.
10. Sky lights must be effectively covered and all lights blacked-out.
11. Keep off the roofs. Damage to the roofs and the danger of accidents during total darkness makes it impossible for the building owners to allow it.
12. Do not use the telephone during the period of the blackout or for 30 minutes thereafter, except for vital necessities, such as calling the fire or police departments, doctors, etc.
13. Follow the instructions given you by the Air Raid Wardens, Police, Auxiliary Police, Firemen and Auxiliary Firemen and all Civilian Defense officers. They have been specially trained for your protection.
14. Learn what to do, what not to do and how to act under a real raid.
15. Failure on the part of even one civilian to carry out the blackout may bring injury or death to many. Such failure can be treated only as a criminal offense.

Be Cool — Be Calm — Be Sensible!

State-wide Blackout Test on Dec. 14

State Civilian Defense Coordinator Walter F. Roberts announces that Governor Griswold has authorized a state-wide test blackout to be held the night of December 14. The test will be held under the supervision of the Seventh Service Command. All communities in the state are to have their blackout machinery in perfect working order by that time, so that the test will be a complete success. There have been a few county-wide tests made already, and many tests of local communities, and in most instances the results have proved to be successful. Every citizen in every community in the state should personally see that the first state-wide test is a success.

More information will be published later on Bruning's blackout set-up, when arrangements are worked out.

Blackout on Dec. 14 Must Be Observed

The blackout test that will be observed on December 14, at 10:00 p.m. is under the authority of the Commanding Officer of the 7th Corps Area. The enforcement of this order is placed in the hands of the mayor or chairman of the boards of cities and villages in this area. They will be helped by the County Civilian Defense Council, but the actual enforcement will be by the local municipal leaders.

In the country the information will be relayed to the people by the leaders of the neighborhood group. This blackout is under the orders of the U. S. Army and must be observed by everyone. All lights must be either turned out or the windows darkened for a period of twenty minutes.—Thayer County Council of Defense.

BRUNING ALL SET FOR TEST BLACKOUT

Members of the Bruning volunteer fire department will serve as Wardens during the Blackout here Monday night. At the Firemen's meeting this week, each member was assigned a sector to patrol.

At ten o'clock, a long blast of the fire siren will mark the beginning of the Blackout. All lights are to go out immediately and not be turned on again until the "all-clear" signal of the siren at 10:20.

Rural folks have received their instructions through the mail, and a leader has been assigned for each community.

This Blackout is official and must be observed.

BLACKOUT COMPLETE AT BRUNING

The Blackout at Bruning Monday night was a complete success, as reported by the 15 Wardens who patroled the town. Cooperation of citizens was 100%, as not a light was visible anywhere.

The Bruning Army Air Field

HOUSING

May 20, 1943 <u>Bruning Banner:</u>

Government to permit 51 new houses in area in Hebron, Bruning and Ohiowa. Bruning and Ohiowa area are called the defense area. Houses must be rented to civilian war workers only. Twenty-six houses rent from $31 to $39.99 month. Twenty-five houses rent from $40-50 a month. Additional charges may be made for utilities or other service."

In June of 1943 the Government announced they would build a housing unit in Bruning. Officially it was called War Housing Project NEB-25064, Bruning, NE. The government bought 19.2 acres of ground in the southeast part of Bruning from Rhine Tjaden. The government proceeded to build 120 family units.

Each building was a rectangular wooden building with a two way roof. This housing facility was called "Blair Park" locally. There were 30 buildings of 4 apartments each. Each apartment opened into the kitchen, with a half wall separating into a living room area, and 2 bedrooms and a bathroom off the kitchen. Streets were built running north and south.

There was a Community Building and a Utility Building. The Federal Public Housing covered everything with Federal Funds. This included light and power, streets and alleys, water main and sewerage. Lt. Lentfer states that he didn't believe Bruning had any kind of city sewerage before this project and the city took over this sewerage facility after the war.

These homes were built for the construction workers, but after they finished building the Base, officers and their wives moved into the housing unit.

Ten apartments were given to the village when they were no longer needed. The Community building was sold to the Legion, then to Vernon Elting for a woodworking shop. It is still standing in 1996 although it is vacant. The housing was sold to Max West in 1973.

E.W. Thomas of Alexandria converted the building north of his Lumber Yard into sort of a dormitory for construction workers. He put in bunk beds and his wife helped him to furnish it with sheets and comforters. She was going to help him keep up this housing unit until the first time she went down to wash the sheets, she found liquor bottles and a drunken worker. She never went down to the unit again.

Every farm house around the area or in town that had a spare bed room had it rented out. Housing was indeed a premium.

The Bruning Army Air Field

THE DAY ROOM

The Day Room was a room on the Air Base where the service men could play the piano, cards, ping pong or checkers, read and just generally relax. A lot of public interest was created about the Day Room. Not only did the surrounding counties become involved in furnishing Day Rooms, but **NINE counties** became involved.

The following articles appeared in **THE HEBRON JOURNAL** on July 29, 1943 and August 5, 1943:

JEFFERSON COUNTY TO FURNISH ONE DAY ROOM

At camp and Hospital Council Committee Meeting of the American Red Cross in Fairbury July 23, the Jefferson County chapter voted to furnish one of the day rooms at the Bruning Army Air Field. The Thayer County Chapter had also promised to furnish a room.

PLANS FOR FURNISHING ONE DAY ROOM
PUBLIC EFFORTS FOR BRUNING ARMY AIR FIELD

The first meeting of the Thayer County Camp and Hospital Service Committee was held at the courthouse last Friday evening. A group of about 40 individuals, representing the various civic and community groups throughout the county attended. Mrs. Perce Rosenbaum, County Chairman, was in charge and outlined the objectives for Thayer County.

Lt. Sidney J. Posner, member of the Bruning Air Field, made a talk concerning the Dayroom's needs at his post and Vernon E. Hungate, Field Director of the American Red Cross at the Bruning Field, spoke on the purposes of the organization of the Camp and Hospital service...

The Camp and Hospital Council serves as a centralized medium for all organizations in the county such as clubs, lodges, churches and schools. Through the Council, donations may be made and articles of furniture contributed.

The following items are necessary to furnish one Dayroom (100x20) at the Bruning Air Field: 6 smoking stands, 12 straight backed chairs, 1 pool table, 1 piano, 3 floor lamps, 8 writing desks, 6 davenports, 6 easy chairs, 1 ping pong table, 2000 Victory Books, 3 card tables and 4 to 7 rugs.

Will you please look through your homes for something you would like to give to furnish this room. Call one of these ladies if you have something to give: Mrs. William J. Hill; phone 336; Mrs. Ferd W. McKenzie, phone 312; or Mrs. Harold Shearer, Phone 197.

Nearly the same article as the above is in the **BRUNING BANNER** except it states also: "This furniture need not be new but in good usable condition. Anyone wishing to make a contribution of furniture and other items may notify any one of the committee and the articles will be collected. Donations may be sent to Mrs. R.E. Collison, chairman. The committee is composed of Mrs. R.E. Collison, Mrs. Virgil Bugbee, Martin H. Philippi and R. J. Liliedoll."

The Bruning Army Air Field

THE HEBRON JOURNAL August 26, 1943:

FURNISHING DAY ROOMS FOR SOLDIERS
LADIES DO GOOD WORK

The south-central Nebraska Camp and Hospital Council met at the Bruning Air Field on Thursday, August 19th with a very good attendance. Hamilton, York, Clay, Webster, Fillmore, Gage, Jefferson, Thayer and Nuckolls counties each had representation and report of the work they are doing.

Thayer County had 55 representatives, twenty-three of whom were from Hebron. The Day Room our county has furnished was completed and opened to the public. It is well furnished and comfortable.

War Department Tells How Air Bases--Like Bruning's--are Built

In the office of nearly every one of the area engineers of the Missouri River Division of the Corps of Engineers, there hangs a cartoon depicting an area engineer receiving orders to build a war effort project on a piece of marshland. His orders from his superior are, "We are in no hurry for this project, you may take your time, just so it is ready for occupancy in ten days."

Under the fast moving pace set by Colonel Lewis A. Pick, the Division Chief, that order it not as far wrong as it would seem at first. What should in ordinary times, take a year to build, must be constructed in one-sixth to one-twelfth the time. Speed, the all essential element in this war, is the living symbol of the officers of the Division.

A close-knit organization, supervised by the Division and directed by the three districts—Kansas City, Missouri; Omaha, Nebraska; and Fort Peck, Montana—sends officers and men from the division and district on a moment's notice to assist an officer in the field to keep the Missouri River Division "ahead of schedule" all of the time. Men and material are shifted just as a commanding officer shifts his men and material in battle.

The construction program, in the nine states of the Missouri River Division, is in reality the battleground of the home forces. Huge maps are the working grounds for each chief of a division. Each hour will change the map. When new installations are authorized, men and material must be shifted. Lines of communications and avenues of transportation opened. An area engineer placed to direct the work.

It matters little whether the order is to build an air base, a satellite field, a cantonment, an ordnance plant, a depot, a warehouse, a hospital, a storage area, a relocation center, or a dog kennel, it all must be constructed at once. The site selected may be far removed from railroads, bus travel, or plane service. These must be installed and lines of communication, hundreds of telephone lines made available.

The material sections may have all of the available material in use at the moment that a new war effort project is authorized. All of the big machines are working at top speed, but the new project must have attention. Material is pulled from several jobs, and machines, taken from this place and that place, are either on the road or on flat cars bound for the new job almost before the area engineer arrived to hold on until something else may be gotten for them.

Real estate men set up their offices and begin to buy the land. Surveyors, in many cases, are on the land almost simultaneously with the real estate men. They are laying out roads, runways, barrack sites, and drainage systems, while real estate men purchase the land. Complete office forces must be recruited and set up by the the area engineer, who in all probability has just finish building a large airport 30 to days ahead of schedule and has left his assistant in charge of mopping up that project while he takes over the new one.

Equipment, material, and manpower must be planned in advance and orders sent out. Trainloads of material must be arriving each day to keep the schedule, and the men busy. To illustrate this, the average small air field must have at least 150 train carloads of material alone each day of the time that they are pouring concrete to keep the pavers busy. These must come in an uninterrupted flow either by train or truck.

Sewerage system must be planned and installed. If sufficient water is not available, then wells must be dug. This may mean that miles of pipe will have to be laid. The local electrical power system is called upon for electricity, but this in practically all cases is supplemented with a power plant of the projects.

Some idea of the magnitude of the job that confronts some of the area engineers, may be realized when it is understood that runways constructed in sixty days or less, that is starting from the time the area engineer arrives throughout the planning stages, the surveying, and the form setting before a yard of paving can be laid, could, if stretched out in a standard 20 foot concrete highway, reach from Omaha to Lincoln.

He still must build his barracks for the men, recreational halls, theatre buildings, commissary, post exchanges, and churches. Roads that will stand years of usage must be constructed along with the rest. Then, he must see that the roads into and away from the area are suitable for the usage to which the user will demand of them.

Hangars for the air bases and shops, along with miscellaneous warehouses, are by no means a small part of the project.

The Division real estate section must work at top speed so that nothing is built on land that does not belong to Uncle Sam. The personnel branch must have available names and suggested persons for the immediate shift to a job. The operations division must know where every piece of machinery and equipment is at all times and to what use it is being put. They, also, must know the exact status of the work of every project so as to be able to suggest changes of equipment. They must know the exact amount of material on hand so the surplus can be moved within the hour if necessary.

The engineering division stands ready with available information as to cost and engineering problems.

The contracts and labor relations of the division must stand ready to facilitate all contracts and assist in the placing of workers on the job.

Because of certain military censorship restrictions, all of this information must be kept a secret.

A little less than a year ago, Colonel Lewis A. Pick was placed in command of this Division. Under his leadership, the organization has grown to perfect teamwork and into a fast moving, hard hitting, efficient division whose motto is the colonel's own making, "Make no decision that will not speed to a successful and efficient end, the job you are assigned."

NEBRASKA

BRUNING ARMY AIR FIELD
BRUNING

Restricted

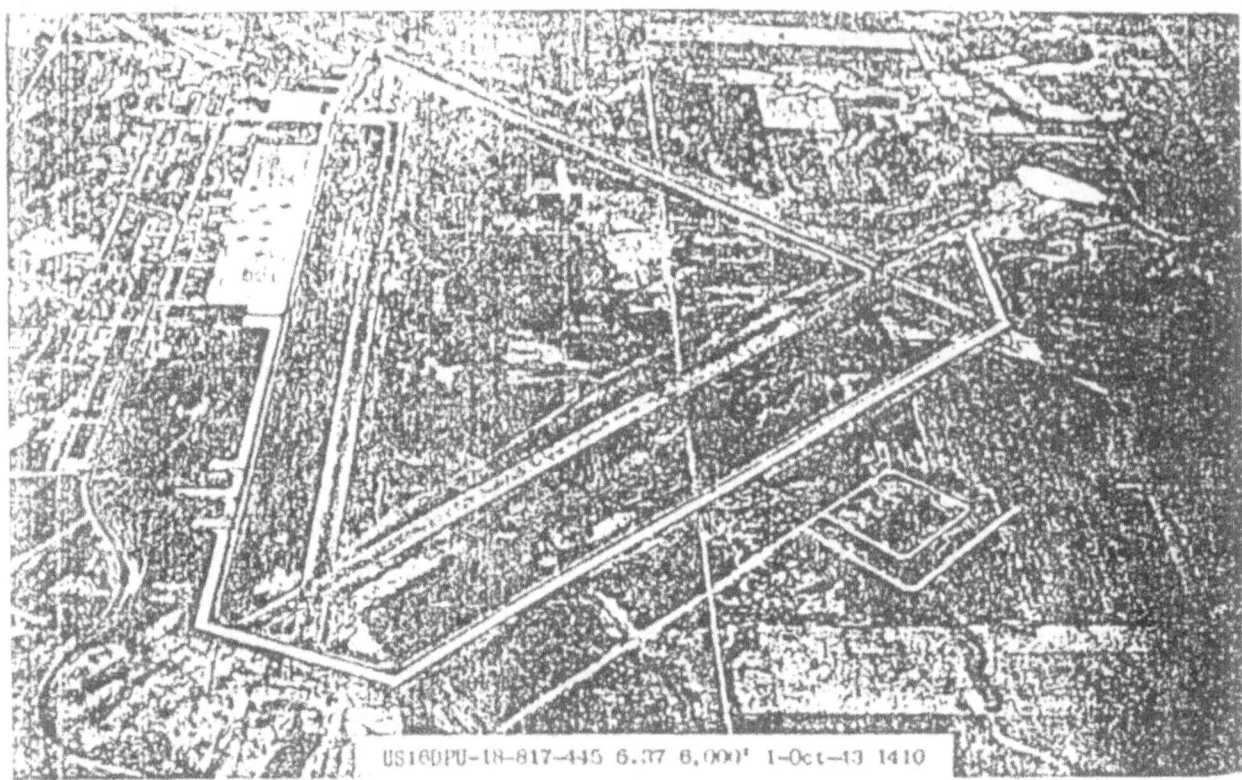

LOCATION:

    FROM CITY - 7.3 mi. E (air line).
    POSITION - Lat. 40°20'08". Long. 97°25'28".
    ALTITUDE - 1,542'.
    CITY POPULATION - 232.

DESCRIPTION:

    TYPE - Army.
    SIZE - 1,720 acres (total area).
    SHAPE - Irregular.
    LANDING AREA - Runways: N/S 6,800' x 150',
      NE/SW 6,800' x 150', NW/SE 6,800' x 150',
      concrete.
    DRAINAGE - Artificial (adequate).
    APPROACH HAZARDS - None within 40/1 glide angle.
    MARKINGS - Tetrahedron (lighted).
    LIGHTING - Beacon (rotating); obst.; contact;
      B-2 runway (portable); flood (stationary).

FACILITIES:

    HANGARS - (1) 225' x 202', door 160'2" x 25'
      (center section 37' x 10'); (2) 202' x
      125', door 160'2" x 25' (center section
      37' x 10'); (1) 149' x 96', door 120'4"
      x 25'5"; wood.
    SHOPS - Major engine repair; major aircraft
      repair.
    GASOLINE -
      At Airport - 73, 91, and 100 octane; 18
        servicing trucks.
      In Vicinity - 91 and 100 octane, 4.0 mi. N.
    OIL -
      At Airport - SAE 50 to 60.
      In Vicinity - SAE 50 to 60, 4.0 mi. N.
    COMMUNICATIONS - Telephone; telegraph; teletype.
    PERSONNEL ACCOMMODATIONS (Transient) -
      At Airport - 25 officers; 50 enlisted men.
      In Vicinity - At Bruning.

March 1945

RADIO FACILITIES:

    RANGE - None.
    TOWER - 396 kcs. and 126.18 mcs. (Cont.
    GND/AIR - None.
    INSTRUMENT APPROACH AND LETDOWN PROCEDU.

WEATHER (Records from Station at Bruning

    PREVAILING WIND - SW, except Dec., Jan.,
      Mar., NW; Apr., Sept., SE.
    PRECIPITATION - Av. mo., 0.42" (Jan.) to
      (June); av. yr., 28.06".
    TEMPERATURE - No data.
    FOG - Mar., Apr.
    FACILITIES (At Airport) - First-order
      station; Army weather teletype, 24
      operation.

TRANSPORTATION:

    AIRLINES - None reported.
    RAILROADS - Burlington Route, at Bruning
      Sidings - Capacity, 15 cars, 6.0 mi. from
      field.
    ROADS - State No. 4, 0.8 mi. S; county road
      0.9 mi. W; improved.
    FACILITIES - Bus service.

OPERATED BY: Army Air Forces.

OWNED BY: U. S. Govt.

Those Who Flew
Bruning Army Air Field
Paul Baker, BAAF's first Control Tower Operator

I was one of the first control operators at the Bruning Army Air Field. I was there about the entire time the field was open. Can you imagine what we Easterners, many from New York City, thought when we saw the sign "Bruning Population 232". Soon it swelled to several thousand as the military personnel arrived.

When Bruning opened it was a B-24 Bomber Base. We couldn't imagine why so many Air Bases were built so close together. To add fuel to the fire, Fairmont and Bruning were both B-24 bases. Several times pilots would say they were wanting landing instructions but they were on the wrong field. After watching for several weeks, we could see they were not ready for combat but they were desperately needed overseas. So many were lost in Europe.

The next year Bruning was converted into a P-47 Fighter Base. Can you imagine taking a young pilot right out of training and putting them in a High Powered Thunderbolt? While I was on duty one flyer crashed on landing and his plane burst into flame near our control tower. Another day, a pilot dove his plane from 16,000 feet straight down into the field.

"We Control Operators were not popular on the Field. Because of the pressures of our work, and the demands that we be in the sharpest mental condition, we never had to stand roll call, inspection, KP or similar army duties. Our furloughs and leaves were not cancelled as the others were.

I found those people of Bruning, Hebron and Fairbury and other small towns were the nicest, warmest, most generous and kindest people I have ever met. We were privileged and fortunate to have spent time there. They say the Lord works in mysterious ways, I'm sure glad he moved me to Nebraska for a time."

Paul Baker, Southbury, Connecticut

All Nebraska Air Fields were built on the same generic plan. The uninsulated barracks each had three coal burning heating stoves in them.

The Bruning Army Air Field Infirmary. Inset: Two Medics in front of the infirmary. Byron Behm picture

Bruning Army Air Field Chapel

Interdenominational Chapel was moved to Filley, NE by the American Lutherans when the base closed. It was then struck by lightening and burned down. Photo --Pastor Tom Aamren.

Th PX at Bruning Army Air Field
Picture from Lorraine Doggett, Chester, NE

The PX at Bruning Army Air Base —Coffee Shop and Soda Fountain
Notice Jute Box selector in center — Picture from Lorraine Doggett

The Bruning Army Air Field Office Workers
L-R: Gladys Currey, Evelyn Hasselbring, Phil Riechert, Marie Christenancy, Frieda ___, Anna Keilwitz, Cecil Huff, Katherine Zetts, Lois Martin. Front row: Hazel Stark, Wilma Garland, Margaret ___, June Brown, Peggy Smith, Lt. William Russell, J.L. Cumberlan, Lt. Stanely Erzar. Picture Lorraine Doggett.

Bruning Army Air Field
Carpenter Workers

The Parachute Unit — Made and packed parachutes

Parachute workers: Back, L-R: Mrs. Johanas (F.D.) Daykin; Opal Junket (P.D.) Fairbury; Unknown, (F.D.); Lucy Hendershot (P.O.) Hebron; Fayetta Simpson (F.D.) Alexandria & Fairbury; Front row: Nice helpful unknown man; Ruth Hohlfeld Lay, (P.O.), Deshler; Jeanne Ray, Hebron (P.O.); Mr. Eisenson, Foreman; Office Worker, Fairbury; Miss Steele, Hebron (F.D.); Irene Wickman (P.O.) supervisor, Fairbury. (F.D. - Fabric Department   P.D. - Parachute Department) Picture from LaVerne Doggett - Chester.

The Bruning Army Air Field Fire Department
Picture from Lorraine Doggett, Chester, NE

Making A Move
Featured in this photo taken in 1957 is the first of two former Fairbury College housing units being raised before its ride from the northwest part of the block between J and K, 11th and 12th streets, to a site north of the college classroom building on Ninth Street, to house classrooms and a library. The buildings were given to the college in 1948 by Bruning Air Force Base.

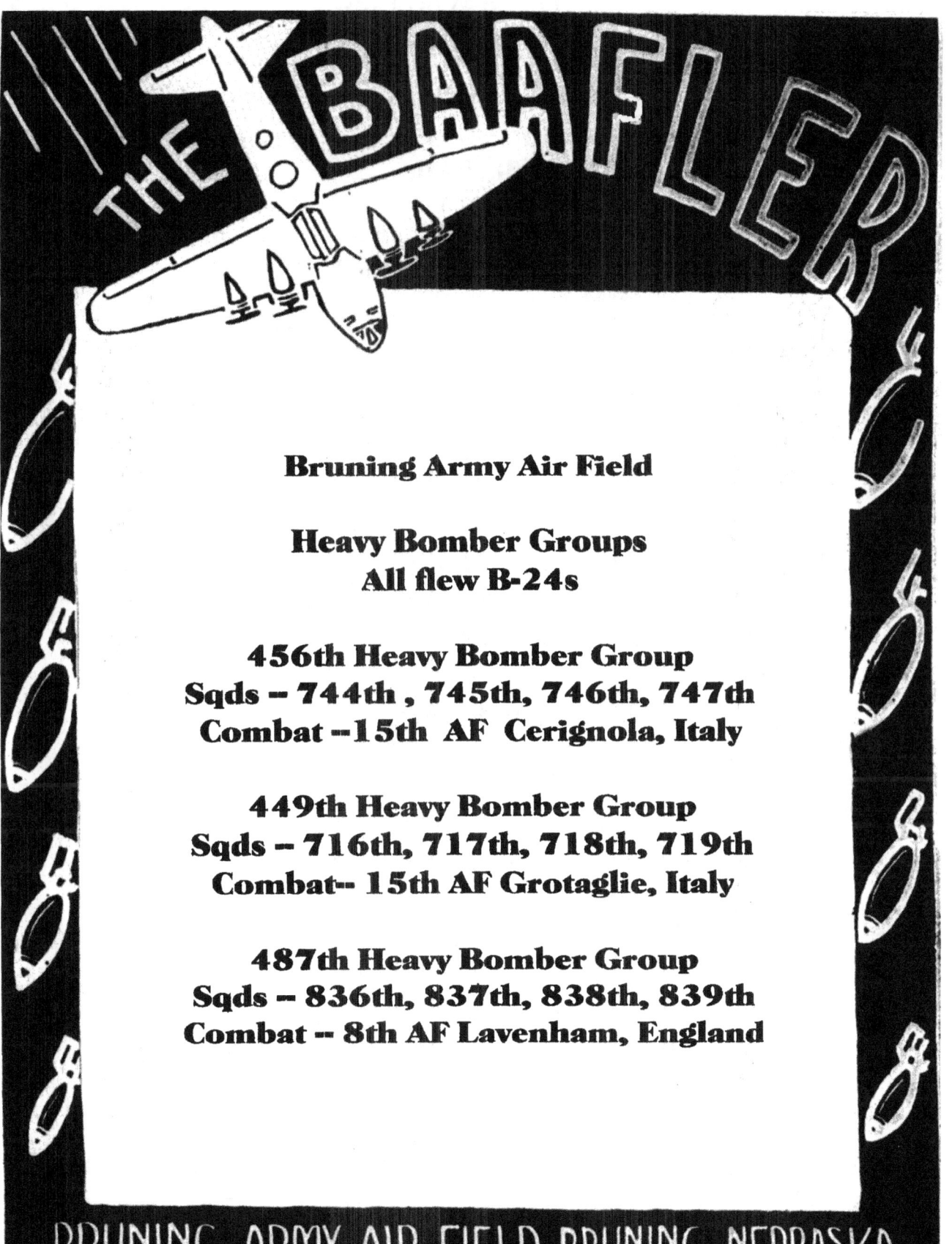

Those Who Flew
B-24s at Bruning AAF

456th Heavy Bomber Group:
Squadrons: 744th, 745th, 746th, 748th

Activated 14 May 1943 Wendover, Utah
21 August 1943—"one B-24 and commanding officer arrived in Bruning"
24 August 1943—"the remainder of men (of 456th) have arrived"
*taken from mimeographed paper ***The Baffler*** published on Bruning Base
28 August 1943 — Flew four B-24Ds over base on Dedication"
"Possibly 30 men to a squadron"— Bill Phillips, KS member of 745th
7 Sept. 1943 — Picture from Merle Hagen of CO shows 73 members of 456th
"Had 4 model crews — each to become a squadron model —744, 745, 746, 747"
One B-24 for each Squadron" Bill Clark — Midway, Kentucky 746th tailgunner.
8 October 1943 — 456th left Bruning — ***from 456th Bomb Group History***

449th Heavy Bomb Group:
Squadrons 716th, 717th, 718th, 719th:

Activated May 1, 1943 at Davis Monthan Field, Tucson AZ
6 September 1942 arrived at Bruning Army Air Base in Nebraska
Brought four B-24Ds from Alamogordo, NM Acquired 44 more B-24D
62 brand new B-24Hs from Ford factory, Willow Run factory
Total 110B-24s at Bruning ***Hollie Wilkes Diary,***
Each squad had approx 22 crews formed and trained at Bruning
Approx 2000 men in all in 449th
17 Nov. 1943 started overseas movement
Flew 61 or 62 B-24Hs from Bruning to Grotagglie, Italy
Information from 449 Book From ***Tucson to Grotagglie*** and Col. Hollie Wilkes, Miss

487th Heavy Bomb Group:
Squadrons 836th, 837th, 838th, 839th

22 Sept. 1943 — Activated Maj. Lancaster took command Bruning Sept. 25, 1943
Middle of Nov. 1943 —113 Officers and 512 enlisted men assigned Bruning
30 Nov. 1943 — 165 officers and1100 enlisted men arrived from Pocatello, ID
Dec. 1943 — 13 more crews from Clovis, NM joined 487th
10 Dec. 1943 — entire group effected movement by air and ground echelon from Bruning to Alamogordo, NM.— all information found in ***The History of 487th Bomb Group***. No mention of number of planes. Accuracy of information questioned by members of 449th

Welcome to our

HOME PAGE

456th Bomb Group Association

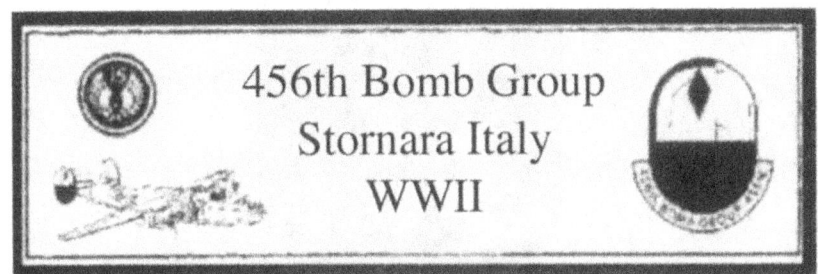

A Brief History Of The 456th Bomb Group

456th BOMBARDMENT GROUP (H) Stornara, Italy 1943-1945

The 456th Bomb Group was formed 14 May 1943.

On 1 June 1943, the 456th Bombardment Group (H) was activated, along with it's four squadrons, at Wendover Army Air Field, Wendover Utah. These Squadrons were designated as the 744th, 745th, 746th and the 747th. The 456th Bomb Group would go into combat in the four-engined B-24 heavy bomber aircraft.

The squadrons were not manned until 14 July 1943 after movement to Gowen Field, Boise Idaho.

HEADQUARTERS, 456th Bombardment Group (H), Office of the Group Commander, Gowen Field, Idaho, 14 July 1943

GENERAL ORDERS No. 1

1. In accordance with the provisions of AR 600-20 the undersigned assumes command of the 456th Bomb Group effective this date.

THOMAS W. STEED Col. AC, Commanding

Thus this the first General Order created the 456th Bomb Group, one of the many who were to defeat Hitler and distinguish themselves in the destruction of the Nazi war machine's ability to conduct war.

456TH BOMB GROUP

Group Patch

456th Heavy Bomber Group

456th Stead's Colts

Colonel Steed's "Flying Colts" flew their first combat mission on February 10, 1944 from their base at Stornarella, just south of Foggia, Italy - as a unit of the 304th Bomb Wing Headquartered at Cerignola. When the war ended in May 1945, the 456th had flown over 200 missions, clobbered over 100 targets in 11 different countries, hitting key rail centers, oil fields and, refineries, aircraft factories, airfields and troop concentrations. Its last mission was a "first" for the 15th Air Force, the 100% bombing of the Tarvisio Motor Transport Depot in northern Italy. During this group achievement, Colonel Steed's men had earned one Distinguished Service Cross, 19 Silver Stars, 215 Distinguished Flying Crosses, over 2,000 Air Medals; and the 456th had been awarded two Distinguished Unit Citations (for clobbering aircraft factories at Wiener-Neustadt, Austria, on May 10, 1944; and for "taking care of" the oil refineries at Budapest, Hungary, on July 2, 1944 and had earned seven campaign streamers.)

Those Who Flew
456th Heavy Bomber Group

"We flew our planes to Italy and then my crew was given a new silver plane over there which stood out among the other Olive drab green planes. This new plane was shot down on our 13th mission and I was a prisoner of war the rest of the war and was one of the first to be freed when the war was over." Bill Clark

Letter from Bill Phillips
Manhattan, Kansas 13 Jan 1997

Thanks for sending the book. (This is the blue book printed by the Historical Society entitled *Bruning Army Air Field* I have spent some time reading various parts of it. I am not sure it refreshed my memory, but I was able to more accurately reconstruct some of the events.

It appears that the 456th Bomb Group with its four squadrons (744th, 745th, 746th, 747th) was a small blip on the total activity at BAAF. The Group and each of the Squadrons are mentioned in one or more of the "Baafler" publications. The first reference I found was on August 14th, (P. 145) when the major discussion centered on the softball team. I am sure this was during the time I referred to in my first letter when I recall so few men per squadron.

Then on August 21st a "Baafler" article stated, "... one of our B-24s with our commanding officer arrived..." As more planes arrived, I am sure the level of activity increased. The August 24th paper indicated the remainder of our men (of the 745th, my squadron) have arrived. "We were there at the time of the dedication on August 28th. The last mention I found of the 456th was in "Bomb News" on September 4th. This had to be not long before we departed for our next phases that lead to Muroc, CA and then to Italy." Bill Phillips

456th Newsletter
by Fred the Ed

"Fred the Ed" the publisher of the 456th Newsletter put in a request for news stories from 456er that were stationed at Bruning. He went through issues of *The Baffler* which was the mimeographed newsletter put out on the Bruning Base in 1943 and found and published several of the paragraphs which mentioned a member of the 456th. Fred noted that the paper seemed so highschoolish but of course, the members were just out of high school. They had not been to war or seen combat..

Here is a sample of some of the items Fred noted:

Sgt. Dentler is working in earnest to become the big heart throb of a certain blonde from QM. *(There was a Daniel Dentler in S-3 from Gettysburg PA, current status deceased)* Of course, you must have noticed him giving her the rush at the dance last Saturday and he hasn't let up yet. Good luck Sarge, you'll need it . . . . .

T/Sgt. Blankenheim made his bid for Group Casanova last Saturday night. Did you notice the smile on his face as the women literally dived into his arms while at the dance? .... rough.

Women? — Our Sergeant Major Zabinsky (Zabu, brother Snafu, ventured into town the other night to keep a date with one of the local Fairbury Belles. I don't know if she was a female grappler or not, but the following morning Zabu reported to work supported by two crutches . . . . (Charles Sabinsky is a current member, perhaps he'll see this when I use it in a newsletter.)

Those Who Flew
Bruning Army Air Field

The 456th Heavy Bomber Group was made up of 4 Squadrons
The 744th, 745th, 746th and 747th

Those Who Flew
Bruning Army Air Field

456th Heavy Bomb Group

In the book ***456th Bomb Group 1943-1945*** published by Turner Publishing Company of Paducah, KY there is only a slight mention of the group being in Bruning stating: "The Air Echelon was reunited with the Group Echelon at Bruning AAF, Nebraska. The men of the Group Echelon, after training in Gowen Field (Boise Idaho), had moved on to Bruning AAF in August" Bruning Army Air field is barely mentioned in the 456th web site. Other official sources say the first echelon arrived in Bruning in July 1943 and left as late as October 1943.

The 456th was important in the Bruning Army Air Field history, as they supplied and flew the B24s which flew over the field in the Official Field Dedication on August 28, 1943 and these planes were presented to the public on that day. Nebraskans lined up for miles to attend this dedication. It was an unusually and unbearably hot day and people were overwhelmed by the heat as the estimated crowd of 25,000 Nebraskans were crowded in and waited in line to get to the field. Nebraska farmers were just coming out of the Depression and their cars were old and many had difficulty creeping along waiting their turn in line. The car radiators boiled, even in the few newest 1941 automobiles as they waited in line. 1941 was the last year cars were available until after the war.

"Fred the Ed" Riley who is the historian for the 456th and who publishes the 456th newsletter put in a request for men who were stationed at Bruning to respond and give more details of being at Bruning. Bill Clark gave this recollection via telephone call June 27, 1997:

Bill Clark Box 657
Midway, Kentucky 40347

"I was a tail gunner in the original 746th Squadron of the 456th Bomber Group. There were four model crews given special training at Bruning Army Air Field. The four groups were squadrons numbered 744, 745, 746, 747. Each squad had but one crew and one plane — a B-24G. These four planes flew in formation over the dedication of the Bruning Air Base on August 28, 1943.

When we came to Bruning there was a small PX and a MP unit. The 15th Air Force had not been organized at that time. Of the original 746th there are 4 men still alive in June 1997. Two of them are in very good shape but the other two are not well.

Some of the officers I remember were Major Golden; Capt. Grueber, " Moose" Crowball, Jack Hannon; Captain Frederick Weston Hyde III who was a West Pointer, and Col. Thomas Stead. These went on and became full pledged squadrons. The movie actor Jimmy Stewart was a member of this 456th group."

487th Bombardment Group (Heavy) Group Markings

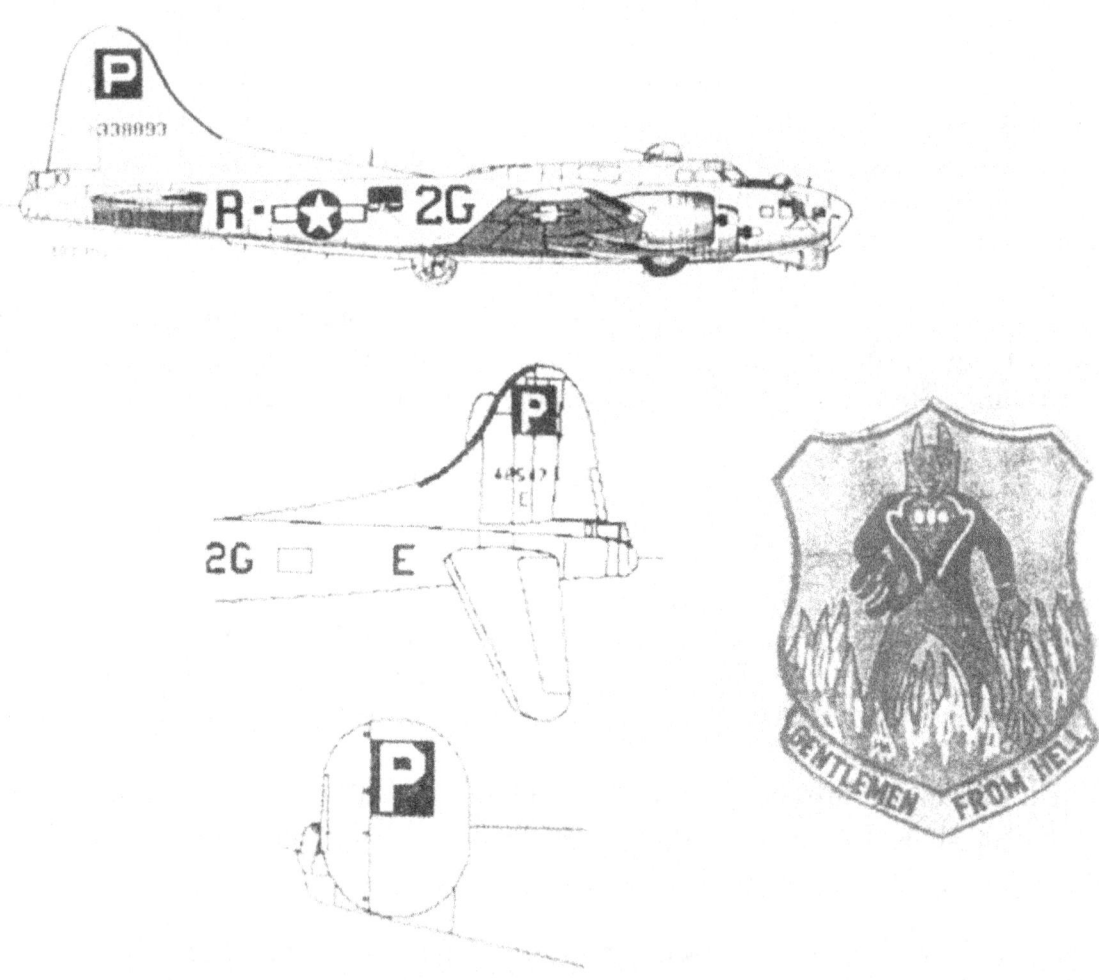

8th AF - 4th Bomb Wing (92nd BW as a B-24 outfit)
487th Bomb Group (square-P)
(836th, 837th, 838th, 839th Bomb Squadrons)
Lavenham, England
Transitioned to B-17s from B-24s

487th Bombardment Group (Heavy)

Activated by Second Air Force on 22 September 1943
Transferred to Eighth Air Force on 15 April 1944
Deactivated by Eighth Air Force on 7 November 1945

Comprised of 836th, 837th, and 838th Bombardment Squadrons. The 8th Anti-submarine Squadron was redesignated to the 839th assigned to the 487th Bomb Group on 1 October 1943.

Bases of Operation
    22 September 1943 - Bruning, Nebraska
    10 December 1943 - Alamogordo, New Mexico
    13 March 1944 - Camp Kilmer, New Jersey
    5 April 1944 - Station 137, Lavenham, Suffolk, England
    25 August 1945 - Drew Field, Florida

Combat Group Commanders
    February 1944 to May 1944 - Lt. Col. Beirne Lay, Jr. (MIA - evaded - returned to duty)
    May 1944 to December 1944 - Col. Robert Taylor III
    December 1944 to May 1945 - Col. William K. Martin
    May 1945 to June 1945 - Lt. Col. Howard C. Todt (Acting CO)
    June 1945 to August 1945 - Col. Nicholas T. Perkins

Missions
    First Mission - 7 May 1944
    Final Mission - 21 April 1945

Total Missions - 185
Sorties - 6,021
Total Tonnage Dropped - 14,641

Aircraft
    Aircraft Used -
    B-24H/J February 1944 to July 1944
    B-17G July 1944 to November 1945

Aircraft Lost-
33 Missing In Action, 24 lost in other operations

Enemy Aircraft Claims-22 destroyed, 6 probable, 18 damaged

The History of the 487th Bomb Group
by Bill Colburn — Atlanta, GA. 487th BG 8AF

On 22 September 1943 an order from Headquarters of the Second Air Force constituted authority for the activation of the 487th Heavy Bomb Group Headquarters. It would be composed of the 836th, 837th, 838th and the 839th Squadrons. The 839th was redesignated to the 8th Antisubmarine Squadron on October 1, 1943.

Major Charles E. Lancaster came to the Army Air Field in Bruning, Nebraska to assume command of the 487th Bombardment Group on 25 September 1943. However, on 10 October 1943 Major Lancaster was absent from Bruning as he and other key personnel attended various courses of instruction at the School of Applied Tactics in Orlando, Florida, Major Cross was in command during his absence.

By the middle of November 1943, a total of 113 officers and 512 enlisted men were assigned to the 487th Bombardment Group Squadron. Commanders and staff had been appointed and organized. Although still in its infancy, the 487th began to assume the identity and functions of an active Bombardment Group.

During the remainder of November the manning of the Group continued at an accelerated pace, seven combat crews from Pocatello, Idaho augmenting the ground personnel who were rapidly approaching authorized strength. 165 Officers and 1100 Enlisted Men were assigned to the 487th Bombardment Group as of 30 November 1943.

Early in December 1943, thirteen more combat crews joined the 487th Bombardment Group from Clovis, New Mexico. On the 10th of December 1943 the entire Group effected a movement by air and ground echelons from the Army Air Field in Bruning, Nebraska to the Army Air Base in Alamogordo, New Mexico where phase training was to be accomplished. As the organization approached authorized strength during December, assignments continued, however, at a diminishing rate, 243 Officers and 1294 Enlisted Men-being assigned as of the close of 1943. Fifty combat crews from Davis-Monthan Field, Tucson, Arizona were assigned to the 487th Bombardment Group early in January 1944. Combat assignment was with the 8th AF at Lavanham, England. They flew B24 aircrafts. Later they flew B17s.

Those Who Flew
Bruning Army Air Field

Merle L. Hagan was born March 25, 1920 in Kirk, CO. He was inducted into the Air Force on March 16, 1942 and was with the original 456th Bomb Group at Bruning, Nebraska. As Merle brought this rare picture of the 456th taken at Bruning to the Thayer County Museum, he said, "I had no idea we were making history at the time."

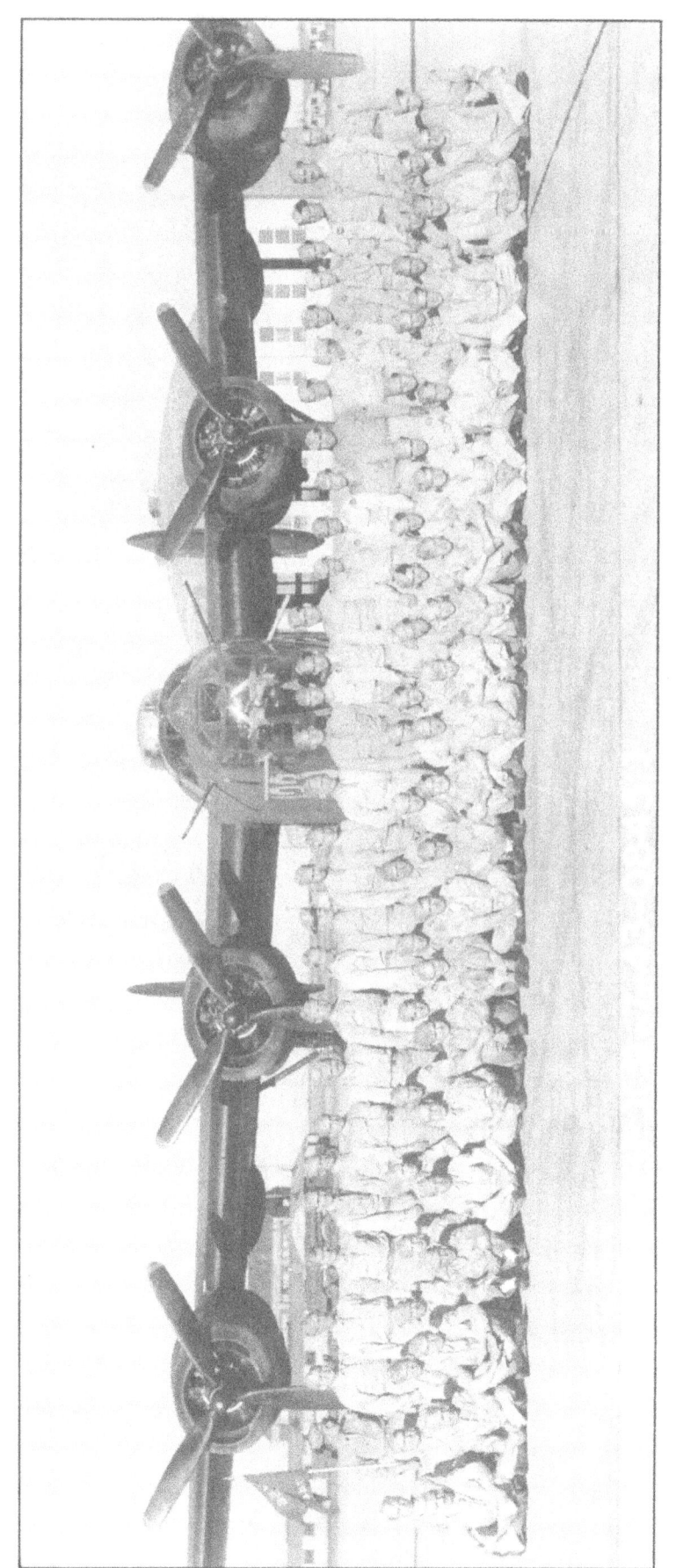

B-24 LIBERATOR #42-52155
COL. "PAT" GENTRY, PILOT
MISSION 65 WEINER NEUSTADT
JU-88 FIRED ROCKET IN ENGINE
CO-PILOT LANHAM INJURED

449TH HEAVY BOMBER GROUP

B-24 Original Drawing

Bill Schlaebitz, a well known architect and artist in Lincoln, NE volunteered to draw a B-24 for the Thayer County Historical Society's second book on the Bruning Army Air Field. We looked for the name of the plane we would honor.

"Things is Rough" was the name of Hartford Fee's plane. In a hand written note he told how he flew over his farm near Coming, Iowa on his way overseas. His mother came out in the yard and waved to him. Think of the emotion she was feeling — here was her son, the pilot, and she was so proud, but on the other hand she knew he was flying into combat and this might be the last time she would see him. We loved the heartwarming story of this farm boy from the Midwest.

"Classy Chassis" was considered for the cover as it was one of the most famous B-24s during the war. It was flown by Ed Sass of the 717th Squadron of the 449th Bomber Group. Unfortunately for Bruning AAF historians, it was not mentioned during the war that this plane flew from the Bruning Base. She was to be brought back to the U.S. but was shot down on her 87th mission.

Mr. Schlaebitz, who was a navigator instructor for the B17 during WWII, was so impressed by the B-24s durability that he chose R.P. "Pat" Gentry's, "Patches" because of the 245 patches she received during the war. The plane was originally named after Lt. Gentry's daughter who was born while he was stationed at Bruning, but was renamed after she had been patched up so many times.

Lt. Col. Gentry was most helpful in sending information to the Thayer County Historical Society about the base. Although in an earlier history written by the 449th Bomber Group, he referred to Bruning as "a God forsaken hell-hole" his later words which he wrote as a reflection of being at Bruning were read at the BAAF Historical marker dedication:

"Looking back from my 80 year old vantage point, Bruning served its purpose very well. We had only a few short weeks to do a critical job. We had to take ten strangers for each crew, put them together as a cohesive unit, give them some basic rudimentary training as a combat team and convince them we could survive at least long enough to reach the combat zone! Had Bruning been other than a quiet rural way station the problems would have been severe. The lack of amenities, urban lights and pleasures, and major distractions was, a blessing in disguise."

The 449th Heavy Bomber Group
Books which have been written about the 449th

Much has been written about the 449th Heavy Bomber Group. Their first book was entitled **_Tucson to Grottaglie_** and printed by Turner Publishing Company. Damon Turner, who served in the 449th, put the book together with the help of his wife, Marie. Col. Jack Randolph supplied the mission records.

Upon seeing the demand for this history, a second book was written and put together entitled **_"And This is Our Story"_**. In 1985 Turner Publishing Company of Paducah, Kentucky printed the two books together in a single volume.

Late Pass is a news letter published regularly by Dick Downey, a former bombardier with the 719th. Dick organized the 449th Association and has collected and printed many stories and personal histories from the 449th HB Group.

A third book entitled **_449th Bomb Group - Grottaglie and Home_** was Published by Turner Publishing Company in 1989. This book is recognized by the beautiful dust cover, a collage of pictures and memorabilia complied by the artist Jim Dietz.

A fourth book entitled. **_"Maximum Effort" A History Of the 449th Bomb Group_** was published by Norfield Publishing, PO Box 16672, Panama FL 32406 and printed by Rose Printing, Tallahassee, FL, in 2000. It was complied and edited by Lt. Col. Richard T. Downey (Ret) and D. William Shepherd. The dust cover of this book is a full color reproduction of the prize-winning painting, "Maximum Effort" commissioned by Hollie Wilkes and painted by James Dietz.

D. William Shepherd wrote **_Of Men and Wings_** about the first 100 missions of the 449th Bombardment Group from January 1944 to July 1944. It was printed in 1996. This is based on the Wartime Diary of Charles A. Shepherd of the 718th Squadron.

Those Who Flew

Books written about the 449th Heavy Bomber Group
(continued)

50 Mission Crush is a personal account by Lt. Col. Donald R. Currier (Ret) and was printed by Burd Street Press, Beidel Printing, Sheppensburg, PA. He has given permission to print an exciting chapter from this book in this volume telling of his flight through the Atlas Mountains getting to Grottaglie.

Stalag-Luft III is a collection of stories and sketches about some of the 363 members of the 449th who became Prisoners of War. Lt. Col. Hollie Wilkes has provided the Thayer County Historical Society with a copy of this booklet. Bob Neary was given permission to keep a dairy while in the camp and drew realistic pictures of the barracks and showed conditions in this POW camp. The 449th commander, Col Darr Alkire was taken prisoner and was placed in this camp.

Escape from Terror by Major Weldon K. Burton was published by Looking Glass Graphics in Murfreesboro, AR in 1995. It is dedicated to his brother Weldon Burton who was lost in action over the Northern Adriatic. It covers the entire story of Stalag Luft III from beginning to end. Staglag Luft meant POW camp for airmen.

The Planes of The 449th Bomb Groups in World War II
Plane history and the nose art of the planes of the 449th Bomb Group has been published by Norfield Publishing and printed by Boyd Brothers both of Panama City, FL. D. William Shepherd compiled this book.

As so much has been published about the heroic 449th HB, a group who gave so much for their country and for our FREEDOM. ***The History*** of ***Thayer County Aviation including the Bruning Army Air Field*** cannot do justice to their achievements, but recommends their history be read from the above volumes mentioned.

Those Who Flew
Bruning Army Air Field

COMMANDING OFFICERS OF 449TH

On the back cover of the 449th book #2 entitled FROM TUCSON TO GROTTAGLIE there are three pictures of the commanders of the 449th with a few words about each of them:

"All were tough courageous leaders. There was no question who was in the lead ship. They were of different temperaments:

Col. Darr Alkire once said "Every time this God damned group goes up on a mission, I'm going to lead it"

Col. Thomas Gent when faced with a tough target said, "Let's go get them men!"

Col. Jack Randolph, under battle conditions, said, "Come and follow me, boys!" Col. Randolph was also called 180 Randolph because after leading the men through flak, he turned around and went back through it again.

It was Col. Darr Alkire who was the Company Commander while the group was at Bruning. There was no question that Col. Alkire was a stern and severe disciplinarian. One young pilot said that he arrived in Bruning, put his gear in the barracks and went up to see the hangars to check out the facilities. While in a hangar a dark figure loomed out of the darkness and yelled, "Lieutenant, why didn't you salute me?" "You are not wearing a coat, and have nothing on your uniform to indicate you are a superior officer, Sir" was the young Lieutenant's answer.

"I am Col. Alkire, the commander of this group and I don't need anything on my uniform. Take a look at this FACE and don't you forget it. Every time you see it, YOU SALUTE!"

Roy Jackson of Minneapolis, MN, a retired Captain of the U.S. Air force wrote:
"Our group commander, Colonel Darr Alkire, joined early in our stay at Bruning. The Colonel had just returned from London where he had been a military observer during the Battle of Britain. He was a fine leader and never failed to impress us that this was "SERIOUS BUSINESS."

In his book entitled "50 MISSION CRUSH", by Lt. Col. Donald R. Currier USAF (retired) written with the help of his wife, Blondie, he has this to say about Col. Alkire: "The first of October 1943, was an eventful day in my life. First I encountered the toughest guy I had yet to meet. I, along with all the other officers of the 449th who had so far reported in, were assembled in the base theatre that morning for a mandatory formation. On the stage all by himself stood our group commander, Colonel Darr H. Alkire.

"He confronted us with a piercing stare and Lo and behold, the place fell as silent as a tomb. When he finally spoke, there was no word of welcome or even an introduction. There really wasn't any need because we Second Lieutenants recognized God wearing those two eagles on his blouse."

Those Who Flew
Bruning Army Air Field

When Col. Alkire began to speak, his message was direct and to the point. I guess everyone there assembled still recalls, his words:

"You young punks with that pot metal on your chests think you're pretty good flyers. Well, you're not! You know nothing of combat flying, but that's what I am here to teach you." Then he got down to business and read us the riot act, scaring the hell out of us in the process. He told us what he expected and how unhappy he would be if he didn't get it. He itemized a series of fines that would be imposed on any officer who, in any way, screwed up. The fines depending on the gravity of the sin, could reach $75 which equal to our monthly flight pay. Father Flannigan's Boys Town, which was in Nebraska, was to be the recipient."

This is the attitude most all the men had towards Col. Alkire. That is, all except for Lt. Col. Hollie Wilkes. Hollie tells quite a different story. He, too, met Col. Alkire for the first time in the number three hangar at Bruning. The two men bonded immediately. Hollie Wilkes was non-commissioned. He was in maintenance. Perhaps it was because he was not a pilot that Darr Alkire felt free to talk to him. And talk they did. They sat on one of the planes and talked for nearly 2 hours upon meeting.

From that moment on, Hollie was Alkire's confidant. Whenever Col. Alkire bawled the men out, (which was often) he would grin and boast to Hollie afterward about the great job he had done scaring and putting fear into the men. That was his strategy. He wanted the men to be afraid of him more than anything else. He wanted the men to fear him more than the enemy. He wanted his men to obey him and they did.

Bruning, to Hollie Wilkes, was hell. They had to learn in just weeks what would normally take 6 months to learn. He remembered going to work one Sunday and not getting to bed until Wednesday without a break from the aircraft maintenance work needed. When he awoke Thursday, his eyes were so swollen he could not open them.

All the tar paper barracks at Bruning had 3 coal burning stoves in them. The draft wasn't set correctly on one of the coal burning stoves. and Hollies eyes were swollen from the smoke. To work from Sunday to Wednesday also shows what perseverance Hollie Wilkes showed even then. Hollie was given a field commission as soon as they got to Italy. Probably being Alkire's best friend also helped but he is an unusual and an outstanding man. He has done much to preserve the history of the 449th.

Hollie Wilkes remained Col. Darr Alkire's confidant until Col. Alkire was shot down and became a Prisoner of War. It is said that when Alkire became a prisoner of war, he took over the POW camp, in the same way he took command of everything. He told the German's they didn't know how to run a POW camp and proceeded to run a strict disciplined POW camp for them. The men were given assignments, they were required to do certain jobs, carefully dole out the Meguro rations methodically and were required to maintain cleanliness as best they could. Once again the men were probably more afraid of Col. Akire than they were of the enemy. Even his captors were afraid of him. Undoubtedly life in that POW camp was better than most.

Darr Alkire was later promoted to Brigadier General.

449th Bombardment Group

The Original Aircraft of the 449th Bombardment Group

The 449th Bombardment Heavy Group was activated May 1st, 1943 at the Davis Monthan Field in Tucson, Arizona by a 2nd Air Force order. After being moved around they were sent to Alamogordo, NM. Col. Darr Alkire took command in Alamorgordo. After the men had just gotten accustomed to the desert area of New Mexico, a special order was given Sept. 6, 1943 that they would move to Bruning Army Air Field in Nebraska. Bruning had been called the Bruning Air Base but had been renamed in April of 1943 by the Secretary of War who said it must now be called the Bruning Army Air Field (BAAF).

When the 449th HB Group came to Bruning from Alamogordo, NM they brought with them older B-24s. One of the planes brought from Alamogordo was a B-24 D model named TARFU which stood for Things Are Really Fouled Up. Other planes were brought in making a total of 110 B-24s at the Bruning Base. Lt. Col. (Ret) Ralph "Pat" Gentry said these planes were of every color — from camouflage, desert tan and green.

Of these 110 planes, 61 brand new B-24H models were flown from the Ford plant at the Willow Run Factory in Detroit, Michigan to the Bruning Army Air Field. The new planes were all painted an olive green and were brought in during the months of October and November 1943. Most replacement planes delivered to the 449th in Italy were not painted. These new 61 aircraft delivered to Bruning were equipped with the latest Sperry site and were distributed to the four squadrons of the 449th HB to be flown to Italy. Fifteen Aircraft were assigned to each of the following squadrons: 716th, 717th, and 718th. Sixteen aircraft were assigned to the 719th Squadron. . .

Most of the combat crews personalized their original aircraft with descriptive names and appropriate nose art. This record of the planes, their numbers and their names has come from Lt. Col. Hollie Wilkes (Ret.) Lt. Col. Dick Downey (Ret), Lt. Col. Pat Gentry (Ret), from records available at the Historical Research Agency, the Internet and from personal correspondence with some of the men of the 449th.

APPENDIX 28
RESTRICTED
HEADQUARTERS BRUNING ARMY AIR FIELD
Office of the Commanding Officer
EXTRACT

SPECIAL ORDERS
No........228

Bruning, Nebr
14 Nov 43

The fol named O and EM of Flight Echelon, 449th Bomb Gp (H) AAF, this sta, processing and will report to the CO thereat.

449th Bomb Gp (H) AAF, Hq

COL DARR H. ALKIRE
MAJ ROBERT C McILHERAN
CAPT CECIL E PETTERSON
CAPT TEDO R CHRISTIAN JR
CAPT THOMAS McNAMARA
1ST LT VINCENT F VALLERO
1ST LT MALCOM L LEVENSON

1ST LT PAUL R NUGENT
1ST LT EDWARD F WESTLAKE
2ND LT DALE LINCOLN
2ND LT ORA T DAWSON JR
2ND LT WILLIAM B MITCHELL
2ND LT RICHARD D CRYSLER

M/Sgt Hollio A Wilkos
T/Sgt Melvin S Cook
M/Sgt William G Braden
S/Sgt Jesse O McCullough
T/Sgt Milton B Coon

S/Sgt John G Anderson
Sgt Julius Moininger
M/Sgt Paul L Floyd
M/Sgt Charles M Herzog

716th Bomb Sq

Crew 6-1 Flt A
2ND LT HAROLD A OIEN
2ND LT PAUL J RUSSELL
2ND LT JUSTIN D McANALLY
2ND LT CHARLES F POPKEN JR
S/Sgt Arthur H Joan
T/Sgt Vincent F Mahoney
S/Sgt Loren E Bunger
Sgt Raymond E Carpenter
S/Sgt Paul R Bumgardner
S/Sgt Clyde C Chafin

Crew 6-2 Flt C
2ND LT EDWARD V DRINAN
2ND LT JAMES H BRUNGER
2ND LT HENRY C SIVEWRIGHT
2ND LT ROBERT L LEVENSON
S/Sgt Frederick E Albright
S/Sgt Donald W Harrington
S/Sgt William A Simmermen
S/Sgt Vernon L Smith
S/Sgt Robert K Parsons
S/Sgt Reginald W Brown

Crew 6-3 Flt B
2ND LT CECIL E KINORD
2ND LT CECIL H HARMON
2ND LT PAUL J CHRISTOFF
2ND LT THOMAS C VENABLE
Sgt Wiliam J Mitchell
Sgt Porter A Chadwick
Sgt Charles W Newton
Sgt Joseph T Coniglione
Sgt Robert L Nairm
Sgt Jack P Bossom

Crew 6-4 Flt B
2nd Lt ROBERT M KENNELLY
2nd Lt ALPHONSE F HANLEY
2nd Lt EDWARD D MILLS
2nd Lt GEORGE F MADDEN
S/Sgt Loyd J Webster
S/Sgt Joseph J Julius
S/Sgt Audrey Salyer
S/Sgt Richard A Carter
S/Sgt Vincent A Smilos
Cpl Richard T Hallum

Crew 6-5 Flt C
2nd Lt GILBERT F BRADLEY
2nd Lt PHILIP J SHERIDAN
2nd Lt KENNETH E EBERSOLE
2nd Lt JOSEPH P McMONIMON
S/Sgt Joseph W Montagna
Sgt Robert F Fisher
Sgt Roland J Prescher
Sgt Herbert R Clements
Sgt Paul S Biggart
Sgt Franklin A Grubaugh

Crew 6-6 Flt A
2nd Lt ROBERT N BRADY
2nd Lt THOMAS J O'KEEFE
1st Lt AMOS L BECHTOLD
2nd Lt GRAHM LITTLE
S/Sgt Benny Adamo

Crew 6-6 Flt A (cont'd)
S/Sgt Palmer J Bashaw
S/Sgt Walter J Maich
S/Sgt Francis L McPherson
Pfc James M Galvin
Pvt Arthur K Sjoborg

Crew 6-7 Flt A
F/O VIRGIL HAMILTON
2ND LT THOMAS J WILDERN
2ND LT HAROLD B NELSON
2ND LT LEONARD WILLNER
Sgt Earl N Roth
Cpl William A Kennedy
Sgt Dale S Blaugh
Sgt John Molnar
Sgt John P Eberhart
Sgt Warren S Snyder

Crew 6-6 Flt A
2ND LT CARL R BROWNING
2ND LT HAROLD R MADSEN
2ND LT NICHOLAS D LANNIN
2ND LT HAROLD P QUISNO
Sgt Lloyd D Lewis
Sqt Elmer G Howell
Sgt Charles L Voogd
Sgt Irwin Weiss
Sgt John E McKeague
Sgt Sherman Barnhill

Crew 6-9 Flt B
2ND LT HARRY W MOORE
2ND LT RES M WILDE
2ND LT WALTER C CATES
2ND LT JAMES W RICKELS
Sgt Gordon D Thornton
Sgt Francis A Kvaltine
Sgt Fernand R Custeau
Sgt James F Milnos
Sgt Thomas J Desmond
Cpl Carl A Shedlock

Crew 6-10 Flt A
2ND LT GEORGE W FOOTE
2ND LT QUENTIN P MADIGAN
2ND LT JOHN J MURPHY
2ND LT ALEXANDER R NELSON
Sgt James W Gorrell
Sgt Albert J Yano
Sgt Harry E Lain
Sgt Walter G Gates
Sgt Harold M Skidmore

Crew 6-11 Flt B
F/O GORDON E POWERS
2ND LT WILLIAM H NOLD
2ND LT WILLIAM M BUFORD
2ND LT ANTHONY J ROSE
Sgt Charles W Horne
Pfc William W Sheldon
Sgt Harold F Young
Sgt Carl E Horne
Sgt William R Mumper
Sgt William E Litzinger

Crew 6-12 Flt B
2ND LT JOHN R FORBES
2ND LT JOHN K PARSHALL
2ND LT STANLEY M GLEASON
2ND LT JOSEPH A PUTRIUS
S/Sgt Steve Szacum
Sgt James P Malone
Sgt Ernest Nahigian
Sgt Richard J Bohrer
Sgt Clemeth J Enyeart Jr

Crew 6-13 Flt D
2nd Lt ROBERT P BIRD
2ND LT ANSON F HUGHES
2ND LT DEANE C MANNING
2ND LT VICTOR S HARRIS
Pvt Oscar I Allison
Sgt Jack K Dixon
Sgt Richard W Leaf
Sgt Edward F Szymanski
Sgt Frank W Watkins
Sgt James M Blake

Crew 6-14 Flt B
2ND LT VINCENT K ISGRIGG
2ND LT ROBERT A GROSS
2ND LT STANLEY E GRZESIK
2ND LT CHARLES V McGILL
S/Sgt John L Zierowicz
S/Sgt Ottavo F Tosti
Sgt Edward I Eisler
Sgt Estel L Warner
Sgl Donald L Ames
Sgt William T Sanders

Crew 6-15 Flt C
2ND LT MARION J MESSENGER
2ND LT FRANCIS H DAVIS
2ND LT BENJAMIN F CAFFEY
2ND LT RAYMOND A ZOELLER
Sgt George C Henry
Sgt Thomas G Cronin
Sgt Harold C Tegtmeier
Sgt Anthony C Massino
Sgt Donald A Peterson

Crew 6-16 Flt D
2ND LT RICHARD W KENDALL
2ND LT JAMES D GUDGER
2ND LT WOODWARD E DAVIS
2ND LT LEONARD W CAPPUCCILLI
S/Sgt John J Cuccia
Sgt Lawrence F Dassinger
Sgt Benjamin E Browning
Sgt Ray C Reneau
Sgt William H Hyde
Sgt Carl A Weisz

Crew 6-17 Flt D
2ND LT RICHARD F ROBERTS
2ND LT CHARLES R DACEY
2ND LT CHARLES F BUNTZ
2ND LT JOSEPH J VITEK
Sgt Fred W Bryant

Crew 6-17 Flt D (cont'd)
Sgt Robert W Dontje
Sgt Everett C Arnold
Sat Harold O Tomey
Sgt James Paterson Jr
Sgt James B McDonald

Crew 6-15 Flt C
2ND LT ROBERT J KAPP
2ND LT ALBERT F BRIDGHAM
2ND LT ERNEST J JOHNSON
2ND LT WALTER A KAESS
Sgt Dennis H Wood
Sgt Charles Anderson
Sgt Cornelius F Moriarty
Sgt Charles C Griffin
Sgt Lloyd T Wright
S/Sgt Daniel Buda

Crew 6-19
CAPT JACK SILVERSTEIN
1ST LT JAMES W RIERSON
2ND LT ALBERT C ALLUMBAUGH
2ND LT OTIS J BOLTON
2ND LT NORMAN J BARBER
1ST LT BURR TARRANT JR
1ST LT RICHARD C NOEL JR
2ND LT GEORGE M HOWARD
2ND LT CLYDE J BECKLEY
2ND LT CHESTER R JONES

Crew 6-20
2ND LT GEORGE RUNKLE
M/Sgt Clarence B Davis
M/Sgt William F Treadway
T/Sgt John L Mazlow
T/Sgt Joseph C Gaus
S/Sgt Kenneth B Bolsins
S/Sgt Andrew Gima Jr
S/Sgt Thourbon D Hanna
S/Sgt Howard P Hubbard
S/Sgt John T King

Crew 6-21
T/Sgt Armand P Dupont
T/Sgt Earl O Vian
S/Sgt Webster W DesJardina
S/Sgt Donald D Scharff
Sgt J.C. Brown
Sgt Harold B Fisher
Sgt Harold B Lipshitz
Sgt John J Morello
Cpl Salvatore A Esposito

Crew 6-22
M/Sgt Leslie Massingill
T/Sgt Victor R Krick
S/Sgt George R Stout
S/Sgt Henry M Bordin
Sgt Jack W Wunderlich
Sgt Eugene J Christian
Sgt John R Allen Jr
Sgt John W Booth Jr
Pfc Herman Ingram

Bruning Army Air Field

716th Squadron (449th BG) Original Aircraft

"THE HEAVENLY BODY"; Tail #58; Serial #42-07708
Delivered to Bruning 15 Oct. '43, assigned to Drinan's crew. Demise: Crashed and burned on an emergency landing during a practice flight, 7/17/44. One killed.

"DUMBO"; Tail #46, Serial #42-07741.
Delivered to Bruning 15 Oct. '43, assigned to Knapp's crew. Demise: Crashlanded 1/14/44 with no casualties at Bari, Italy, with Kendall's crew aboard. Circumstances of Loss: As the group headed out over the Adriatic, on the first leg of its flight to the target at Mostar, Yugoslavia, Kendall's crew aboard plane #741 was forced to jettison the bomb load and turn back after the "electrical system went out" and two engines failed. When the engines of ship #741 "cut off over Adriatic, the pilot was able to throttle the intermittently the number-2 and number-3 engine sufficiently to see land. Pilot warned the crew to be ready and gave sign to the gunners who parachuted successfully. Six men stayed with the ship and when Bari Airport was sighted the pilot dove ship with no power and came in for landing. Made a wheel down landing, rolled about 2,000 feet when left gear gave way gradually. Plane turned on left wing and ball turret which could not be retracted and dug into ground ripping the fuselage. The open bomb bay doors were ripped off. Dumbo was the first plane to be recovered for salvage.

"BRADY'S GANG"; Tail #47, Serial #42-07769.
Delivered to Bruning 25 Oct. '43, assigned to Brady's crew. Demise: Downed 1/31/44 by fighter attacks over Udine, Italy with Brady's crew aboard. 2 KIA, 8 POW, and 3 evaded to allied territory. Circumstances of Loss: As the formation prepared to rally to the left immediately after bombs were released, Brady's Gang was hit by flak. The ship was seen to "go into a steep dive, level momentarily, then crash into a mountain side."

"DEVIL'S HENCHMEN"; Tail #48, Then #63; Serial #42-52089.
Delivered to Bruning 18 Oct. '43, assigned to Messenger's crew. Demise: Transferred to 15th AF Depot for major overhaul in mid-44; subsequently reassigned to another Bomb Group, post war salvaged 6/23/45; one of the very few original 449th ships to survive the war.

"MAW STRICKNINE"; Tail #49, Serial #42-52104.
Delivered to Bruning 1 Nov. '43, assigned to Powers' crew. Demise: Transferred to Goioa, Italy, 15th AF Depot for major overhaul in mid-44; subsequently reassigned to another Bomb Group, post-war salvaged 8/16/45; one of the very few original 449th ships to survive the war.

"SLICK CHICK"; Tail #50, Serial #42-52110.
Delivered to Bruning 27 Oct. '43, assigned to Roberts' crew.
Demise: Transferred to 15th AF Depot 2/22/44 and returned 5/5/44. Later transferred to Depot again and subsequently reassigned to another Bomb Group; post-war salvaged 11 Aug. '45.

"GHOST OF THE OMAR"; Tail #51, Serial #42-52140 Delivered to Bruning 31 Oct. '43, assigned to Browning's crew. It was Named after a lounge in the Continental Hotel in Kansas

City, Missouri where the crews got to spend their last nights with their wives before going overseas. Demise: Downed on 9 June '44 with Collins' crew aboard. 10 POW, 1 evaded. Circumstances of Loss. After rendezvousing with the other Groups, the 449th formation headed northward up the middle of the Adriatic enroute for Munich, Germany. As the formation passed over the city of Udine in northern Italy, Ghost of the Omar -- with Collins' crew aboard -- was hit by flak. The damage was not thought at first to be severe enough to abort the mission, and the Ghost continued northward with the formation until -- some three miles west of Salzburg -Collins' crew realized they would have to turn back. The Ghost "left the formation dropping down very low but under control with the two inboard engines smoking." No chutes were seen at that time and the Ghost was soon lost from sight by the other planes in the formation. Collins' crew was subsequently forced to bail out.

"PISTOL PACKIN' MAMA"; Tail #52, Serial #42-52146.
There were two Pistol Packin' Mamas in the 449th. The other was spelled with two m's. "Pistol Packing Mama" with the words, "Lay that pistol down Babe, Lay that pistol down" was a hit song during this time. She was delivered to Bruning 1 Nov. '43, assigned to Bradley's crew. Demise: Downed on 2/22/44 with Bird's crew aboard. 10 POW. Circumstances of Loss. On 22 February 1944, the 449th attacked the Obertraubling Aircraft Factory at Regensburg, Germany. They met stiff resistance in the form of both fighters and flak. The fighters scored direct hits on ship #52. When the last of the fighters broke off the engagement, Bird's crew began the struggle to keep their heavily damaged B-24 airborne but realized they had to bail out 50 miles from Ghas.

"SOPHISTICATED LADY"; Tail #53, Serial #41-29214.
Delivered to Bruning 26 Oct. '43, assigned to R. Bird's crew. Demise: Downed by fighters on 2/25/44 with Bradley's crew aboard. 1 KIA, 9 Evaded. {Circumstances of Loss. On 25 February 1944, the 449th attacked the ME-109 factory at Regensburg, Germany. As the bombers rallied left off the target and emerged from the flak, the 449th formation came under heavy attack from an enemy fighter force. The enemy fighters were "extremely aggressive" and "pressed home their attacks with great vigor." The fighters scored direct hits on Sophisticated Lady forcing Bradley's crew to immediately feather the number-1 and number-2 engines. As the aircraft lost altitude, Bradley's crew was forced to bail out. Nine chutes were seen.

"BLIND DATE"; Tail #54, Serial #42-29243. Delivered to Bruning 9 Nov. '43, assigned to Kennelly's crew. Demise: Downed by heavy flak and fighter attack 4/12/44 with Beam's crew aboard. 4 KIA, 6 POW. Circumstances of Loss. On 12 April 1944, the 449th attacked the aircraft factory at Wiener-Neustadt, Austria. Coming off the target, the 449th was attacked by some 25 to 30 enemy fighters. At the "tail-end Charlie" position in C-section of the 449th formation, the number-3 engine of ship #54 was seen to burst into flames as a "single very aggressive fighter" pressed home the attack. Beam's crew was forced to immediately bail out as the "ship went into a spin." Six chutes were seen and the aircraft was last seen "going down in flames."

"STINKY THE B. T. O."; Tail #55; Serial #42-64462 "**B**ig-**T**ime **O**perator" Delivered to Bruning 9 Nov. '43, assigned to Oien's crew. Demise: Blew up 2/22/44 under fighter attack with Browning's crew aboard, 3 KIA, 7 POW. Circumstances of Loss. On 22 February 1944, the

449th attacked the Obertraubling Aircraft Factory at Regensburg, Germany. They met stiff resistance in the form of both fighters and flak. Enemy fighters scored direct hits on ship #55 which was seen to explode.

"THE WISE VIRGIN"; Tail #56; Serial #41-28616.
Delivered to Bruning 28 Oct. '43, assigned to Kinerd's crew. Demise: Kinerd's crew forced to bail-out due to heavy combat damage 2/22/44. No casualties. Circumstances of Loss: On 22 February 1944, the 449th attacked the Obertraubling Aircraft Factory at Regensburg, Germany. They met stiff resistance in the form of both fighters and flak. The enemy fighters scored direct hits on ship #56. However, Kinerd's crew was able to keep the ship airborne until they reached southern Italy. Kinerd's crew successfully bailed out over friendly territory near Bari, Italy.

"RAMP TRAMP"; Tail #57, Serial #42-07700.
Delivered to Bruning 21 Oct. '43. Assigned to Moore's crew.
Demise: Downed with Moore's crew aboard 2/22/44. 7 KIA, 4 POW. #42-07700. Circumstances of Loss: On 22 February 1944, the 440th ran into stiff resistance in the form of both fighters and flak. During the final minutes of the fighter attack on the 449th formation, enemy fighters scored direct hits on ship #57, Ramp Tramp manned by Moore's crew caught fire and subsequently exploded in the air.

"MISS LEE DING"; Tail #75; Serial #42-07737.
Delivered to Bruning 18 Oct. '43, assigned to Isgrigg's crew. Demise: Downed 6/26/44 with Sullivan's crew aboard. 2 KIA, 8 Evaded. Tail #60, then Circumstances of Loss: On 26 June 1944, the 449th attacked the aircraft factory at Schwechat, Austria. Over the target, the Group encountered "intense, accurate, heavy flak" which damaged 26 aircraft. As they emerged from the flak field, Lt. Sullivan and his copilot struggled to maintain control of ship #75 as the number-1 engine refused to feather after being knocked out by flak. As ship #75 begin to fall astern the formation, planes #67 and #15 also dropped out of formation to form an escort. The three ships formed up and began trailing behind the 449th formation. No enemy fighters spotted the three stragglers. An hour later, ships #67 and #15 handed off the escort job to a formation of friendly fighters. Ship #75, still unable to feather the number-1 engine could not make it back across the Adriatic Sea to Italy. Sullivan's crew bailed out over Yugoslavia.

"727"; unnamed; Tail #59 Serial #42-07727.
Delivered to Bruning (date unknown), assigned to Forbes' crew. Demise: Downed 2/25/44 with Forbes' crew aboard. All 10 KIA. Circumstances of Loss. On 25 February 1944, the 449th attacked the ME-109 factory in Regensburg, Germany. As the bombers rallied left off the target and emerged from the flak, the 449th formation came under heavy attack from an enemy fighter force. The enemy fighters were "extremely aggressive" and "pressed home their attacks with great vigor." Ship #59 was "last seen under control with the engine smoking and falling back just after the target."

APPENDIX 29

717th Bomb Sq

Flight Echelon
CAPT ARTHUR B SWAN
1ST LT GEORGE W GORDON
1ST LT EDWARD J SASS
2ND LT FRANK HENGGENER
2ND LT WILBUR N RASMUSSEN
2ND LT CHESTER F LORRILORD
T/Sgt Jerold O Shepard
S/Sgt Wesley Gurney
Sgt Otto J Wench
Cpl Raymond V Blankenship

Crew #7-1
2ND LT HAROLD R LOUGHRAN
2ND LT ROY H JACOBSEN
2ND LT GEORGE D YOUNGCLAUS
2ND LT STEPHAN E PATER
T/Sgt Otho Hoover
S/Sgt Edger H Adcock
S/Sgt George E Bailey
S/Sgt James T Holt
Sgt Adolph J DiMinno
Pvt Charles E Wagner, Jr

Crew #7-2
2ND LT JOHN H STARR
2ND LT ROBERT W SAMSON
2ND LT PAUL IHEVINNE
2ND LT JOE R SMITH
T/Sgt George E Radcliff
T/Sgt Edward J Byer
S/Sgt Bill Tom
S/Sgt Colombo Simeone
S/Sgt Thomas Mikolajczyk
Pfc Porter H Singleton Jr

Crew #7-3
2ND LT WARREN H RIDGWAY
2ND LT JOSEPH C WHITLOCK
2ND LT JOHN P McCARTHY
2ND LT GEORGE H PARKS
S/Sgt George T Potts
S/Sgt Jack B Newman
S/Sgt LeRoy E Tripp
Sgt Frank A Rim
Sgt John P Colson
Cpl L A Flinn

Crew #7-4
2ND LT BRYCE GRAY JR
2ND LT CARL W WILES
2ND LT JOSEPH I RESNICK
2ND LT PAUL J NELSON
T/Sgt William B Miller
S/Sgt Richard D Rosen
Sgt Lummy W Richardson
Sgt John Curr
Sgt Michael Litvinoff
Sgt Anthony Gorka

S/Sgt Frank J Kroll
Sgt Ellsworth R Daniels
Sgt Pasquale Olivette
Sgt Reinert J Thoensen
T/Sgt Gerald W Hansen
S/Sgt John P Creed Jr
2ND LT JOHN R CLINE
T/Sgt Kermit L Frische
S/Sgt LeRoy Crumpler
Sgt Harry L Oates

Crew #7-5
2ND LT JACOB F KURY
2ND LT FRANK A COOPER
2ND LT JAMES B CALDWELL
2ND LT GEORGE W BUTLER
S/Sgt Leo J Gibbo
Sgt James F Linkley A
Sgt Robed L Young
Sgt James C Piland
Sgt Gordon F Hoore
Sgt Wesley J Butts

Crew #7-6
2ND LT WILLIAM C BONTLEY JR
F/O KELLER J BLANCHARD
2ND LT GLENN F JOHNNSEN
2ND LT JOHN S GALATI
S/Sgt Loren W Massey
Sgt Gerard J Plourde
Sgt Donald C Eck
Sgt Leroy L Compson Jr
Sgt Nunzie Tripaldi
Sgt Alfred J Gallant

Crew #7-7
2ND LT FELIX C FOWLER
2ND LT LANCELOT L MINOR JR
2ND LT JACK R BARBOUR
2ND LT HOWARD E ORGERA
T/Sgt John Chonka
S/Sgt Percival A Chadwick Jr
S/Sgt Donald H Harrington
Sgt Eldon W Sweeney
Sgt Guido N Brazzale
Pvt Allen J MacEacherin

Crew #7-8
2ND LT HARTFORD FEES
2ND LT JAMES K HUBBARD
2ND LT JOHN J LACASTRO
2ND LT OSCAR MENAKER
S/Sgt Ahti A Poole
S/Sgt Harold Phillips
S/Sgt Charles N Holcomb
S/Sgt Charles D Hostetler
S/Sgt Joseph R Horner
Pvt Peter Chalkus

Crew #7-9
2ND LT GIFFORD T HEMPHILL
2ND LT NELSON D WOOD
2ND LT ROBERT FELDMAN
2ND LT JOHN D PUFF
T/Sgt Francis J Tolisano
S/Sgt Dominic D Lombardelli
S/Sgt Angelo P Melchiarre
Sgt D C Powell
Sgt Orel M Harper
Pvt Eugene W Briggs

2ND LT EDDIE A COPE
M/Sgt Robert J Batdorf
T/Sgt Edward E Zachary
S/Sgt William M Hendrickson
S/Sgt James C Henderson
S/Sgt John P Celibi
S/Sgt William A Cover
S/Sgt Robert Kohn
S/Sgt Peter Zuzzola
S/Sgt William C McCahill

Crew #7-10
2ND LT HOWARD D JEUTTER
2ND LT THEODORE KAKOWSKI
2ND LT JOHN R GAGNON
2ND LT WARREN W PARADIES
S/Sgt Stamati G Kithriotis
S/Sgt Walter F Salinsky
S/Sgt Milton J Verret
Sgt Herbert H Batterton
Sgt Hayden O Payne Jr
Sgt John P Micera

Crew #7-11
2ND LT HENRY J McINVALE JR
2ND LT BENJAMIN R DIETRICH
2ND LT LESTER E FIESTER
2ND LT GORDON I FIELDS
S/Sgt Anthony J Ponticelli
Sgt Harold Cook
Sgt Ralph G Edwards
Sgt Ray V Copley
Sgt Joseph Fastiggi
Sgt Arthur J Cordeira

Crew #7-12
2ND LT VERNON H SAMUELSON
2ND LT LEROY T DAVIDSON
2ND LT DONALD A BECKER
2ND LT LAWRENCE O ECKL
Sgt Montague Harrison
Sgt Joseph L Bowman
Sgt William B Aaron Jr
Sgt John C Bennett
Sgt Lenville D Ashworth
Sgt Lincoln Abraham

Crew #7-13
2ND LT ALBERT O GEMINDER
2ND LT JOSEPH W BROWN
2ND LT THOMAS E TAYLOR
2ND LT JOHN F DEVINE
T/Sgt Fred McColough
S/Sgt Anthony R Franklin
S/Sgt Kenneth E Yarian
S/Sgt William V Czerwinski
S/Sgt George I Parker
S/Sgt George A Deringer

2ND LT FREDERICK ESPER
2ND LT VICTOR KESSLER
2ND LT WILLIAM T McDONALD
M/Sgt Frank P Kocher
S/Sgt Michael O Roth
Sgt Raymond C Logies

Crew #7-14
2ND LT JOHN W OLSON
2ND LT HERBERT W GREEHALGH
2ND LT WALTER SIEWERT
2ND LT EDWARD C DEREN
T/Sgt Glennard O Chapman
T/Sgt Oliver E Cameron
S/Sgt Lester E Seeback
S/Sgt Cornelius A Lauve
S/Sgt Benny E Cellilli Jr
Pvt Donald E Miller

Crew #7-15
2ND LT LAWRENCE D SIES
2ND LT FREDERICK T YORG
2ND LT JOHN S DOUGLAS
2ND LT THOMAS NASSER
T/Sgt Howard L Finch
S/Sgt William G Smith
S/Sgt Marion L Nelms
S/Sgt Data C Christensen
Sgt Marlen E Ellefson
Pvt Clyde C Buller

Crew #7-16
2ND LT ELLIOTT A THOMPSON
2ND LT LLOYD J SMITH
2ND LT ROSS L BUSH
2ND LT JAMES H GALLIHER
Sgt Stem Babiec
Sgt Wayne W Ross
Sgt Lloyd G Buehrer
Sgt Samuel W Scott
Cpl Tony P Lopez
Pvt Arnold R Cain

Crew #7-17
2ND LT ALFRED C MORTON
2ND LT JOHN R MARSHALL
2ND LT FELIX C FORSHAGE
2ND LT JAMES IN CAMPBELL
Sgt Bay Walter
Sgt Eulalio B Lobato
Sgt Jim Shanahan
Sgt Francis J Horres
Sgt Clement Godiez
Sgt Gilman C Allen

Crew #7-18
2ND LT WILSON H JONES
2ND LT JAMES R BARBER
2ND LT ROBERT FAUCHENBACH
2ND LT STANLEY P BURCZAK
S/Sgt Elmer E Mechan
S/Sgt George B Welch
Sgt Calvin B Willocks
Sgt Chester Umperovitch
Sgt Paul D Zickler
Pfc Billy R Price

Original planes of the 717th Sq. of the 449th

"LURCHIN' URCHIN"; Tail #34; Serial #41-29223.
Delivered to Bruning 28 Oct. '43, assigned to Kury's crew. Demise: Downed over Aviano, Italy, 1/31/44 with Group C. O. Alkire flying as Group Lead with part of Thompson's crew and selected lead crewmen aboard. 3 KIA, 8 POW. Circumstances of Loss. Over Aviano airfield the 449th experienced "intense, accurate, heavy flak." As the formation prepared to rally left after the bomb drop, Lurchin' Urchin' fell victim to the flak. Ship #34 was seen to "go into a steep glide apparently out of control." Nine chutes were seen.

"CINNSY'S MARGIE"; Tail #35; Serial #42-07723.
Delivered to Bruning 20 Oct. '43, assigned to Samuelson's crew. Demise: Made an emergency landing at Tarquina, Italy, on 12 Aug. '44. Crew returned to base. The ship was repaired by a mobile maintenance crew and reassigned to another Bomb Group.

"HOLY JOE"; Tail #36; Serial #41-29225
Delivered to Bruning 1 Nov '43, assigned to Fowler's crew. Demise: Crashed on take-off with Ivers' crew aboard 3/29/44. 2 KIA, 8 injured. Circumstances of Loss. On 29 March 1944, the 449th set out to bomb the marshalling yards at Bolzano, Italy. Between 0740 and 0804 hours, 35 B-24s --each carrying ten, 500-pound bombs -- rolled down the runway at a little less than one-minute intervals and struggled into the air. The operations log shows that the 30th aircraft to roll down the runway was ship #36 with Ivers' crew aboard. Just at the instant ship #36 lifted off the runway, one of the four engines suddenly quit. It was the kind of situation which every pilot and crew member feared most -- a fully-fueled, bomb-laden bomber losing an engine at the moment of take-off. Lt. Ivers had no option but to attempt a crash landing. Two of the crew died in the ensuing crash. The other eight were injured.

"THE TEMPTRESS"; Tail #37 Serial #42-52107;
Delivered to Bruning 29 Oct. '43, assigned to Juetter's crew. Demise: Crashed on take-off 2/23/44 due to engine failure with a full bomb load. All 10 members of Juetter's crew KIA when bomb load exploded. Circumstances of Loss: On 23 February 1944, the 449th attacked the ball-bearing plant at Steyr, Austria. Between 0700 and 0800 hours, the 449th aircraft rolled down the runway and began to assemble into formation. Even before the total formation could complete forming-up disaster struck. Ship #37 -- manned by Jeutter's crew -- "crashed to the ground one mile north of Fragagnano, a town about ten miles south of Grottaglie." All ten crew members died in the violent crash.

"RELUCTANT LIZ"; Tail #38; Serial #41-28596.
Delivered to Bruning 19 Oct. '43, assigned to Bontley's crew. Named because the pilot took his wife, Liz, for a very illegal flight over the Bruning area. Liz was very reluctant to do this. Lt. Col. Hollie Wilkes has donated a video to the Thayer County Museum showing an interview with Liz as she explained going for that initial flight over the Bruning countryside. Her husband obtained a small A uniform for her, and when the guard was at the far end of the field she ran across the runway and got into the plane and flew over the farm house where she was staying.

Demise of the plane: Downed 4/4/44 with Bontly's crew aboard. 2 KIA, 8 POW. Circumstances of Loss. "ATTACK BUCHAREST MARSH YARDS" read the operational order for 4 April 1944 which sent the 449th on its most famous, memorable, and costly mission. Twenty-eight ships of the 449th, unescorted and unaccompanied by other groups, attacked the marshalling yards. "Approximately 80 to 100 enemy aircraft attacked the formation" as the 449th departed the target. The ferocious air battle lasted for an hour and a half. At the "tail-end Charlie" position in the high box of the second section, ship #38 "was seen to be mortally hit by enemy aircraft fire just after the target. Ten men reportedly bailed out immediately and the aircraft fell out of control.

"PEERLESS CLIPPER"; Tail #39; Serial #42-29216.
Delivered to Bruning 21 Oct. '43, assigned to Sie's crew. Named for the sponsoring company, Peerless Woolen Mills, Chattanooga, Tennessee. Demise: Lost in a 3-aircraft, mid-air collision over Steyr, Austria, 2 April '44 with Kury's crew aboard. 11 KIA . Other aircraft involved in the mid-air collision were "SUPERSTITIOUAL-O-WISHUS" Ship #45, with Starr's crew aboard and "MISS BEHAVIN" ship #43 with Geminder's crew aboard. Of the 31 men in the three aircraft, 30 KIA & 1 POW.] Circumstances of Loss. Over Steyr, Austria, on 2 April 1944, the 449th was attacked by some 60 to 70 enemy fighters. The enemy fighters aggressively pressed home their attacks with rockets, cannons, and aerial bombs. In the 'B' section of the 449th formation, disaster struck with stunning swiftness. "At 1235, over the target of Steyr, three B-24s collided, one sliding into another sideways. Both hit the front of a third plane and tore off the nose right in back of the pilot seat." Two of the ships "broke in pieces and fell down, no chutes being seen." The crew of the third ship began bailing out. Seven chutes (one on fire) were reportedly seen and the ship crashed five miles south of the target. By at least one account, the aircraft which initially lost control "sliding into another sideways" was struck by an aerial bomb dropped from an enemy aircraft above the 449th formation. This was never confirmed. Regardless of what started this chain reaction of aircraft crashing into each other, ship #45, ship #39, and ship #43 were gone in minutes.

"THUNDER BAY BABE"; Tail #40; Serial #42-07623.
Bruning 15 Oct. '43, assigned to Ridgeway's crew. Demise: Lost over Yugoslavia, 3/23/44 with Ridgeway's crew aboard. 6 KIA, 4 POW. Circumstances of Loss: On 23 March 1944, the 449th set out in the early morning to attack the fighter production plant at Steyr, Austria. However, some 30 miles south of Zagreb, Yugoslavia, an impenetrable weather front was encountered. As the formation maneuvered in an attempt to go around and over this weather front, Fees' crew aboard ship #44 observed that ship #40 -- Thunder Bay Babe --was "behaving erratically, but under control". Unable to overcome "impossible weather conditions", the decision was made to abort the mission. As the Group began the long sweeping turn to reverse course, ship #40 was observed "falling out of formation and disappearing into the undercast. It did not complete the turn-back, and no chutes were seen."

"OLD IRONSIDES"; Tail #47; Serial #42-52170.
Delivered to Bruning 10 Nov. '43, assigned to McInvale's crew. Demise: Downed by flak near Belgrade, Yugoslavia, 5/18/44 with McInvale's crew aboard. All 9 crew evaded. Circumstances of Loss. On 18 May 1944, the 449th set out to attack the marshalling yards at Ploesti. However, after encountering impassable weather near the Yugoslavian coast, the 449th diverted

to the alternate target of Belgrade, Yugoslavia. As the formation pressed across Yugoslavia, ship #47 -- Old Ironsides was seen lagging behind the main formation. Well before the IP was reached, ship #47 called on the command frequency requesting the course heading back to base. Shortly thereafter, all contact was lost with ship #47. It was later learned that McInvale's crew had been forced to bail out over Yugoslavia.

"SHACK HAPPY"; Tail #41; Serial #42-07744.
Delivered to Bruning 19 Oct. '43, assigned to Morton's crew. Demise: Downed 5/5/44 on Ploesti mission with Morton's crew aboard. 4 KIA, 6 POW. Circumstances of Loss. "Today we went on a big one. The boys knew it was a 'double-credit' from the moment they walked into the briefing room for there was that long string leading straight to Ploesti." "Beginning at target area and continuing for period of about 12 minutes approximately 25 to 30 enemy aircraft attacked the formation." The aggressive, frontal attacks wreaked havoc as the German fighters flashed through the 449th formation. While the 449th was rallying to the left coming off the target, ship #41 turned right, away from the formation, calling on the radio that the control cables were shot away by the flak over the target. "He was not out of control and was last seen in a big sweeping turn just south of the target." The copilot, bombardier, ball-turret, and waist gunner were killed in the ensuing action as the German fighters pounced on the crippled B-24. As ship #41 went down in flames, the remaining crew members bailed out.

"DRAGON LADY"; Tail #42; Serial #42-52134.
Delivered to Bruning 17 Nov. '43, assigned to Olson's crew. "Terry and the Pirates" was a very popular comic strip written by Milton Caniff in the 1940s. The "Dragon Lady" was the seductive temptress in the comic. Demise: Overshot landing 2/22/44 due to combat damage and hit a stone wall with Morton's crew aboard. No injuries. Ship was salvaged. Circumstances of Loss. On 22 February 1944, the 449th attacked the Obertraubling Aircraft Factory at Regensburg, Germany. They met stiff resistance coming from southern Italy. The damaged aircraft overshot the field and hit a stone wall.

"MISS BEHAVIN"; Tail #43; Serial #42-52086.
Delivered to Bruning 31 Oct. '43, assigned to Loughran's crew. Demise: Lost in a 3-aircraft, mid-air collision over Steyr, Austria, 2 April '44 with Geminder's crew aboard. All 10 crew KIA. Other aircraft involved in the mid-air collision were "SUPERSTITIOUS AL-O-WISHUS" (Ship #45, with Starr's crew aboard) and "PEERLESS CLIPPER" (ship #39 with Kury's crew aboard). Of the 31 men in the three aircraft, 30 KIA & 1 POW. Circumstances of Loss. Over Steyr, Austria, on 2 April 1944, the 449th was attacked by some 60 to 70 enemy fighters. The enemy fighters aggressively pressed home their attacks with rockets, cannons, and aerial bombs. In the 'B' section of the 449th formation, disaster struck with stunning swiftness. "At 1235, over the target of Steyr, three B-24s collided, one sliding into another sideways. Both hit the front of a third plane and tore off the nose right in back of the pilot seat." Two of the ships "broke in pieces and fell down, no chutes being seen." The crew of the third ship began bailing out. Seven chutes (one on fire) were reportedly seen and the ship crashed five miles south of the target. By at least one account, the aircraft which initially lost control "sliding into another sideways" was struck by an aerial bomb dropped from an enemy aircraft above the 449th formation. This was never confirmed. Regardless of what started this chain reaction of aircraft crashing into each other, ship #45, ship #39, and ship #43 were gone in minutes

"THINGS IS ROUGH"; Tail #44; Serial #42-52091.
Delivered to Bruning 20 Oct. '43, assigned to Fees' crew. Hartford Fee was elated to learn he was to be transferred to Bruning as his home town was Coming, Iowa. Before going overseas, he flew "Things Is Rough" over their Iowa farm and his mother came out into the yard and waved to him. What great pride she felt to see her son and his plane but at the same time felt the anguish of worry that he was going into combat. Demise: Transferred to the 15th AF Depot for major maintenance. Subsequently transferred to another Bomb Group. Post-war salvage, 8/13/45. One of the few 449th original ships to survive the war.

"SUPERSTITIOUS AL-O-WISHUS"; Tail #45 Serial #42-52136.
Delivered to Bruning 27 Oct. '43, assigned to Starr's crew. Demise: Lost in a 3-aircraft, mid-air collision over Steyr, Austria, 2 April '44 with Starr's crew aboard. All 10 crew KIA. Other aircraft involved in the mid-air collision were "MISS BEHAVIN" (Ship #43 with Geminder's crew aboard) and "PEERLESS CLIPPER" (ship #39 with Kury's crew aboard). Of the 31 men in the three aircraft, 30 KIA & 1 POW. Circumstances of Loss. Over Steyr, Austria, on 2 April 1944, the 449th was attacked by some 60 to 70 enemy fighters. The enemy fighters aggressively pressed home their attacks with rockets, cannons, and aerial bombs. In the 'B' section of the 449th formation, disaster struck with stunning swiftness. "At 1235, over the target of Steyr, three B-24s collided, one sliding into another sideways. Both hit the front of a third plane and tore off the nose right in back of the pilot seat." Two of the ships "broke in pieces and fell down, no chutes being seen." The crew of the third ship began bailing out. Seven chutes (one on fire) were reportedly seen and the ship crashed five miles south of the target. By at least one account, the aircraft which initially lost control "sliding into another sideways" was struck by an aerial bomb dropped from an enemy aircraft above the 449th formation. This was never confirmed. Regardless of what started this chain reaction of aircraft crashing into each other, ship #45, ship #39, and ship #43 were gone in minutes.

"MIASIS DRAGON"; Tail #46 Serial #42-52172;
Delivered to Bruning 9 Nov. '43, assigned to Gray's crew. Demise: Downed 4/4/44 with Tyler's crew aboard. 10 KIA. Circumstances of Loss. "ATTACK BUCHAREST MARSH YARDS" read the operational order for 4 April 1944 which sent the 449th on its most famous, memorable, and costly mission. Twenty-eight ships of the 449th, unescorted and unaccompanied by other groups, attacked the marshalling yards. "Approximately 80 to 100 enemy aircraft attacked the formation" as the 449th departed the target. The ferocious air battle lasted for an hour and a half. Ship #46 Tyler's crew -- "was seen to be mortally hit by enemy aircraft fire and burst into flame just after the target."

"CLASSY CHASSY"; Tail #33 and #48; Serial #42-52157.
Delivered to Bruning 9 Nov. '43, assigned to Geminder's crew. First 449th ship to complete 50 missions without an early return. One of the most publicized planes during the war was to return to US for display and to sell war bonds. Demise: Downed by flak 11/22/44 with Ludtke's crew aboard. 2 KIA, 7 POW, 1 evaded.

Bruning Army Air Field
718 Bombardment Squadron — Nov. 1943

Those with dots on their forehead were killed in combat
Pictue from Cornelius A. Reisdorf, Cape Coral, FL
(4th from right, bottom row)

Back row: Grimmer (pilot), Rhodes (co-pilot), Roth (navigator), Martin (bombardier). Front row: Cece (nose turret gunner), Dannison (engineer), Murray (radio operator and waist gunner), Grane (bubble turret gunner), Sherman (tail turret gunner), Hollingsworth (waist gunner). Donated by Barbara Roth

APPENDIX 30

718th Bomb Sq

Crew 8-1-A
2ND LT HENRY N SILVERS
2ND LT DUFFEY A CARTER
2ND LT MICHAEL A BIRBIGLIA
2ND LT JOHN T McVICARS
Cpl Julius V Stewart
S/Sgt Mayo E Eavenson
Cpl. Herbert J McBay
Cpl Gene Stedman
S/Sgt Lewis J Warner
Cpl Stephen Morrison

Crew 8-2-A
2ND LT JAMES W MINOW
2ND LT WALLIS L WEBB
2ND LT ARNOLD KOHLER
2ND LT RAYMOND A MANN
S/Sgt Wayne A Walther
Sgt Robert E Kruse
S/Sgt Willard Livingston
Sgt Stephen B Smith
S/Sgt Ernest R Bago
Cpl Donald W Dohass

Crew 8-4-A
2ND LT STEVEN PETZ
2ND LT JOSEPH C PAYSON
2ND LT GEORGE B SKIDMORE
2ND LT JAY T VAN SICKLE
T/Sgt Henry L Spence Jr
Sgt Dyron Booth
S/Sgt Wendel E Plooger
Sgt George Evans
Sgt John M Caswell
Sgt Hobbard D Davis

Crew 8-6-A
2ND LT PAUL R HARPER
2ND LT S D SERMERSHEIM
2ND LT WILLIAM K MANN JR
2IND LT ROBERT S BOREN
S/Sgt Demetre Barns
Sgt Harold L Tombro
Sgt Robert W Williams
Sgt Joseph F Clark
Sgt Donald Clark
Sgt Dan R Brown

Crew 8-7-B
2ND LT THOMAS E CHANDLER
2ND LT ROBERT N WINTER
1ST LT HETER IHRIE
2ND LT DAVID D LIVINGSTONE
T/Sgt Edward J Fechko
Sgt Charles J Murphy
S/Sgt Roland V Vickery
Pfc Charles B Tibbetts
Sgt John C Wood
S/Sgt Edward J Lucy

Crew 8-8-B
2ND LT DALE E ROGERS
2ND LT LEONARD RESNICK
2ND LT WARREN H KINNE
2ND LT ROBERT A HOGGATT
S/Sgt Arthur K Turekian
Sgt Stanley Mawrytko
S/Sgt Willard Schreiber
Sgt Saul D Goodman
Sgt John F Spinney
S/Sgt Alfred H Sildar

Crew 8-9-B
2ND LT HARRY A CARTER
F/O FRANK E STERNER
2ND LT ALBERT J KANZE
2ND LT RICHARD L SUK
S/Sgt Maynard C Manske
Sgt John L Durbin
S/Sgt Retonoi Pollogrino
Sgt Adolph M Commers
Sgt Robert W Leonard
Sgt Glen W Greene

Crew 8-10-D
2ND LT FLETCHER S PORTER
2ND LT THOMAS H TURNER
2ND LT RICHARD S HOWE
2ND LT JAMES C CADY
Sgt Roy F McDean
Sgt Charles Shepherd
Sgt Robert R Rosefield
Sgt George A Bobeck
Sgt Edgar Van Kouren
Sgt Charles J Schroer

Crew 8-13-C
2ND LT RAY C STALEY
2ND LT ROBERT K SCHAITZ
2ND LT GEORGE E McMULLEN
2ND LT RICHARD BLAISDELL
S/Sgt Clyde F Flowers
Sgt John Fraer
S/Sgt Cesco C Vannater
Sgt James R Mitchell
S/Sgt David H Godfrey

Crew 8-14-C
2ND LT HAYWARD S WHEELER
2ND LT WILLIAM N JARRELL
2ND LT NORMAN F TAYLOR JR
2ND LT OSCAR J BLOCH
Sgt Earle A Whidden
Cpl Benedict E Vital
Sgt Reeve A Samson
Sgt Robert A Borucki
Sgt Myron A McLay
Sgt Clarence M Shoarer

Crew 8-15-C
2ND LT HAROLD C WINGFIELD
2ND LT HAROLD E VENNELL
2ND LT JOSEPH O BRAUD
2ND LT CHARLES A FOSKETT
Sgt Fred O Nelson
Cpl Charles W Robinson
Sgt Joseph R Fritsche
Sgt Duane R Peterson
Cpl George F Mahn
Pvt William C Kopetchny

Crew 8-16-C
2ND LT ARNOLD V LARSON
2ND LT JAMES A WILSON
2ND LT ROBERT J WEBER
2ND LT GEORGE B HOYLE
Sgt Gerald K King
Sgt Reginald L Ferguson
Sgt Absolam H Kelly
Sgt Frank Manning
Sgt Milo B Burks
Sgt Jim Y Horn

Crew 8-2-D
1ST LT JOHN W WOOD JR
2ND LT SYLVAN H LUBIN
2ND LT DONALD R CURRIER
2ND LT ROBERT B FENTON
Sgt Wilfred C Ayers
Sgt William E Granowski
S/Sgt Norbert J Kneis
Sgt Gilbert H Smith
Sgt Dennin J Bauers
S/Sgt Harry C Smith

Crew 8-5-D
2ND LT BEN N KENDALL
2ND LT RICHARD C PELKEY
2ND LT HARRY B McGUIRE
2ND LT PERSHING J HILL
Sgt Gerald W Herrington
Sgt Given C Grooms
Sgt Harold T Thompson
Sgt Nick Gavalas
Sgt Charles A Lamarca
Sgt Harvey E Gann

Crew 8-11-D
2ND LT WARREN A STEWART
2ND LT CORNELIUS REISDORF
2ND LT ROLAND D RICKERT
2ND LT SAMUEL GOLDENBERG
S/Sgt Eugene A Ward
Sgt Jack C Faulhaber
Sgt Paul F Hadley
Sgt Richard R Bach Sr
Sgt John E Bash
S/Sgt Lucius J Hamel

Crew 8-12-D
2ND LT DAVID A RASBACH
2ND LT ELMER SCHNACKENBERG
2ND LT WILLIAM H GARDTNER
2ND LT JOHN E ASBURY
Sgt Paul G Fleming
Sgt Thomas T Hager
Sgt Robert E Bell
Sgt Joseph R Leraci
Sgt Harry W Herwig Jr
Sgt John N Rensheim

Crew 8-17-D
2ND LT HAROLD E PICKARD
2ND LT ALVIN L FERLBERG
2ND LT ROOM A McELDOWNEY
2ND LT GEORGE W HALZEL
S/Sgt John V Gegoulis
Sgt Harris P John
Pfc Patrick H Hoavey Jr
Sgt Danile H Mahoney
Sgt Theodore J Henze
Sgt Robert O Hansen

Crew 8-18
1ST LT WILLIAM C NOSKER
1ST LT REXFORD E TOMPKINS
2ND LT HERBERT D MARTIN
2ND LT THOMAS J E JOBIN
2ND LT JOHN H WITE JR
2ND LT GEORGE M D RICHARDS
2ND LT DONALD L BOHANNON
2ND LT ROBERT O BULLIS
1ST LT DONALD P ULLMAN
1ST LT JESS C BENNETT

Crew 8-19
M/Sgt Harry E May
T/Sgt Earl G Filsinger
T/Sgt Michael F Urbanek
S/Sgt John H Dixon
S/Sgt Palmer D Miller
S/Sgt John Loasia
S/Sgt Domnic G Gafarelli
S/Sgt Robert E Muller
Sgt J 8 Kempson
2ND LT GEORGE W A CHUDYK

Crew 8-20
Sgt James A Wells
S/Sgt Edward L Buffington
Sgt Joseph E Skalak
Sgt Caleb W Hogsed
Sgt Francis L Weaver
S/Sgt Terry J Lavergno
Sgt George R Dennis
S/Sgt John N Clark
Sgt Floyd J Lawell
T/Sgt Ish I Katzoff

Crew 8-21
Sgt Earl G Smith
T/Sgt George C Worthington
M/Sgt Bernard Kessler
S/Sgt Harold F Haggerty
T/Sgt Gordon H Shaw
Sgt Carman J Viaforo
Sgt Victor Teicher

718th Squadron (449th BG) Original Aircraft

"VENI, VIDI, VICI"; Tail #17; Serial #42-52150.
"Veni, Vidi, Vici" is Latin for "I came, I saw, I conquered." Delivered to Bruning 5 Nov. '43, assigned to Silvers' crew. Demise: Downed by flak 5/17/44 with Silvers' crew aboard. 7 KIA, 3 POW. Tail #17; Serial #42-52150. A photo was taken of Veni, Vidi, Vici. "With the number-2 engine totally shot away by flak, Ship #17 begins its final descent over Orbetello, Italy. 17, May 1944. There was a direct hit by flak shell on #2 engine blowing the engine off and firing the ship" The pilot, Lt. H. Silvers and the copilot, Lt. Thomas Turner "held the aircraft under control-- straight and level until the crew could bail out. The B-24 peeled out of formation to avoid damage to other aircraft." The wing collapsed and seven members of Silver's crew, including both pilots, perished in the ensuing crash. In the post-mission debriefing, the Squadron C. O. referred to the controlled manner in which ship #17 peeled out of the formation thereby avoiding other aircraft and allowing time for crew members to begin bailing out as "the finest piece of flying ever seen."

"41-29217"; Tail #18; Serial #42-29217.
Later called Dumbo #2. Dumbo was a flying elephant. Delivered to Bruning circa Oct./Nov. '43, assigned to Kendall's crew. Demise: Downed 1/30/44 by flak and fighters over Udine, Italy, with Kendall's crew aboard. 9 KIA, 1 POW. Circumstances of Loss. On 30 Jan. 1944, thirty 449th aircraft bombed the German airfield at Udine, Italy. At 1228 hours, "immediately after bombs were away," enemy fighters, "variously estimated as 20 to 50" in number, furiously attacked the 449th formation. The enemy fighters, "mostly ME-109s with a sprinkling of FW-190s, attacked from all positions of the clock, and most of the time from below. Some attacked in 2's and 3's abreast. Attacks were pressed to within 200 and 300 yards." The attacks were "concentrated on the lower flight of the first section" which was "apparently ... left uncovered from above when the second section in making the turn for the IP swung wide over the first section while there was straggling in this flight itself." Within minutes after the beginning of the attack, three ships in the low flight of the first section were mortally damaged by the enemy fighters. Ship #18 was "reported ... to go down just south of the target." The copilot was 2nd Lt. Fletcher Porter, the original pilot of Big Noise From Kentucky.

"HOT ROCK"; Tail #20, Serial #41-29218.
Delivered to Bruning 22 Oct. '43, assigned to Petz's crew. Demise: Sent to 15th AF Depot for major repair. Subsequently transferred to another Bomb Group. Post-war salvage 3 June '45. One of the original ships to last out the war.

"461"; Tail #21; Serial #42-64461.
Delivered to Bruning (unknown). Demise: Damaged by flak 4/23/44 over Vienna RR yards with Rouse's crew aboard. Crashlanded in Yugoslavia. The crew torched the ship. 1 KIA, 9 Evaded. Circumstances of Loss. Thirty 449th aircraft bombed the enemy aircraft factory at Schwechat, Austria, at 1455 hours on 23 April 1944. The flak wreaked havoc on the 449th formation. Four B-24's fell victim to the deadly barrage. Ship #21 "dropped back in the formation with the

number- 1 engine smoking and feathered" as Rouse's crew struggled to keep the bomber airborne. Ship #21 was last seen just south of Zagreb, Yugoslavia, losing altitude. Being too low to bail out and unable to climb due to combat damage, Rouse's crew landed ship #21 in a field in Yugoslavia. The radio operator was killed in the action. After setting the ship afire, the other nine crew members contacted partisan forces and successfully evaded.

"HARPER'S FERRY"; Tail #22; Serial #41-28621. Delivered to Bruning 6 Nov. '43, assigned to Harper's crew. Demise: The 718th sent her to the 15th Air Force Depot in December of 1944. Post-war salvage 8/16/45. One of the few 449th original ships to survive the war.

"SINNERS DREAM"; Tail #23; Serial #41-28605.
Delivered to Bruning 9 Nov. '43, assigned to Chandler's crew. Demise: Downed over Udine, Italy, 1/30/44 with Chandler's crew aboard. 6 KIA, 5 POW. Circumstances of Loss. On 30 Jan. 1944, thirty 449th aircraft bombed the German airfield at Udine, Italy. At 1228 hours, "immediately after bombs were away," enemy fighters, "various enemy fighters estimated to be 20 to 50" in number, furiously attacked the 449th formation. The enemy fighters, "mostly ME-109s (ME stood for Messerschmitt) with a sprinkling of FW-190s, attacked from all positions of the clock, and most of the time from below. Some attacked in 2's and 3's abreast. Attacks were pressed to within 200 and 300 yards." The attacks were "concentrated on the lower flight of the first section" which was "apparently left uncovered from above when the second section in making the turn for the IP swung wide over the first section while there was straggling in this flight itself " Within minutes after the beginning of the attack, three ships in the low flight of the first section were mortally damaged by the enemy fighters. Ship #23 was observed "to spiral to earth and crash" just after the target.

"PISTOL PACKIN MAMMA"; Tail #24; Serial #41-28597.
Delivered to Bruning 19 Oct. '43, assigned to Dale Roger's crew. Demise: Downed 4/16/44 over Brasov, Rumania, with Roger's crew aboard. 1 KIA, 9 POW. Circumstances of Loss. The marshalling yard at Brasov, Rumania, was the 449th's target on 16 April 1944. As the 449th departed the target, they came under attack by enemy fighters. Three 449th aircraft, ships #24, #29, #36 fell victim to the fighters. All three aircraft were reportedly beginning to "straggle" in the rear of their formations when they were "attacked by the enemy fighters." Details of the losses were sketchy. However, aboard ship #24, the top-turret gunner was killed as the enemy fighters pressed home their attacks. Crews were observed bailing out of the three stricken bombers, all of which "went out of control and crashed."

"DAISY MAE"; Tail #25; Serial #41-07726.
Delivered to Bruning 15 Oct. '43, assigned to Carter's crew. "Lil Abner" was a very popular comic strip in the newspapers at that time. Daisy Mae was Lil Abner's girl friend. Received ground damage during the night of 8 Jan. '44 when an RAF Beaufighter lost control on landing and ran into her. The ship was repaired, put back into service, and flew combat missions until 1 Aug. '44 at which time it was salvaged.

"BIG NOISE FROM KENTUCKY"; Delivered to Bruning 5 Nov. '43, assigned to Porter's crew. Demise: Downed by flak on 5/5/44 over Bor, Yugoslavia, returning from Ploesti mission with Harper's crew aboard. 1 POW, 9 Evaded. Tail #26; Serial #42-52149. Circumstances of

Loss. Thirty-eight 449th B-24s attacked the marshalling yards at Ploesti, Rumania, on 5 May 1944. Over the target, the 449th was pounded by "intense, accurate, heavy flak." As they emerged from the flak, some 25 to 30 enemy fighters attacked the formation. Four B-24s fell victim to the flak and fighters. When the enemy fighters broke of the attack, the remaining thirty-four B-24s closed up the formations, and, with the feeling that the worst part of the mission was behind them, began the long flight home. An hour after departing Ploesti -- as the formation passed directly over Bor, Yugoslavia -- flak again appeared in the sky around the lead section. The flak squarely bracketed ship #26. Both the number-3 and number-4 engines were knocked out. Lt. Paul Harper -- realizing that his plane was mortally damaged -- gave the order to bail out. At 1508 hours the crew bailed out. Big Noise "went into a spiral glide and crashed with blinding flash." The position was noted as 4350N - 2113E.

"EVERYBODY'S BABY"; Tail #27 Serial #42-07756.
Delivered to Bruning 25 Oct. '43, assigned to Stewart's crew. Demise: Damaged in a ground accident in early March 1944. While taxiing across the muddy field at Grottaglie, the right wheel of ship #27 struck a deep hole. The shock of striking the hole caused major damage to the trut and right wing. Ship #27 subsequently became a "spare parts" ship.

"YE OLDE RUGGED CURSE"; Tail #28; Serial #42-07762.
Delivered to Bruning 31 Oct. '43, assigned to Rasbach's crew. Demise: Combat damaged 2 April '44 by fighters over Steyr, Austria; Rasbach's crew made emergency landing at Foggia, Italy. Ship salvaged for spare parts. Circumstances of Loss: The aircraft components factory at Steyr, Austria, was the 449th's target on 2 April 1944. At high noon -- as the lead elements of the 449th formation approached the IP -- sixty to seventy enemy fighters attacked the 449th formation. Ship #28 suffered heavy damage as the "very aggressive" ME-109's some of which "came within 100 feet of the top turret," raked the length of the B-24 with 20-mm cannon fire. The number-1 engine, waist section, and flight deck were riddled. The shell fragments which richocheted through the aircraft wounded four crewmen. Flying on three engines, ship #28 managed to make it back Italy and to make an emergency landing at Foggia. The combat damage was so severe that the ship was salvaged for spare parts.

"HELLS-A-POPPIN"; Tail #29; Serial #42-52166.
Delivered to Bruning 9 Nov. '43, assigned to Staley's crew. "Hells a Poppin" was a very popular movie during 1943. Demise: Downed 4/16/44 over Brasov, Rumania with Temchulla's crew aboard. 3 KIA, 7 POW. Circumstances of Loss: The marshalling yard at Brasov, Rumania, was the 449th's target on 16 April 1944. As the 449th departed the target, they came under attack by enemy fighters. Three 449th aircraft, ships #24, #29, #36 fell victim to the fighters. All three aircraft were reportedly beginning to "straggle" in the rear of their formations when they were "attacked by the enemy fighters." Details of the losses were sketchy. Three crewmen aboard ship #29 were killed during the action as the enemy fighters pressed home their attacks. Crews were observed bailing out of the three stricken bombers, all of which "went out of control and crashed."

"730"; Tail #30; Serial #42-07730.
Delivered to Bruning circa Oct./Nov. '43, assigned to Wheeler's crew. Demise: Downed 1/30/44 over Udine, Italy, when rammed by a ME-109. 10 KIA. Circumstances of Loss: On 30 Jan. 1944,

thirty 449th aircraft bombed the German airfield at Udine, Italy. At 1228 hours, "immediately after bombs were away," enemy fighters, "variously estimated for 20 to 50" in number, furiously attacked the 449th formation. The enemy fighters, "mostly ME-109s with a sprinkling of FW-190s, attacked from all positions of the clock, and most of the time from below. Some attacked in 2's and 3's abreast. Attacks were pressed to within 200 and 300 yards." The attacks were "concentrated on the lower flight of the first section" which was "apparently ... left uncovered from above when the second section in making the turn for the IP swung wide over the first section while there was straggling in this flight itself." Within minutes after the beginning of the attack, three ships in the low flight of the first section were mortally damaged by the enemy fighters. Ship #30 was "seen to explode and go into a spin" when "it was rammed by an ME-109, one of the B-24s engines being afire at the time of the collision.

"SLEEPY TIME GAL"; Tail #31 & 29 Serial #42-07745;
"Sleepy Time Gal" was a popular song in the 1940's. Delivered to Bruning 19 Oct. '43, assigned to Wingfield's crew. Demise: Downed 2/23/44 by fighters. 7 KIA, 3 POW. Circumstances of Loss. The 23rd of February 1944 saw the 449th attack the aircraft factory at Steyr, Austria. As the formation approached the target shortly before noon, "30 to 40 ME-109, ME-110, and JU- 88" attacked the 449th. The enemy fighters, attacking from the rear, scored direct hits on ship #31 which "was seen to wing over at the target and go into a steep dive" from which it never recovered.

"WHITE FANG"; Tail Serial #41-28606.
Delivered to Bruning 27 Oct. '43, assigned to Pickard's crew. Demise: Downed 1/14/44 over Mostar, Yugoslavia, with Pickard's crew aboard when struck by bombs from another aircraft in the formation. 9 KIA, 2 POW. #32; Circumstances of Loss: Operational Order Number 2 for January 14th 1944 identified the target for the day as the "TOWN OF MOSTAR." At this point in time, the 449th had not lost a plane and crew over an enemy target. Although "two ME-109s attacked the formation" and "flak over the target was heavy and moderate," the Group's first combat loss was not directly attributable to enemy action. The Group formation "followed the route but missed the IP and missed the target -- 5 miles north" with the result that the formation "circled before the bomb run began." During the circle maneuver, the 449th formation came unglued. Aircraft lost their positions relative to each other with disastrous results. When bombs were released, ship #606 with Pickard's crew was directly below the bomb bay of ship #737. The first two bombs in the string struck ship #606 amid ships causing the ship to explode in mid-air in a "huge ball of fire, smoke, and debris."

"WOODS CHOPPER"; Tail #35, #19, #44; Serial #42-07750. Delivered to Bruning 20 Oct. '43, assigned to John Wood's crew. Demise: Crashed 2 July '44 four miles north of home base, out of fuel, with Kirkland's crew aboard returning damaged. 3 KIA. Circumstances of Loss: On 2 July 1944 when it crashed just short of the runway at Grottaglie with Kirkland' crew aboard returning damaged from a mission to Budapest, Hungary. In his book **"50 *Mission Crush*"** Donald Currier wrote that a sergeant said he would paint the nose art on the plane for $20.00. The original nose art showed an axe descending upon the neck of Tojo. The already severed head of Hitler is seen to the right. In April 1944, a Wing inspector ordered that the caricatures of Tojo and Hitler be painted over -- the reason, to avoid offending the enemy. For another $5.00, the artist painted individual pictures under the windows of the

APPENDIX 31

719th Bomb Sq

Crew 9-1-AC
2ND LT ROBERT D EASTERS
2ND LT CHARLES M SWIFT
2ND LT DONALD B VAN LIER
2ND LT JAMES A GOFORTH
T/Sgt Floyd B Caldwell
Sgt Walter H Hauser
Sgt Sylvan R Lazarus
S/Sgt Carl H Cobb
S/Sgt Frank E Boudroau
Sgt Raymond P Sunderland

Crew 9-2-D
2ND LT GEORGE T FERGUS JR
2ND LT JAMES R KERVIN
2ND LT JOE B TRUEMPER
2ND LT HENRY B FINCH
S/Sgt Ruben C Phillips
Sgt Russell H Bolden
Sgt George F Littlejohn
Sgt Donald Walker
Sgt Edward S Cooley
Sgt Vito Corso

Crew 9-3-A
2ND LT JOHN C WOODLE
2ND LT WILLIAM C BRYAN
2ND LT VERNON C DICKSON
2ND LT HOWARD R MOREY
Sgt Lewis M Rush
S/Sgt Doyce V Burt
S/Sgt Frank I Sumpter
Sgt Vernon C Caldwell
Sgt William D Fink
Pvt Clifford H Williams

Crew 9-4-A
2ND LT JAMES C GRIMMER
2ND LT JOHN J ROADES
2ND LT MARTIN E ROTH
2ND LT JOSEPH MARTIN
Sgt Gerald V Danison
Stg Wesley I. Cease
S/Sgt Donald E Murray
S/Sgt Warren W Hollingsworth
Sgt Willard S Sherman
Sqt Frederick N Crain

Crew 9-5-A
2ND LT ELMER C MEADE
2ND LT KENNETH A KEELER
2ND LT RICHARD W SAWYER
2ND LT HUGH P MARTIN
S/Sgt Frank D Vitrano
Sgt Fidel P Guorroro
Sgt Harold E Hays
Sgt Sam M Graci
Sgt Clifford A Kirschler
Sgt Russell J Lindhorst

Crew 9-6-DC
2ND LT WILLIAM T PHILLIPS
2ND LT LYLAN W LACY
2ND LT JOHN J WALSH
2ND LT JAMES R CLARY
Sgt Marvin P Martin
Sgt Virgil W Kitchens
Sgt Thomas F Walsh
Sgt Earl Baxter
Sgt Edgar R Pohlo
Sgt Edward J. Walsh

Crew 9-7-BC
2ND LT SHELDON I ZIMMERMAN
2ND LT PAUL A LAHR
2ND LT DUNCAN W McDONALD
2ND LT GERALD MURRAY
Sgt Waldo A Wineinger
Sgt Mark S Turkiowicz
Sgt Elbert Hopponstodt
Sgt Thomas Pollogrino
Sgt Robert E Goorlitz
Sgt Andrew D Survilla

Crew 9-8-0
2ND LT RICHARD GARRISON
2ND LT JAMES SMALL
2ND LT ALVIN P GOLDBERG
2ND LT EDWARD R DARNINSKI
S/Sgt James E Post
Sgt Robert Manman
Sgt Lawrence I Green
S/Sqt David M Grey
Sgt Raymond Richardson

Crew 9-9-A
2ND LT JOHN M McCORMICK
2ND LT CHARLES R LYNCH
2ND LT WILFRED STAGHAN
2ND LT ROBERT E LAUBER
Sgt Arthur Van Arkel
Sgt Charles Cheatham
Sgt Theodore Thompson
Sgt Howard Schattler
Sgt Ivan L Elsrod
Sgt Boyd D Thietton

Crew 9-10-B
2ND LT CLARENCE
2ND LT DONALD F HOUSE
2ND LT GEORGE F McSTEEN
2ND LT JOHN C GRAY
Sgt Joseph LaBrunda
Sgt Meddle Brouillette
Sgt Walter Clayton
Sgt Angelo P Gervasi
Sgt Thomas Munley
Sgt William J Irwin

Crew 9-11-D
2ND LT JOSEPH W GEISEL
2ND LT FREDERICK KRUCKMEYER
2ND LT DAVID W TACK
2ND LT JOHN B GAWLEY
Sgt Manuel Medoiros
Sqt J D Beatty
Sgt Clyde J Deorge
Sgt John J Johnson
Cpl Maurico L Matott
Sgt Walter J Dillon

Crew 9-12-D
F/O WILLIAM R THIEME
2ND LT EDWARD J O'ROURKE
2ND LT GILBERT MALRAIT
2ND LT FRANCIS L BECK
Sgt Mark J Ehert
Sgt Guy E Blakely
Sgt Homer E Edgar
Sgt Louis N Lannon
Sgt Karl Vaagen
Sgt Ingmar Hippe

Crew 9-13-CC
2ND LT RALPH P GENTRY
2ND LT DONALD C LAPHAM
2ND LT ROY A DEGAUGH
2ND LT EDWARD V BUNDERSON
T/Sgt Howard J Carlson
Sgt Edward J Matya
Sgt Martin Eggleton
Sgt Elmer R Shane
Sgt Roy R Ferguson
Sgt Fred A Route

Crew 9-14-C
F/O RAYMOND B WOLTKEMP
2ND LT LEO F VALDER
2ND LT JAMES Y HAMBLEY
2ND LT RAYMOND W WADE
Sgt Sam Nahman
Sgt Thomas W Rich
S/Sgt Wilson H Wiley
Sgt James H Bunnell
Sgt Emmanuel P French

Crew 9-15-C
1ST LT ANTHONY D POLINK
2ND LT FORREST A RINGLE
2ND LT GEORGE B BOYLES
2ND LT JOHN L ZIMMERMAN
S/Sgt George Rothenburg
Sgt Clinton J Wilson
S/Sgt John P Sickley
Sgt Angelo Bursio
Sgt. John H Jarrard
S/Sgt Edward Laver Jr

Crew 9-16-B
2ND LT SHELBY McARTHUR
2ND LT WILLIAM C HOLLAND
2ND LT JERRE F LOGEN
2ND LT FREDERICK OSTROM
S/Sgt Isaac M Spence
Sgt Joseph Druther
Sgt Albert T Bosch
Sgt Harold Fox
Sgt Preston Farish
Sgt John J Morris

Crew 9-17-C
2ND LT SIDNEY A STEPHENS
2ND LT JAMES N SCHINDLER
2ND LT LAWRENCE HEVERLE
2ND LT HENRY A WILTSE
2ND LT RICHARD F ROBERTS
SGT Lloyd J Starr
Pvt George W Morrison
Sgt John H Yuhas
Sgt Dawsey L Shriner
Sgt Percy J LeBlanc

Crew 9-18
CAPT DAVID DECOUNCILL
2ND LT ROBERT D McFARLAND
2ND LT MICHAEL J O'NEIL
2ND LT CHARLES R ST JOHN
M/Sgt Bernard J Brady
S/Sgt Rudolph Leskovar
Sgt Leo W Rosset
Pfc John E Ruppel
Sgt John W Borton
Sgt Leo C Austin

Crew 9-19
1ST LT HIERO F HAYS
2ND LT JOHN J SCHUMAN
2ND LT LEO L OGUREK
1ST LT EARL McDANIEL
T/Sgt Francis W Harris
S/Sgt Clarence E Lambertz
Sgt Carl S Gibson
Sgt Morlon V Painter
Sgt Robert A Kolezar
Sgt Marshall Stoner

Crew 9-20
2ND LT GEORGE W PARKER
2ND LT CHARLES D CROMMON
1ST LT PAUL C EVILSIZOR
T/Sgt Harold G Sauer
M/Sgt Frank N Crabbe
S/Sgt Bill Baker
S/Sgt Arnold K Knutson
Sgt Morgan F LeRoy
S/Sgt Frank Kazanowski

Crew 9-21
S/Sgt George A Busonik
Sgt Edward F Kullman
S/Sgt Elwin J DePew
Sgt Frederick I Ross
Sgt Raymond H Lara

crew stations. Under John's window was "Long John". Lubin's window featured "Pisonia". Ayers showed "Gumbo" and Currier had "Blondie" which was the name of the girl who became his wife and who helped him write his book and a pair of dice with a "6"and a "4" on it. Permission to copy a chapter from Currier's book describing the exciting flight over the Atlas mountains is found in this book.

719th Squadron (449th BG) Original Aircraft

"PUDGY 11"; Tail #01 Serial # 42-07747
Delivered to Bruning 9 Nov. '43, assigned to 719th Operations Staff and Squadron C. O. David Council. Demise: Crashed 8 Dec. '43 into a mountain in the Atlas Range of North West Africa during movement overseas. 14 KIA. Circumstances of Loss. The Group began movement overseas on 16 November 1943. The individual airplanes of the air echelon headed for Italy by a route which took them to Florida, thence to Puerto Rico, Trinadad and Brazil. The Atlantic crossing was made between Brazil and Dakar, Africa. From Dakar the Group flew north to Morroco, then east to Tunsia, and finally north across the Mediterrean Sea to southern Italy. In North Africa, They had to negotiate a flight through the Atlas Mountain Range. By the first week in December, the individual aircraft formed a long, unending chain stretching from Topeka to North Africa. Such a massive movement of men and equipment was certain to produce mishaps. Tragedy struck the Group for the first time on the 8th of December. Captain David Councill, C. O. of the 719th Squadron, and twelve others died when ship #01 struck a mountain peak in the Atlas Mountains of North Africa.

"STAR EYES"; Tail #02; Serial #41-29203. Delivered to Bruning 28 Oct. '43, assigned to Meade's crew. Demise: After at least 70 missions, the ship was heavily damaged and salvaged for parts on 3/19/45.

"LOS LOBOS"; Tail #03; Serial #42-07761.
"Los Lobos " is Spanish for the wolves. During WWII, men who were on the prowl for women were referred to as wolves. Delivered to Bruning 25 Oct. '43, assigned to Polink's crew. Demise: Heavily damaged 10 Feb. '44 making a return landing with a load of fragmentation bombs. Several bombs broke loose on the landing. Ship salvaged for spare parts. No injuries.

"JUANITA"; Tail #04 Serial #42-52126. Delivered to Bruning 28 Oct. '43, assigned to Woltkamp's crew Demise: Downed 1/16/44 by fighters with Woltkamp's crew aboard. Circumstances of Loss. On the morning of 10 Feb. 1944, twenty-three 449th B-24s attacked the German airdrome near Osoppo in northeastern Italy. Although there were "no attacks by enemy planes" and "no flak over the target area," ship #4 with Woltkamp's crew was "lost after the target." Reportedly, ship #4 "ditched in the Adriatic sea about 25 miles from Venice, Italy. "It was subsequently learned that five of the crew members perished, and the remaining five became POWs.

"SUNSHINE"; Tail #05; Serial #42-52106.
Delivered to Bruning 23 Oct. '43, assigned to Stephen's crew. Demise: Damaged 3/29/44 by flak over North Italy with Hemphill's crew aboard. Crew attempted to make it to Switzerland.

Misidentified destination and landed at a German airfield at Venegono, Italy. Crew became POWs. Aircraft was subsequently used for propaganda purposes by the Luftwaffe. Circumstances of Loss: On 29 March 1944, between 0740 and 0821 hours, thirty-eight 449th B-24s took off to make an attack on the marshalling yard at Bolzano, Italy. The last ship to take-off -- ship #5, Sunshine, with Hemphill's crew aboard -- was destined on this day to a fate which was unique among 449th aircraft. Thirty-six of the aircraft reached the target and dropped 87-1/2 tons of bombs on the target area. By 1530 hours, thirty-five of the 449th aircraft had returned to base. The missing aircraft was Sunshine. Its fate was a mystery to Group personnel. In the months to come, it would be learned that Sunshine, flying at the very rear of the 449th formation, was hit by flak over the target which knocked out two engines. Hemphill's crew knew they could not make it back to southern Italy. The safe haven of Switzerland, however, was less than 75 miles away. Therefore, rather than bail out, the pilots turned westward and began trading distance for altitude in an attempt to make it to a Swiss airfield. A few minutes later, what was believed to be an airfield in Switzerland was located, and Hemphill brought Sunshine in for a safe landing. Ironically, it was not Switzerland. It was northern Italy. The entire crew was immediately taken prisoner, and turned over to the Germans. Sunshine, completely intact, was taken over by the Luftwaffe for propaganda purposes. Among 449th aircraft, it was a unique fate.

"BETTY JEAN"; Tail #06; Serial #41-28625.
Delivered to Bruning 6 Nov. '43, assigned to Phillip's crew. Demise: Downed 1/19/44 by flak over Perugia, Italy, with Phillip's crew aboard. 6 POW, 4 Evaded. Circumstances of Loss: The enemy reconnaissance base at Perugia, Italy, was the 449th target on 19 Jan. 1944. There were no attacks by enemy aircraft. However, the "heavy, moderate-to-intense, accurate flak" mortally damaged ship #6, Betty Jean. When last seen by other aircraft in the formation, ship #6 was "heading for the east coast and still going down -- number-3 feathered and number-4 on fire." Nine chutes were seen. It was subsequently learned that all ten members of Phillips' crew successfully bailed out. "Seven became POWs and three successfully evaded. Although Betty Jean was the Group's fifth loss on a combat mission, she may well have been the first Group aircraft actually brought down by enemy flak.

"TWO TON TESSIE"; Tail #07 Serial #42-52117. Delivered to Bruning 27 Oct. '43, assigned to Fergus crew. Demise: Downed 5/29/44 with Fergus's crew aboard. 10 POW. Circumstances of Loss ; Enroute, to Wiener-Neustadt on 29 May 1944, some 20 minutes before reaching the IP, the radio operator aboard ship #7 called in on the command frequency saying they were "having trouble with turbos." The Group leader instructed ship #7 to jettison their bomb load. After dropping its bombs, ship #7 was able to maintain position in the formation. However, just as the Group was reaching the IP, ship #7 dropped out of the formation and turned back alone. Ship #7 was apparently still under control when it turned back, and no chutes were seen. "This aircraft was not seen after that time" by any of the Group aircraft. It would later be learned that ship #7 fell victim to enemy fighters after the turn back. All ten members of Fergus' crew succeeded in bailing out safely and subsequently became POWs.

"PAPER DOLL"; Tail #08; Serial #42-07691
Brought to Bruning 15 Oct. '43, assigned to Garrison's crew. "Paper Doll" was a very popular song during WWII. The words started, "I want to buy a paper doll that I can call my own, a doll

that other fella's can not steal" Demise: Downed by fighters on 4/4/44 over Bucharest with Garrison's crew aboard. 7 KIA, 3 POW. Circumstances of Loss. "ATTACK BUCHAREST MARSH YARDS" read the operational order for 4 April 1944 which sent the 449th on its most famous, memorable, and costly mission. Twenty-eight ships of the 449th, unescorted and unaccompanied by other groups, attacked the marshalling yards. "Approximately 80 to 100 enemy aircraft attacked the formation" as the 449th departed the target. The ferocious air battle lasted for an hour and a half. Five minutes after bombs were away, ship #8 was observed to go down "in a controlled dive to 10,000 feet" with "the right wing badly shot up" then "caught fire, rolled on back and crashed."

"GUARDIAN ANGEL"; Tail #09; Serial #42-07715
Brought to Bruning 15 Oct. '43, assigned to Woodle's crew.
Demise: Downed 2/22/44 by flak and fighters over Regensburg, Germany, with Woodle's crew aboard. 11 POW. Circumstances of Loss: On 22 February 1944, the 449th attacked the Obertraubling Aircraft Factory at Regensburg, Germany. They met stiff resistance in the form of both fighters and flak. The enemy fighters scored direct hits on ship #9. Guardian Angel was mortally damaged and forced to fall out of formation. It was last sighted settling into the cloud cover under heavy attack by the pursuing fighters.

"MIGHTY MOUSE"; Tail #10 Serial #41-28594;
Delivered to Bruning 20 Oct. '43, assigned to Frone's crew. Demise: Ditched at sea 1/15/44 with Frone's crew aboard. 4 bailed out and became POW's, 6 who remained with the ship were KIA. Circumstances of Loss: The 449th attacked the marshalling yard at Prato, Italy on 15 January 1944. The 449th formation departed Grottaglie, crossed southern Italy on an almost due east course to the Isle of Capri, there taking up a northwesterly course which roughly paralled the Italian coastline. Shortly after passing the Isle of Elba, ship #10 suddenly lost power in two engines. Only two options were open -- either bail out or attempt a ditching at sea. Evidently crew members were given a choice. Four crew members successfully bailed out, and were subsequently picked up by rescue boats. The six who chose to remain with the ship died in the ditching.

"BETTY ANN"; Tail #11; Serial #41-292175.
Delivered to Bruning 20 Oct. '43, assigned to Thieme's crew. It was originally called "Battlin' Betty Ann" after the pilot's wife, Mrs. Betty Ann Thieme. Demise: One of the three 719th ships lost during the overseas movement in December 1943. Ship encountered severe icing conditions over west Africa. Crew was forced to bail out on 15 Dec. '43. Thirteen bailed out successfully, 1 KIA when chute failed to open. Circumstances of Loss: The Group began movement overseas on 16 November 1943. The individual airplanes of the air echelon headed for Italy by a route which took them to Florida, thence to Puerto Rico, Trinadad and Brazil. The Atlantic crossing was made between Brazil and Dakar, Africa. From Dakar, the Group flew north to Morroco, thence east to Tunsia, and finally north across the Mediterrean Sea to southern Italy. In north Africa, they had to negotiate a flight through the Atlas Mountain Range. By the first week in December, the individual aircraft formed a long, unending chain stretching from Topeka to North Africa. Such a massive movement of men and equipment was certain to produce mishaps. Near Meknes, North Africa, ship #11 encountered severe icing conditions forcing the crew to bail out. All bailed out successfully except Captain Hiero Hays whose parachute failed to open.

"HASSAN THE ASSASSIN"; Tail #12; Serial #41-29237.
Delivered to Bruning 6 Nov. '43, assigned to Zimmerman's crew. Enroute overseas in December 1943, the ship was damaged landing in Puerto Rico necessitating that the ship be grounded for extensive repairs. The crew proceeded to Italy by "hitch-hiking" on various transports en route with space available. Final Demise: Ship repaired and transferred to 459th Bomb Group, where it was renamed "TAMERLANE II". Crashed 3/17/44 in Austria.

"DIXIE BELL"; Tail #13; Serial #41-29193.
Delivered to Bruning 1 Nov. '43, assigned to Grimmer's crew. Demise: Downed 4/4/44 over Bucharest with Kendall's crew aboard. 2 KIA, 8 POW. Circumstances of Loss. "ATTACK BUCHAREST MARSH YARDS" read the operational order for 4 April 1944 which sent the 449th on its most famous, memorable, and costly mission. Twenty-eight ships of the 449th, unescorted and unaccompanied by other groups, attacked the marshalling yards. "Approximately 80 to 100 enemy aircraft attacked the formation" as the 449th departed the target. The ferocious air battle lasted for an hour and a half. Shortly after the target, ship # 13 was observed to fall out of formation with the number-3 engine on fire. Nine chutes were seen.

"LONESOME"; Tail #14; Serial #42-07732.
Delivered to Bruning 19 Oct. '43, assigned to Geisel's crew. Named "Lonesome" because all the men on this crew were bachelors. Demise: Transferred to 15th Air Force Depot after 41 missions. Subsequently reassigned to another Bomb Group. Post-war salvage, 8/16/45. One of the few original Bruning ships to survive the war.

"PATCHES" or "LIL LASSIE"; Tail #15; Serial #42-52155.
Delivered to Bruning 9 Nov. '43, assigned to "Pat" Gentry's crew. This ship was named "Lil Lassie". Gentry intended to rename it "Sweet Sue" after his daughter who was born on September 6, 1943. However, after a few missions, it was patched with 245 aluminum squares rivetted over flak and bullet holes with contrasting colored metal so that it was given the name "Patches". There were two "Patches". The other was a replacement plane #AC 41-29428. Demise for 52155: Transferred to 15th AF Depot. Subsequently reassigned to another Bomb Group. Salvaged after crashlanding 7 Aug. '44.

"MAUI MAID"; Tail #16; Serial #41-28623.
Delivered to Bruning 10 Nov. '43. This plane was named after Col. Alkire's wife who was from Hawaii. With Group Commanding Officer, Col. Darr Alkire as lead pilot, this ship led the overseas flight from Bruning, Nebraska to Morrison AAF, Florida, and from there overseas by the southern route in December 1943. Col. Alkire's crew was made up of the Group HQs staff, operations, and support personnel. Alkire and crew landed at Grottaglie, Italy, as the first 449th bomber on the field. This ship flew a few missions with other crews. Demise: Ground accident, ran into an embankment. No injuries. Ship salvaged for spare parts.

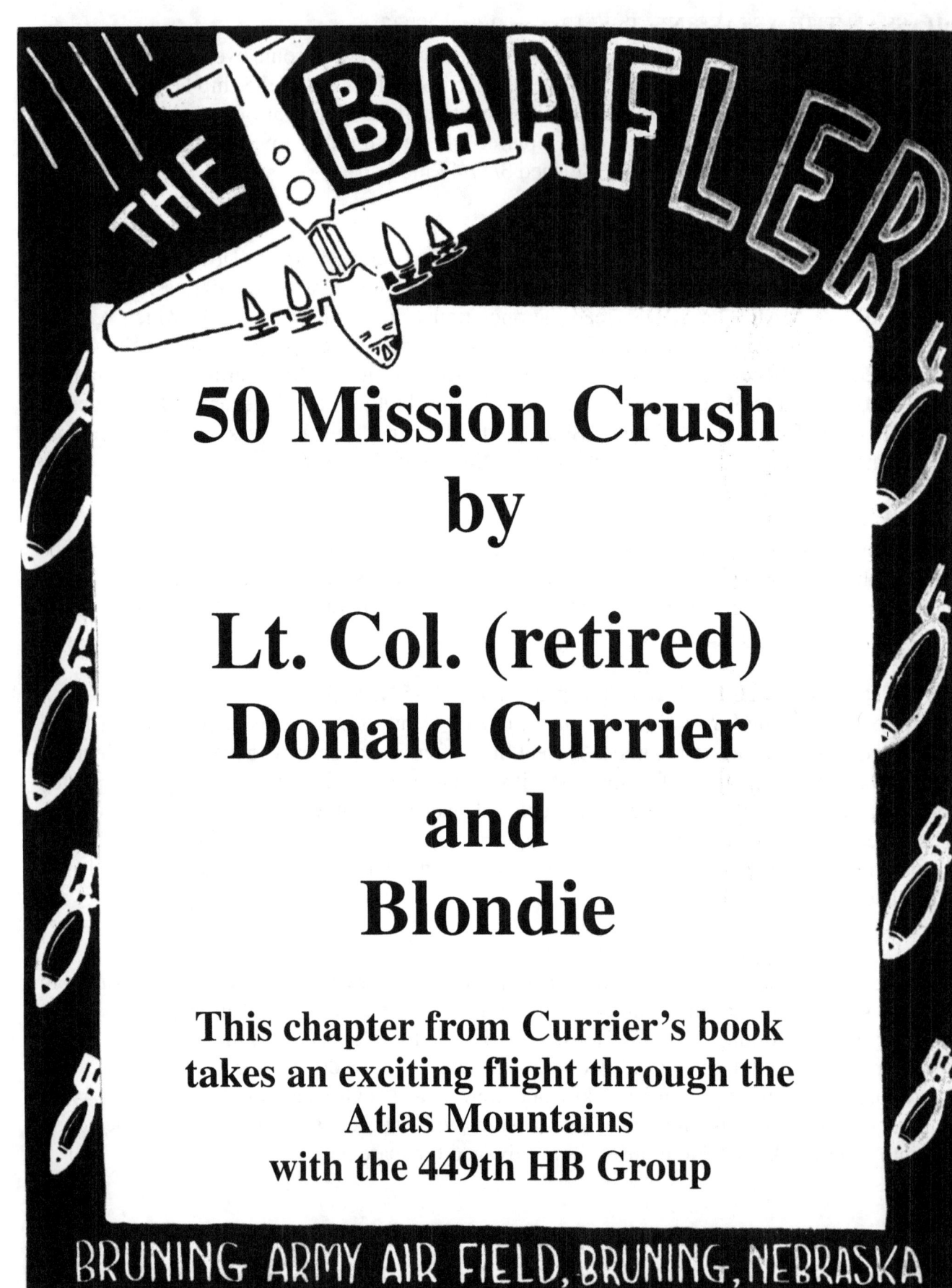

50 Mission Crush
by Lt. Col. Donald R. Currier (ret)

Donald Currier was a member of the 449th HB Group stationed at Bruning. With the help of his wife, "Blondie", he wrote a personal account of his war experiences. Of the 17 crews of the 718th Squadron which trained together at Bruning, ten were shot down in the first 6 months. His crew was one of the 62 B-24s which flew from Bruning to Italy. In Chapter 5 of his book, *50 Mission Crush,* he tells of a part of the perilous journey just getting through the Altas Mountains. He has graciously given us permission to copy it.

CHAPTER 5

We Close In On The War

To be greeted by a guy with a flit gun after your first flight across the Atlantic was somewhat deflating. I guess the Africans were afraid of catching something from Brazil--what that could be that they didn't already have, I couldn't imagine. In any event, after being fumigated, we disembarked from the "Chopper". It had been a long night--about twelve hours flying time. They took us to some tents and showed us where the mess hall was. We were hungry. The Army Air Corps did not believe in pampering its airmen. Except for the several candy bars we had bought on our own, we hadn't eaten for fifteen hours.

We stayed in Dakar for two days. Muller went over the "Chopper" with a fine-tooth comb and pronounced her OK. It was good to have Muller with us on this trip. He was a superb crew chief, but a white knuckle flyer. I can still see him hunkered down on the flight deck his ears cocked to the engines' tune and his eyes on the gas gauges. I figured that if it were humanly possible for a crew chief to keep us flying, Muller could do it. And he had the greatest possible incentive to do it. His ass was on board, too.

The next leg of our journey was North to Marrakech, Morocco. If ever a plane needed to be in good shape and a crew on the qui vive, this was the leg. Twelve hundred nautical miles from the jungles of West Africa over the virtually unexplored emptiness of the Sahara to the grim starkness of the Atlas Mountains which we could not fly over and had to penetrate--this was a real moment of truth. When we were briefed for the trip and given maps, I could hardly believe what I was hearing. There were only five visible checkpoints for reference in those twelve hundred miles! The maps covering a large portion of the Spanish Sahara were almost blank. Even the variance was not known over most of the way, and, of course, wind data was nil. In navigation school these factors were applied to all dead-reckoning problems, but here the briefer just gave us the "educated guess" on these values and told us to adjust it whenever we got a visual fix.

We started out and for the first hundred miles, we were right on the predicted course and hit the first checkpoint "close enough for government work." The next point, however, was a big black rock sticking up from the desert emptiness three hundred miles up the line. The briefer guaranteed that we would see it if we were anywhere near. It was supposed to be five miles east of our course. Waiting for that rock to appear was a tense period. I had a predicted time, but when that ran out--no rock. The problem was that we were looking in the wrong direction. The rock finally showed ten minutes later and about seven or eight miles to the west of course. Obviously, something was wrong with our wind data.

I made some course corrections and we pressed on to the next checkpoint--another four hundred miles beyond. You can't imagine the vast emptiness of this land! There was nothing--no roads, no villages, no rivers in this area. The ground was mostly flat, but one could see the hint of hills on the horizon--or maybe they were mirages. Our briefers were not optimistic about our chances if we went down here. They told us at all costs to stay with the plane and to be very very careful how we behaved if we were found by tribesmen. Some would help us and some would kill us for whatever we had. The odds were about fifty-fifty for either outcome.

We continued on, our eyes straining for the predicted checkpoints. Next was a basaltic escarpment a few miles to the west of course and, beyond that, a dim but well-used caravan trail crossing a deep wadi. By the Grace of God, we found them, made such course adjustments as needed, and droned on to the key checkpoint of the trip--the tiny desert town of Tindouf.

If you perceive the Sahara to be mostly brown, it was. But so was the town of Tindouf--a tiny island of humanity nestled in a vastness so great that it was nearly lost to the eye from any distance. Furthermore, it took on the color of the desert mud from which it was constructed, and brown on brown is not easy to spot. Apparently this had been a problem for earlier aerial passersby because--lo, and behold--just east of town was a big White circle with a "T" in the center. Now THAT's a checkpoint!

The next leg of the trip was only about sixty miles as I recall, but it was a most critical leg. It took us, at eight thousand feet, right up to the forbidding face of the Atlas Mountains that formed an impenetrable barrier to further Northern progress. The Atlas towered to fourteen thousand feet, and the trick was to negotiate them at eight thousand. Why? Because we carried no oxygen and humans don't function too well above twelve thousand feet without oxygen. How were we to get through the mountains? There was a pass used for centuries by camel caravans that wound its way through the jagged peaks to emerge in a lush oasis lined with date palms and guarded by the walled palace of the sultan.

Now, camels could take their time to thread their way through that rocky path, but airplanes must maintain flying speed. We flew straight for the mountains at one hundred fifty-five miles per hour. The closer we got, the more antsy John got. He could see that our time was running out and that either we bumped into the mountains or did a "three-sixty" and got out of there.

"Are you sure we're on course?" he kept asking me. I tried to reassure him that all was well. With such a precise checkpoint at Tindouf and such a short leg to fly, the chance of being off course and missing the pass was very low. But, the damned thing was impossible to see until you got right on top of it.

At almost the last possible moment, John shouted, "I got it!" and he wheeled the "Chopper" into a rather tight left and began to let down. We twisted and turned through the rocky gorge, losing altitude all the way until we saw the greenness of the oasis. What a sight! The airfield was a few miles beyond. John "greased" her in. I, for one, was darned near wiped out. I devoutly hoped that I'd never see that route again. When we finally got to our base, we learned that Dave Council, Squadron Commander of the 716th Squadron and his crew, were lost trying to make it through the Atlas Mountains.

Who would ever guess that Africa could be freezing cold? Not we pilgrims from the West! But it was. We once again were ushered to a tent complex and issued some bedding. The bunks in the tent were nothing but a netting of ropes--no mattresses or other creature comforts. The blankets and sheets they gave us were supposed to make us comfy. They didn't. When the sun set at Marrakech, it turned unbelievably cold. The moisture content of the desert air was practically zero and, when the sun went down, there was nothing to hold the heat of the day.

The first night we shivered and shuddered all night long. When morning came and we were still held there, we got into our baggage to find some more appropriate clothing to wear. Since leaving the States, we'd been in summer time. We slept in our skivvies and had no problems. But now we needed more. I found what I thought was the perfect solution--my heated flying suit.

In the early days, bomber crew members riding in positions that required only a limited degree of mobility were issued heated flying suits which got their heat by plugging into the electrical system of the B-24. The suits were a handsome robin's egg blue color and were designed to be worn under a coverall-type flying suit. The suits even had heated feet and gloves. They were supposed to be worn only on missions, but they looked darned attractive as underwear in the frigid nights in North Africa. I, and several of the others, dug them out of the baggage racks and put them on. I didn't take mine off for nearly a month.

When we arrived at Marrakech, we still didn't know where we would end up. England and the Eighth Air Force was a good possibility, but so was the Thirteenth Air Force in the China-Burma-India Theater. You got there via the same route. Another possibility was Italy and the Fifteenth Air Force, although we knew very little about it. It had only recently been organized and begun operations in Italy. We awaited the next route briefing with great anticipation. Alas, it revealed nothing, except to direct us to Algiers and to a famous airfield-Maison Blanche.

The city of Algiers, which we were fortunate to have the chance to visit, was no desert town. It was a cosmopolitan city on the Mediterranean with wide avenues, attractive buildings and parks, and even hotels--most of which had been appropriated by the Army higher brass for their comfort and pleasure. Algiers was a French city without a doubt, from the language of the people to the names of the streets and the menus in the restaurants. But, it was a city of contrasts. While many of the people dressed in conventional Western garb, the natives wore long, white, shapeless robes that covered them from neck to ankles. These robes looked for all the world like mattress covers we used on our bunks. Maybe they were. The Yanks had been here for over a year and were well dug in. I could visualize some very rich Supply Sergeants placing huge orders through channels for mattress covers.

We were lucky to find a room in a small "two-star" hotel on a side street for the one night they allowed us in town. We did, however, get a chance for a real hot shower and a comfortable bed with a spring mattress which seemed like heaven compared to our recent lodgings. It was the first decent time we'd had since leaving Puerto Rico--which seemed like ages ago even though it had been less than three weeks. Algiers picked us up tremendously.

The next leg of the trip was going to be very revealing as to our ultimate goal. We would either be setting a course North or we could forget England. They briefed us for Tunis, so that ruled out the Eighth Air Force for us. OK, we could live with that. The stories we'd heard about flying out of England against Fortress Europe hadn't been all that enticing. Now it was either the Fifteenth or the CBI.

We were at the top of Africa, close to the sea, and the amount of human activity was great. Lots of cities and towns and land features would make navigating a cinch. We headed out for Tunis with the sea to our left and the desert to the right. The habitable part of North Africa was a relatively narrow band along the Mediterranean. But, what a history had been lived out there from earliest days to the present!

As we moved across the North African landscape, we soon began to see signs of war recently fought. We noted heavily damaged towns and lots of abandoned, burned-out vehicles. From the air, it, was also very easy to pick out the final results of the massive air battles which had taken place overhead. Crashed and burned aircraft were visible where they had fallen. What had happened to the gallant airmen on both sides who had flown them? One could not tell if they lay entombed in the wreckage or had lived to fight another day. It was a sobering thought.

When we approached Tunis and prepared to land, the carnage of war lay all around. The field was a one-directional runway of pierced steel planking. Surrounding the base was the biggest aircraft junk pile we'd ever seen. We glimpsed the carcasses of just about every plane that had fought there. Most of them we'd only seen in pictures during our aircraft recognition classes in training. There were scores of German planes, from giant JU-52's to Stukas and ME-109's. There were Hurricanes and Spitfires. There were planes with French and, Italian markings--most of which looked woefully obsolete beside our newer American types. But, there were some of those there, too, in that aerial graveyard. It looked to us like all of those planes had simply been bulldozed off the field to keep it operational after bombing attacks. That, indeed, was the case.

We stayed only one night at Tunis, but it was memorable. Since we had arrived early in the afternoon, we had time to get to our assigned quarters, get cleaned up, and change into our "suntans." We got a bite to eat and were then ready to explore. The closer we got to the war zone, the more relaxed were the rules. We had no restrictions on going into town from Marrakech on. It was simply a matter of finding some transportation. At Tunis, we found that there was a "six-by" truck going in, so most of us hopped aboard -all but Syl Lubin and Red Bauers, our ball gunner. They said they would follow later. We got directions as to where to catch a bus back to the base and its schedule. We were ready for some fun.

Tunis was another Frenchified North African city but with significant Arab influences. Its architecture reflected the mixture. Further, there were a lot more Arabs and a lot fewer French, Americans, etc. We soon felt its mysterious presence.

We officers found what looked like a decent cafe and went in for dinner. The other crewmen took off for further sightseeing. After eating a quite good dinner, we ordered some of the local champagne. It was cheap enough, but it had a pinkish cast that made it look sort of rusty. A few bottles of this tasty wine combined with the warmish temperature of the very crowded room soon got to Fenton, who was not much of a drinker. We figured that we were reaching the end of our long trek and had not done at all badly flying the whole route by ourselves. Staggering to his feet, Fenton loudly proclaimed a toast to us assembled. We cheered and raised our glasses.

As Fenton's arm went up, it kept right on going. The liquid flew over his head and splashed all over the nicely pressed "pinks and greens", of an American Army full Colonel sitting at a table behind him! A very tense few moments ensued as the Colonel wiped himself off, saying awfully bad things about all flyers in general and about us in particular. Rear-echelon "ground-pounders" tended to react that way towards the Air Corps. We left. The eagles on his blouse seemed to indicate that that was the right thing to do.

After walking around a bit to clear our heads, we decided that we must see what a real-life Casbah looked like. Tunis had one, and a British soldier directed us to it with some very serious warnings about sticking together and staying away from side alleys. The Casbah was just a section of town inhabited by the native Arabs. In the daytime, it teemed with all sorts of people shopping in the stalls and making lots of noise. At night, when we were there, it was quiet and sort of creepy, at least to me. I kept looking around for characters like Pepe le Moko and Peter Lorre. What we saw were men in their flowing robes silently sliding along the near-empty streets looking at us suspiciously. It suddenly occurred to me that, at least for the present, we represented the power structure. No one bothered us, and we left without incident. About midnight, we found the bus going back towards tile base and I boarded it. It had been an interesting night.

As usual, Silly did it a might differently. He and Red noticed a jeep parked near Base Headquarters with the key in it. They appropriated it and drove merrily off to town. There they abandoned the jeep as possibly a tad "warm," and proceeded to enjoy Tunis and its many pleasures. They covered the town like a blanket, meeting some other air crewmen and carousing until all hours. They were secure in the assurances of these other guys that they had a truck and would give them a ride back to base. When the night was over, they all piled into the truck and were deposited at the base. There was only one problem: Tunis had two air bases and their friends of the night were at the other one! Silly and Red limped into our base at six-thirty A.M., just in time to report for the briefing for our next stop on our road to war.

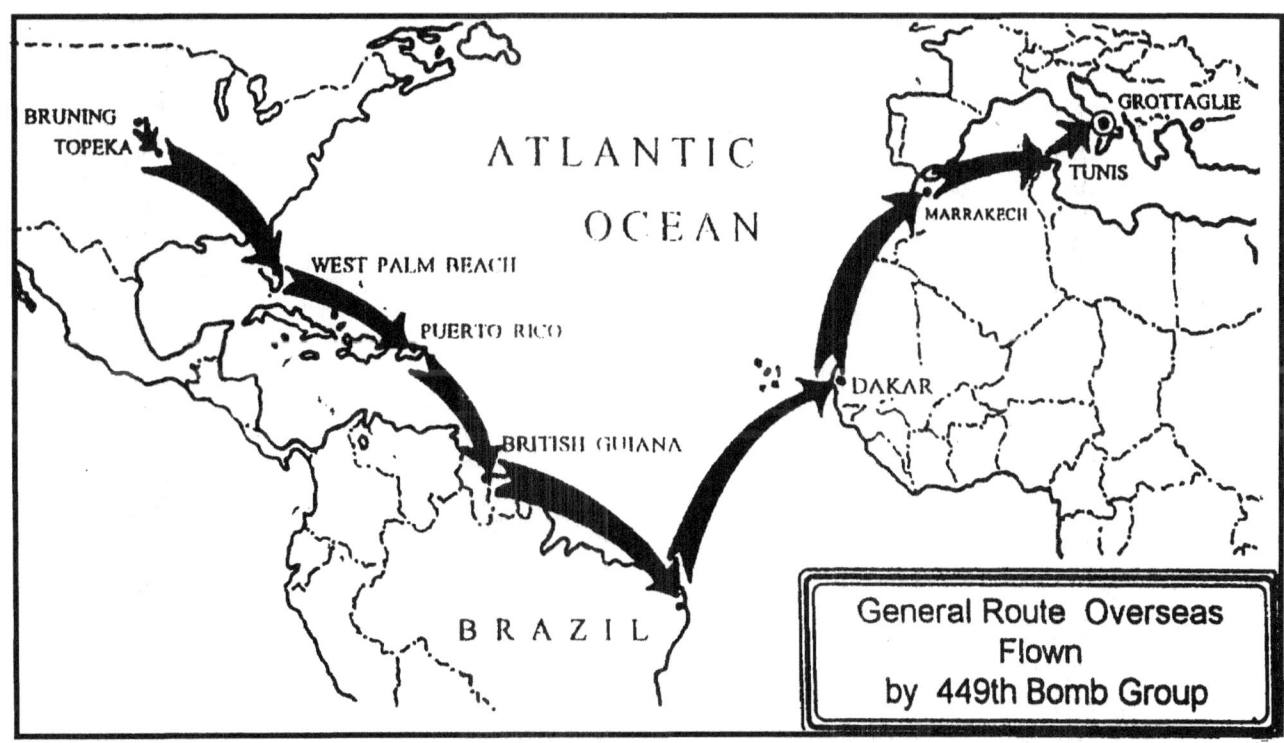

Route taken from Of Men and Wings

Crew of the "Chopper"

449th Bomb Group Association

DECEASED MEMBERS THAT WERE KIA IN WWII AND RETURNED TO PRIVATE CEMETERIES IN THE USA BY FAMILY REQUEST

NAME	POS.	DATE	SQ	MISSION PILOT	MACR#
Acampora, Albert (NMI)	G	28 Feb. 45	716	Hanson	12511
Allen, Henry L.	CP	25 Feb. 44	716	Knapp	02617
Arieff, Ellis (NMI)	B	09 Dec. 44	719	Caldwell	01576
Ballou, Ralph G.	G	09 Dec. 44	719	Caldwell	10576
Bashaw, Palmer J.	RO	31 Jan. 44	176	Brady	02300
Batterton, Herbert H.	G	02 Apr. 44	717	Kury	04024
Bauers, Dennin J.	G	16 Apr. 44	718	Temchulla	04039
Belcher, John W.	RO	04 Apr. 44	719	Thieme	03978
Belyea, Robert G.	unk	21 May 44	717	Brown	none
Block, Oscar J.	PH	15 Aug. 44	718	Betzen	15099
Bornstein, Seymour (NMI)	CP	09 July 44	716	Westbrook	none
Boss, Richard C.	unk	21 May 44	717	Brown	none
Brix, Vigo	CP	18 Aug. 44	719	Watson	none
Brogger, James	G	07 Feb. 45	719	Trailkill.	12072
Brown, Al K.	CP	05 May 44	717	McInvale	none
Brown, Don R.	G	14 Jan. 44	718	Pickard	02070
Brown, Donald P.	RO	01 Mar. 45	717	Farrington	12745
Burnette, Hubert R.	G	01 Mar. 45	717	Farrington	12745
Burnham, Donald W.	N	12 Apr. 44	716	Beam	04034
Bzan, Andrew M.	G	18 Aug. 44	719	Watson	none
Caldwell, James B.	N	02 Apr. 44	717	Kury	04024
Caldwell, Julian L.	P	09 Dec. 44	719	Caldwell	10576
Campbell, James W.	B	05 May 44	717	Morton	04714
Carchia, Joseph (NMI)	G	07 Feb. 45	719	Thrailkill	12072
Chandler,, Thomas E.	P	30 Jan. 44	718	Chandler	02404
Chernak, Paul P., Jr.	G	07 Feb. 45	719	Thrailkill	12072
Cohen, Bernhard A.	RO	27 Aug. 44	716	Weiss	08251
Colson, John P.	G	24 Mar. 44	717	Ridgway	03469
Colwell, Albert A.	G	27 Aug. 44	716	Weiss	08251
Cordeira, Arthur J.	G	04 Apr. 44	717	Bontley	03701
Corliss, William W.	RO	05 May 44	716	White	04667
Cox, James S.	G	28 Feb. 45	716	Hanson	12511
Davis, Kenneth W.	G	23 Nov. 44	717	Ball	none
Doyle, Fowler C.	CP	09 Dec. 44	719	Caldwell	10576
Eaton, Robert	CP	11 Oct. 44	717	Wright	none
Eavenson, Mayo E.	FE	17 May 44	718	Silvers	05052
Ebert, Mark J.	FE	04 Apr. 44	719	Thieme	03978
Eiselewski, Edward J.	G	07 Apr. 44	716	Bell	03979
Elmore, Bruce (NMI)	unk	09 July 44	716	Westbrook	none
Engle, James W.	G	29 Mar. 44	717	Ivers	none
Englehardt, Richard (NMI)	B	27 Aug. 44	716	Clabaugh	none
Fetting, Edward A.	P	02 Apr. 44	717	Fetting	04025
Firth, John E.	unk	21 May 44	717	Brown	none
Frones, Clarence M.	P	15 Jan. 44	719	Frones	02397
Gallagher, James H.	B	31 Jan. 44	717	Alkire	02403
Garrison, Richard C.	P	04 Apr. 44	719	Garrison	03703
Gegoulis, John W.	G	14 Jan. 44	718	Pickard	02070
Geminder, Albert O.	CP	02 Apr. 44	717	Fetting	04025
Gibbo, Leo J.	G	02 Apr. 44	717	Kury	04024
Godioz, Clement (NMI)	6	05 May 44	717	Morton	04714

449th Bomb Group

NAME	POS.	DATE	SQ	MISSION PILOT	MACR#
Gray, Bernie A.	CP	16 July 44	719	Crossley	none
Hays, Hiero F.	P	15 Dec. 43	719	Hays	none
Hayslett, Harry (NMI)	G	07 Feb. 45	719	Thrailkill	12072
Hebda, J.S.	G	08 Jan. 45	716	Bivins, J.K.	none
Heiskell, Roger L.	unk	17 Sep. 44	716	unk	none
Hill, Preston J.	Cy	01 Mar. 45	716	Farrington	12745
Hollingsworth, Warren W.	G	04 Apr. 44	719	Kendall	04205
Holohan, John E.	N	07 Feb. 45	719	Thrailkill	12072
Home, Charles W.	G	12 Apr. 44	716	Beam	04034
Howell, Elmer G.	RO	21 Feb. 44	716	Browning	02636
Jarrell, William N.	CP	30 Jan. 44	719	Wheeler	02579
Jeutter, Howard B.	P	23 Feb. 44	717	Jeutter	none
Johnson, Howard R.	RO	26 May 44	718	Warner	05435
Johnson, William D.	N	17 May 44	719	Silvers	05052
Jones, It. W.	CP	09 Jan. 45	716	Bivins, J.K.	none
Kirkland, Cecil	11	02 July 44	718	Kirkland	none
Knapp, Robert J.	11	25 Feb. 44	716	Knapp	02617
Lacastro, John J.	N	24 Mar. 44	717	Ridgway	03469
Lain, Harry E.	G	24 May 44	716	Foote	05370
Lannin, Nicholas D., Jr.	13	22 Feb. 44	716	Browning	02636
Lapierre, Antonio (NMI)	G	04 Apr. 44	719	Garrison	03703
Ledbetter, John	FE	02 July 44	718	Kirkland	none
Lemak, Bela W.	CP	22 Feb. 44	716	Moore	02613
Lewis, Ballard C.	G	04 Apr. 44	717	Tyler	03699
Lopez, F.	N	08 Jan. 45	716	Bivins, J.K.	none
Lopez, Tony P.	G	31 Jan. 44	717	Alkire	02403
Ludtke, Lester L.	P	22 Nov. 44	717	Ludtke	10044
Madigan, Quentin P.	CP	24 May 44	716	Foote	05370
Mahoney, Daniel 1-1.	G	14 Jan. 44	718	Pickard	02070
Maiewski, Paul E.	G	07 Feb. 45	719	Thrailkill	12072
Malrait, Gilbert A.	N	04 Apr. 44	719	Thieme	03978
Marshall, John R.	CP	05 May 44	717	Morton	04714
Mazur, E.J.	B	08 Jan. 45	716	Bivins, J.K.	none
McCool, Lawrence R.	CP	17 July 44	716	Bolt	none
McDaniel, Thomas J.	none	Oct. 43	719	none	none
McDonald, James B.	6	23 Apr. 44	716	Roberts	04199
Merritt, Charles E.	N	04 Apr. 44	717	Tyler	03699
Mikolajcxyk, Thomas (NMI)	G	02 Apr. 44	717	Starr	03995
Moore, Charles C.	FE	05 Sep. 44	716	Alexander	none
Murray, Donale D.	RO	04 Apr. 44	719	Kendall	04205
Nehigian, Ernest (N M 1)	G	25 Feb. 44	716	Forbes	03203
Nixon, Arthur E.	G	II June 44	716	Gudger	06021
O'Rourke, Edward J.	CP	04 Apr. 44	719	Thieme	03978
Ornstein, Adolph (NMI)	B	04 Apr. 44	719	McCormick	03702
Pagliaro, Rocco (NMI)	G	29 May 44	718	Henggeler	05458
Parks, George H.	B	02 Apr. 44	717	Starr	03995
Parshall, John K., Jr.	CP	25 Feb. 44	716	Forbes	03203
Peck, Robert K.	N	15 Aug. 44	718	Betzen	15099
Perlberg, Alvin L.	CP	14 Jan. 44	718	Pickard	02070
Perri, Frank (NMI)	RO	11 June 44	716	Gudger	06021
Peterson, Duane R.	unk	08 May 44	719	none	none
Peterson, Warren (NMI)	unk	16 July 44	719	Crossley	none
Porter, Fletcher S.	CP	30 Jan. 44	718	Kendall	02711
Radcliff, George E.	G	02 Apr. 44	717	Staff	03995

449th Bomb Group

NAME	POS.	MISSION DATE	SQ	PILOT	MACR#
Reneau, Roy C., Jr.	G	22 Feb. 44	716	Moore	02613
Repeta, Henry S.	G	12 Apr. 44	716	Beam	04034
Rich, Thomas W.	G	31 Jan. 44	719	Woltkamp	02325
Ridgeway, Warren H.	111	24 Mar. 44	717	Ridgway	03469
Ronsheim, John	G	15 Aug. 44	718	Betzen	15099
Russ, William E.	CP	02 July 44	719	Kirkland	none
San Antonio, Louis S.	unk	16 July 44	719	Crossley	none
Saunders, Walter C.	G	26 June 44	719	Harton	none
Scarborough, Clement B.	G	22 Nov. 44	717	Ludtke	10044
Schmitt, Harold F.	CP	15 Aug. 44	718	Betzen	15099
Shaw, William B.	B	17 Oct. 44	719	Trumbull	none
Smith, Joe R.	B	24 Mar. 44	717	Ridgway	03469
Starr, John R.	P	02 Apr. 44	717	Staff	03995
Strom, Melvin R.	Ph	07 Feb. 45	719	Thrailkill	12072
Sweeney, Eldon W.	G	04 Apr. 44	717	Tyler	03699
Tharpe, Harold D.	PH	12 Apr. 44	716	Beam	04034
Thieme, William M., Jr.	P	04 Apr. 44	719	Thieme	03978
Thornton, Gordon G.	FE	22 Feb. 44	716	Moore	02613
Tibbetts, Charles R.	G	30 Jan. 44	718	Chandler	02404
Tinder, James L.	G	05 July 44	716	Haywood	none
Toney, Harold O.	G	23 Apr. 44	716	Roberts	041199
Turpin, Adolph (NMI)	G	28 Feb. 45	716	Hanson	12511
Tyler, Everett F.	P	04 Apr. 44	717	Tyler	03699
Tyrell, Thomas J.	B	09 July 44	716	Westbrook	none
Vadez, Dario	G	23 Apr. 44	718	Driggers	none
Verret, Milton J.	G	23 Feb. 44	717	Jeutter	none
Visciglia, Frank E.	FE	29 Dec. 44	706	Willding	10890
Vital, Benedict E.	G	30 Jan. 44	708	Wheeler	02479
Wagner, Edward S.	B	19 Aug. 44	719	Watson	none
Warner, Lewis J.	G	17 May 44	708	Silvers	05052
Warsa, Frank C.	G	27 July 44	708	Progar	none
Watson, Henry N.	P	18 Aug. 44	719	Watson	none
Weinstein, Chester (NMI)	RO	07 Feb. 45	719	Thrailkill	12072
Weisbrod, Joseph C.	B	04 Apr. 44	717	Tyler	03699
White, Howard K.	CP	14 July 44	709	Geisert	06823
Widenhofer, Robert F.	G	13 Apr. 44	719	Rustad	04096
Williams, Walter D.	RO	02 Apr. 44	707	Fetting	04025
Wilson, Clinton J.	G	04 Apr. 44	719	Polink	03879
Winter, Robert N.	CP	30 Jan. 44	718	Chandler	0244404
Witt, Gerald S.	P	17 Oct. 44	719	Witt	none
Wood, Dennis H.	FE	25 Feb. 44	716	Knapp	026617
Yaksh, Ernest J.	G	15 Aug. 44	718	Betzen	15099
Zieman, Lawrence E.	G	15 Aug. 44	718	Betzen	15099

449th Bomb Group

MEMBERS OF THE 449TH BOMB GROUP WHO ARE INTERRED OR COMMEMORATED ON THE TABLETS OF THE MISSING

ARDENNES AMERICAN CEMETERY

NAME	RANK	SER. NO.	SQD.	STATE	DATE/DEATH	LOCATION
Adams, Donald R.	S SGT	33376690	717	N.Y.	02 Apr. 44	C - 29 - 3
Anderson, Charles W.	S SGT	16101350	716	ILL.	25 Feb. 44	C - 38 - 19
Antonakos, George C.	I LT	0-668695	719	N.C.	07 Feb. 45	B - 36 - 50
Beck, Francis L.	2 LT	0-688298	719	ILL.	04 Apr. 44	A - 21 - 19
Bosch, Albert T.	S SGT	12157155	719	N.Y.	04 Apr. 44	A - 40 - 23
Braud, Joseph O.	2 LT	0-755168	718	LA.	23 Feb. 44	C - 28 - 16
Brouillette, Meddie P.	S SGT	15335428	719	IND.	04 Apr. 44	C - 12 - 32
Bursio, Angelo J.	S SGT	19024949	719	CAL.	04 Apr. 44	A - 33 - 8
Butter, George W.	2 LT	0-747574	717	CONN.	02 Apr. 44	C - 2 - 53
Byer, Edward J.	T SGT	17129474	717	KANS.	02 Apr. 44	D - 35 - 4
Clough, Nelson., Jr.	SGT	36415075	717	MICH.	05 May. 44	B - 32 - 47
Donavon, Gerald T.	S SGT	32218454	717	N.Y.	02 Apr. 44	C - 14 - 55
Eck, Donald C.	S SGT	35599307	717	O1110	04 Apr. 44	B - 41 - 9
Goldberg, Alvin M.	2 LT	0-755221	719	N.Y.	04 Apr. 44	B - 31 - 51
Hale, Hubert H.	SGT	38444111	719	ARK.	13 Apr. 44	A - 29 - 4
Harlander, Edward A.	SGT	12038066	716	N.J.	05 May. 44	B - 23 - 21
Harrell, William M.	SGT	34689984	718	GA.	23 Feb. 44	C - 29 - 8
Hollederer, George E.	T SGT	32673185	717	N.Y.	02 Apr. 44	C - 25 - 17
Kieskowski, Edward	2 LT	0-806084	717	ILL.	16 Apr. 44	B - 16 - 8
Laine, Robert W.	S SGT	39558516	716	CAL.	05 May. 44	B - 16 - 1
Lhevinne, Paul	2 LT	0-809657	717	CAL.	02 Apr. 44	C - 27 - 16
McCaslin, Ralph J.	S SGT	20312270	717	PA.	02 Apr. 44	C - 33 - 8
Monahan, Robert E., Jr.	SGT	15097376	718	KY.	16 Apr. 44	D - 5 - 46
Norris, Harold W.	S SGT	32391035	717	N.J.	04 Apr. 44	A - 29 - 21
Parker, George 1.	S SGT	34149983	717	TENN.	04 Apr. 44	C - 5 - 56
Paterson, James Jr.	S SGT	11097126	716	R.I.	23 Apr. 44	D - 11 - 56
Quisno, Harold P.	2 LT	0-690713	716	CAL.	22 Feb. 44	B - 32 - 57
Reed, Norman R.	SGT	20347617	719	MD.	13 Apr. 44	A - 8 - 8
Samson, Robert W.	2 LT	0-684055	717	ILL.	02 Apr. 44	C - 26 - 19
Sickley, John F.	T SGT	38224758	719	L.A.	04 Apr. 44	A- 11 - 18
Smith, Edward C.	SGT	35528636	716	OHIO	12 Apr. 44	C - 20 - 11
Stagman, Wilfred L.	2 LT	0-690689	719	IOWA	04 Apr. 44	C- 19-4
Sunderland, Raymond P.	S SGT	35416016	719	OHIO	04 Apr. 44	B - 38 - 52
Thrailkill, Edwin M.	CAPT.	0420481	719	ILL.	07 Feb. 45	B - 14 - 12
Turekian, Arthur K.	T SGT	32498967	718	N.Y.	16 Apr. 44	B - 24 - 1
Vose, Ralph I., Jr.	2 LT	0-682533	717	PA.	02 Apr. 44	C - 34 - 4
Wood, John S.	S SGT	32738251	717	N.Y.	29 May 44	C - 3 - 46
Zimmerman, Sheldon J.	2 LT	0-746504	719	N,Y.	04 Apr. 44	C - 6 - 44

FLORENCE AMERICAN CEMETERY

NAME	RANK	SER. NO.	SQD.	STATE	DATE/DEATH	LOCATION
Allumbaugh, Albert C.	CAPT	0-749178	716	Mont.	27 Aug. 44	G - 1 - 17
Ames, Warren F.	2 LT	02063326	716	Mass.	02 Mar. 45	
Anderson, Gerald E.	2 LT	0-694295	716	Minn.	07 Apr. 44	
Betz, Edward H.	2 LT	02001248	716	N.Y.	28 Feb. 45	D-8-2

Continued on next page

Names without a grave location are for memorial tablets only.

449th Bomb Group

FLORENCE AMERICAN CEMETERY

NAME	RANK	SER. NO.	SQD.	STATE	DATE/DEATH	LOCATION
Potts, George T.	T SGT	13029046	717	PA.	24 Mar. 44	F- 1-41
Reed, Wayne Z.	S SOT	12239141	716	N.Y.	27 Aug. 44	D- 13-2
Samson, Reeve A.	T SGT	12168472	718	N.Y.	30 Jan. 44	C - 9 - 30
Sanetta, Emit	S SGT	33695246	717	PA.	19 Feb. 45	
Sapadin, Milton S.	S SGT	32815432	716	N.Y.	26 Aug. 44	
Schievink, Harold E.	2 LT	0-830710	718	MICH.	26 Dec. 44	
Schulze, Walter J.	SGT	32429497	716	N.Y.	07 Apr. 44	
Scott, Samuel W.	S SGT	16162379	717	ILL.	31 Jan. 44	D - 4 - 28
Silvers, Henry N., Jr.	1 LT	0-747345	718	N.J.	17 May 44	0-10-44
Sjoberg, Arthur K.	SGT	16086643	716	MICH.	31 Jan. 44	B-9-8
Thompson, Harold T.	S SGT	39455478	718	IDA.	30 Jan. 44	
Velker, John, Jr.	S SGT	33719238	717	MD.	19 Feb. 45	
Way, Edward J.	S SGT	32914821	718	N.J.	26 Dec. 44	
Wheeler, Hayward S.	1 LT	0-80391g	718	CAL.	30 Jan. 44	A- 10-46
Whidden, We A.	T SGT	31095586	718	MASS.	30 Jan. 44	D - 4 - 43
Whitlock, Joseph C.	2 LT	0-691021	717	LA.	24 Mar. 44	B - 13 - 45
Whitson, Curtis E.	SGT	14133872	716	TENN.	07 Apr. 44	
Woltkamp, Raymond B.	FLT O	T-121614	719	OREG.	16 Jan. 44	A - 5 - 10
Wood, John C.	SGT	33490280	718	PA.	30 Jan. 44	F - 9 - 38

LORRAINE AMERICAN CEMETERY

NAME	RANK	SER. NO.	SQD.	STATE	DATE/DEATH	LOCATION
Carter, Richard A.	SGT	33193493	716	D.C.	25 Feb. 44	D - 18 - 38
Cleary, James J., Jr.	2 LT	0-694334	717	CAL.	02 Apr. 44	B - 16 - 27
Englehart, Willis L.	2 LT	0-701581	719	CAL.	14 July 44	B-30-6
Flory, William R.	S SGT	18150872	717	LA.	01 Apr. 44	A - 30 - 49
Foote, George W.	1 LT	0-900332	716	MICH.	24 May 44	C - 5 - 69
Frankovic, Peter J.	SGT	19124638	719	MONT.	13 Apr. 44	A - 32 - 28
Gorrell, James W.	T SGT	13127196	716	PA.	24 May 44	G - 8 - 25
Griffin, Charles C.	S SGT	14085205	716	FLA.	25 Feb. 44	A - 26 - 56
Kozekowski, Felix D.	T SGT	32916625	716	N.J.	02 Mar. 45	K - 20 - 13
Kury, Jacob F.	1 LT	0-690657	717	PA.	02 Apr. 44	K - 27 - 36
MacDonald, Thomas A	2 LT	02069072	716	N.Y.	31 Mar. 45	G - 9 - 19
Moore, Gordon F.	S SGT	18155756	717	TEX.	02 Apr. 44	K - 50 - 27
Moore, Harry W.	1 LT	0-746399	716	CAL.	22 Feb. 44	B - 30 - 36
Phillips, John F.	FLT O	T-061358	717	MICH.	02 Apr. 44	G - 17 - 22
Plourde, Gerard J.	SGT	31179937	717	R.I.	02 Apr. 44	A - 14 - 39
Post, James E.	T SGT	32214994	719	N.Y.	04 Apr. 44	K - 29 - 38
Rost, Kenneth C	S SGT	37668121	716	IOWA	01 Mar. 45	K - 30 - 29
Rustad, Warren N.	2 LT	0-689359	719	WASH.	13 Apr. 44	A- 16-44
Simeone, Colombo	S SGT	11091523	717	MASS.	02 Apr. 44	A - 28 - 15
Stout, George R.	S SGT	39614047	716	MONT.	22 Feb. 44	C - 14-83
Szacun, Steve	S SGT	36514773	716	MICH.	25 Feb. 44	E - 44 - 20
Woods, Ernest	S SGT	12167848	717	N.Y.	02 Apr. 44	F - 12-23
Wright, Loyd T.	S SGT	16150377	716	KY	25 Feb. 44	D - 4 - 17

LUXEMBOURG AMERICAN CEMETERY

NAME	RANK	SER. NO.	SQD.	STATE	DATE/DEATH	LOCATION
McEldowney, Robert A.	2 LT	0-755157	718	T.H.	14 Jan. 44	E-4-5

Names without a grave location are for memorial tablets only.

449th Bomb Group

RHONE AMERICAN CEMETERY

NAME	RANK	SER. NO.	SQD.	STATE	DATE/DEATH	LOCATION
Boehnke, Elmer J.	S SGT	37549911	718	S. DAK.	26 May 44	D-2-19
Merrifield, Lawrence	CPL	37652254	718	IOWA	26 May 44	
Miller, Robert W.	T SGT	20601580	718	ILL.	26 May 44	
Slusher, Robert C.	S SGT	35099211	718	OHIO	26 May 44	
Smith, Charles F.	CPL	16125346	718	ILL.	26 May 44	
Spyres, Claude E., Jr.	2 LT	0-701331	718	ARK.	26 May 44	
Sterner, Frank E.	2 LT	01683531	718	PA.	26 May 44	
Tanner, Harold W.	2 LT	0-699537	718	LA	26 May 44	
Warner, Gerald E.	2 LT	0-691327	718	S. DAK.	26 May 44	

SICILY+ROME AMERICAN CEMETERY

NAME	RANK	SER. NO.	SQD.	STATE	DATE/DEATH	LOCATION
Allen, James G., Jr.	1 LT	0-808107	718	TENN.	15 Aug. 44	F - 14 - 21
Austin, Lynford A -	2 LT	0-823818	716	MICH.	17 Nov. 44	
Bach, Richard P., Jr.	SGT	32489211	718	N.J.	14 Jan. 44	E - I - 35
Baldwin, Francis G., Jr.	1 LT	0-828910	719	OHIO	09 Dec. 44	J - 12 - 66
Bartlett, William W.	2 LT	02060763	716	MASS.	17 Nov. 44	
Battagliola, William	S SGT	31121085	718	CONN.	13 Oct. 44	
Bell, John L.	2 LT	0-806960	716	TEX.	07 Apr. 44	
Betzen, Leo A.	2 LT	0-696625	718	KANS.	15 Aug. 44	F - 13 - 25
Biggart, Paul S.	S SGT	35374636	716	IND.	25 Feb. 44	
Blakely, Ralph, Jr.	2 LT	0-720142	719	TENN.	30 Dec. 44	
Brown, Joseph W.	1 LT	0-684482	717	OHIO	20 May 44	G - 14 - 26
Carlson, Charles L.	2 LT	0-706695	718	CAL.	15 Aug. 44	F- 11 -29
Chattermole, Gerald W.	CPL	33804720	717	PA.	30 Oct. 44	F-8- 15
Ctapsaddle, James R.	S SGT	35235052	719	OHIO	10 Aug. 44	J - 14 - 62
Clark, Clifford C.	2 LT	02062739	716	MO.	04 Dec. 44	F - 3 - 5
Conboy, Thomas W.	1 LT	0-760788	717	CAL.	01 Aug. 44	A - 3 - 28
Cooper, Frank B.	2 LT	0-776955	716	CONN.	17 Nov. 44	
Dehn, Arnold A.	CPL	17156344	716	MINN.	17 Nov. 44	
Dietrich, Benjamin R.	1 LT	0-691139	717	CAL.	21 May 44	G- It -26
Doelfel, George H.	S SGT	33667794	718	PA.	15 Aug. 44	F- 10-29
Erickson, Donald A.	T SGT	39408284	719	CAL.	09 Dec. 44	B - 4 - 36
Feeney, Daniel It.	CPL	36601518	719	ILL.	30 Dec. 44	
Fiester, Lester E.	2 LT	0-690394	717	PA.	05 May 44	D - 8 - 27
Franklin, Merle E.	CPL	18163671	716	OKLA.	17 Nov. 44	
Franz, George W., Jr.	CPL	33709276	716	PA.	17 Nov. 44	
Gagnon, John R.	2 LT	0-755220	717	S. DAK.	23 Feb. 44	D - I I - 10
German, Darrell E.	2 LT	02001247	716	OHIO	28 Feb. 45	H - 2 - 37
Goodman, Lawrence L.	2 LT	02068916	719	N.Y.	30 Dec. 44	
Graffigna, William G.	2 LT	0-689525	716	MO.	07 Apr. 44	
Graves, C. Stuart	PVT	32383193	716	N.Y.	04 July 44	F- 12-2
Henze, Theodore J.	SGT	38236573	718	ARK.	14 Jan. 44	E - 15 - 54
Heyer, Walter C.	CPL	39211210	719	WASH.	30 Dec. 44	
Hoff, Robert C.	T SGT	38345183	718	TEX.	26 Dec. 44	
Johnstone, James M.	CPL	33715286	718	PA.	26 Dec. 44	
Julian, Henri H., Jr.	2 LT	0-928243	719	ARK.	30 Dec. 44	
Kephart, Clyde A.	T SGT	33718556	718	MD.	26 Dec. 44	
Kertis, William G.	1 LT	0-819686	719	PA.	17 Oct. 44	G - 2 - 25
Kita, Peter	CPL	13082444	718	D.C.	26 Dec. 44	
Kjera, Lynn J.	SGT	37568325	719	N. DAK.	14 Nov. 44	C - 3- 44

Names without a grave location are for memorial tablets only. *Continued on next page*

449th Bomb Group

SICILY+ROME AMERICAN CEMETERY

NAME	RANK	SER. NO.	SQD.	STATE	DATE/DEATH	LOCATION
Knox, John P.	2 LT	0-830618	716	MASS.	02 Mar. 44	
Kolezar, Robert A.	T SGT	13116148	719	PA.	30 Dec. 44	
Krueger, Milton C.	CPL	37471825	719	S. DAK.	30 Dec. 44	
MacEacherin, Allen J.	PFC	11086910	717	MASS.	23 Feb. 44	F - 13 - 55
Maraldo, Walter J.	2 LT	0-701621	716	N.Y.	09 July 44	E- 11 -21
Marfisi, Charles A.	S SGT	42022151	719	N.Y.	18 Aug. 44	F - 4 - 29
Marple, Albert E.	2 LT	02061112	719	N. DAK.	09 Dec. 44	F - 7 - 38
McCubbin, Lawrence W.	CPL	37681646	719	MINN.	30 Dec. 44	
Montgomery, Alexander	T SGT	11122280	718	CONN.	15 Aug. 44	F - 14 - 25
Mumford, Joseph F.	CPL	12145787	716	N.Y.	17 Nov. 44	
Nosse, Rudolph J.	SGT	35521547	719	OHIO	04 Dec. 44	F-4-2
Okonieski, Chester	WOJG	W2125542		PA.	17 May 44	E - 9 - 37
Orchard, Fred S.	1 LT	0-715801	719	OHIO	26 Dec. 44	
Orrico, Charles J.	SGT	19149689	718	N.J.	04 Oct. 44	E - 6 - 51
Paradies, Warren W.	2 LT	0-751928	717	N.Y.	23 Feb. 44	D - 2- 20
Perrine, Ray L.	CPT	39609839	718	OHIO	26 Dec. 44	
Resnick, Leonard	2 LT	0-805674	718	N.J.	05 Apt. 44	D - 14 - 23
Roberts, Gwinn O.	SGT	34353986	716	GA.	17 Nov. 44	
Roe, Leroy C.	CPL	36881119	719	MICH.	30 Dec. 44	
Shaw, William E.	2 LT	0-773342	717	OREG.	17 Oct. 44	J - 6 - 59
Shestack, Thomas 9	S SGT	35729302	718	IND.	31 Jan. 44	F - 3 - 2
Sijewic, Anthony	CPL	32965926	716	N.Y.	17 Nov. 44	
Sims, Delos L.	CPL	34926730	719	MISS.	30 Dec. 44	
Stewart, Alton H.	S SGT	06256379	716	ILL.	09 June 44	E - 7 - 45
Sweebe, Wayne L.	2 LT	02059863	716	OHIO	17 Nov. 44	
Trapp, Leonard E.	FLT O	T-007078	719	WIS.	30 Dec. 44	
Turley, Robert D.	2 LT	0-758110	717	MINN.	21 May 44	G - 6- 36
Westbrook, Hubert M.	2 LT	0-812343	716	TENN.	09 July 44	G - I - 54
Wooldridge, Kenneth L.	PFC	33533820	717	VA.	21 May 44	G - 14 - 59
Wright, Joseph F.	CPL	37478258	716	IOWA	04 Dec. 44	D- 1 -33

Names without a grave location are for memorial tablets only.

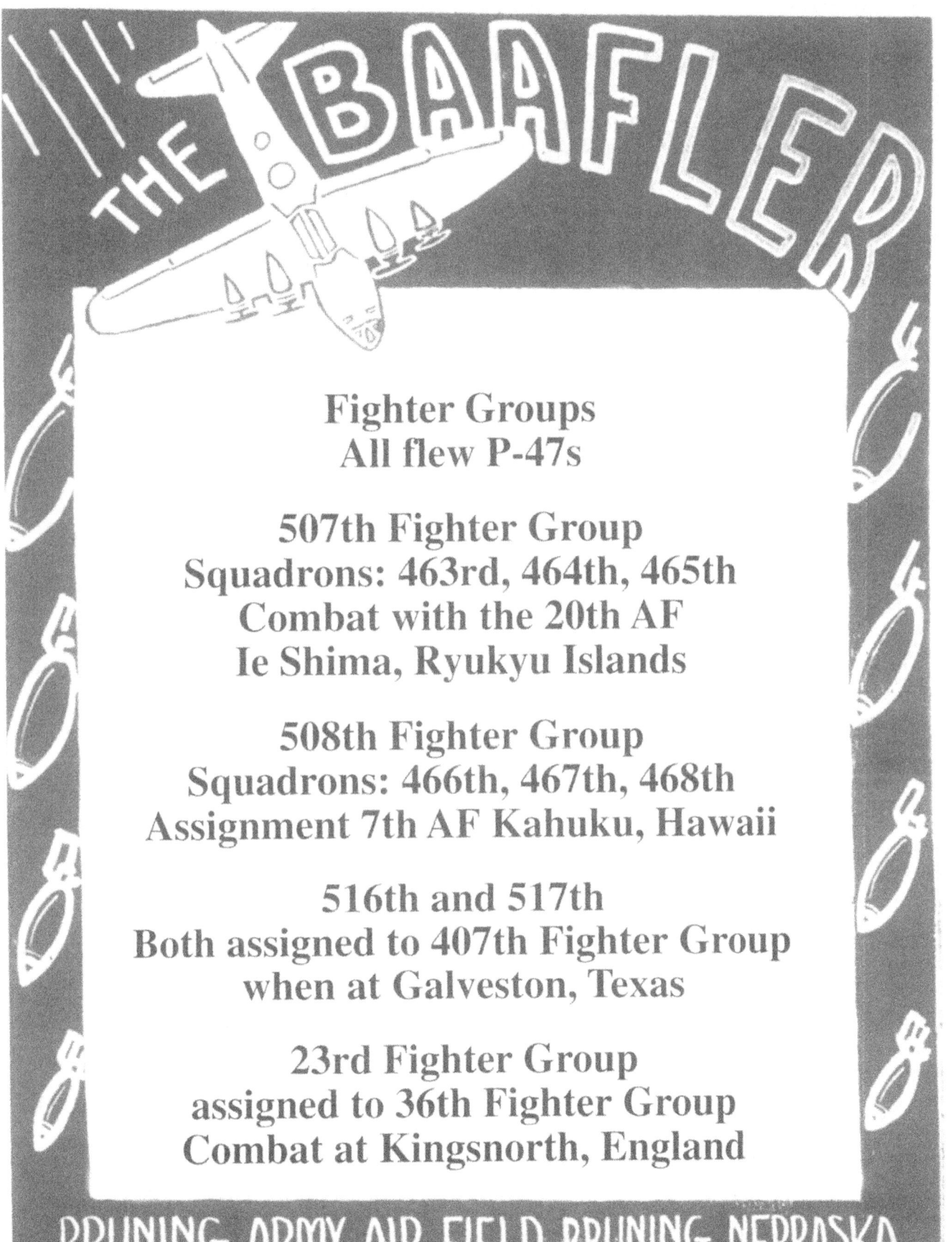

Those Who Flew
507 Fighter Group
465th, 463rd 464th Fighter Squadrons

ACTIVATED: Bruning AAF, Nebraska, 23 October 1944
TRAINED: Dalhart AAF, Texas, 14 December 1944 to 30 April 1945
STAGED: Fort Lawton, Seattle, Washington, May 1945
EMBARKED: From Seattle, Washington aboard the U.S.A.T. Cape Canso 1630 22 May 1945
ENROUTE: Pearl Harbor, 30 May-- 2 June 1945
          International Date Line --7 June 1945
          Eniwetok, Marshall Islands -- 11 - 12 1945
          Ulithi, Caroline Islands 17-18 June 1945
ARRIVED: Ie Shima, Ryukyus Islands -- 24 June 1945

COMBAT MISSIONS

DATE	TYPE OF MISSION	DESTINATION
1 July 1945	Combat Air Patrol	Kyushu, Japan
2 July 1945	Combat Air Patrol	Local (Ryukyus)
3 July 1945	Combat Air Patrol	Kyushu, Japan
4 July 1945	Combat Air Patrol	Kyushu, Japan
5 July 1945	Photo Escort	South Kyushu, Japan
6 July 1945	Photo Escort	South Kyushu, Japan
7 July 1945	Bombing	Gato Retto, Japan
7 July 1945	Dumbo	Koshki, Japan
8 July 1945	Combat Air Patrol	Local
9 July 1945	Escort	Kyushu, Japan
10 July 1945	Photo Escort	Ashiya Air Field, Japan
10 July 1945	Dumbo	Koshki, Japan
10 July 1945	Dive Bombing	Sasebo, Japan
11 July 1945	Combat Air Patrol	Local
12 July 1945	Photo Escort	Tsurvki, Japan
12 July 1945	Dumbo	Kyushu, Japan
12 July 1945	Photo Escort	South Kyushu, Japan
12 July 1945	Search (for Flattop)	Kyushu, Japan
16 July 1945	Dive Bombing	Hokiura, Japan
17 July 1945	Escort Bombing	Shanghai, China
18 July 1945	Dive Bombing	Miyakonojo
21 July 1945	Dive Bombing	Amami
22 July 1945	Dive Bombing	Shanghai, China
24 July 1945	Escort (Bombing)	Shanghai, China
27 July 1945	Dive Bombing	North Kyushu, Japan
28 July 1945	Escort	Sasebo, Japan
28 July 1945	Strafing (Fighter Sweep)	South Kyushu, Japan
28 July 1945	Escort	Kyushu, Japan
29 July 1945	Escort	Kure, Japan
30 July 1945	Strafing (Fighter Sweep)	East Kyushu, Japan
31 July 1945	Escort	Kammon Tunnel, Japan
31 July 1945	Escort	Miyazski, Japan
31 July 1945	Escort	Kanoya, Japan
2 Aug 1945	Photo Escort	East Kyushu, Japan
5 Aug 1945	Dive Bombing	Trumizu, Japan
6 Aug 1945	Photo Escort	Kyushu, Japan
7 Aug 1945	Dive Bombing	Kago Shima, Japan
8 Aug 1945	Escort	Kyushu, Japan
9 Aug 1945	Strafing (Fighter Sweep)	Yamata, Japan
10 Aug 1945	Bombing	Kumanmoto, Japan
11 Aug 1945	Dumbo	West Kyushu, Japan
11 Aug 1945	Dive Bombing	Inland Sea
12 Aug 1945	Dive Bombing	Miyakzaki, Japan
13 Aug 1945	Bombing Strafing (Fighter Sweep)	Korea
14 Aug 1945	Dumbo	Korea
15 Aug 1945	Search Mission	Korea

The *History of The 507th Fighter Group*

The 507th Fighter Group was organized in 1944 in Bruning, Nebraska, the core of manpower originally taken from the 262nd AAF Base Unit at Bruning Air Force Airfield. The 262nd AAF Base Unit was a fighter training group, teaching combat fighter tactics to newly commissioned pilots as replacements in combat units in the European and Pacific Theatres.

On December 12, 1944, the 507th was shipped to Dalhart AAF, Dalhart, Texas, for intensive training in preparation for overseas assignment in the Asiatic-Pacific Theatre. Following the four months of combat training for long range escort, strafing, dive bombing, etc., four to five months of delays and traveling, the 507th arrived on Ie Shima July 1945 to begin its intended purpose. We were assigned to the Twentieth Air Force but operated with the seventh Air Force based on Okinawa.

Beginning on July 1 and ending on August 15, 1945 (the day the war ended), the 507th flew forty-six missions. There were 1492 sorties flown, 367 were bomber escorts, 178 photo escorts and 115 dumbo escorts. The group flew 351 dive bombing sorties, 254 fire bomb sorties (napalm) and 135 fighter sweeps.

The 507th had ninety-five P-47 aircraft and 150 pilots. The pilots logged over 8700 combat hours (July 1 - August 15) and destroyed thirty-eight aircraft in the air, fired over 600,000 rounds of 50 caliber ammunition, dropped more than 480,000 pounds of CP bombs, 70,000 gallons of napalm fire bombs and consumed a million gallons of gasoline.

Within the 2,000 mile radius, the 507th planes struck Kumamoto, Kanoya, Miyazaki, Yawata, Kure, Kamnon Tunnel, Sasebo, Trumizu, Korea, Kago Shima, and Shanghai, China.

The 507th suffered 13 casualties due to these combat missions. Pilots averaged 55.8 combat hours and 9 1/2 completed sorties for the forty-six days of combat.

The 507th Group was awarded the Asiatic-Pacific ribbon with three battle stars China Offensive, Ryukus Campaign and the Air Offensive Japan Campaign. The 507th also received the Presidential Unit Citation and many pilots received the Air Medal.

The 507th has continued as a unit since the end of World War II, with only the 465th squadron on active status, based at Tinker Field in Oklahoma City. In 1993, the 507th Group and 465th Squadron was deactivated and the personnel moved into a tanker unit still based at Tinker Field.

***507th Fighter Group Memorial Plaque
mounted on the
USAF Academy Cemetery Memorial Wall
Colorado Springs, Colorado***

507TH FIGHTER GROUP

Lest We Forget   The Buddies We Lost

Lost In Training

Second Lt. Glenn W. Dexter
Second Lt. Alden L. Kaylor
Flight Officer Jack F. Anderson

Lost in or Associated with Combat

First Lt. George W. Bradley
Second Lt. Willis E. Bean
Capt. Lanham C. Connally
First Lt. Walter R. Frederik
Second Lt. Earl G. Graham
Flight Officer Paul Lynn
Flight Officer Joseph B. Lawhon
Second Lt. William L. McDaniel, Jr.
Flight Officer Neal T. McGinnis
First Lt. Frank W. Merneck
First Lt. John R. Ranger

Those Who Flew
Bruning Army Air Field

Dewaine Erickson, Wilcox, NE
At Bruning Army Air Field

507th Historian
Http://www.geocities.com/bruningairfield/index.html

Those Who Flew
Bruning Army Air Field

Memories of members of the 507th Fighter Group

Memories of Dewaine Erickson

This history started Dewaine on the role of being the Official Historian for the 507 th Fighter Group and from that start he made the 507th website
http://www.geocities.com/bruningairfield/index.htmI

The 507th Fighter Group was activated in October 1944 after training for several months at the Bruning Air Base. To take advantage of better conditions for flying, the group was shipped to the Dalhart, Texas air base in December.

Further training and preparations for overseas were made at Dalhart. In late March 1944, one group of pilots and enlisted men departed to Camp Stonemas in California, then boarded a Navy aircraft carrier with the group's P-47 planes. The remainder of the group had a free train ride to Fort Lawton in Seattle, Washington.

We then boarded the Cape Canso, a former cargo ship made by Kaiser. We found our way below to five high hammock type bunks that became our living area for the next five weeks. The first day or so out we encountered rough seas. Most of the group became seasick, spending considerable time leaning over the rail or down below "barfing" (as it is called today) in the head.

Stand up eating took practice at the 42 inch high counter. One had to hold the tray with one hand and eat with the other or find himself eating from his neighbors tray as it moved from side to side with the roll of the ship. Food was acceptable when you consider alternatives "C-rations", or snacks at the ship's PX. I bought a Babe Ruth candy bar, ate part of it until I found little worms eating the remaining portion.

It became necessary to use salt water for bathing and shaving when fresh water became short. Washing clothes was done by tying them to a rope and dropping them over the side to dangle in the sea water. One guy lost two pairs of coveralls.

The stop at Pearl Harbor for fuel and provisions gave us our first view of destruction - the battle ship Arizona lay submerged near where we docked.

Another stop was in the Ulithi Island group where hundreds of ships were anchored. We docked just off Mog Mog (yes, Mog Mog), went ashore for rest and recreation. Some A-rank beer, some swan and some played ball. About a week later, we went ashore on Ie Shima just off the northern end of Okinawa. Ie Shima is about five miles long and two and one-half miles wide.

Destruction of the island was complete. The people, mostly farmers who were not killed in the attack were moved to the north part of the main island off Okinawa. A few Japanese military were holed up in caves on the single 600 foot high mountain.

We slept on the ground with a rock for a pillow until two man tents came. C and K rations were served a few days.

Those Who Flew
Bruning Army Air Field

Memories of Dewaine Erickson *(continued)*

Getting planes ready for combat became the first order of business. We soon settled into a work routine to keep the planes operational for flights each day. The first few nights brought bombing runs by Japanese bombers. The sky lit up with exploding shells and tracer bullets. The weather was usually clear, hot and dry. We wore boots and boxer shorts. Our mess hall was made out of ammunition crates was adequate. Food was delicious except for the so called butter, it had the consistency of drywall compound. Orange marmalade became a serious problem, I still dislike the taste. The cooks did a masterful job disguising spam.

One day a small group of us in the same squadron became deathly sick. We were conveyed in a meat wagon to a medical field hospital tent. It was determined that we had eaten tainted sausage that morning for breakfast. Upon coming to my senses I thought I must be hallucinating, a school classmate was giving me an IV injection.

Later in our stay, beer and pop in bottles became available. But there was no refrigeration so we hung a bottle with wire onto a gasoline drain cock under the airplane. The dripping of 100 octane fuel evaporated on the bottles causing it to cool the liquid.

With the dropping of the bombs on Hiroshima and Nagasaki, the war ended. Shortly Ie Shima became the landing spot for two Japanese planes carrying envoys for signing the agreement to cease hostilities. Both planes were painted white with large green crosses on the fuselage. This group then boarded a US C-54 for a flight to the Philippine Islands to meet with General MacArthur. It took several months to place in motion the program of dissolving units and returning home all members of the military. Those with the longest service and highest number of points were returned first. Planes and war material were left in place or pushed into ravines rather than returned to the US. Industry at home did not want the excessive supplies of war.

After spending six weeks on detached service in Shanghai, China in the spring of 1946 I was returned to the US through the Panama Canal, New York City and discharged at Fort Leavenworth, Kansas.

Dewaine R Erickson
P O Box 118
Wilcox NE 68982

EARLE M. CRAIG, JR.
P. O BOX 2638
MIDLAND, TEXAS 79702-2638
915-682-8244
915-682-6805 FAX

2 May 1996

Mr. Dewaine R. Erickson
P. O. Box 118
Wilcox, NE 68982

Dear Dewaine:

In the fall of 1944, I joined the 463rd Squadron 507th Fighter Group at Bruning, Nebraska.

Unfortunately I will be unable to attend the reunion at Fairmont in June and I have almost no meaningful anecdotes to report. My few vivid recollections however of Bruning that fall and early winter are:

1. it seemed to be the coldest spot on Earth;

2. the air was the clearest I had ever experienced - - - from 20,000 feet one could see forever; and

3. the pungent odor from the coal-burning pot-bellied iron stoves was homey and comforting. It reminded me of my own home near Pittsburgh in western Pennsylvania.

Again, sorry to miss the reunion but have a great time. Best regards.

Sincerely yours,

Earle Craig

EMCjr/lre

Those Who Flew
Bruning Army Air Field

Dewaine Erickson, Wilcox, NE
Dewaine has been a great consultant to the Thayer County Historical Society
Taken from the Holdredge Daily Citizen 11-11-99

Wilcox man says memories of WWII more vivid today

By JACK DONOGHUE

WILCOX--Until a few years ago, Dewaine Erickson didn't talk about his World War II experience.

"As you get older, I guess you remember more," said Erickson. "And the memories are more vivid."

Those memories are especially vivid today.

"I think there ought to be more programs for young people to tell them of the sacrifices other people have made," he said. "When I look at those who didn't come back and even the ones who did, I had it easy," said Erickson.

He said his sacrifice was "only three years of my time."

The 1940 Wilcox grad served as an engineer with the 465th Fighter Squadron. The unit was stationed on the tiny island of IeShima, off the northern end of Okinawa, from June of 1945 to December that year.

"We were supposed to maintain the planes to fly escort for the B-29's, but we were never used for that," said Erickson. "We flew military missions to the southern islands of Japan, and as far away as Shanghai and Korea."

Erickson said there were 90 P-47 planes and about 150 pilots with the 465th, and there were other U.S. military units on the island.

He said until tents were delivered, they slept on the ground with a rock for a pillow.

"Getting planes ready for combat was the first order of business, and we settled into a routine to keep the planes operational," said Erickson.

"The first few nights brought bombing runs by Japanese bombers," he recalled. "The sky lit up with exploding shells and tracer bullets."

He said the destruction of the island was complete.

"The people, mostly farmers, were moved to the north part of the main island off Okinawa," said Erickson. "A few Japanese military were holed up in caves on the single 600-foot high mountain."

DEWAINE ERICKSON

Erickson said after bombs were dropped on Hiroshima and Nagasaki to end the war, IeShima became the landing spot for the two Japanese planes carrying envoys who would sign the agreement to cease hostilities.

"The bombs were just a terrible thing," said Erickson. "But think of the lives that were saved."

Erickson thinks particularly of the five other men from Wilcox who were stationed on Okinawa.

He thinks, too, of the lives lost; and all the memories are closer to home since he saw the movie "Saving Private Ryan".

"Everybody should see that "Saving Private Ryan,'" said Erickson. "That movie tells all about what war is like."

Erickson worries that a lot of the younger people don't understand the significance of Veteran's Day.

"I don't think people today know what it means," he said. "I think everybody should."

"We don't want any more wars,' sighed Erickson.

Those Who Flew
Bruning Army Air Field

The Way It Was
Corrine Baruth Kautzman

Corrine Baruth was only 18 when her father drove her to Geneva, Nebraska where Lt. Woodrow Miller and Sgt. Cecil G. Stewart were conducting interviews as a part of a detachment of Air Force Personnel from Topeka. KS. Here is part of her experiences as a secretary at the Bruning Air Field.

During the hot summer of 1944, we had a severe electrical storm. I'd worked late and missed my car pool. Lt. Miles raced up to the bus stop in his convertible and slammed on the brakes "Get In!" he said hurriedly. "There's been a helluva plane crash near Omaha. All twenty-seven P47 pilots on their way to gunnery practice in South Dakota were killed as well as the pilot of the C47. Lightening hit the plane. The "old man" (Base Commander) says the rail and meal tickets have to be ready by 0800 tomorrow. A convoy of servicemen will pick up the bodies at Omaha and escort them home for burial."

As I got into the convertible, "Red", Lt. Mile's female Irish Setter, challenged my right to enter the vehicle. A very possessive dog, Red had the reputation of not liking women in the car when she was with Lt. Miles. Finally, by giving the dog a scolding, and Lt. Miles holding her, I climbed into the car. When we got to the office, Sergeant Stewart was busy making reservations. I remember it being a very hot, sultry night. June bugs clustered and banged on the window screens trying to get inside to the light. We had three fans running trying to keep us cool. About 7 p.m., Lt. Miles took me to the Officers Club for a bite to eat. We came back to the office and worked throughout the night.

About 2 a.m., he called me into his office to take dictation. When he finished, I stood up, snapped my steno book shut as I had done hundreds of times. However, a June Bug had crawled inside the steno pad without my knowledge. There was a sharp crunching sound as the bug's body was crushed between the paper pages. Over tired from lack of rest for more than twenty one hours, hot and over wrought from typing all the rail tickets for the escorts and the dead bodies of the young pilots, (some I knew), and realizing the fragility of life, crushing the June bug put me over the edge and I went to pieces. Lt. Miles (a bachelor) and Sergeant Stewart (married) stood dumbfounded, unaware the June bug's crushed body inside my steno pad was causing my hysteria. All they could think to do was let me cry, get me a glass of water, have me finish my work, then get a staff car and send me home.

In the fall of 1944, farmers in northeastern Nebraska complained that P47's were flying under telephone wires scaring horses and livestock to run into barbed wire fences. Some animals were badly injured and had to be destroyed. The planes were traced to Bruning Army Airbase. The offending P47 pilots were brought up for court martial. My sister, Evelyn Baruth Prchal, worked in the civilian personnel office as a payroll clerk. When a call came in from the Courts and Boards office frantically searching for someone who knew shorthand for a trip to Norfolk,

Those Who Flew
Bruning Army Air Field

When personnel's call came, I was leaving work for the day. Hearing how desperate they were, I agreed to go and said "I'll pack tonight and be ready to go when I get to work in the morning". "Oh, no", they said. "You have to leave in a half hour." Silly me. I forgot the Air Corps always wanted it yesterday. Every objection I raised on leaving that evening, they countered. Someone in personnel loaned me a coat. They had orders cut so I could obtain a toothbrush, toothpaste and deodorant from the Post Exchange. At 5:30 p.m., I crawled into the staff car with my little paper sack, borrowed money for meals and hotel and a borrowed raincoat. I didn't know it, but my big adventure was about to begin.

It was a cool, crisp fall Nebraska night for the trip. We got to Norfolk about 10:30 p.m. stopping along the way to eat dinner. I ate with the Major and the Captain. Our driver, a private, ate alone at the counter. My first lesson in the division of enlisted men and officers. Although hotel reservations had been made before we left Bruning, the desk clerk would not allow me to check in without luggage. The Major and Captain showed him the orders, explained why I had a sack and no luggage, but the clerk was immovable in his decision.

He tartly suggested I get a room at another hotel and called. There was a room. As I was leaving, I remember the Captain hesitated, his sense of chivalry believing they should see me safely to this hotel. But the Major had other ideas, he called to the Captain to "come along" and they went to their rooms. I was a young, inexperienced traveler, but I knew as I neared railroad tracks, it was a hotel used by railroad men. The room was clean and functional. It had a lavatory, a chest of drawers, a straight chair, bed, and no phone in the room. A bare 100 watt light bulb glaring overhead was the only light. The bathroom for all rooms on the second floor was at the end of the hall. The scary thing was the lock on my door was broken. I made my first mental black mark against the Major.

The private sped off in the staff car when I walked into the hotel so I was stranded. I used the shared bathroom at the end of the hall, came back to my room and pushed the chest of drawers in front of the door, washed out my undies and crawled into bed in my slip. The one light blanket on the bed was not sufficient against the cold Nebraska fall weather, but I wasn't about to put on my borrowed rain coat and trudge down to the desk to get another blanket. I draped the raincoat over me as best I could for extra warmth and tried to sleep, hoping the chest of drawers would discourage any intruder.

Heavy clomping of boots in the hall sounded through the night as railroad men came or left for work. When I finally looked at my watch, it was 6 a.m. The staff car was picking me up at 7:30 a.m. so I got up and dressed. My underwear was still damp. I put it on. I was very tired and had a lousy night. I finished dressing, put on my raincoat, took my paper sack and went downstairs to the desk to inquire about a place nearby to eat. At 7:30 the staff car drew up in front of the hotel. The Major and Captain looked well rested. The young private yawned alot as we set out for our first interview of the day. The first stop was at a well kept farm. The farmer, in his late thirties declined to give testimony against the young pilots. I cannot quote him exactly after all these years, but his conversation went something like this:

"I'm thirty nine years old, have five children, a wife and a farm whose food I produce helps feed the troops. So in my way I guess, I'm helping with the war effort although I'd like to be in the

Those Who Flew
Bruning Army Air Field

service. I won't testify against these boys even thought I suffered some livestock loss. As I see it, the low flying under the telephone lines may save their lives in combat." He folded his arms over his chest and learned against the barn. He'd said all he intended to say. As we drove away, the Major or, who gave me the impression he thought everyone west of the Hudson river was illiterate, said in a surprised tone "He was pretty smart for a farmer." Coming from farm stock myself, my blood was boiling, but I kept silent. That was when I made the second big mental black mark against the Major.

Most of the other farmers talked openly about their grievances. I took down the testimony and but the Major and Captain were still cruising the area for more testimony. About 7 p.m. we went into Norfolk for supper. My fatigue was overwhelming by this time. I thought we were through for the day, but the Major said "After we eat, we'll finish with the last two farmers. At 10:30 p.m. I finished the last of the transcription. There was disagreement from the farmer on several items in the transcription. I apparently had flubbed it up. The Major was extremely irritated as he corrected it. I was too tired to care. As we left Norfolk, the Major and Captain snuggled down in the back seat and promptly fell asleep. The private yawned dangerously. I talked to him for several hours to try and keep him awake. Now, utterly exhausted, I quit trying. I ceased caring if we had an accident and I was killed. I laid my head back against the front seat and fell asleep.

About 6 a.m. and 12 miles out of Beatrice, Nebraska it began to rain. I heard a "bump, bump, bump" noise. The Major and Captain roused from sleep. "Flat tire", announced the private as he got out in the rain to change it. Later he crawled back in the car soaking wet. "Bump, bump, bump went the noise as we started.

"Another flat tire?" demanded the Major.

"No sir, I think I left the flat tire on and took off a good tire," offered the private. "What!" yelled the Major. "Were you out'tom cattin' around last night instead of sleeping?"

The Major was silent the remainder of the trip after the private responded to his tirade. "No Major" the private said. "They didn't give me any per diem for the trip. I haven't had much food since we left and I had to sleep in the car in Norfolk. All I had was my light jacket and it got really cold. I couldn't sleep." I related to his story of no sleep as I mentally added my third black mark against the Major for not showing responsibility for his personnel.

That day I learned the true meaning of an army slogan: "Just do your job and never volunteer for anything." Working at Bruning Army Airfield was a unique experience. For a young, unpretentious girl who had never been too far from home, it opened up a new world for me. I met many people and learned about different parts of the country, customs and human nature never learned in books. Our area had suffered from the aftermath of the Great Depression, drought and grasshoppers. The jobs that were created by the base helped revive our economy. After the base closed, people transferred to new locations. When the war ended, they were absorbed by industries, manufacturing goods needed by the American consumers who had made do or done without throughout the war years.

Those Who Flew
Bruning Army Air Field

In November of 1944, my sister and I left the Bruning Army Air Base for New York City. We worked for the Army Signal Corps for almost a year. We came back to Nebraska in late 1945. My sister went to Omaha and worked for War Assets. I worked at the Lincoln Army Airfield until they closed, then transferred to Forbes Air Base in Topeka, KS. I was bumped by a veteran's widow and left the government to begin work for the Kansas State Highway Commission. On November 24, 1949, 1 married Louis N. Kautzman, Jr., a former 1st Lt. in the infantry's Americal Division that fought in the South Pacific at Guadacanal and Fiji Islands. We have a daughter, Cynthia Sue Kautzman Smith, born September 14, 1954 and a grandson, Austin Louis Michal Smith, born September 30,1991 -The End

Epilogue:
Several years ago when visiting my niece, Pauline Baruth Niederklein of Daykin, NE, she asked if I would care to revisit Bruning Army Air Base. As we entered the area where M.P.'s once checked our passes, I thought about our car pool. At first, guards believed drivers were alone, but when they stopped at the gate, five additional heads popped up. We used the commuting time to sleep, for we often worked seven says a week.

A few crumbling cement foundations remained, part of a hanger and a barracks with a tree and swing set in the back yard. My niece told me the barracks housed several families. The men worked at the feed lot. The concrete runways where B24's and P47's once thundered down for takeoff were fenced and filled with assorted breeds of feeder cattle. My last memory of Bruning Army Airfield, as we drove away, was the lone Longhorn steer. He was a standing sentinel atop a mountain of manure overlooking a place built fifty-four years ago to teach rudiments of death and bring destruction at another time and at another place.

Copyright remains with author. Permission to print granted to Thayer Co. Historical So.

THE USO GIRL
by Corrine Baruth Kautzman

A temporary wartime airbase built near Bruning, Nebraska, was one of hundreds that sprang up throughout the United Stated during World War II. USOs were organized in surrounding towns, my hometown of Fairbury, NE included, to offer some social life for the service men stationed there.

My name was submitted as a possible candidate for the Fairbury "Kaydettes" along with 25 or 30 other girls. The persons put in charge of selecting candidates were particular about the character of the girls. After your name was submitted, you appeared before the USO board for an interview. Even though the chaperons on the board had known the Girl's parents for years, and the girls all their lives, they rigidly followed all the rules.

As a member, you were given a pale green card with "USO Kaydettes" and you name written on it and signed by a chaperon. You couldn't go inside the USO without your card even though the chaperon at the door had shared a cup of rationed coffee with your mother that morning.

After the base became operational, army buses picked up the girls and chaperons from the surrounding towns each Wednesday night. We traveled at the wartime speed of 35 miles an hour to conserve precious tires and gas in an unairconditioned bus. Many carefully groomed

Those Who Flew
Bruning Army Air Field

girls boarded the bus carrying a paper sack. The girls removed a chiffon scarf from it to protect their hair for the long trip as bus windows were flung open wide for ventilation. Before you went into the dance, you dropped your scarf in the sack and put it, on your seat to reclaim on the trip home. At the base, the chaperons stood guard on each side of the walk as we left the bus to go inside to the dance.

The dance started at 8:00 pm and we had an excellent band made up of musicians who had once played with Benny Goodman, Tommy Dorsey, Glenn Miller and other famous bands. On hot summer nights, your dance partner (hoping for one kiss) might suggest you step outside to get a breath of cooler air. He not only didn't get the kiss, he couldn't even step off the side walk with you, 4 or 5 chaperons were supervising to see that your virtue was not compromised.

The dance ended at 10:30 and the USO girls reboarded the buses under the watchful eyes of the chaperons for the return to town. There was lots of singing and laughing as the bus made its way down highway 4 and 15. Some girls reported they'd met a new heart throb. Others cheerfully rubbed bruised feet, the result of inexperienced dance partners braving the dance floor to hold a pretty girl in their arms.

But it was a tiresome trip home after a long day. To insure an extra 40 winks, some of us devised shortcuts to speed up bedtime preparation. The sacks we'd left on our seats earlier not only contained the scarves we'd used to deep us neat on the trip to the base but had another set of supplies for the return trip--face cream, astringent, and a washcloth to remove makeup. Also inside were curlers or bobby pins and the little jar of water to wet the hair before setting. We were not the same well-groomed girls getting off the bus in town as we were getting on. Instead we resembled creatures from another planet, heads covered with metal curlers or bobby pins and skin devoid of makeup and shiny with face cream.

Once home, we brushed our teeth and dropped into bed exhausted, counting on our morning shower to revive us for another day. As we began to fall asleep with dance tunes of "Pennsylvania 6-5000", "Tuxedo Junction", "Moonlight Serenade" and "the A Train" whirling through our heads, our last thoughts were of what we were going to wear to the local USO dance held in Fairbury on Saturday night.

507th Fighter Group

WORLD WAR TWO

463RD   464TH   465TH

3729 Wren Ave.
Ft Worth, TX 76133
(817) 292-0889

10 July 1996

Mrs. Burdette Priefert
RR1 Box 47
Belvidere, NE 68315

Dear Mrs. Priefert:

Received a copy of the Bruning AAF History. That certainly was a task getting the information together going back over fifty years. Congratulation on a job well done.

Enclosed is a copy of the orders sending the 516th & 517th Ftr. Sqdns. from Galveston AAF to Bruning in March of 1944. We became the 262nd Combat Crew Training Squadron. In October 1944 most of us joined the 507th Ftr. Gp. and moved to Dalhart. Sorry I did not send these orders with the 507th orders.

The article written by Corrine Baruth Kautzman was very interesting to me. Especially the part about the trip to Norfolk to take statements from farmers of the area about low flying aircraft scaring their animals & etc. I was the leader of the flight that hit the power line and fright caused a man to fall off his tractor and all the women were mad that the electricity was cut off & could not do their washing. The two students were given a Court Martial. We went to Colorado Springs, CO for the Court Martial. The Major (Lawyer) defending the two Lieutenants tried to put the blame on me.

Tell Corrine I am sorry for all the hardship we caused her by having to make the trip to Norfolk. But, those were the good old days when we were young and having fun.

I am looking forward to seeing James & Dorothy Bunker and Dewaine & Bonnie Erickson in September at the 507th reunion in Cleveland, Ohio. Wish I could have attended the reunion, but had to attend a family reunion in Houston that weekend.

Thanks for all your hard work representing the 507th and the other organizations of the Base.

Sincerely,

Clyde J. Whaley
Clyde J. Whaley
Fin. Off. 507th Ftr. Gp.

8524 North Harrison Court
Kansas City, Missouri 64155
August 20, 1996

Mr. Clyde Whaley
And Members of the 507 Fighter Group
3729 Wren Avenue
Ft. Worth, Texas 76133

Gentlemen:

Virginia Priefert forwarded me a photo copy of Mr. Whaley's letter to her, knowing I would be interested in Mr. Whaley's point of view of the Norfolk, Nebraska incident. Virginia and I marvel how fate got the book in the hands of the leader of the low flying aircraft that terrorized the Norfolk area and raised such ire in the hearts of the housewives in that community.

Mr. Whaley, you and the men of the 507th Fighter Group flying over Norfolk, were unsuspectingly dealing with a most formidable enemy, almost equal to the Germans or the Japanese, the Nebraska rural housewives on their Monday washday. I know of what I speak. My mother belonged to such a washday sisterhood on Little Sandy Creek (5 miles south of Daykin or 4 1/2 miles east of Alexandria, Nebraska), near the Bruning Airfield. The determination of this Monday sisterhood left such a lasting impression on me, several years ago I was compelled to write an account of it in memory of my mother. I enclose a copy of the story. After reading the story, you will see what lengths otherwise honest kind, good women would stoop to. As I see it, you barely missed being drawn and quartered.

As for the hardship you caused me in having to make that trip, I'm certain I grew from that life experience. It took young men such as yourself and the men of the 507th fighter Group, with courage, daring and bravado to do a difficult job. Because of the sacrifice made by you, the 507th and our country's other armed services, including my dear husband, I've been blessed with a good life and I thank you for it. I shutter to think what it might have been if the outcome of the war had been different.

Sincerely Yours
(signed) Corrine Baruth Kautzman

Enclosure

Those Who Flew
Corrine Baruth Kautzman *(continued)*

"AND STILL CHAMPION"

An undeclared war took place every Monday morning among the housewives on Little Sandy Creek. The winner was the first to have a batch of laundry stretched on the clothesline.

Mom, a born competitor, held the winning title for the years of 1932 and '33. But one Monday morning, the gas motor for the washing machine wouldn't start, threatening her impeccable record.

With stricken look, Mom raced to the barn where Dad was harnessing horses.

"What's wrong Cora?" he asked

"Gus, you have to come immediately and fix the washing machine," she said breathlessly, tugging at his shirt.

"I don't know much about engines," Dad said, giving the strap he was buckling a final yank. Mom gave Dad an imploring look.

Knowing how Mom felt about this absurd contest and how hard she worked at it, Dad left the horse and came to the house. He knelt by the gas engine and tried a series of adjustments. Mom stood expectantly waiting for life to quiver into the balking machine. Losing his temper, Dad resorted to pushing, pounding and finally swearing, but the stubborn gas engine refused to budge.

"I'm sorry Cora" he said giving Mom a comforting hug, "But motors are beyond me. You'd better get a repair man. " Abject defeat clouded Mom's face as Dad headed back to the barn.

My sister and I, eating our cornflakes at the kitchen table, watched Mom roll and unroll the edge off her apron in frustration. Suddenly, she sprinted upstairs, calling down to my sister and me from the top step.

"Evelyn, get a clean, wet rag and wipe the clothesline. Corrine, get the clothespin bag from the laundry room and hurry!"

Within a minute, she raced back downstairs, grabbed the clothes pin bag from my hands, and shot out the door.

From her vantage point at the top of the backyard hill, Mom surveyed the neighbors' clotheslines. No laundry was yet in sight. Moments later, the winner and still champion of the Little Sandy Creek hoisted her victory flag. Four dry clean white sheets, fresh from the linen closet whipped briskly in the early morning wind.

By Corrine Baruth Kautzman

Soldier's Personal Stories
James Bunker written by Dorothy Bunker
Milligan, NE

James Adam Bunker was born 6/24/1924 at Montrose (Lee Co.) Iowa, the eldest son of Isaac Johnson Bunker and Martha Ellen (Value) Bunker. He worked in a restaurant & on farms before enlisting. His basic training was at Amarillo AAF, Texas and transferred to Pocatello AAF and Bruning, AAF where he met and married DOROTHY KOCA of Tobias, who worked for Civil Service at the airfield.

Jim reported 12/11/1944 to Dalhart AAF, TX before overseas departure 5/22/1945 from Seattle, WA and was in the Asiatic-Pacific Theatre, enroute to Hawaii on to Ie Shima and Okinawa, Ryukyi Islands when the Japanese surrendered and signed peace treaty aboard the Battleship USS Missouri near their airfield.

He returned to Camp Stoneman, CA and discharged at Ft. Douglas, Utah 4/6/1946. He served as sergeant with the 507 Fighter Group, 463rd Fighter Squadron serving 2 yrs. 4 mo. He received the American Theatre of operations service ribbon, Asiatic-Pacific Service Ribbon with 3 Battle Stars, Good Conduct Medal, Victory Medal, Distinguished Unit Badge with Oak Leaf Clusters and Expert Carbine Medal.

He belongs to tile Geneva, NE V.F.W., Post 7102, Milligan, NE, American Legion HSSK Post 240 and the Bunker Family Association of America.

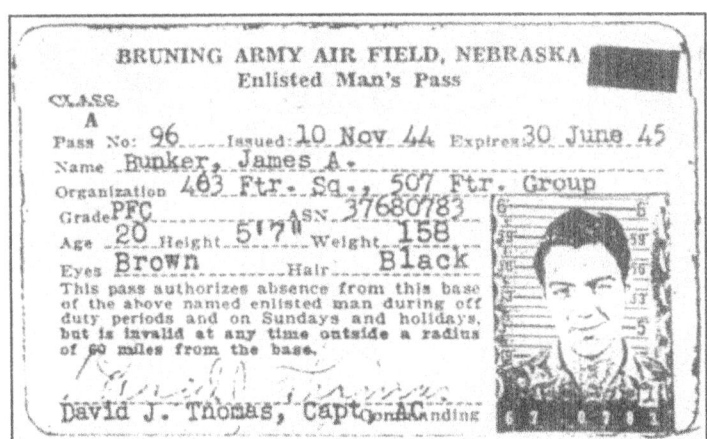

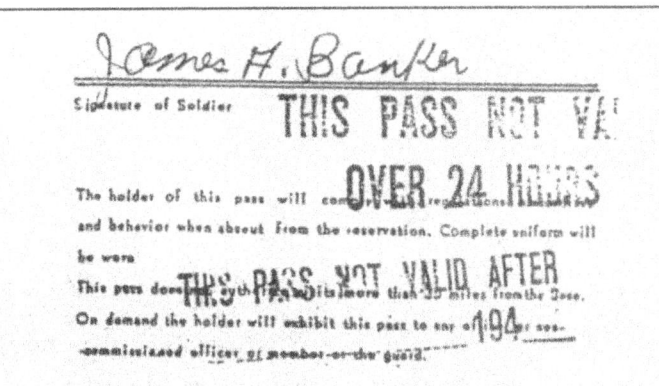

James A. Bunker

Those Who Flew
507th Fighter Group
Ie Shima

After the A-bombs were dropped at Hiroshima and Nagasaki, Ie Shima became the landing spot for the two Japanese planes carrying the envoys to sign the peace treaty. These Japanese planes were painted white with green crosses on them. A C-54 then carried them to the Philippines and from there they were taken to the USS Missouri to sign the peace treaty.

Pictures by Dewaine Erickson

507th FIGHTER GROUP ASSOCIATES
P.O. Box 163
Watkinsville, GA 30...
Tel. (706) 769-6236 or ...

IN MEMORIAM
507TH FIGHTER GROUP
HEADQUARTERS
463RD 464TH 465TH
SQUADRONS
BRUNING, NE DALHART, TX IE SHIMA
WORLD WAR II
PRESIDENTIAL UNIT CITATION - KOREA
WESTERN PACIFIC CAMPAIGN
BATTLE STARS: - JAPAN
- RYUKYUS
- CHINA

June 3, 1996

Virginia Priefert, President
THAYER COUNTY HISTORICAL SOCIETY
RR1, Box 47
Belvedere, NE 68315

Dear Ms. Priefert:

I received your correspondence of May 24, 1996, and am writing to give you permission to copy 507th Fighter Group Materials for resale at the Museum in Belvedere, Nebraska.

As you know, the 507th Fighter Group, composed of a Headquarters Detachment, 463rd Squadron, 464th Squadron, and the 465th Squadron, was formed at the Bruning, Nebraska Air Base. After our organizational process, we then went to Dalhart, TX Air Base for our overseas training. From there we shipped to the Pacific Theatre as our combat area.

I was the assistant to the 507th Chaplain, but these duties commenced after we went to Dalhart, so I'm not familiar with the Chapel Service schedule at Bruning Air Base.

I called Clyde Whaley, the Finance Officer of the present day 507th Fighter Group Associates, Inc., and he will mail you a roster today. I also phoned Bill Jenner at O'Fallon, Illinois, and asked him to try to find a roster for you. (Bill was the group's weatherman.)

Enclosed herewith are some other materials regarding the 507th, along with a picture of a bronze plaque that was installed at the Air Force Academy in Colorado in July of 1994.

Sincerely,

James H. Mosbey, Jr
Adj., 507th FGA, Inc.

JHMjr/cm

Enclosure

cc: Clyde Whaley, Finance Officer; Bill Jenner; Dorothy Bunker

Those Who Flew
Bruning Army Air Field

Major Arthur T. Rice

Major Robert F. Hemphill

The CO was a pretty cool cucumber. If you recall the kind of Joe who could make a long-range flight over Korea. have his turho blow oil him, all oil-leak cover the canopy. Tojos all over the sky, and somehow get the outfit back on the pinpoint of Ie Shima, change his mildewed flying suit, comb his hair and look as refreshed as if he had just stepped out of cocktail lounge on the top of the Mark. We have done quite a bit of research on the subject and to our knowledge no one ever saw him rattled: and God knows he had the provocation.

You saw the medium-sized ultra-reserved man walking to his ship with clean-shaven face and trim mustache, perhaps thought him a grim product of a grim business, a difficult guy to get to know. In a sense, that may have been true but both GIs and Officers have been known to sit down with him and have a good old-fashioned gabfest sprinkled liberally with a dry sense of humor. Just in case you weren't fortunate enough to trap him yourself, he filled out one of those Personal History forms—the kind you filled out at least 748 times, from basic training on. Here are of the answers. His father is a farmer and his mother is a "farmerette." There are two other boys in the family—one a farmer and the other an electrical engineer

The demarcation between maintenance and flying is concentrated in the person of the Operations Officer who gets the right men in the right planes at the right time. Taking what Engineering hands him, he is responsible more than any other man for getting the stuff that pay-offs over the target.

It's a job calling not only for a high degree of flying skill, but the human attributes of leadership, tact, vision, infinite patience, and certain characteristics of the disciplinarian. Major Hemphill brought these to his job and added to the amalgam something not necessarily essential, but helpful—a sense of humor.

Major Hemphill was born twenty-eight years ago in the little town of Blair, Nebr., son of a dentist. His sister, Janet, is a hostess for United Air Lines, so flying is in the family blood. Graduating from Blair high school in 1936, he, attended Dana College in Blair for two years and received his A. B. degree from the University of Nebraska in 1941. Concurrently with his liberal arts course. He spent two years studying law at the university.

ROBERT F. HEMPHILL
4842 Johnson Point Road, NE
Olympia, Washington 98516-9152
(3601491-5710

THE "FLYING ERECTOR SET, aka RUGGEDY ANNE

The P-47N aircraft No. 182 on its hardstand in this picture was on Ie Shima in the Ryukyu Islands, combat location of the 507th Fighter Group. It was the Jug which I flew as operations officer of the 465th Fighter Squadron, and it was a faithful bird which I love even to this day.

It had a unique history leading to its double name before it launched into combat. Our squadron and aircraft were off-loaded from "jeep" carrier USS Roi to Majuro Atoll in the Marshall Islands, standing by to fly forward into the active combat theater. Before reaching the Marshalls, the Roi encountered violent weather, such that the ship's inclinometer at storm peak registered a roll of 37 degrees, theoretically enough to capsize, we were informed. All came through well save jug No. 182. It had been tied down on the hangar deck, and a nearby finger lift tug broke its moorings in the storm, and before it could be corralled, had careened back and forth, severely damaging the tail cone, right wing tip, and one of the propeller blades of 182.

Squadron commander Major Arthur T. Rice and squadron engineering officer, Captain Alan D. Duff, Jr. surveyed the damage. Duff suggested that since the squadron faced an indeterminate waiting period on Majuro, it would be a good thing for his crews to have a maintenance challenge to deal with: how about good old banged-up 182?

And so it happened that 182 and the other more fit aircraft were floated ashore by barge and subsequently Duff and associates performed their magic. A tail cone was found somewhere and installed, a new right wing tip and its securing members were fashioned from metal stock, and a propeller blade was obtained from Marine Air Group 13 on Majuro, which was equipped with F-4U Corsairs, having similar propellers.

I was called one morning to test hop No. 182. After the usual walk-around, and astonishment at what had been wrought, I boarded, cranked it up, taxied out, checked mags, and was off. It flew beautifully, all gauges in the green, Next came a stall series, and a surprise. No. 182 stalled out 3-to-4 knots slower than book standard. Our unanimous postflight verdict: the stall bonus was derived from the skilled handicraft and negotiation proficiency of the 465th maintenance force.

I proudly welcomed No. 182 into our active roster and named it as indicated. Ruggedy Anne, on the right side cowling, received only one complaint, and that from my late wife whose middle name was Anne. She questioned whether "ruggedy" suitably described her. She had a point - and I had one hell of an aircraft.

Robert F. Hemphill
Colonel, USAF Retired
May 19, 1997

Those Who Flew
507th Fighter Group
456th Fighter Sqd.

A Special Photograph: Iwo Jima

In June 1945 the 465th Fighter Squadron, 507th Group flying P-47s was temporarily based on Majuro Atoll, Marshall Islands, awaiting orders to move forward into the active combat zone. Also located on Majuro was Marine Air Group 13 flying F-3U Corsairs, with whom friendly liaison was established.

One day the MAG 13 commander mentioned to Major Art Rice, 465th commander, that a "pretty good" picture from the USMC assault and capture of Iwo Jima had come through channels enroute to rear headquarters. Rice expressed interest, and saw that it was indeed a great photograph, the original Joe Rosenthal shot of the Iwo Flag raising on Suribachi, ultimately a Pulitzer prize winner and often called the greatest WW II photograph. At Rice's request the Marine commander had two extra prints made, one for Rice and one for me.

I have long treasured it, dim and faded as it has become and am please to present a copy of that "made from the original negative" Rosenthal shot.

Robert F. Hemphill
Colonel, USAF retired
May 19,1997

Those Who Flew

Colonel Robert F. Hemphill
From War to Peace

Robert F. Hemphill, who was with the 507 Fighter Group, writes Children stories and Poetry. One of his children's book is entitled **Harrison Bunny and the Black Mysterious Gang.** It was illustrated by Karl Karpa. He also writes poetry and has compiled a book entitled **Hand Me Downs**. It is composed of Poetic Impressions by various members of the Hemphill & Jenkins families. Here are two poems taken from that book:

FRIENDS

So many things are puzzling,
but this I know is true
my world is full of sunny lanes
because I've walked with you.

You've given me as treasures
the gem of friendship rare:
the shining light of faith and love,
the knowledge that you care

You've helped me grow less earthbound
in looking high above,
to the light that never fails us-
to the truth that God is love.

And so -- my days are happy-
I've wealth untold, 'tis true
because God planted friendship
deep in the heart of you.

"*Poetic Impressions*" by Robert F. Hemphill's mother

FLYING THOUGHTS

Because he's wearing silver wings,
I see in every plane that flies
my brown-eyed son at its controls
winging his way through ageless skies.

And so -- each time I see a ship
flashing its beauty through the air
I say, "Please bless the pilot Lord,
and keep him flying there."

OUR FIRST JUGS
(P-47Ns)

Virginia Priefert received this information from Marshall Golden, just before this book went to press.

I am from Newington, Connecticut and arrived at the Bruning Army Air Field on October 10, 1943 coming from Tinker Air Base in Oklahoma City. I was assigned to the 464th of the 507th and worked in the sub depot in the north hangar of the base where we did the housekeeping for the base. I married my beautiful secretary, Loretta Vonderhaar from Hebron, Nebraska.

I was there when the 449th were there and after they moved out the P-47s of the 23rd came in. Forty-five new P-47s arrived for the 507th and when the first one came in, I was really surprised when the pilot took the helmet off displaying beautiful red hair — it was a woman. Those planes were brought in from Republic Manufacturing by women. I can't say enough for the work the women did during that time.

Horace Young and Jim Gill showing their field expedient washing machine on Ie Shima.

Horace Young gasing his P-47 after a flight.

Those Who Flew
507th Fighter Group
Ie Shima
pictures by Dewaine Erickosn

One of the white Japanese planes with green crosses carrying the envoys to sign the peace treaty when WW II was over. They landed on Ie Shima and then were taken by an American C-54 to the Philippines and on to Douglas McArthur.

A Peace plane went off the runway as it took off...Crew is working on brake.

464TH IKE'S BOYS 507TH FG

IE SHIMA, THE FIRST STEP

TOWARD WORLD PEACE —

IT DOESN'T COST MUCH TO GO FIRST-CLASS (A)
OR
"Smile Pretty"

36th Fighter Group

Brucheville, Manche, France
April 9, 1990
Dedication of Monument
to the 36th Fighter Group
Don Worthley Photograph
(Don's hand on monument)

The 36th Fighter Group
was made up of 3 Fighter Groups:

The 22nd was stationed at Scribner, NE

The 23rd Squadron was stationed at
the Bruning Army Air Field

The 53rd was at Ainsworth, NE

36th Fighter Group

Midland, Texas—September 29, 1995
Plaque dedicated to the Pilots of the 36th
Fighter Group killed in action during WW II
Placed in Gen. Doolittle Garden of
The Confederate Air Force
Don Worthley, Photograph

Midland, Texas—Sept. 29, 1995
L-R: Don Worthley—Member of 36th Fighter Group
Nancy Farbsten—who traced down the last relative
of 1st Lt. Roger T. Lane
Linda Shine—from the Smithsonian Air & Space
who unveiled the plaque dedicated to the
36th Fighter Group
Tom Glenn—Master of Ceremonies
Don Wortley, Montesano, WA Photographs

History of the 36th Pursuit Fighter Group

Excerpts of the History of the 36th Fighter Group as given to the Thayer County Historical Society on October 8, 1989 by Don Worthley:

The 36th Pursuit Group was formed February 1, 1940 at Langley Field, Virginia with the Headquarters and the 22nd Pursuit Squadron. The 22nd, the 23rd, 32nd and 34th were formed at Brooks Field San Antonio, Texas. There were 500 recruits sent to Brooks Airforce Base between October and December 1939.

Col. H. P. K. Walasley was a cadet at Brooks and graduated in August of 1940 and commanded the 23rd for its duration at Brooks Airforce Base. The 23rd & 32nd were transferred to Langley Field, Virginia November 13, 1940 to join the 22nd and make the 36th complete.

The 36th Pursuit Troop was transferred to Puerto Rico January 2, 1941 and sailed on the USS Chateau Thiery from Newport Beach, Virginia and docked at Ponce, Puerto Rico and was assigned to Losey Field.

Each squadron had 5 aircraft P-36s. The group had a T-6 air craft and a B-10 twin engine bomber. About 30 P40Cs were assigned to the group in April 1941. About two months later the group received a number of P-40Es.

The 23rd spent five months in the Virgin Islands. The squadron returned to Losey Field in late October 1941. In November 1941 the group was assigned P-39s. In 1943 the 32nd was transferred to Trinidad and the group returned to the states in May 1945 and was joined by the 53rd squadron.

The Commanding Officers of the 36th were:

Major Ned Schran--1939-1942
Major Harrington--- 1942
Col. William Curry--1943 and was replaced some time later by Paul Douglas.

The 36th trained at several points throughout the U.S.A. in 1943:

The 22nd at Scribner, NE
The 23rd Squadron was stationed at the Bruning Army Air Field, Bruning NE
The 53rd was at Ainsworth, NE

In 1943 departed the U.S.A. March 23, 1944
Arrived Liverpool, England April 5, 1944

Departed Liverpool, England April 5, 1944
Arrived Omaha Beach Wednesday July 20, 1944

The 36th Fighter Squadron Schedule (continued)

Arrived St. Marie Dumont, France Wednesday July 26,1944
Departed St. Marie Dumont, France Wednesday September 6, 1944

Arrived LeMans, France, Wednesday September 6, 1944
Departed LeMans, France, Sunday September 24, 1944 at 7:00 A.M.

Arrived Epernay, France, Sunday September 24, 1944 at 5:30 P.M
Departed Epernay, France, Wednesday October 3,1944 at 4:00 P.M.

Arrived Reims, France, Wednesday October 4, 1944 at 6:30 P.M.
Departed Reims, France, Oct. 28. 1944

Arrived Louvane, Belgium, Saturday October 28, 1944 at 11:30 P.M.
Departed Louvane, Belgium, Wednesday March 28, 1945 at 12:30 P.M.

Arrived in Eschnweiler, Germany, Wednesday March 28, 1945 at 5:30 P.M.
Departed Eschnweiler, Germany, Monday April 9, 1945 at 2:00 P.M.

Arrived Coblenz, Germany, Monday April 9, 1945 at 7:30 P.M.
Departed Coblenz. Germany, Saturday April 21, 1945 at 11:30 A.M.

Arrived Kassell, Germany, Saturday April 21. 1945 at 8:00 P.M.

After the war in Europe ended, the men of the 36th soon started their journey home and the 36th Fighter Group of WW II, was deactivated in 1947.

This group was awarded Battle Honors for outstanding performance of duty against the enemy on 1 Sept. 1944, when learning the enemy was making a withdrawal through a gap at Clamancy, France. They divided into two groups and covered all roads on which the enemy might withdraw. The 36th flew from dawn to dusk at low altitude through intense & accurate enemy anti-aircraft fire. They destroyed many enemy vehicles. They returned to base and rearmed and returned four times to destroy the enemy column and destroyed a column of enemy vehicles and ammunition dump on the fourth mission. This was a decisive blow at the enemy transportation and personnel at an important time in the campaign in Northern France.

visiting around / By JOHN ED PEARCE
NOVEMBER 26, 1978

Sweet bird of youth

War was hell, but many young pilots of the 36th Fighter Group got this glimpse of heaven as their beloved bird — the P-47 — soared the blue

A reunion of some of World War II's daring young men

WORLD WAR II veterans of the 36th Fighter Group, U.S. Air Force, held a reunion a few weekends ago out at the Ramada Inn on Louisville's Hurstbourne Lane. I dropped in to see what happens when old fliers get together, and found pretty much what you would expect. A fair amount of drinking and a large amount of reminiscing.

Some brought their wives and children; some came alone. Some took buses on guided tours to Churchill Downs and other points of interest;

JOHN ED PEARCE is a *Magazine* staff writer.

some partied. After a rather sedate dinner meeting on Friday night, at which it was announced that the association now has 215 names on its mailing list, meaning that it has found that many of the old boys, and that next year's meeting will be in Phoenix, partying broke out. By 10 o'clock Saturday morning, when the sightseeing buses rolled away with the pure at heart, the hospitality room was already awash with beer and recollections of people and places of yesteryear.

One thing everyone seemed to remember fondly was the P-47, the

stubby fighter plane that pilots of the 36th flew against the Germans. It was, the aging pilots agreed, one helluva fine plane, not especially pretty, but capable of taking a lot of punishment and bringing its pilot back to base.

"It was tough," said Bob Ferris, stocky, gray-haired ex-pilot from Dubuque, Iowa, who looks pretty tough himself, but found a lot to laugh about. "We liked it much better than the P-51, the Mustang. For escort duty, the 51 was better, faster and more maneuverable, but that wasn't what we were doing primarily. We were mainly do-

The sweetest bird: The World War II pilots of the 36th Fighter Group have fondest memories of the spunky P-47, shown above in a wartime photograph.

ing ground-support, strafing and dive-bombing right ahead of the troops on the front lines. We flew 51s on escort out of England before D-Day, but then went to the P-47. Our group went with the troops at Omaha Beach and followed them right on into Germany."

"LeMans was the first place we were based in Europe," added Bill Holekamp. "As soon as they found a flat place they'd put down pierced planking, that steel matting with holes in it, and that was the airfield. That 47 could land on anything." Holekamp, who operated a seed-cleaning business in Comfort, Texas, after leaving the Air Force in 1945, was with Ferris in the 23rd Squadron, and rates as an old-timer, having joined the squadron when it was flying P-40s in Puerto Rico.

"We don't have too many of the 51 guys left," Ferris explained, "because we lost them. The 51 was good for escorting bombers, and if you got hit you'd have enough altitude to bail out. But in our work we went in so low that what we faced generally was ground fire, so we needed a plane that could take it, and the 47 could. You took a hit in the cooling system of the 51 and in seconds the ethylene went, the engine froze, and you went down. But that big radial engine on the 47 could take a lot of punishment, and as long as it was running, the 47 was a nice-handling plane. Of course, it didn't fly much once that engine stopped. It was a big bull of a fighter plane.

"Remember that big Polish kid?" Ferris asked, and Holekamp nodded solemnly. "He'd been sick, and he wanted to fly more missions to catch up with the other guys he had come in with. He only had 12 missions. Well, he was up this one day and this Focke-Wulf got on his tail and just shot hell out of him — bullets went over his shoulder, under his seat, between his legs, shot out his instrument panel, shot out his radio, riddled his canopy, hit his engine, wings, went all through that cockpit. You never saw anything like it. But he got it back. I saw him when he came down, and I said to the doc, that kid will never fly again. He was like a zombie sitting in that plane, looking at nothing, not moving. Couldn't talk. Couldn't even get a Purple Heart out of it, didn't have a scratch. But he was shot, his nerves gone. We had to junk the plane, it was shot up so bad. But it got him back."

"You couldn't go wrong landing that 47," added Holekamp. "Carl Curry landed one, and we had to go over pick it up, put on a new wing, new undercarriage, new engine, new canopy. Just shot to hell. But it flew."

"Mine was the same way," said Ferris. "Took a 40 millimeter hit that blew my 500-pound bomb right off and came up through the wing, so that the guns were hanging out, all the ammunition dangling. Looked like somebody had punched holes in the cockpit with a butcher knife, but I wasn't hit. I flew it around and stalled it to see how it would land, and brought it right in. Holes all over that damn thing.

"Talk about luck; there was this Berkwist, from Minneapolis, went in so low on a bombing run that he got hit by his own bomb blast, creased his forehead. Only man I know got the Purple Heart from his own bomb."

The parade of recollections was interrupted by the arrival of Alfred Fiumara, of Pittsburgh, who was engineering officer of the 23rd Squadron, and has made every reunion since the first in 1972. The reunions, he says, are getting bigger every year. "I bet I saw 10 new faces just last night," he said.

Ken "Kayo" Myers, a former crew chief who enlisted from Chenoa, Ill., but now works with delinquent boys for the Indiana Department of Corrections after retiring with more than 20 years of service with the Air Force, wandered over to ask if the others were going on the bus trip. Myers is setting up next year's meeting in Phoenix. Nobody really cares where the reunion is, he says; they'll go, no matter where it is.

"We don't know how many of us are still alive," said Bill Holyfield, of Mobile, Ala. "Every time we get in touch with somebody, he knows somebody, and the list keeps growing. The 36th is still active, see, but what we're talking about is the period from 1939 to '46. A group is about a thousand to twelve hundred men, and in that seven-year period a lot of men went through. Some have died, no doubt. We're getting older, you can see. All in our 50s, 60s. Most of the guys are looking good, though."

A chartered bus pulled up outside the motel, and Irene Hess, of Louisville, who handled publicity for the reunion, called for everyone to get on board. A couple of dozen men and women pushed out the door. A tall, athletically built man in a brown suit, smoking a curved-stem pipe, hurried to join them. Horace Bamberg, said Bob Ferris.

"He's a career man," he explained. "Funny thing about him. He was flying a dive bombing mission one day, I think we were at LeMans then. Anyhow, he got his controls shot away, and he was down two or three hundred feet. So he trims the plane up with his tabs to climb the best it will, gets rid of his canopy and stands up in his seat,

Continued

Sweet bird of youth Continued

and when the plane gets as high as he thinks it's going to, he jumps.

"Well, he says everything sort of went into slow motion. The plane was just mushing along, and he had to wait until he got clear of it before he pulled his ring, and it seemed to take a long time. Finally, it left him, and he jerked his ring and just as his parachute streamed out, his feet went through the top branches of this tree. Luckily, the chute caught and jerked him to a stop about 12 feet from the ground, and there he swung, and the Germans started shooting at him. So he figures this is no place to watch a war, so he drops out of his chute, and starts crawling toward what he hopes are the Americans, and sure enough, a U.S. patrol picks him up.

"He's feeling pretty good about things, when up comes this combat photographer and asks him if he'll go back and get back into his parachute harness and pose for a picture. With the Germans still blasting away. Nutty guy. Horace said no thanks, he didn't think so."

A short, ramrod-straight, gray-haired man marched into the lobby, glanced around crisply and marched out to the bus.

"That's Col. Bull Curry," says Myers, "the commander of the 36th.

" '... just as his parachute streamed out, his feet went through the top branches of this tree.' "

He wasn't the only commander, you understand, but for these people here, when you say commander, they mean Bull Curry. The things that make for a top outfit, and ours was, is the caliber of the line chief, and of the commander. And as a commander, Curry was just about the best. He always flew with a slide rule, trying to find ways to get more out of that plane. No one in the Air Force knew more about the 47 than Bull Curry. The 36th spawned a lot of commanders for other groups because of him."

Myers was a charter member of the 36th, serving in Puerto Rico before the group was formed at Brooks Field, Texas, and Langley Field, Va., in 1940. Like most of the others, he got out in 1945, but civilian life didn't seem as good to him, and in 1950, he went back in and served until 1965, when he retired. In the meantime, he earned degrees in education at the University of Maryland and Indiana University, and began civilian life working with delinquent boys. He is now commander of the 36th Fighter Group Association.

"Why do we come back? Oh, to see the guys, I guess. Some of the wives were talking last night about the old-timers who were together back in Puerto Rico, and they said they were really closer than brothers, and I guess that's about right. You don't forget."

"I heard one day that there were some guys down in Dayton from the 36th," said William Shisler, of Columbus, Ohio, "so I went down there. I hadn't seen anyone from the old outfit for almost 30 years, and all of a sudden there we were, facing each other. I knew them all, just like time hadn't passed. So we decided to get everyone we could together in Atlanta. There were 14 of us there, then 65 the next year. We're just starting to grow."

Shisler, who was dressed in a burgundy suit ("They call me the Red Baron," he said with a laugh), worked in a war plant before joining the Air Corps in 1942. "I'd been a boxer, and had to get my nose fixed," he related, "and then they found my pulse was too high. So I got a doctor to give me something that quieted it down, and they took me. Got out in '45, never had a scratch on me. Then I joined the Air Guard, and one day on a training mission this P-51 cuts my plane in two, right behind the cockpit. I bailed out. Had time to swing about once before I hit the deck. I love these reunions. Get together with the guys, meet their wives, see what's happened to us all."

He and his wife left to get some breakfast, and the others wandered toward the hospitality room. Bob Ferris sat in an easy chair, facing the bar. Swede Reyman, Bill Holyfield, a dozen others were telling stories and laughing happily. "Have a drink," a man hollered. We're into our third beer and fifth lie." That brought a burst of laughing.

"You remember Compton, crewed for Capt. Miles?"

"Sure."

"Killed himself."

"You're kidding."

"Nope. Got to drinking. Couldn't handle it. Shot himself."

"Remember Dunlap? Used to take his false teeth out, and somebody found them and hid them?"

"What was the name of that guy down in Puerto Rico was messing around with that gook's wife? Anyhow, the gook caught him, hit him over the head with a machete. I don't think he really wanted to kill him, but he damn near did. Well, anyhow, this guy always rode a white horse; he'd come riding into the base in full uniform on this white horse. Well, somehow he managed to get on his horse and the horse brought him back to the base,

---

"The drinks were flowing, and more and more was heard the word 'remember?' "

---

and he bled on that horse so much the horse looked like a red and white horse. Live? Oh, sure. Wasn't hurt too bad, I think, but he sure bled like hell. I don't think he ever did go back to see that woman."

"Let's see, where did we go after England? LeMans, then Tours, then where? Yeah, Juvincourt, then Aachen. I remember one time we got a three-day pass into Paris, ran into this bunch of women. Stayed 14 days on a three-day pass. Boy, you had to have money. Expensive as hell, that place."

"They ain't cheap here, for that matter." Loud, derisive laughter.

"How would you know? You still chasing women? Hell, that's like a dog chasing a car. If he catches it, he can't drive." More laughter.

Sweet bird of youth Continued

"We were the first outfit into France," recalled Swede Reyman. "We had this one guy in our outfit went nuts. Became a killer, went out hunting people to shoot. Shoot people off bicycles. Had to send him back to the States."

"We were flying right with the troops," said Bob Ferris. "Sometimes flying five or six missions a day. Go out at daylight, sometimes not get back until after dark. But the guys liked it, most of them. I remember this one guy — remember him? — cried like hell when he had to leave the outfit.

"A lot of the time we spent shooting up trucks, tanks, trains, anything to let the troops move. Used to call us the trainbusters. The only time we couldn't help the troops was during the Battle of the Bulge, when they really needed us. Couldn't get off the ground because of the fog and snow. No ceiling at all. If you did get up, you couldn't see anything. We were grounded about 10 days, right during the worst of it. Man, that was frustrating. Scary, too. When the Germans broke through, it looked like they were coming right for us. We had orders to burn all the planes if we were attacked; didn't have anything to fight with. A flier with no plane isn't much of a fighter."

One of the men stretched and complained of his arthritis. Others laughed and mentioned ailments of their own. The drinks were flowing, and more and more was heard the word "remember?" And more and more it seemed that maybe the word was, more than anything else, the answer to why the men were there. For war is not a pretty thing, or pleasant, but for those who survive it, it is like nothing else a man can experience. To have met the terrifying challenge of war gives a man a glimpse of life and himself that he can never forget.

Because life, for most of us, is a thing of few peaks and many sloughs, of boredom, if not of pain. And so men remember the times, the places, the moments of peril when life stood its tallest. And they draw together, in a kind of love, so that they may remind each other, and try to touch again, across the gulf of years, the young men who used to be, before time took youth away. ❏

23RD FIGHTER SQDN

ADAMS, GEO & FLORA, PO BOX 88101, COLORADO, SPRINGS 80908, (719) 495-2155
ADAMS, NATHAN & MAGGIE, 2411 WINDING WAY, VALDOSTA, GA 31602, (912) 244-0238
ADIE, BILL & GLORIA, 4032 NE 23RD ST, PORTLAND, OR 97212, (503) 284-2648
ALDRICH, BILL, 3938 McNEAL DR., PETERSBURG, MI 49270
ANDERSON, ANDY SCOTTYE, 143 DALEVIEW CR, RUSSELLVILE, KY 42276, (502) 726-800
ANDREWS, ANDY & LANELL 3935 LANDSDOWN PL, LAS VEGAS 89121
ARCHY, CHARLES J, 1013 E HIGH ST, MT PLEASANT, MI 48858
BALDWIN, CHUCK & PEGGY, 408 TERRACE CR, LAMESA, TX 79331, (806) 872 8070
BAMBURG, H E "BAM" & PEGGY, 1415 ROBIN DR, SHERMAN, TX 75092, (903) 893-0203
BARNISKI, RAYMOND, RT #1, BOX 25, OMAHA, AK 72662
BARNARD, CONWAY, P.O. BOX 721, LOVINGTON, NM 88260
BENNER, WILLIAM & GRACE, 3602 JOHN COURT, ANNADALE, VA 22003
BEVANS, DOUG & BETTY, 3049 EBANO DR, WALNUT CREEK, CA 94590 (510) 934-5317
BLACK, LEO & STELLA, 2438 NEWPORT AVE, OMAHA, NE 68112, (402) 455-7781
BLUMBERG, BEN & JANE, 309 SPAULDING CT, FRANKLIN, TN 37064, (615) 646-2747
BOLAND, J R, RT #4 BOX 102, BLAIRSVILLE, GA 30512
BRIENT, CHARLES H, 9306 NONA KAY DR, SAN ANTONIO, TX 78217 (210) 824-7678
BROHM, RICHARD E, 4044 CRAWFORD LANE, LOUISVILLE, KY 40218
BROOKS, GEO-ROGDELL, 4710 MARIGOLD, LOUISVILLE, KY 40213 (502) 969-7512
CLOUD, BILL, 4725 MIDLANE DRIVE, HILLIARD, OH 46401, (614) 444-1191
COHEN, JACK & IVA, 1612 BROADWAY, GARY, IN 46407, (219) 885-4030
DARNLEY, JIM & ANN, P O BOX 513, ALTOONA, FL 32702, (904) 669-5500
DAVIS, JR PATRICK W, 6713 WOLKE COURT, MONTGOMERY, AL 36116
DELANEY, WM & BETTY, 537 CRESS CREEK CT, CRYSTAL LAKE, IL 60014, (815) 455-9543
DIXON, JACK & MAXINE, 103 SIR ARTHUR DR, LAS VEGAS, NV 89110, (702) 452-2054
DOBRICK, TED & LORRAINE, W5963 CO A, ELKHORN, WI 53121, (314) 475-7476
DRIEFKE, DON & BETTY, 2920 MARBLE SPR, BARNHART, MD 63012, 314-475-7478
ERICSON, ELDON & BETTY, 1460 SUNSET RD, RIO RANCHO, NM 87124, (505) 892-9321
EVERSOLE, GORDON, W 4714 E 28TH ST, KANSAS CITY, MO 64177
EYLER, KEN, 2301 S DIVISADERO ST, VISALIA, CA 93277
FIUMARA, AL-MILLIE, 756 SOMERVILLE DR, PITTSBURGH, PA 15243 (412) 279-1905
FOLEY, F M-MARGARET, 29 MEADOW-GLENN RD, NORTHPORT, NY 11768, (516) 269-9454
FRAHLMAN, D P & SUE, 4217 PARK LANE, DECATUR, IL 62521, (217) 423-2014
FRANKLIN, D R & GRACE, 410 MAGNOLIA DR, YUMA, AZ 85354 (520) 342-3173
FRIEND, WILLIE F, 3032 CORONA, ENGLEWOOD, CO 80110 (303) 761-2096
GAILER, FRANK & M, 7 DARTFORD LANE, SAN ANTONIO, TX 78257, (210) 698-0475
GAUNT, WILLIAM & DOROTHY, 10112 TULIP ST, PINELLAS PARK, FL 34666
GEDRITES, FRANK & MARGARET, 7570 ANGLERS LA, DAYTON, OH 45414 (513) 890-9756
GOOD, DON & MARGARET, 2292 S SHERMAN ST, DENVER, CO 80210 (303) 744-7390
HARTMAN, WILLIAM, ATHENS, WI 54411
HEIN, WILLIAM, P O BOX 58, ALTAMOUNT, IL 62411, (618) 483-5871
HESS, ERNEST & IRENE, 1116 CHESLEY DR, LOUISVILLE, KY 40219, (502) 969-6189
HIGHSMITH, AUBREY, 6946 HOVENKAMP, FT WORTH, TX 76114
HOECK, WAYNE & JOANN, 1013 SW 17TH ST, WILLMAR, MN 56201, (612) 235-0770
HOLEKAMP, JIM & E, 3310 VILLAGE FALLS CT, KINGSWOOD, TX 7739 (713) 359-3885
HUFF, ENICE & EDNA, 1614 FIELD DRIVE, ENID, OK 73703, (405) 237-5199
HUGHES, BEN- MARJORIE, 945 RIDGE RD, HOMEWOOD, IL 60430
JOHNSON, ELLA-RANDY, 207 CUMBERLAND RD, WAXAHACHIE TX 75165, (214) 937-1855 KLINE, TED & MILLIE, 5153 SYCAMORE RD, CHEYNNE, WY 82001, (307) 638-6164
LaFOUNTAIN, JOHN-GRETA, 200 TOMAHAWK TR, MICH CITY, IN 46360, (219)-874-6359 LARSON, HAROLD, 650 W McARTHUR, EAU CLAIRE, WI 54701
MAGUSSON, M & EDITH, 1305 E 54TH ST, SIOUX FALLS SD 57103 (605) 334-6662
MARSHALL, PHIL & LINDA, 1209 NEWPORT AVE, AUSTIN, TX 78753 (512) 836-3094
MARTIN, JIM & VI, 524 BLACKROCK RD RR3, COVENTRY, RI 02816 (401) 821-2510

McELROY, JOSHUA-MILDRED, 3520 NEW ERA Dd, MUSCATINE, IA 52761 (319) 263-1876
MINGUCCI, AL-DOROTHY, 106 W 26111 ST, SHIP BOTTOM, NJ 00006, (609) 494-3973
MONTGOMERY, RALPH-BETTY, 76911 ASCALON, PALM DESERT, CA 92211, (619) 360-1753
MOORE, JR JOHN- FLORENCE, RT #8 BOX 170, FAYETTEVILLE, TN 37334, (615) 433-4180
NALLIA, BOB-JEAN, 120 DESERT ROSE DR, HENDERSON, NV 89015, (705) 564-1460
PATER, ROLAND-EVELYN, 2909 GLENDALE, RACINE, WI 53403, (414) 554-1757
PAVILONIS, AL-FRANCIS, 9184 PARAGON WY, BOYNTON BCH, FL 33437, (407) 364-5526
POULIOT, ALPERT S, 102 SUN RIDGE WAY, REDLANDS, CA 92373, (714) 793-5780
QUEEN, CHARLES & TINA, 2101 EXPOSITION BLVD, AUSTIN, TX 78703 (512) 473-2392
REYMAN, SWEDE & ALLEN E, 4420 E OSBORNE RD, PHOENIX, AZ 85018 (602) 840-1661
ROBASON, RUBY, 106 JUNIPER ST, MANSFIELD, TX 76063, (917) 473-4579
RUEHLEN, LANE & MARY, 3011 ARNOLD AVE, TOPEKA, KS 66614 (913) 273-0343
RUSK, BOB & ADELA, 1002 S JUNCTION AVE, MONTROSE, CO 81401, ( ) 249-4393
SCHIERHORST, AL & PAT, 2401 LAUDER DR, MAITLAND, FL 32751, (407) 629-6438
SCOTT, LLOYD P O BOX 634, HARRAH, OK 73045-0634, (405) 391-2404
SEALE, JON & LUCY, N-41 McKINLEY/PARKVILLE, GUAYNABO, PR 00969 (809) 789-248
SHAUGHNESSY, J & DELORES, 1230 HILLCREST DR, FREEPORT, IL 61032, (815) 235-3845
SHEARER, CLIFTON & JOANN, RT #5 VILLAGE RD, PITTSBURG, TX 75686
SHORT, JIM-MATHILDE, 5205 SADDLE RIDGE TR, SAN ANTONIO, TX 76904, (915) 949-5676
SHUMAKER, BOB & FRAN, 2319 BRANDONN RD, COLUMBUS, OH 43221, 614-486-9028
SLAUGHTER, E M & MARTHA, P O BOX 752, LAMAR, SC 29069, (803) 326-5810
SYNWOLT, RICHARD, RT 01 BOX 65, NORMANGEE, TX 77871, (409) 396-6036
THOMAS, BOB & NADINE, 12189 ROBERT GLN, SAN ANTONIO, TX 70252, (210) 622-9732
TOUPS, HERMAN & IVA, 506 CALVIN ST, LUFKIN, TX 75901, (409) 634-5385
UHLMAN, BILL & JEAN, P O BOX 236, EATONVILLE, WA 90329, (206) 832-6206
VAN CLEVE, CALVAN, RT #1 BOX 216, ROCKDALE, TX 76567
VOEGTLIN, RAY, 720 N 17 DR, STURGEON BAY, WI 54235, (414) 746-0326
WALL, ED & LILLIAN, 14311 SKYFROST #30, DALLES, TX 75253, (214) 557-7929
WASHBURN, FRANK, 800 CORTEZ LANE, FOSTER, CA 94404, (415) 349-6853
WATKINS, JACK & TONI, 1200 PENN, BIG SPRING, TX 79720, (915) 263-2558
WERTS, DEAN & RUTH, RT #1 BOX 126, RUSELLI, IA 50238, (515) 535-4923
WILKERSON, NATHAN, 15203 W US HWY 160, ASH GROVE, MD 65604, (417) 672-2773
WILSON, CHESTER & WILMA, RT #1 BOX 635, CHETOPA, KS 67336, (316) 236-7486
WORRELL, RONALD & BARBARA, 419 S FOURTH ST, DEKALB, IL 68115, (815) 756-6582
WORTHLEY, DON & BETTY, 625 HIGHLAND DR, MONTESANO, WA 98563, 249-3250
WRIGHT, JR PHIL- JOAN, 1011 RIVER DR 101, LIVINGSTON, MT 59047, 406-22-3597

"A cigarette? Doggone it, I've almost forgotten what smoke looks like!"

THIS PAGE IS UNCLASSIFIED

MONTHLY AIRCRAFT STATUS REPORT

WAR DEPARTMENT
AAF FORM NO. 111A
TENTATIVE 11-4-42

(This ...et to be detached before writing and used a... work sheet)

Page 1 of 3 Pages

Air Force or Air Service Area: 2nd Air Force
Command: 72nd Fighter Wing
Group: 262nd CCTS (F)
Squadron: _____

Detachment: _____
Depot, Subdepot, or Modification Center: _____
Station Name: Bruning AAF, Nebraska
Date of Report: 15 June 1944

TYPE, MODEL, AND SERIES	ARMY AIR FORCES SERIAL NUMBER	FLYABLE OPERATIONAL	FLYABLE NOT OPERATIONAL	GROUNDED MAINTENANCE OR REPAIR	GROUNDED MODIFICATION	GROUNDED AWAITING PARTS	GROUNDED OTHER REASONS	MAJOR USE (See Code)	ENTER "A" IF AIRCRAFT IS ACCEPTED BUT AWAITING FACTORY DELIVERY	COLUMN FOR USE OF AIR FORCE OR COMMAND (NOT REQUIRED BY HQ. A.A.F.)
A	B	C	D	E	F	G	H	I	J	K
B-24D	42-40336			123				P		
RB-24E	42-7167			113				P		
RB-24E	42-7295			106				P		
RB-24E	42-7346	X						P		
RB-24E	42-7407			112				P		
AT-23A	41-18097				10			Q		
P-47D	42-8022	X						E		
P-47D	42-8036			1				E		
P-47D	42-8044			1				E		
P-47D	42-22399					22		E		
P-47D	42-22400	X						E		
P-47D	42-22571	X						E		
P-47D	42-22572			2				E		
P-47D	42-22575	X						E		
P-47D	42-22577			51				E		
P-47D	42-22579	X						E		
P-47D	42-22581	X						E		
P-47D	42-22585	X						E		
P-47D	42-22999	X						E		
P-47D	42-23001	X						E		
P-47D	42-23002	X						E		
P-47D	42-23003	X						E		
P-47D	42-23004	X						E		
P-47D	42-23007	X						E		
P-47D	42-23008	X						E		
P-47D	42-23009	X						E		
P-47D	42-23010	X						E		
P-47D	42-23012	X						E		
P-47D	42-23013	X						E		
P-47D	42-23015	X						E		

CODE FOR MAJOR USE—Column 1:

(A) Flying School Training
(B) Technical School Training
(C) Transition Flying Training
(D) Operational Training Unit
(E) Replacement Combat Crew Training
(F) Anti-submarine Duty
(G) Hemisphere Defense Other Than Anti-submarine Duty
(H) Cargo Transport
(I) Troop Carrier
(J) Passenger Transport
(K) Being Ferried
(L) Individual Flying
(M) Towing Targets
(N) Experimental Use
(O) Service Testing
(P) Held for Repair; Maintenance; or Awaiting Parts for Repair
(Q) Held for Modification
(R) Held for Completion
(S) Other Uses (explain in footnote)

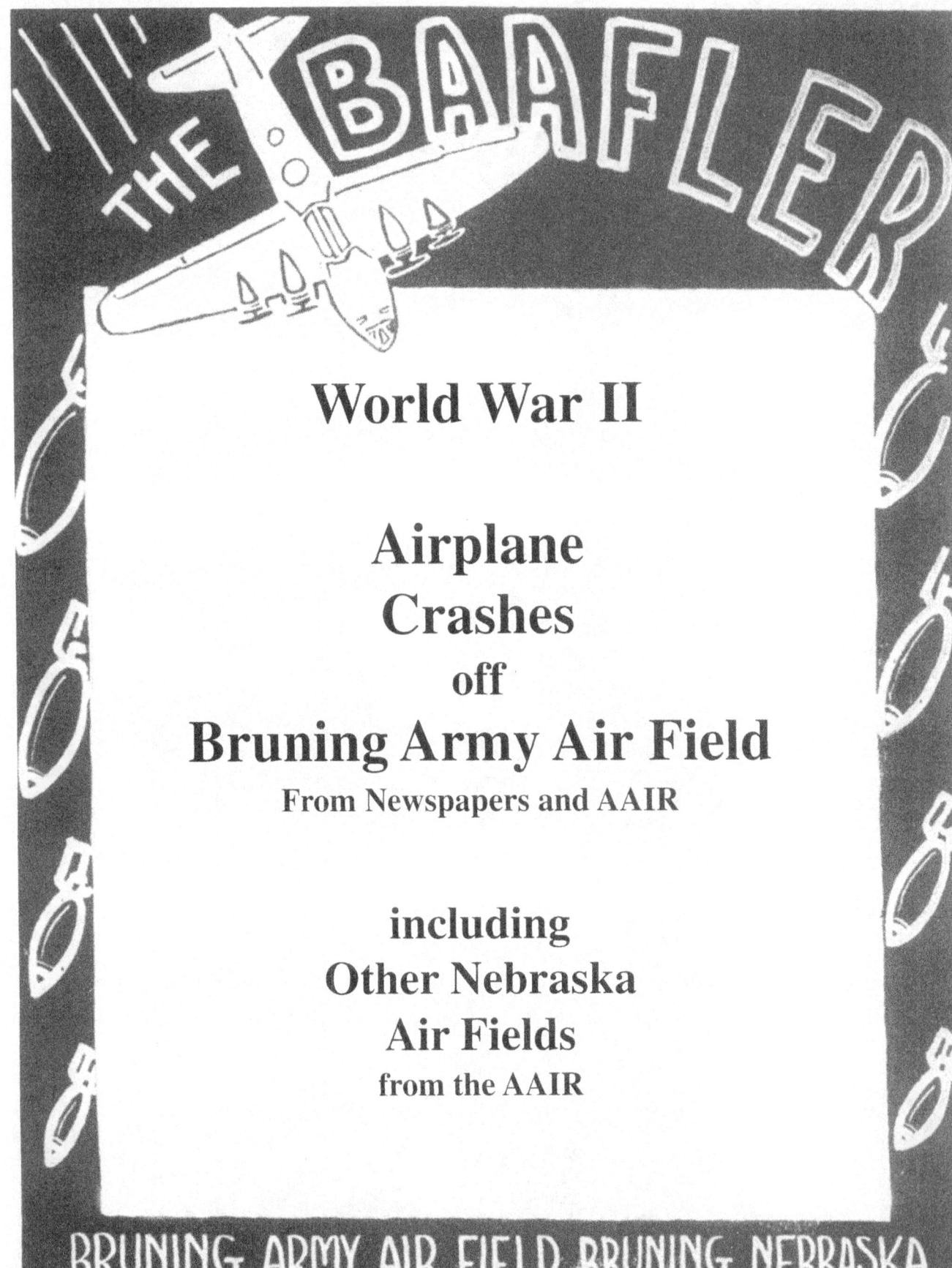

Bruning Army Air Field Accidents

P-47 and B-17 Collision

A plane crash, with eight fatalities, occurred in the Bruning Army Air Field area on 12 July 1944. A formation of B-17s from the Sioux City, Iowa AAB were to fly into the Bruning area and the P-47 fighter group from the Bruning AAF were to practice attacking the B-17 -- a combined training interception. The crash occurred 2 miles southeast of Daykin, NE. at 0848 CWT.

In the official U. S. Army Report of Aircraft Accidents the nature of the accident was a collision in full flight. The cause of the accident is given as 100 percent pilot error as the "Pilot (of the P-47) did not 'break-off' soon enough and collided with the B-17." However, the pilot had been experiencing plane malfunction up until that time.

The name of the P-47 pilot was 2nd Lt. Charles F. Jewett, C-763214 of the 262nd FPTS Sq. 1 from Bruning AAF. As he made no attempt to bail out, it was concluded he was knocked unconscious on the initial hit. His plane was a P47D-11RA, serial number 42-23008.

According to Lt. Charles. H. Hughes, who was in the second flight of the P-47 formation, Lt. Jewett called the leader of the P-47 formation and said he was having supercharger trouble and could not control it and so he dropped back.

Later he radioed that he thought the supercharger was working again and he would rejoin the formation. According to Lt. Hughes, Jewett made an attack, which was almost head-on, but misjudged his distance. Lt. Hughes wrote, "Although the element leader wasn't making a head-on attack, the bombers made a turn into the attacking element and Lt. Jewett being behind and out of position was pulled into a head on attack. According to Hughes, Lt. Jewett made a quarter roll when his wing hit the bomber wing and sheered a wing off both the bomber, and the fighter plane. The bomber rolled over and then went into a flat spin. At about 6 or 7 thousand feet the bomber disintegrated into pieces.

The pilot of the B-17F was Lt. Jack C. Schmidt, 0-729913, who was flying plane No. 42-30944 from the Sioux City AAB at Sioux City, IA of the 2nd AF 224 th CCTS Section 11. Lt. Schmidt was also killed.

The Copilot was Lt. Wallace E. R. Clements, 0-82415610, and although the plane was pointing straight down, he was able to get his chute on and went out the nose hatch. He dislocated his left ankle, dislocated his back, and received a laceration above the left eye.

Cpl. Leonard J. Rizzuti, 19199801, in the tail of the B-17, got his chute on despite the spinning of the plane and jumped to safety with no injury.

Cpl. Salvador V. Halcon, 39133418, the waist gunner, was thrown to the floor by the ammunition boxes, which fell on top of him. He freed himself, got his chute and went out where the plane had split in half with no injuries.

The seven men in who B-17 who were killed were:
Lt. Jack C. Schmidt -- 0-79923, the pilot on the B-17
Lt. Frank A. Remke - 0-723 745, the navigator on the B-17
Lt. Joseph Silverstein -- 0-772752, the bombardier on the B-17
Cpl. Frank E. Weddell 15335587, the engineer on the B-17
Cpl. Frank Cassanova 16116134, the radio operator on the B-17
T/St Charles L. Strickland -- 18063455, gunner on the B-17
Pfc. Edward D. Wieland -- 35067897, gunner on the B-17

Damage to Property reports were taken by Lt. Robert W. Rogers from the farmers on whose farms the wreckage fell. Gustav Drees of Daykin received $10 for damage to water tank and $5.00 for damage to corn crop when the P-47 crashed on his farm. Karl Sheele of Powell, NE, asked for no damage; Lawrence Schmidt of Powell, asked for $50.

262ND FIGHTER PILOT TRAINING STATION
SQUADRON I
BRUNING ARMY AIR FIELD

Bruning, Nebraska,
12 July 1944.

SUBJECT: Aircraft Accident.

TO: All concerned.

When the formation took off, Lt. Jewett was in the first flight, and my position was in the second. While climbing to altitude I heard Lt. Jewett call the leader and say he was having supercharger trouble and couldn't control it and at the same time I saw him drop back. After a while he called and said he was rejoining the formation. I did not see him again until we were in position on the bombers and the other flight began their pass. Lt. Jewett was behind his element leader when his flight began their pass. I looked up to my element leader and then back at the bombers just in time to see Lt. Jewett hit. It looked like he had done a quarter roll when his wing hit the bomber's wing and shearing a wing off the bomber, and the fighter plane. I didn't see Lt. Jewett again after that, but observed the bomber rolling over and then go into a flat spin. At about six or seven thousand the bomber disintergrated into pieces. From the way Lt. Jewett hit the bomber he was making an attack that was almost head on and misjudged his distance. Although the element leader wasn't making a head on attack the bombers made a turn into the attacking element and Lt. Jewett being behind and out of position was pulled into a head on attack.

CHARLES H. HUGHES,
2nd Lt., Air Corps,
Trainee Pilot.

Editor's note: Charles Hughes married Virginia McKenzie, well known music teacher in Thayer County. He was assigned to the 86th Squadron of the 79th Fighter Group. They fought on the "Forgotten Mediterranean Front" making the advance in Northern Italy. The 79th had only minimal support and materials as they fought over the Pennines Mountains overlooking the Po Valley. Making 52 missions, Hughes was one of only three left in his group, according to his wife. He was highly decorated. His daughter, Betty Edzards of Bruning, NE said she knew nothing of her late father's military career as it was always considered to be "too painful to talk about".

We are searching for more information at this time on how many men from Bruning were in the 79th Fighter Group. Perhaps there were on other survivors.

Plane Crashes --WWII

STATEMENT OF CREW MEMBER (B-17)

Bruning, Nebraska
12 July 1944

I was in the tail when the P47 hit us. I saw a flash and the ship rocked violently. The plane started to spin and I started to go back to the escape hatch. I had trouble getting there because the plane was in a spin and was forcing me further to the rear. I put on my chute and jumped out, waited a brief moment before pulling the rip chord. When the chute opened I was close to the ground for I had only a quick look around before I hit the ground. While I was coming down I noticed the ship in two parts and the copilot and armor gunner had parachuted safely. The main fuselage came quite close to the co-pilot. I couldn't say for sure whether it hit him or not.

/s/ Leonard J. Rizzuti,
LEONARD J. RIZZUTI

Bruning, Nebraska
12 July 1944

I was in the left waist. Suddenly I was thrown to the floor by the crash. It happened so fast I didn't know what happened. The plane began jumping then, and I tried reaching for my chute. But the force of gravity was too great. I was thrown against the ammunition boxes; they fell on top of me. I finally freed myself. The plane seemed to level off for a second, and I clamped my chute on which was beside me. I walked towards the part where the plane was split in half in front of the tail turret and managed to jump clear.

/s/ Salvador V. Halcon
SALVADOR V. HALCON

STATEMENT OF CREW MEMBER (B-17)

I was in Co Pilot seat when P47 came in for attack. He was making a head on attack from above. He hit the outboard panel of the right wing. The plane flipped over and went into a spin. The plane spun three or four times and I then felt a very severe jolt, it threw the Pilot and myself against the windshield of the plane. It was then that the plane must have broken in two. It was very hard for me to get out of my seat. the plane was pointing straight down. I finally got my chute, which was under the seat, and went out the nose hatch.

/s/ Wallace E. R. Clements
WALLACE E. R. CLEMENTS
2nd Lt., A.C.

P-47 and B-17 Collision (continued)
12 July 1944
Debris falling near Daykin and Powell, NE

Bruning AAF plane crashes

Lt. Thomas L. Clark

Vernida (now Messing) and Jeanne (now Kerwood) Michel's were playing upstairs and their mother was hanging up clothes on the clothes line. Suddenly a P-47 crashed in their yard. Mrs. Michels rushed upstairs to get the girls and then ran to get their father who was in the field working. He had seen the crash and thought it had hit their house. The Michels did not have a telephone at that time.

Later Lt. Clark's father wrote to the Michels asking them to tell how bad their son was injured. This is Mrs. Michels hand written reply:

Powell, Nebr.
Oct. 4, 1944

T. L Clark
Sunburst, Mont.

Dear Sir:
   In reply to your letter of Sept 10 asking how bad the face and body were crushed, of your son. One leg and one arm were blown off from the explosion near by. The top part of his head was torn off and his jaw was crushed but his nose was still on. I left as soon as we had the fire put out on his body as the plane was burning quite badly. The Ambulance came soon and we were not allowed to be near after that.

I don't suppose it would of been so bad if it hadn't exploded as he had 275 or more gallons of gasoline in the plane. I don't suppose you will ever receive the billfold as the commanding officer said they would not send it, but you would receive the money and any valuable papers that were in it. It was pretty burnt too.

Sorry to tell you how bad it was, We felt badly too as the plane crashed near our house. We consider ourselves lucky. He was headed north and the wind was from the south. Had it been the opposite no doubt all the buildings would of burned.

It is understood you are a doctor so you no doubt would be able to take more than some of the rest of us.

We hope this war will be over soon, and after that, we might be able to see each other sometime.

Mrs Walter Michels. (Dorothy)

Bruning Air Plane Crashes

Lt. John Wagner

According to the Official Aviation Report of Aircraft Accidents, Lt. John Wagner was killed Aug. 9, 1944 "when he made a 'wingover' after which he dove straight down at about a 70 degree angle into the ground where ship crashed and burned."

In the Official Report there are statements from these witnesses who all testified that the plane went straight down with the motor roaring.:

Glen Birky, Shickley, NE
Ray Kennel and Edward Kennel
Henry Chris Waterman

DESCRIPTION OF ACCIDENT

(Brief narrative of accident. Include statement of responsibility and recommendations for action to prevent repetition)

An aircraft accident involving P47D-11RA, 42-23044, piloted by John A. Wagner, Jr., 2nd Lt., AC, occured three (3) miles East of Shickley, Nebraska on 9 August 1944. The pilot was killed.

Investigation and evidence shows that the pilot (Lt. Wagner) called to the ship with him before starting a descent from approximately 19,000 feet. According to statement of pilot who was with him, Lt. Wagner sounded perfectly normal. Lt. Wagner's ship started a normal descent with a speed estimated to be between 300 to 350 miles per hour, and in a dive estimated at approximately 45° to 60° angle. The plane following Lt. Wagner's ship pulled away and lost sight of it at about 9,000 feet. He then looked for Lt. Wagner's plane in question and saw a small fire.

Evidence from the crash shows the plane dove into the ground at a 60° angle or higher angle at high speed under full power. Possible cause of the accident would be the pilot cutting the throttle clear back at low altitude, causing him to lose control of aircraft. There is also the possibility the pilot may have lost consciousness from unknown cause, and also the possibility of locked control from unknown cause.

The engineering officer terms the aircraft a complete loss and recommends it for survey.

Since no definite facts and evidence are available as to the exact cause of the accident, the aircraft accident committee finds the cause and responsibility for the accident as undetermined.

The accident is Group I.

Signature _____
RICHARD E. HOLCOMBE, Major AC
_____
RICHARD H. REATY, Captain AC
_____
JOHN W. ALLISON JR., Lt. AC

Date August 12, 1944

Letter written to parents on Aug. 6, 1944. He was killed Aug. 9.

BRUNING OFFICERS' CLUB ... ARMY AIR BASE
BRUNING, NEBR.

Sunday eve.

Dear Folks,

Just down after flying most all this afternoon in the World's fastest and best fighter plane, the THUNDERBOLT P-47. Yours truly can now be classed as a Thunderbolt pilot which in the Air Forces is about the highest honor. I flew it for the first time just this last week and during that first flight found it is the sweetest thing in the air. With a top speed of well over 400 miles per hr. it is able to climb at the unbelieveable rate of 4,500 ft per min. Its biggest thrill is landing as we set her down on the runway at 150 miles per hour and that's really travelling on the ground. Besides this, all I've been telling you, it has the best combat record and is the safest fighter plane in combat by recently released government figures.

But all this is not from what I've read because I have flew it and seen for myself and also find it is not even hard to fly. Yesterday Major Johnson an ace P-47 pilot who has just returned from Europe talked to us about his experiences in combat. Ralph will probably know about him as he is the Major Johnson who has 27 aerial victories and considered one of the leading aces of the war. From what he has been through in the Thunderbolt it is almost impossible to be shot down and it can out climb, out speed, out shoot, out dive, and turn inside any other plane allied or enemy. Talking about shooting it has 8 fifty cal. guns, four in each wing, that will blow any thing to pieces. Then as for taking punishment it is well protected by a more plate which makes it so safe. Well this a lot of letter to brag to you about my plane but I want you all to know all about it. I was up cruising around this afternoon, up by Omaha, Lincoln, Kansas City etc. and all of these big cities are one hundred to two hundred miles from our field and I could fly to any one of them from here in a matter of a few minutes. Yes it is a long jump from the little P-19 Fairchild you saw me fly at Sikeston to the 2,000+ (military secret) horse power ship I'm now flying.

Well I didn't have much to write about so I thought all this might interest you. I couldn't be happier as I am doing just what I have been working for for the last two years. Will sure be glad to see Daddy Thursday and will have a nice visit I know. Will write you all about it. I really enjoy your letters and hope this finds you all well and as happy as I am.

All my love,
John

P.S.- Pardon my awful writing

HEADQUARTERS
Bruning Army Air Field
Office of the Summary Court Officer
Bruning, Nebraska

September 11, 1944

Mr. John A. Wagner, Sr.
c/o Mrs. Dora Weir
52 County Line Road
Westerville, Ohio

Dear Mr. Wagner:

    The death of your late son came to me as a great shock and to all of his comrades. The end came suddenly and without suffering. The Commanding Officer of this Base has appointed me to take charge of all of his personal effects. I have received from the Commanding Officer of his squadron all of his personal effects and those that he had at the time of his death were forwarded to me by the Intelligence Officer at the Sioux City Army Air Base. A Special Order from this Headquarters was issued requesting all persons who had any claims against or property belonging to him to get in touch with me. I have paid all outstanding claims and have turned over a check to the General Supply Officer of this Base who should forward the same to you within the next few days. There is attached a list of the articles shipped and money forwarded and after you have checked them, I would like you to sign at the bottom of each page and return the list to me as a receipt so that I can render a proper report of my doings to the Commanding Officer. I have included a copy of the list with the articles shipped to you.

    If there is any difficulty concerning the 6 months' additional pay payable on death of an officer, please feel free to get in touch with me at any time. The Personal Affairs Officer of this Base, Captain Tatnall, is also willing to do anything he can in his power to straighten out either of these two matters.

    May I express my own personal sympathy in your loss. The entire Base at this Field grieves with you and yours. If you are in doubt or wish any explanation about anything concerning the effects or your legal rights, please feel free to call upon me for any additional information you may desire.

    Sincerely yours,

    JOSEPH O. ROCHELEAU
    1st Lt., Air Corps
    Summary Court Officer

JOR/bej
Incl: 1-List of articles shipped.

Those Who Flew
Bruning Army Air field
Alexandria Argus --Sept 7, 1944 (page 365 Bruning AAf History)
20 Year Old P-47 Instructor Dismissed

Dear Mrs. Priefert:

I just received a book from Dewain Erickson entitled "Bruning Army Air Field History" and I have briefly gone through all of its pages. I am the individual mentioned on page 365, that then 2nd Lt. Alvin J. Luongo. Having been a part of the Bruning story I will herein relate my personal part in Bruning Army Air Field.

The 407th trained at Galveston fully expecting to move, as a Group to some overseas assignment. As I then understood it, the policy was changed and it was decided that enough Groups were in place and only replacement pilots would now be sent. The 407th was disbanded and since we had more P-47 time than any others then in the States we were divided into two groups to form two Fighter Pilot Training Schools. Half went to Pocatello, Idaho and my half went to Bruning.

My log book indicates that I flew a P-47 to Bruning on 3-8-44. 1 had an orientation flight on 3-9-44 and my first flight as an instructor on 3/10. I was in the yellow nose squadron, Flight C, and 1st Lt. Ben H. Nicholls was the CO. A pilot named Trumbower was assistant and when he left about 2 Months later I was assigned as assistant to Nicholls. John Hallmark was our Squadron CO. Major Holcombe was the School C/O. Col. McAllister was the Base CO but had absolutely nothing to do with the School or its operations.

July 15, 1944 was my final flight in the P-47. I led a flight of 3 planes and during the flight I buzzed the City of Beatrice.

During the low passes over the City .I came near the County Court House and the Sheriff or someone near him read the numbers on the planes of my two students. This information was relayed to Bruning and McAllister ordered all planes to be recalled. I was too low and 40 miles away to receive this recall so that when I returned to the base our flight was the last to land. Ben Nicholls met me on the flight line and we immediately reported to McAllister. He informed me and the two students that we were grounded, restricted to the base and that he was recommending the 3 of us for Courts-martial. I reminded McAllister that the two students were obliged to follow me and he said that would not be for him to decide. As it turned out, I was court-martialled and the two students were compelled to testify against me. The Courts-Martial was short and sweet, the board found me guilty and I was sentenced to "dismissal from the service and forfeiture of all pay due or to become due". To be final, the Courts-Martial had to go through all channels and be reviewed and thus I received pay as well as my promotion to 1st Lt. My approved dismissal never came through until 12-23-44. Once again a civilian I was required to register for the draft and the following May of '45 I was again in the army as a buck private in the infantry. My military career ended early in 1946.

Alvin J. ("Lu") Luongo

340 Oak Center Place,
Valdosta, GA 31602
7 Dec. 2000

Those Who Flew
Bruning Army Air Field

List of plane crashes off Bruning Field

	Home Base	Pilot's Name	Plane	Mishap location
1	Bruning AAF	Dobony, John --Buffalo, NY	P47D	2 1/2 mi NE Ohiowa
2	Bruning AAF	Jaeger, William D. -- Skokie IL	Trainer	2 1/2 Mi. NE Ohiowa
3	Bruning AAF	Mrenak, Frank M. --McDonough, PA	trainer	2 1/2 mi. NE Ohiowa
4	Bruning AAF	Mastin, I Richard	CAP	near Bruning
5	Bruning AAF	Miles, Albert E.	P-47D	Witchita, KS
6	Bruning AAF	Hurd, Edgar W.	P-47D	Bruning, NE
7	Bruning AAF	Brace, John L.	P-47D	Bruning, NE
8	Bruning AAF	Thomas J. Mc Daniel -- DC	auto	on Base - 449th HB
9	Bruning AAF	Dulgarian, Dick G.	P-47D	Bruning, NE
10	Bruning AAF	Steiner, Joseph R.	P-47D	Bruning, NE
11	Bruning AAF	Harriman, Donald M.	P-47D	near Bruning
12	Bruning AAF	Leoni, Albert G.-- Cincinnati, OH	P-47D	on the Bruning Field
13	Bruning AAF	Robbins, George F. -- Erie, PA.	P-47D	East of Cordova, NE
14	Bruning AAF	Maxson, James L.	P-47D	Bruning, NE
15	Bruning AAF	Bennet, Doewin J.	P-47D	Bruning, NE
16	Bruning AAF	Hildebrand, John R.	P-47D	Bruning, NE
17	Bruning AAF	Williams, Thomas A.	P-47D	Bruning, NE
18	Bruning AAF	McCarthy, John T.	P-47D	Bruning, NE
19	Bruning AAF	Washburn, William F.	B17G	Bruning, NE
20	Bruning AAF	Trumbower, Frederick W.	P-47D	Bruning AAF
21	Bruning AAF	Smith, Levi W.	P-47D	Bruning AAF
22	Bruning AAF	Brethen, Richard H.	P-47D	Irving, Kansas
23	Bruning AAF	Cox, Richard C.	P-47D	Herkimer, KS
24	Bruning AAF	Thurston, William A.	P-47D	9 mi SW Tecumseh, NE
25	Bruning AAF	Mercer, Roger N.	P-47D	AAB Alamogordo NM
26	Bruning AAF	Trumbower, Frederick W.	P-47D	Bruning AAF
27	Bruning AAF	Giles, Ralph E.	P-47B	Brock, NE
28	Bruning AAF	Lee, Wayne B.	P-47D	Bruning AAF
29	Bruning AAF	Peschken, Stanley	P-47G	code 96-169 (Bruning)
30	Bruning AAF	Ramirez, Lose	P-47D	code 96-169 (Bruning)
31	Bruning AAF	Hearn, William D.	P-47D	code 76-119
32	Bruning AAF	Peterson, Don M.	P-47G	code 96-169 (Bruning)

Those Who Flew
Bruning Army Air Field

List of plane crashes off Bruning Field
(continued)

	Home Base	Pilot's Name	Plane	Mishap location
33	Bruning AAF	Boutwell, William C	P-47D	code 96-169 (Bruning)
34	Sioux City, IA	Charles L. Strickland--gunner	B-17F	2 1/2 mi. E of Daykin, NE
35	Sioux City, IA	Wieland, Edward D. --gunner	B-17F	2 1/2 mi. E of Daykin, NE
36	Sioux City, IA	Frank A. Remke --navigator	B-17F	2 1/2 mi. E of Daykin, NE
37	Sioux City, IA	Cassanova, Frank --radio operator	B-17F	2 1/2 mi. E of Daykin, NE
38	Sioux City, IA	Weddell, Frank E. -- engineer	B-17F	2 1/2 mi. E of Daykin, NE
39	Bruning AAF	Jewett, Charles F.	P-47D	2 1/2 mi. E of Daykin, NE
40	Bruning AAF	Jolley, Clayton R. Selma, CA	P-47D	cornfield near Bruning
41	Sioux City, IA	Joseph Silverstein--bombardier	B-17F	2 1/2 mi. E of Daykin, NE
42	Sioux City, IA	Leonard J. Rizzuti -- tail gunner	B-17F	2 1/2 mi. E of Daykin, NE
43	Sioux City, IA	Halcon, Salvador V--waist gunner	B-17F	2 1/2 mi. E of Daykin, NE
44	Sioux City, IA	Schmidt, Jack C.--Pilot	B-17F	2 1/2 mi. E of Daykin, NE
45	Sioux City, IA	Clements, Wallace --Co-pilot	B-17F	2 1/2 mi. E of Daykin, NE
46	Bruning AAF	Gehr, Richard O.	P-47D	Bruning, NE
47	Bruning AAF	Knight, Charles E.	P-47D	Bruning, NE
48	Bruning AAF	Erichson, George E.	P-47D	between Daykin & Powell NE
49	Bruning AAF	Keller, Gerald C.	P-47G	Air Force code 76-151
50	Bruning AAF	Clark, Thomas L.-- Sunburst, MT	P-47D	Powell or 4 mi E of Alex
51	Bruning AAF	Acree, Thomas buried in Fairbury, NE	C-47	6 miles SW of Naper, NE
52	Bruning AAF	Albert, John F -- Chicago, IL	C-47	6 miles SW of Naper, NE
53	Bruning AAF	Armstrong, William C.-- Nashville MD	C-47	6 miles SW of Naper, NE
54	Bruning AAF	Arnett, Willard F. Jr-- West Virginia	C-47	6 miles SW of Naper, NE
55	Bruning AAF	Blakeslee, Herbert, A. --Eddyville, NE	C-47	6 miles SW of Naper, NE
56	Bruning AAF	Boechman, George E.--Charlotte, N.C.	C-47	6 miles SW of Naper, NE
57	Bruning AAF	Bohle, Robert K Co Pilot --Chicago, IL	C-47	6 miles SW of Naper, NE
58	Bruning AAF	Brown, Jack L. --	C-47	6 miles SW of Naper, NE
59	Bruning AAF	Brown, Richard E.	C-47	6 miles SW of Naper, NE
60	Bruning AAF	Burke, James C. Jr --Norfolk, Mass.	C-47	6 miles SW of Naper, NE
61	Bruning AAF	Clarkson, Donald J.--Kansas, City Mo.	C-47	6 miles SW of Naper, NE
62	Bruning AAF	Hemphill, Lloyd L --Crane, Mo.	C-47	6 miles SW of Naper, NE
63	Bruning AAF	Hutslar, Orson H.	C-47	6 miles SW of Naper, NE
64	Bruning AAF	Johnson, Arthur --San Francisco. CA	C-47	6 miles SW of Naper, NE

Those Who Flew
Bruning Army Air Field

List of plane crashes off Bruning Field
(continued)

	Home Base	Pilot's Name	Plane	Mishap location
65	Bruning AAF	Jolley, Clayton R. Selma, CA	C-47	6 miles SW of Naper, NE
66	Bruning AAF	Jolley, Leonard C. Selma CA	C-47	6 miles SW of Naper, NE
67	Bruning AAF	Keller, Gerald C.	C-47	6 miles SW of Naper, NE
68	Bruning AAF	Lytle, Jack E.	C-47	6 miles SW of Naper, NE
69	Bruning AAF	Meadows, Stanley J. Sioux Rapids	C-47	6 miles SW of Naper, NE
70	Bruning AAF	Nesbitt, Robert E. Jr.	C-47	6 miles SW of Naper, NE
71	Bruning AAF	O'Malley, Bernard W. --Indiana	C-47	6 miles SW of Naper, NE
72	Bruning AAF	Paladino, Anthony J.	C-47	6 miles SW of Naper, NE
73	Bruning AAF	Patterson, Bruce S.	C-47	6 miles SW of Naper, NE
74	Bruning AAF	Pope. Lelan Alex	C-47	6 miles SW of Naper, NE
75	Bruning AAF	Porter, Charles V.--Texas	C-47	6 miles SW of Naper, NE
76	Bruning AAF	Roberts, Leslie B	C-47	6 miles SW of Naper, NE
77	Bruning AAF	Roberts, Pat N. Jr	C-47	6 miles SW of Naper, NE
78	Bruning AAF	Sehorn, LaVon	C-47	6 miles SW of Naper, NE
79	Bruning AAF	Dickey, Robert O.	P-47	cornfield 2 mi. E shickley
80	Bruning AAF	Wagner, John A. --Ohio	P-47	3 mi. E of Shickley

Chronological List of plane crashes off Bruning Field

Base	Name	Plane	Location	Status	Date
Bruning AAF	Dobony, John -- Buffalo, NY	P47D	2 1/2 mi NE Ohiowa	1st fatality	Febr. 1944
Bruning AAF	Jaeger, William D. -- Skokie IL	Trainer	2 1/2 Mi. NE Ohiowa	1st fatality	Febr. 1944
Bruning AAF	Mrenak, Frank M.-McDonough, PA	trainer	2 1/2 mi. NE Ohiowa	lived	Febr. 1944
Bruning AAF	Mastin, I Richard	CAPatrol	near Bruning	killed	Febr. 18, 1944
Bruning AAF	Miles, Albert E.	P-47D	Witchita, KS		Febr. 25, 1944
Bruning AAF	Hurd, Edgar W.	P-47D	Bruning, NE		Oct. 10, 1944
Bruning AAF	Brace, John L.	P-47D	Bruning, NE		Oct. 12, 1944
Bruning AAF	Thomas J. Mc Daniel -- DC	auto	on Base - 449th HB	killed	Oct. 12, 1944
Bruning AAF	Dulgarian, Dick G.	P-47D	Bruning, NE		Oct. 16, 1944
Bruning AAF	Steiner, Joseph R.	P-47D	Bruning, NE		Oct. 22, 1944
Bruning AAF	Harriman, Donald M.	P-47D	near Bruning		Sept. 14, 1944
Bruning AAF	Leoni, Albert G. -- Cincinnati, OH	P-47D	on the Bruning Field	killed	Sept. 14, 1944
Bruning AAF	Robbins, George F. -- Erie, PA.	P-47D	East of Cordova, NE	killed	Sept. 14, 1944
Bruning AAF	Maxson, James L.	P-47D	Bruning, NE		Sept. 16, 1944
Bruning AAF	Bennet, Doewin J.	P-47D	Bruning, NE		Sept. 22, 1944
Bruning AAF	Hildebrand, John R.	P-47D	Bruning, NE		Sept. 25, 1944
Bruning AAF	Williams, Thomas A.	P-47D	Bruning, NE		Sept. 26, 1944
Bruning AAF	McCarthy, John T.	P-47D	Bruning, NE		Sept. 9, 1944
Bruning AAF	Washburn, William F.	B17G	Bruning, NE		Sept. 8, 1944
Bruning AAF	Trumbower, Frederick W.	P-47D	Bruning AAF	lived	March 12, 1944
Bruning AAF	Smith, Levi W.	P-47D	Bruning AAF		March 12, 1944
Bruning AAF	Brethen, Richard H.	P-47D	Irving, Kansas		March 16, 1944
Bruning AAF	Cox, Richard C.	P-47D	Herkimer, KS		March 16, 1944
Bruning AAF	Thurston, William A.	P-47D	9 mi SW Tecumseh, NE		March 19, 1944
Bruning AAF	Mercer, Roger N.	P-47D	AAB Alamogordo NM		March 21, 1944
Bruning AAF	Trumbower, Frederick W.	P-47D	Bruning AAF		March 29, 1944
Bruning AAF	Giles, Ralph E.	P-47B	Brock, NE		March 30, 1944
Bruning AAF	Lee, Wayne B.	P-47D	Bruning AAF		March 30, 1944
Bruning AAF	Peschken, Stanley	P-47G	code 96-169 (Bruning)		July 07, 1944
Bruning AAF	Ramirez, Lose	P-47D	code 96-169 (Bruning)		July 04, 1944
Bruning AAF	Hearn, William D.	P-47D	code 76-119		July 05, 1944
Bruning AAF	Peterson, Don M.	P-47G	code 96-169 (Bruning)		July 07, 1944
Bruning AAF	Boutwell, William C	P-47D	code 96-169 (Bruning)		July 08, 1944

Chronological List of plane crashes off Bruning Field
(continued)

Base	Name	Plane	Location	Status	Date
Sioux City, IA	Charles L. Strickland--gunner	B-17F	2 1/2 mi. E of Daykin, NE	killed	July 12, 1944
Sioux City, IA	Wieland, Edward D. --gunner	B-17F	2 1/2 mi. E of Daykin, NE	killed	July 12, 1944
Sioux City, IA	Frank A. Remke --navigator	B-17F	2 1/2 mi. E of Daykin, NE	killed	July 12, 1944
Sioux City, IA	Cassanova, Frank --radio operator	B-17F	2 1/2 mi. E of Daykin, NE	killed	July 12, 1944
Sioux City, IA	Weddell, Frank E. -- engineer	B-17F	2 1/2 mi. E of Daykin, NE	killed	July 12, 1944
Bruning AAF	Jewett, Charles F.	P-47D	2 1/2 mi. E of Daykin, NE	killed	July 12, 1944
Bruning AAF	Jolley, Clayton R. Selma, CA	P-47D	cornfield near Bruning	lived	July 12, 1944
Sioux City, IA	Joseph Silverstein--bombardier	B-17F	2 1/2 mi. E of Daykin, NE	killed	July 12, 1944
Sioux City, IA	Leonard J. Rizzuti -- tail gunner	B-17F	2 1/2 mi. E of Daykin, NE	lived	July 12, 1944
Sioux City, IA	Halcon, Salvador V--waist gunner	B-17F	2 1/2 mi. E of Daykin, NE	lived	July 12, 1944
Sioux City, IA	Schmidt, Jack C.--Pilot	B-17F	2 1/2 mi. E of Daykin, NE	7 killed	July 12, 1944
Sioux City, IA	Clements, Wallace --Co-pilot	B-17F	2 1/2 mi. E of Daykin, NE	lived	July 12, 1944
Bruning AAF	Gehr, Richard O.	P-47D	Bruning, NE		July 14, 1944
Bruning AAF	Knight, Charles E.	P-47D	Bruning, NE		July 28, 1944
Bruning AAF	Erichson, George E.	P-47D	between Daykin & Powell NE		July 29, 1944
Bruning AAF	Keller, Gerald C.	P-47G	Air Force code 76-151	lived	July 30, 1944
Bruning AAF	Clark, Thomas L.-- Sunburst, MT	P-47D	Powell or 4 mi E of Alex	killed	July 31, 1944
Bruning AAF	Acree, Thomas buried in Fairbury, NE	C-47	6 miles SW of Naper, NE	killed	August 03, 1944
Bruning AAF	Albert, John F -- Chicago, IL	C-47	6 miles SW of Naper, NE	killed	August 03, 1944
Bruning AAF	Armstrong, William C.-- Nashville MD	C-47	6 miles SW of Naper, NE	killed	August 03, 1944
Bruning AAF	Arnett, Willard F. Jr-- West Virginia	C-47	6 miles SW of Naper, NE	killed	August 03, 1944
Bruning AAF	Blakeslee, Herbert, A. --Eddyville, NE	C-47	6 miles SW of Naper, NE	killed	August 03, 1944
Bruning AAF	Boechman, George E.--Charlotte, N.C.	C-47	6 miles SW of Naper, NE	killed	August 03, 1944
Bruning AAF	Bohle, Robert K Co Pilot --Chicago, IL	C-47	6 miles SW of Naper, NE	killed	August 03, 1944
Bruning AAF	Brown, Jack L. --	C-47	6 miles SW of Naper, NE	killed	August 03, 1944
Bruning AAF	Brown, Richard E.	C-47	6 miles SW of Naper, NE	killed	August 03, 1944
Bruning AAF	Burke, James C. Jr --Norfolk, Mass.	C-47	6 miles SW of Naper, NE	killed	August 03, 1944
Bruning AAF	Clarkson, Donald J.--Kansas, City Mo.	C-47	6 miles SW of Naper, NE	killed	August 03, 1944
Bruning AAF	Hemphill, Lloyd L --Crane, Mo.	C-47	6 miles SW of Naper, NE	killed	August 03, 1944
Bruning AAF	Hutslar, Orson H.	C-47	6 miles SW of Naper, NE	killed	August 03, 1944
Bruning AAF	Johnson, Arthur --San Francisco. CA	C-47	6 miles SW of Naper, NE	killed	August 03, 1944
Bruning AAF	Jolley, Clayton R. Selma, CA	C-47	6 miles SW of Naper, NE	killed	August 03, 1944
Bruning AAF	Jolley, Leonard C. Selma CA	C-47	6 miles SW of Naper, NE	killed	August 03, 1944

Chronological List of plane crashes off Bruning Field
(continued)

Base	Name	Plane	Location	Notes	Date
Bruning AAF	Keller, Gerald C.	C-47	6 miles SW of Naper, NE	killed	August 03, 1944
Bruning AAF	Lytle, Jack E.	C-47	6 miles SW of Naper, NE	killed	August 03, 1944
Bruning AAF	Meadows, Stanley J. Sioux Rapids	C-47	6 miles SW of Naper, NE	28 killed	August 03, 1944
Bruning AAF	Nesbitt, Robert E. Jr.	C-47	6 miles SW of Naper, NE	killed	August 03, 1944
Bruning AAF	O'Malley, Bernard W. --Indiana	C-47	6 miles SW of Naper, NE	killed	August 03, 1944
Bruning AAF	Paladino, Anthony J.	C-47	6 miles SW of Naper, NE	killed	August 03, 1944
Bruning AAF	Patterson, Bruce S.	C-47	6 miles SW of Naper, NE	killed	August 03, 1944
Bruning AAF	Pope. Lelan Alex	C-47	6 miles SW of Naper, NE	killed	August 03, 1944
Bruning AAF	Porter, Charles V.--Texas	C-47	6 miles SW of Naper, NE	killed	August 03, 1944
Bruning AAF	Roberts, Leslie B	C-47	6 miles SW of Naper, NE	killed	August 03, 1944
Bruning AAF	Roberts, Pat N. Jr	C-47	6 miles SW of Naper, NE	killed	August 03, 1944
Bruning AAF	Sehorn, LaVon	C-47	6 miles SW of Naper, NE	killed	August 03, 1944
Bruning AAF	Dickey, Robert O.	P-47	cornfield 2 mi. E Shickley	killed	August 08, 1944
Bruning AAF	Wagner, John A. -- Ohio	P-47	3 mi. E of Shickley	killed	August 09, 1944
Bruning AAF	Washburn, William B.	B17G	Bruning AAF		Sept. 08, 1944
Bruning AAF	McCarthy, John T.	P47D	Bruning AAF		Sept. 09, 1944
Bruning AAF	Leoni, Albert G.--Cincinnati OH	P\47D	Bruning AAF Field	killed	Sept. 14, 1944
Bruning AAF	Robbins, George -Erie PA	P47D	East of Crodova, NE	killed	Sept. 14, 1944
Bruning AAF	Harriman, Donald M.	P-47D	near Bruning		Sept. 16, 1944
Bruning AAF	Maxson, James L.	P-47D	Bruning, NE		Sept. 22, 1944
Bruning AAF	Bennet, Dorwin J.	P-47D	Bruning, NE		Sept. 26, 1944
Bruning AAF	Hildebrand, John r.	P-47D	Bruning, NE		Sept. 26, 1944
Bruning AAF	Hurd, Edgar W.	P-47D	Bruning, NE		Oct. 12, 1944
Bruning AAF	Brace, John L.	P-47D	Bruning, NW		Oct. 12, 1944
Bruning AAF	Mc Daniel, Thomas J.	auto	on base --449th H.B.	killed	Oct. 12, 1944
Bruning AAF	Dulgarian, Dick G.	P-47D	Bruning, NE		Oct. 16, 1944
Bruning AAF	Steiner, Joseph R.	P-47D	Bruning, NE		Oct. 22, 1944

Alphabetical listing of men who crashed off Bruning Field

Base	Name	Aircraft	Location	Status	Date
Bruning AAF	Acree William F.	C-47	Near Naper, NE	killed	August 03, 1944
Bruning AAF	Albert, John F.	C-47	Near Naper, NE	killed	August 03, 1944
Bruning AAF	Armstrong, William C.	C-47	Near Naper, NE	killed	August 03, 1944
Bruning AAF	Arnett, Willard F. Jr	C-47	Near Naper, NE	killed	August 03, 1944
Bruning AAF	Bennet, Doewin J.	P-47D	Bruning, NE		Sept. 22, 1944
Bruning AAF	Blakeslee, Herbert, A	C-47	Near Naper, NE	killed	August 03, 1944
Bruning AAF	Boechman, George E.	C-47	Near Naper, NE	killed	August 03, 1944
Bruning AAF	Bohle, Robert K Co Pilot	C-47	Near Naper, NE	killed	August 03, 1944
Bruning AAF	Boutwell, William C	P-47D	code 96-169 (Bruning)		July 08, 1944
Bruning AAF	Brace, John L.	P-47D	Bruning, NE		Oct. 12, 1944
Bruning AAF	Brethen, Richard H.	P-47D	Irving, Kansas		March 16, 1944
Bruning AAF	Brown, Jack L.	C-47	Near Naper, NE	killed	August 03, 1944
Bruning AAF	Brown, Richard E.	C-47	Near Naper, NE	killed	August 03, 1944
Bruning AAF	Burke, James C. Jr	C-47	Near Naper, NE	killed	August 03, 1944
Sioux City, IA	Charles L. Strickland --gunner	B-17F	2 1/2 mi. E of Daykin, NE	killed	July 12, 1944
Bruning AAF	Clark, Thomas L.-- Sunburst, MT	P-47D	Powell or 4 mi E of Alex	killed	July 31, 1944
Bruning AAF	Clarkson, Donald J.	C-47	Near Naper, NE	killed	August 03, 1944
Bruning AAF	Cox, Richard C.	P-47D	Herkimer, KS		March 16, 1944
Bruning AAF	Dickey, Robert O.	P-47	cornfield 2 mi. E shickley	killed	August 08, 1944
Bruning AAF	Dobony, John --Buffalo, NY	P47D	2 1/2 mi NE Ohiowa	1st fatality	
Bruning AAF	Dulgarian, Dick G.	P-47D	Bruning, NE		Oct. 16, 1944
Sioux City, IA	Wieland, Edward D. --gunner	B-17F	2 1/2 mi. E of Daykin, NE	killed	July 12, 1944
Bruning AAF	Erichson, George E.	P-47D	between Daykin & Powell NE		July 29, 1944
Sioux City, IA	Frank A. Remke --navigator	B-17F	2 1/2 mi. E of Daykin, NE	killed	July 12, 1944
Sioux City, IA	Cassanova, Frank --radio operator	B-17F	2 1/2 mi. E of Daykin, NE	killed	July 12, 1944
Sioux City, IA	Weddell, Frank E. -- engineer	B-17F	2 1/2 mi. E of Daykin, NE	killed	July 12, 1944
Bruning AAF	Mrenak, Frank M. --McDonough, PA	trainer	2 1/2 mi. NE Ohiowa	lived	
Bruning AAF	Gehr, Richard O.	P-47D	Bruning, NE		July 14, 1944
Bruning AAF	Giles, Ralph E.	P-47B	Brock, NE		March 30, 1944
Bruning AAF	Harriman, Donald M.	P-47D	near Bruning		Sept. 14, 1944
Bruning AAF	Hearn, William D.	P-47D	code 76-119		July 05, 1944

Alphabetical listing of men who crashed off Bruning Field
(continued)

Base	Name	Aircraft	Location	Status	Date
Bruning AAF	Hemphill, Lloyd L.	C=47	Near Naper, NE	killed	August 03, 1944
Bruning AAF	Hildebrand, John R.	P-47D	Bruning, NE		Sept. 25, 1944
Bruning AAF	Hurd, Edgar W.	P-47D	Bruning, NE		Oct. 10, 1944
Bruning AAF	Hutslar, Orson H.	C=47	Near Naper, NE	killed	August 03, 1944
Bruning AAF	Jaeger, William --Skokie, IL	trainer	2 1/2 mi NE Ohiowa	1st fatality	
Bruning AAF	Jewett, Charles F.	P-47D	2 1/2 mi. E of Daykin, NE	killed	July 12, 1944
Bruning AAF	Johnson, Arthur	C=47	Near Naper, NE	killed	August 03, 1944
Bruning AAF	Jolley, Clayton R. Selma, CA	P-47D	cornfield near Bruning	lived	July 12, 1944
Bruning AAF	Jolley, Clayton R. Selma, CA	C=47	Near Naper, NE	killed	August 03, 1944
Bruning AAF	Jolley, Leonard C. Selma CA	C=47	Near Naper, NE	killed	August 03, 1944
Sioux City, IA	Joseph Silverstein--bombardier	B-17F	2 1/2 mi. E of Daykin, NE	killed	July 12, 1944
Bruning AAF	Keller, Gerald C.	P-47G	Air Force code 76-151	lived	July 30, 1944
Bruning AAF	Keller, Gerald C.	C=47	Near Naper, NE	killed	August 03, 1944
Bruning AAF	Knight, Charles E.	P-47D	Bruning, NE		July 28, 1944
Bruning AAF	Lee, Wayne B.	P-47D	Bruning AAF	killed	March 30, 1944
Sioux City, IA	Leonard J. Rizzuti -- tail gunner	B-17F	2 1/2 mi. E of Daykin, NE	lived	July 12, 1944
Bruning AAF	Leoni, Albert G.-- Cincinnati, OH	P-47D	on the Bruning Field	killed	Sept. 14, 1944
Bruning AAF	Lytle, Jack E.	C=47	Near Naper, NE	killed	August 03, 1944
Bruning AAF	Mastin, I Richard	CAP	near Bruning	killed	February 19, 1944
Bruning AAF	Maxson, James L.	P-47D	Bruning, NE		Sept. 16, 1944
Bruning AAF	McCarthy, John T.	P-47D	Bruning, NE		Sept. 9, 1944
Bruning AAF	Meadows, Stanley J. Sioux Rapids	C-47	Near Naper NE	28 killed	August 03, 1944
Bruning AAF	Mercer, Roger N.	P-47D	AAB Alamogordo NM		March 21, 1944
Bruning AAF	Miles, Albert E.	P-47D	Witchita, KS		February 25, 1944
Bruning AAF	Nesbitt, Robert E. Jr.	C=47	Near Naper, NE	killed	August 03, 1944
Bruning AAF	O'Malley, Bernard W.	C=47	Near Naper, NE	killed	August 03, 1944
Bruning AAF	Paladino, Anthony J.	C=47	Near Naper, NE	killed	August 03, 1944
Bruning AAF	Patterson, Bruce S.	C=47	Near Naper, NE	killed	August 03, 1944
Bruning AAF	Peschken, Stanley	P-47G	code 96-169 (Bruning)		July 04, 1944
Bruning AAF	Peterson, Don M.	P-47G	code 96-169 (Bruning)		July 07, 1944
Bruning AAF	Pope. Lelan Alex	C=47	Near Naper, NE	killed	August 03, 1944
Bruning AAF	Porter, Charles V.	C=47	Near Naper, NE	killed	August 03, 1944
Bruning AAF	Ramirez, Lose	P-47D	code 96-169 (Bruning)		July 04, 1944

Alphabetical listing of men who crashed off Bruning Field
(continued)

Base	Name	Aircraft	Location	Outcome	Date
Bruning AAF	Robbins, George F. -- Erie, PA.	P-47D	East of Cordova, NE	killed	Sept. 14, 1944
Bruning AAF	Roberts, Leslie B	C-47	Near Naper, NE	killed	August 03, 1944
Bruning AAF	Roberts, Pat N. Jr	C-47	Near Naper, NE	killed	August 03, 1944
Sioux City, IA	Halcon, Salvador V--waist gunner	B-17F	2 1/2 mi. E of Daykin, NE	lived	July 12, 1944
Sioux City, IA	Schmidt, Jack C.--Pilot	B-17F	2 1/2 mi. E of Daykin, NE	7 killed	July 12, 1944
Bruning AAF	Sehorn, LaVon	C-47	Near Naper, NE	killed	August 03, 1944
Bruning AAF	Smith, Levi W.	P-47D	Bruning AAF		March 12, 1944
Bruning AAF	Steiner, Joseph R.	P-47D	Bruning, NE		Oct. 22, 1944
Bruning AAF	Thomas J. Mc Daniel -- DC	auto	on Base - 449th HB	killed	Oct. 12, 1944
Bruning AAF	Thurston, William A.	P-47D	9 mi SW Tecumseh, NE		March 19, 1944
Bruning AAF	Trumbower, Frederick W.	P-47D	Bruning AAF	lived	March 06, 1944
Bruning AAF	Trumbower, Frederick W.	P-47D	Bruning AAF		March 29, 1944
Bruning AAF	Wagner, John A.	P-47	3 mi. E of Shickley		August 09, 1944
Sioux City, IA	Clements, Wallace --Co-pilot	B-17F	2 1/2 mi. E of Daykin, NE	killed	July 12, 1944
Bruning AAF	Washburn, William F.	B17G	Bruning, NE	lived	Sept.. 8, 1944
Bruning AAF	Williams, Thomas A.	P-47D	Bruning, NE		Sept. 26, 1944

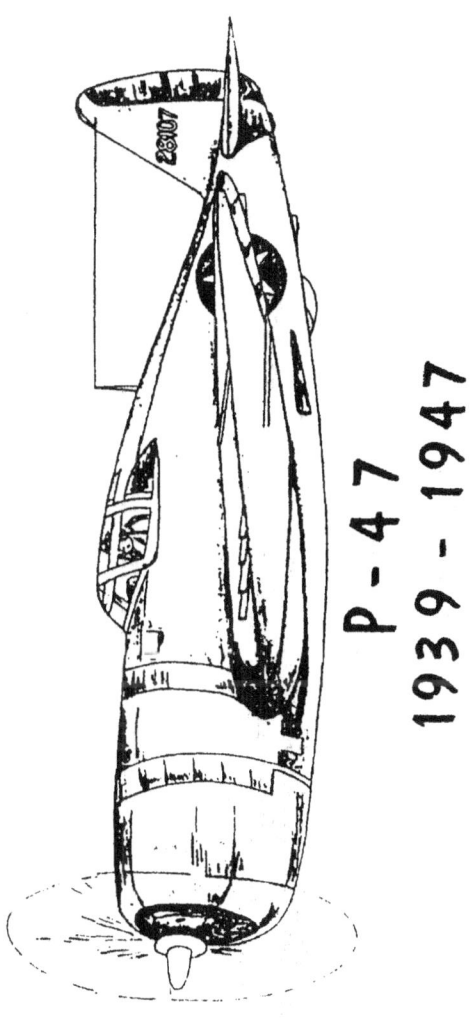

P - 4 7
1939 - 1947

Plane Crashes --WWII

Nebraska Accident Report List

FILECODE	YEAR	AIRCRAFT	SERNO	PILOT	MISHAPLOC	HOMEBASE
42-02-09-27	42	B-26A	41-7354	STARR, JOHN V JR	NASHVILLE, TN	OMAHA, NE
42-03-05-19	42	AT-17A	FJ-146	ANDERSON, HARRY R	MORSE BLUFF, NE	HENSLEY FLD, TX
42-06-11-11	42	F-2	40-684	BAUSCH, WILLIAM C	LINCOLN, NE	LOWRY FLD, CO
43-01-06-12	43	AT-9	41-5785	FOSTER, VICTOR H	OXFORD, NE	LOWRY FLD, CO
43-01-29-07	43	B-26B	41-18069	TAYLOR, THOMAS H	OFFUTT FLD, OMAHA, NE	GLENN L MARTIN, NE
43-02-08-40	43	B-17	42-5298	ADAMS, WILLIAM C	AAB, AINSWORTH, NE	AAB, AINSWORTH, NE
43-02-13-20	43	B-17F	42-29612	ROBINSON, GEORGE A	ORLANDO AB, ORLANDO, FL	KEARNEY, NE
43-02-14-03	43	B-26B	41-18018	TALL, LEONARD C	2 MI NE ROCHESTER, IN	OFFUTT FLD, NE
43-02-16-20	43	BT-13A	42-42287	ROWBOTTOM, HARRY E	PALMDALE ARPT, 3 MI NE	LANCASTER, CA
43-02-18-49	43	B-17F	42-29582	SPINNING, KENNETH W	BRAYMER, MO	KEARNEY, NE
43-02-19-10	43	B-17F	42-29568	KNAPHUS, NED D	HUTCHINSON, KS	KEARNEY, NE
43-02-20-24	43	C-47	41-19484	TERKEURST, JAMES A	GRAND RAPIDS ARPT	ALLIANCE, NE
43-02-20-39	43	L-4A	42-38413	HUSKWY, WILLIAM M	LINCOLN AB, LINCOLN, NE	DALHART, TX
43-02-20-39	43	L-3A	42-2835	VALDES, ERNEST A	LINCOLN AB, LINCOLN, NE	DALHART, TX
43-02-23-60	43	CG-4A	42-61163	MENTEMEYER, FREDERICK H	ALLIANCE AAB, NE	ALLIANCE AAB, NE
43-02-25-35	43	C-53	41-20135	SPEAKMAN, D C	ALLIANCE AAB, NE	ALIANCE AAB, NE
43-02-25-46	43	C-53	41-20116	DEHONEY, JOHN M	BROKEN BOW, NE	SEDALIA WARRENSBURG, MO
43-02-25-46	43	CG-4A	42-77051	ROSS, J	BROKER BOW, NE	SEDALIA, WARRENSBURG, MO
43-03-27-56	43	AT-12	41-17531	ELLIOTT, R R	AAB, GRAND ISLAND, NE	NEW CASTLE AAB, DE
43-03-28-37	43	PQ-8	42-96834	WILLIAMS, WILLIAM T	FREMONT, NE	MEMPHIS, TN
43-03-31-38	43	C-47A	42-23397	EUSTON, MILTON K	ALLIANCE AAB, ALLIANCE, NE	ALLIANCE AAB, ALIANCE, NE
43-04-05-42	43	B-17	42-5321	MORRISON, CYRIL S	AAB SCOTTSBLUFF, NE	AAB SCOTTSBLUFF, NE
43-04-08-49	43	B-17F	42-29879	ZUCKER, RAYMOND J	KEARNEY AAF, NE	KEARNEY AAF, NE
43-04-14-62	43	B-17F	42-25113	BARNESON, JOHN	AAB AINSWORTH, NE	AAB AINSWORTH, NE
43-04-20-54	43	B-26C	41-34093	BAYNE, HARRY C	SCOTT FLD, IL	NCAAB, NE
43-05-04-19	43	C-53	42-215547	STANTON, ROY S	KIMBALL, NE	ALLIANCE, NE
43-05-08-10	43	L-3B	42-36308	TUCKER, JACK C	8 MI SE, AAB, ALLIANCE, NE	AAB, ALLIANCE, NE
43-05-08-11	43	C-47A	42-92024	PAIR, ROBERT H	2 MI N TINKER FLD	AAB, ALLIANCE, NE
43-05-19-49	43	L-4A	42-15210	MESSINGHAM, LAVERN A	8 MI SW ANGORA, NE	AAB, ALLIANCE, NE
43-05-28-06	43	L-3B	42-36258	EDWARDS, CHARLES B	NEAR MUN ARPT	ALLIANCE, NE
43-05-30-14	43	B-24D	42-40808	REEVES, JOHN R	SELFRIDGE FLD, MI	LINCOLN, NE
43-06-14-86	43	C-53D	42-686770	PEARLMAN, EDWIN J	ALLIANCE AAF, NE	ALLIANCE AAF, NE
43-06-21-95	43	C-53	42-68727	STANLEY, DEAN A	AAB ALLIANCE, NE	ALLIANCE, NE
43-06-27-04	43	B-17F	42-30417	BOLON, LEONARD L	RANDOLPH, VT	GRAND ISLAND, NE
43-06-30-04	43	B-26	41-18334	WOODRICK, VICTOR H	OFFUT FLD, OMAHA, NE	AAFPS DODGE CITY, KS
43-07-16-48	42	L-3C	42-60297	GELDBAUGH, CECIL W	OSHKOSH, NE	CASPER, WY
43-09-13-33	42	L-4A	42-36708	BAXTER, RONALD E	VORTH PLATTE, NE	GOODLAND, KS
43-10-04-21	42	B-14D	41-23655	SANNY MAX J	2 MI S, 2I MI E WAYNE, NE	SIOUX CITY, IA
43-10-18-01	42	B-34	AJ-282	SYVERSON, WOODROW W	CHADRON MUN ARPT, NE	CHADRON, NE
43-10-19-03	42	B-24D	41-11771	GODLEWSKI, JOHN T R	OMAHA MUN ARPT, NE	TOPEKA AAB, KS
43-10-22-24	42	L-2A	42-35924	MAGIN, LEWIS H JR	OMAHA MUN ARPT, NE	NASHVILLE, TN
43-11-17-10	42	B-26B	41-18062	CARPENTER, ROY W	OFFUTT FLD, OMAHA, NE	NCAAB, WILMINGTON, DE
43-11-21-23	42	L-4A	42-36417	JACOBS, DAN J	LINCOLN AIR BASE, NE	LOVE FLD, TX
43-12-14-51	42	AT-17B	42-2881	PITCHER, CHARLES S	NEAR CORTLAND, NE	ST JOSEPH, MO
43-12-17-25	42	AT-6C	42-32075	FERGUSSON, DAVID V	LINCOLN AIR BASE, NE	LINCOLN AIR BASE, NE
43-12-24-06	42	B-26B	41-17994	ROSITUS, ALBERT E	AAFSFS, JACKSON AAB, MS	OFFUTT FLD, OMAHA, NE
44-01-04-09	44	C-53D	42-68780	KEMPSON, NORMAN W	AGATE, NE	AAB, ALLIANCE, NE
44-01-06-17	44	B-24E	42-7398	TIPPIN, ROBERT G	7 MI S, 1 MI W HUGO, CO	HARVARD, NE
44-01-09-06	44	C-53D	42-68837	DUCHARME, PAUL J	AAB, ALLIANCE, NE	AAB, ALLIANCE, NE
44-01-10-55	44	CG-4A	42-46583	HODGES, CLARK C	ALLIANCE, NE	AAB, ALLIANCE, NE
44-01-12-26	44	P-47D	42-22343	LIGHTWINE, J W	BIGGS FLD, TX	AINSWORTH, NE
44-01-13-62	44	P-39Q	44-2941	LUTES, DONALD P	SIDNEY, NE	GREAT FALLS, MT
44-01-20-30	44	B-24E	41-20109	FRIEDMAN, SAMUEL L	AAB, HARVARD, NE	AAB, HARVARD, NE
44-01-20-46	44	C-47A	42-100663	WINAND, HOWARD G	AAB, ALLIANCE, NE	AAB, ALLIANCE, NE
44-01-24-57	44	RA-25	42-79830	WALSH, EDWARD J	AAB, ALLIANCE, NE	HILL FLD, OGDEN, UT
44-01-28-62	44	C-47A	43-30668	WAYNE, THEODORE R	GREENSBORO MUN, NC	ALLIANCE, NE
44-01-30-34	44	B-17G	42-32042	GITTINS, CLARENCE E	AAB, GRAND ISLAND, NE	AAB, GRAND ISLAND, NE
44-01-30-41	44	B-24H	41-28753	CONARROE, WARREN E	MC COOK AAB, MC COOK, NE	MC COOK AAB, MC COOK, NE
44-01-31-55	44	L-2C	43-2868	FARNSWORTH, MAXWELL P	MUN ARPT, ALLIANCE, NE	MUN ARPT, ALLIANCE, NE
44-02-01-15	44	B-24H	42-7651	HARGOVE, GRAHAM C	30 MI S HASTINGS, NE	PUEBLO AAB, CO
44-02-02-03	44	B-17G	42-38119	JONES, ALBERT	KEARNEY AAB, NE	KEARNEY AAB, NE
44-02-02-20	44	B-17G	42-31904	BOND, LESLIE A	GRAND ISLAND AAF, NE	GRAND ISLAND AAF, NE
44-02-05-13	44	P-47D	42-8175	FANSLAU, EARNEST W	AINSWORTH AAB, NE	AINSWORTH AAB, NE
44-02-08-01	44	B-17F	42-30933	SALMONS, WILLIAM T	3 MI N 1 MI W EMERSON, NE	SIOUX CITY FLD, IA
44-02-14-32	44	C-47A	42-23866	AARON, BENASH	OMAHA MUN ARPT, OMAHA, NE	AAB, ALLIANCE, NE
44-02-14-43	44	BC-1A	39-838	GROW, JACK W	AINSWORTH AAB, NE	AINSWORTH AAB, NE
44-02-17-12	44	P-47D	42-8019	PADGETT, WALTER F	AINSWORTH AAF, NE	AINSWORTH AAF, NE
44-02-17-49	44	B-24J	42-73385	BUTTON, WARREN F	MUN ARPT, N PLATTE, NE	PETERSON FLD, CO
44-02-18-22	44	B-25G	42-65117	TRECEK, MILTON	MUN ARPT, OMAHA, NE	CLOVIS AAB, NM
44-02-21-07	44	C-47A	42-23776	BRZOSTOWSKI, ALFRED L	15 MI SSE CRAWFORD, NE	AAB, ALLIANCE, NE
44-02-24-03	44	B-24J	42-73341	KAPLAN, WILLIAM	MC COOK AAB, MC COOK, NE	MC COOK AAB, MC COOK, NE
44-02-24-18	44	B-24D	42-40179	NEEL, BILLIE B	MC COOK AAB, MC COOK, NE	MC COOK AAB, MC COOK, NE
44-02-25-01	44	C-47A	42-101000	BUDROE, GEORGE E	AAB, ALLIANCE, NE	AAB, ALLIANCE, NE

Plane Crashes --WWII

Nebraska Accident Report List

44-02-25-07	44 B-24J	42-73391	PATCHING, GEORGE E	MC COOK AAB, MC COOK, NE	MC COOK AAB, MC COOK, NE
44-02-25-24	44 B-17G	42-38203	TALBERT, HOWARD T	GRAND ISLAND AAF, NE	GRAND ISLAND AAF, NE
44-02-25-42	44 P-47D	42-23279	MILES, ALBERT E	WICHITA, KS	BRUNING AAF, NE
44-02-26-07	44 AT-18A	42-55515	VOTAW, VIRGIL L	LINCOLN AAF, NE	ELLINGTON FLD, TX
44-03-01-69	44 B-24H	42-94791	BALLANGEE, CHESTER E	FAIRMONT AAF, GENEVA, NE	FAIRMONT AAF, GENEVA, NE
44-03-06-15	44 P-47D	42-23017	TRUMBOWER, FREDERICK W	BRUNING AAF, BRUNING, NE	BRUNING AAF, BRUNING, NE
44-03-06-34	44 B-17G	42-97224	MARQUETTE, DONALD K	5 MI NE MAXWELL, IA	KAAF, KEARNEY, NE
44-03-06-83	44 B-17G	42-97221	BIRONG, PHILLIP H	NE SE RNWY, KAAF, KEARNEY, NE	KAAF, KEARNEY, NE
44-03-06-83	44 B-17G	42-32060	O BRIEN, JOHN J	NE SE RNWY, KAAF, KEARNEY, NE	KAAF, KEARNEY, NE
44-03-06-87	44 B-17G	42-107071	HANNAFORD, VERNON L	KAAF, KEARNEY, NE	KAAF, KEARNEY, NE
44-03-08-61	44 B-24H	42-94731	CORP, LYNN J	8 MI E HANCOCK, IA	AAF, HARVARD, NE
44-03-08-61	44 B-24H	41-28826	MUELLER, ROBERT H	8 MI E HANCOCK, IA	AAF, HARVARD, NE
44-03-08-80	44 B-17G	42-107058	BUTTORFF, RICHARD D	AAF, GRAND ISLAND, NE	AAF, GRAND ISLAND, NE
44-03-12-09	44 P-47D	42-23010	SMITH, LEVI W	BRUNING AAF, BRUNING, NE	BRUNING AAF, BRUNING, NE
44-03-12-23	44 B-24H	41-28830	WODZINSKI, FRANK T JR	LAAF, LINCOLN, NE	LAAF, LINCOLN, NE
44-03-16-16	44 P-47D	43-25371	BRETHEN, RICHARD H	IRVING, KS	BRUNING AAF, BRUNING, NE
44-03-16-17	44 P-47D	42-23013	COX, RICHARD C	HERKIMER, KS	BRUNING AAF, BRUNING, NE
44-03-19-08	44 P-47D	42-23050	THURSTON, WILLIAM A	9 MI SW TECUMSEH, NE	BRUNING AAF, BRUNING, NE
44-03-21-67	44 P-47D	42-23075	MERCER, ROGER N	AAB, ALAMOGORDO, NM	BRUNING AAF, BRUNING, NE
44-03-25-74	44 C-47A	42-24128	HINTON, RICHARD H	AAB, ALLIANCE, NE	AAB, ALLIANCE, NE
44-03-25-74	44 C-45A	42-23829	SHERLAND, PHILLIP P	AAB, ALLIANCE, NE	AAB, ALLIANCE, NE
44-03-29-44	44 C-53C	43-2022	RAPIN, GEORGE E	AAB, ALLIANCE, NE	AAB, ALLIANCE, NE
44-03-29-46	44 P-47D	42-23009	TRUMBOWER, FREDERICK W	BRUNING AAF, BRUNING, NE	BRUNING AAF, BRUNING, NE
44-03-30-57	44 C-47	42-32809	PICKUP, JOHN W	AAB, ALLIANCE, NE	AAB, ALLIANCE, NE
44-04-09-513	44 B-17G	42-97854	WILLIAMSON, GEORGE L, J	LAGEONS FJORD, GREENLAND	GRAND ISLAND, NE
44-04-10-36	44 B-25D	41-29841	DANIELS, HINTON C	TECUMSEH, NE	ROSECRANS FLD, MO
44-04-13-07	44 B-24E	42-7035	ABRAHAM, STANLEY NMI	MCCOOK AAF, MCCOOK, NE	MCCOOK AAF, MCCOOK, NE
44-04-16-36	44 B-17G	42-102464	STEELE, DAVID A JR	RUNWAY KEARNEY AAF, NE	KEARNEY AAF, NE
44-04-19-56	44 B-17G	42-102567	GRAHAM, CLARK G	GRAND ISLAND AAF, NE	GRAND ISLAND AAF, NE
44-04-20-43	44 UC-78	43-7628	HENERY, WILLIAM MOORE	10 MI SW LIMON, CO	LINCOLN AAF NE
44-04-21-27	44 UC-78B	43-32187	BERNARD, BOBBIE L	BLACKLAND AAF, TX	BLACKLAND AAF, NE
44-04-23-10	44 UC-78	42-58334	LAMKIN, JAMES E	MCCOOK AAF, NE	PETERSON AAB, CO
44-04-24-34	44 B-24J	44-40436	BAKER, JOSEPH R	MCCOOK AAF, NE	LOVE FLD, TX
44-04-26-28	44 C-47A	42-23693	KRUEGER, MERLYN W	ALLIANCE AAF, NE	ALLIANCE AAF, TX
44-04-27-22	44 B-24J	44-40287	BOWDEN, WILLIAM W	MCCOOK AAF, NE	MCCOOK AAF, NE
44-04-28-86	44 RA-24A	42-54426	ZETHREN, GEORGE W	MUN ARPT, FREMONT, NE	SHERMAN FLD, KS
44-04-29-17	44 RB-24E1	41-28413	ANDERSON, VIRGIL D	15 MI SW MERNA, NE	KIRTLAND FLD, NM
44-04-30-04	44 P-47B	42-23062	GILES, RALPH E	BROCK, NE	BRUNING AAF, NE
44-04-30-12	44 P-47D	42-23023	LEE, WAYNE B	BRUNING AAF, NE	BRUNING AAF, NE
44-07-02-13	43 L-4B	43-884	FERGUSSON, DAVID V	ASHLAND, NE	LINCOLN AB, NE
44-07-02-35	43 CG-4A	42-62870	GILSON, MILO E	ALLIANCE AAB, NE	ALLIANCE AAB, NE
44-07-02-36	43 CG-4A	42-61906	MOEN, VIRGIL C	ALLIANCE AAB, NE	ALLIANCE AAB, NE
44-07-02-37	43 CG-4A	42-61884	KAUFMAN, ROBERT V	ALLIANCE AAB, NE	ALLIANCE AAB, NE
44-07-03-05	43 B-17F	42-3379	DAVIS, DAVID J	WHITE CITY, KS	KEARNEY, NE
44-07-04-21	43 B-24D	42-41009	WESTROM, CLIFFORD M	LINCOLN AAB, LINCOLN, NE	LINCOLN AAB, NE
44-07-06-32	43 CG-4A	42-56644	MALLOY, JAMES J	ALLIANCE AAB, NE	ALLIANCE AAB, NE
44-07-06-33	43 CG-4A	42-56692	PIELDRSZCZAH, JOSEPH	ALLIANCE AAB, NE	ALLIANCE AAB, NE
44-07-06-37	43 CG-4A	42-261389	COWAN, CORNELL T	ALLIANCE AAB, NE	ALLIANCE AAB, NE
44-07-06-88	43 CG-4A	42-43629	KLEIN, BENJAMIN	ALLIAMCE AAB, NE	ALLIANCE AAB, NE
44-07-07-15	43 B-26	41-32032	SCOTT, HERBERT W	OFFUTT FLD, OMAHA, NE	NEWCASTLE AAB
44-07-09-22	43 L-3C	43-1563	BELL, JOSEPH W	3 MI W WALDO, KS	AAB, KEARNEY, NE
44-07-09-32	43 C-53	42-268747	LIGHT, JACK T	RAPID CITY AAB	ALLIANCE, NE
44-07-10-02	43 C-47A	42-23801	PATE, JAMES H	SEDALIA AAF, WARRENSBURG, MO	AAB, ALLIANCE, NE
44-07-10-03	43 C-53	42-68785	CHAPMAN, THEODORE K	HEMINGFORD, NE	AAB, ALLIANCE, NE
44-07-10-03	43 C-47	42-23786	HUNTER, JOHN R	HEMINGFORD, NE	AAB, ALLIANCE, NE
44-07-11-12	43 C-47	42-23795	O'DONALD, DANIEL W	AAB, ALLIANCE, NE	AAB, ALLIANCE, NE
44-07-11-13	43 CG-4A	42-62019	COWAN, CORNELL T	ALLIANCE AAB, NE	ALLIANCE AAB, NE
44-07-12-36	43 C-47A	42-23743	KILLGORE, DOYLE S	ALLIANCE AB, NE	ALLIANCE AB, NE
44-07-15-02	43 C-47	42-23726	MISER, JACK	AAB	ALLIANCE, NE
44-07-17-52	43 B-17F	42-30614	WEIHE, JOSEPH W	SCOTTS BLUFF, NE	GORE FLD, MT
44-07-18-34	43 L-3B	42-36306	MURRAY, PAUL J	ANGORA, NE	AAB, ALLIANCE, NE
44-07-18-42	43 B-17F	42-5761	NESTLE, RALPH M	VALENTINE, NE	WATERDOWN, SD
44-07-19-98	43 CG-4A	42-62073	MCGEE, JAMES C	ALLIANCE AAB, NE	ALLIANCE AAB, NE
44-07-22-59	43 CG-4A	42-611351	GAMET, JOSEPH M	ALLIANCE AAB, NE	ALLIANCE AAB, NE
44-07-22-61	43 CG-4A	42-77049	INGLISH, CHARLES H JR	ALLIANCE AAB, NE	ALLIANCE AAB, NE
44-07-23-29	43 CG-4A	42-61370	CARROLL, RAY D	ALLIANCE AAB, NE	ALLIANCE AAB, NE
44-07-26-14	43 CG-4A	42-61448	PAYNE, DONALD E	PAXTON, NE	ALLIANCE AAB, NE
44-07-26-31	43 CG-4A	42-61452	KYTLE, RALPH W	ALLIANCE AAB, NE	ALLIANCE AAB, NE
44-07-27-30	43 CG-4A	42-53132	STULL, LEE T	ALLIANCE AAB, NE	ALLIANCE AAB, NE
44-07-27-31	43 CG-4A	42-37049	RUSZALA, EDWARD J	ALLIANCE AAB, NE	ALLIANCE AAB, NE
44-07-27-89	43 C-60	42-55870	TUIS, G S	MC COOK AAB, MC COOK, NE	TINKER FLD
44-07-28-23	43 CG-4A	42-26204	NETTEKOVEN, ROBERT O	ALLIANCE AAB, NE	ALLIANCE AAB, NE
44-07-28-27	43 CG-4A	42-6411	PUTZ, ADAM H	ALLIANCE AAB, NE	ALLIANCE AAB, NE
44-07-29-07	43 B-17	42-29588	FITZER, HOMER D	AAF, KEARNEY, NE	AAF, KEARNEY, NE

Plane Crashes -- WWII

Nebraska Accident Report List

44-07-29-20	43 CG-4A	42-61397	DIETZ, HOWARD J	ALLIANCE AAB, NE	ALLIANCE AAB, NE
44-07-31-11	43 C-47A	42-23839	STEVENSON, CHARLES W	TAYLOR FLD, 57TH FTD	AAB, ALLIANCE, NE
44-07-31-34	43 AT-17B	42-39140	KESTERSON, J D	4 MI W OGALLALA, NE	AAB DOUGLAS, AZ
44-08-02-43	43 B-17F	42-30534	SHAW, COAD C	SIOUX CITY AAB, IA	KEARNEY, NE
44-08-04-13	43 UC-78	43-7411	SCOTT, JAMES P	KIMBALL, NE	TINKER FLD
44-08-05-73	43 CG-4A	42-62138	TREICHAK, MICHAL A	AAB	ALLIANCE, NE
44-08-06-78	43 B-17F	42-30577	FITZER, HOMER D	KEARNEY FLD	KEARNEY FLD, NE
44-08-07-46	43 B-17F	42-3160	DUFF, LAWRENCE H	AAB	KEARNEY, NE
44-08-08-09	43 C-53	42-68735	AMES, F K	AAB	ALLIANCE, NE
44-08-08-32	43 C-53D	42-68773	BRETT, PEYTON H	TROY, OH	ALLIANCE, NE
44-08-11-100	43 CG-4A	42-77035	KULASA, JOE L	FT ROBINSON, NE	AAB, ALLIANCE, NE
44-08-11-101	43 CG-4A	42-61427	HIDECANAGE, STANLEY A	FT ROBINSON, NE	AAB, ALLIANCE, NE
44-08-11-103	43 CG-4A	42-61443	RAGONA, JAMES	FT ROBINSON, NE	AAB, ALLIANCE, NE
44-08-11-104	43 CG-4A	42-79205	ROWAN, JAMES P	FT ROBINSON, NE	AAB, ALLIANCE, NE
44-08-11-106	43 CG-4A	42-279024	PAYNE, DONALD E	FT ROBINSON, NE	AAB, ALLIANCE, NE
44-08-11-107	43 CG-4A	42-246683	HOWARD, JOHN E	FT ROBINSON, NE	AAB, ALLIANCE, NE
44-08-11-108	43 CG-4A	42-77107	ROWAN, JAMES P	FT-ROBINSON, NE	AAB, ALLIANCE, NE
44-08-11-110	43 CG-4A	42-60046	RAWLINS, ALEXANDER	FT ROBINSON, NE	AAB, ALLIANCE, NE
44-08-11-111	43 CG-4A	42-46552	DAWSON, KECK R	FT ROBINSON, NE	AAB, ALLIANCE, NE
44-08-11-112	43 CG-4A	42-73538	CLARK, JONATHAN	FT ROBINSON, NE	AAB, ALLIANCE, NE
44-08-11-113	43 CG-4A	42-46595	LE VASSEUR, JEROME F	FT ROBINSON, NE	AAB, ALLIANCE, NE
44-08-11-114	43 CG-4A	42-62120	SEIPLE, HARVEY L	FT ROBINSON, NE	AAB, ALLIANCE, NE
44-08-11-115	43 CG-4A	42-52812	LEE, C M	FT ROBINSON, NE	AAB, ALLIANCE, NE
44-08-11-116	43 C-47	42-24075	MCCLEAN, G K	AAB	ALLIANCE, NE
44-08-11-117	43 CG-4A	42-261128	NETTEKOVEN, R O	FT ROBINSON, NE	AAB, ALLIANCE, NE
44-08-11-118	43 CG-4A	42-26974	MALLOY, JAMES J	AAB, ALLIANCE, NE	AAB, ALLIANCE, NE
44-08-11-26	43 CG-4A	42-78991	CHRISTENSEN, H A	AAB	ALLIANCE, NE
44-08-11-51	43 CG-4A	42-79207	LA PLANTE, LEO J	FT ROBINSON, NE	AAB, ALLIANCE, NE
44-08-11-52	43 CG-4A	42-277117	RUSZALA, EDWARD J	FT ROBINSON, NE	AAB, ALLIANCE, NE
44-08-11-93	43 CG-4A	42-62054	GAMET, JOSEPH M	FT ROBINSON, NE	AAB, ALLIANCE, NE
44-08-11-95	43 CG-4A	42-79031	DIETZ, HOWARD J	FT ROBINSON, NE	AAB, ALLIANCE, NE
44-08-11-96	43 CG-4A	42-77036	RAINES, OSCAR T	FT ROBINSON, NE	AAB, ALLIANCE, NE
44-08-11-97	43 CG-4A	42-62049	GILSON, MILO E	FT ROBINSON, NE	AAB, ALLIANCE, NE
44-08-11-98	43 CG-4A	42-61357	FENICK, STEPHEN A	FT ROBINSON, NE	AAB, ALLIANCE, NE
44-08-11-99	43 CG-4A	42-61147	TAYLOR, DALTON W	FT ROBINSON, NE	AAB, ALLIANCE, NE
44-08-12-66	43 CG-4A	42-77041	LEWIS, ETHEL L	FT ROBINSON, NE	AAB, ALLIANCE, NE
44-08-12-67	43 CG-4A	42-46615	DOELGER, LEON C	FT ROBINSON, NE	AAB, ALLIANCE, NE
44-08-12-68	43 CG-4A	42-62042	MCANALLY, EARL W	FT ROBINSON, NE	AAB, ALLIANCE, NE
44-08-12-69	43 CG-4A	42-61891	WILDER, LEON C	FT ROBINSON, NE	AAB, ALLIANCE, NE
44-08-12-70	43 CG-4A	79216	DIXON, JACK H	FT ROBINSON, NE	AAB, ALLIANCE, NE
44-08-17-04	43 B-17F	42-30542	EDNEMANO, ERNEST H	6 MI N WOOD RIVER, NE	KEARNEY AAB, NE
44-08-22-52	43 C-84A	42-61528	HUFF, EMMETT H	ALLIANCE, NE	ALLIANCE, NE
44-08-24-102	43 B-17F	42-30759	NICKELHOFF, RICHARD	AAB	KEARNEY, NE
44-08-28-20	43 B-17E	42-3309	GIMPERLING, JOHN E	HARVARD, NE	AAB, HARVARD, NE
44-08-28-20	43 B-17F	42-30774	ROWLAND, DAVID	HARVARD, NE	AAB, HARVARD, NE
44-08-28-20	43 B-17F	42-30239	TWITCHELL, ROBERT R	HARVARD, NE	AAB, HARVARD, NE
44-08-31-13	43 B-17	42-5451	MCRAVEN, JAMES A	2 MI NE KEARNEY AAB	KEARNEY AAB, NE
44-09-02-56	43 B-17	42-29564	INGLIS, HARLAN K	AAB	Kearney, ne
44-09-06-21	43 B-24D	41-24057	GEIL, LORIN D	STINSON FLD, TX	MC COOK, NE
44-09-11-48	43 B-17F	42-5775	SCHNEIDER, WILLARD G	AAB	Kearney, ne
44-09-13-05	43 B-17F	42-29966	KEHM, ROBERT L	1 ! MI E OSBORNE, KS	Kearney aab, ne
44-09-17-70	43 B-17G	42-31048	MCLEAN, JOHNNY C	MUN ARPT, NORTH PLATTE, NE	CHEYENNE, WY
44-09-22-22	43 B-25D	42-87195	WALBORN, E D	OFFUTT FLD, OMAHA, NE	GLENN L MARTIN - NE CO
44-09-25-09	43 B-17F	42-30530	BARROWS, HAYDEN W	COLUMBUS, TX	AAB, KEARNEY, NE
44-09-29-11	43 C-53D	42-68788	CARDIE, WILLIAM	ALLIANCE, NE	AAB, ALLIANCE, NE
44-09-30-02	43 B-17F	42-29569	MARCY, CHARLES H	8 MI SE CAMPBELL, NE	AAB, HARVARD, NE
44-09-30-63	43 B-17G	42-31094	HOWARD, MELVIN J	MUN ARPT, N PLATTE, NE	GORE FLD, GREAT FALLS, MT
44-10-02-18	43 B-24E	42-7182	SLATER, WILLIAM C	FAIRMONT AAF	GENEVA, NE
44-10-02-46	43 P-39N	42-18897	SUTTON, EDWIN R	GRAND CTRL ARPT, GLENDALE, CA	AINSWORTH, NE
44-10-05-69	43 B-24H	41-29138	LARSON, HAROLD R	AAB, GRAND ISLAND, NE	AAB, MITCHELL, SD
44-10-10-04	43 B-24H	41-29181	BURR, CECIL C	5 MI SW WAYNE, NE	FAIRMONT AAB, GENEVA, NE
44-10-11-56	43 B-17F	42-3467	HUGHES, HAYDEN T	AAB	HARVARD, NE
44-10-11-66	43 B-24E	42-7155	ROACH, JACK L	7 MI W, 2 MI N SCOTTSBLUFF, NE	AAB, SCOTTSBLUFF, NE
44-10-14-01	43 P-39	42-9101	HUBBARD, GLENN A	AAB, CASPER, WY	AINSWORTH, NE
44-10-14-13	43 B-24	42-72830	BOLES, JOHN R	MC COOK, NE	AAB, TOPEKA, KS
44-10-15-01	43 B-17F	42-30025	VAN SYCKLE, LEON G	BROKEN BOW BMB RNG, NE	AAB, KEARNEY, NE
44-10-22-04	43 B-17G	42-31190	JOHNSON, HOWARD E	PONCA CITY, OK	AAB, HARVARD, NE
44-10-24-06	43 B-17G	42-39862	GUYNN, ASHLEY M	HARVARD AAB	HARVARD AAB, NE
44-10-26-61	43 B-17F	42-6043	ELY, KENNETH E	AAB	KEARNEY, NE
44-10-29-68	43 B-17F	42-6072	PIEH, HENRY	AAB	KEARNEY, NE
44-11-10-36	43 RB-26	41-27666	ARMOSKA, RAYMOND	LINCOLN AB, NE	LINCOLN AB, NE
44-12-01-16	43 C-53	42-15547	MURPHY, RICHARD P	20 MI S HYANNIS, NE	AAB, ALLIANCE, NE
44-12-01-58	43 AT-6A	41-292	FAWCETT, WILLIS A	LINCOLN AAF, NE	LINCOLN AAF, NE
44-12-05-05	43 P-47C	41-6567	SPENCER, ARTHUR D	AAB, SCRIBNER, NE	AAB, SCRIBNER, NE

Falcon Field Station Box 22049
Mesa, AZ 85277
(480-218-8198)
www.sonic.net/azfuller

AAIR
Aviation Archaeological Investigation and Research

Plane Crashes -- WWII
Nebraska Accident Report List

44-12-05-21	43 CG-4A	42-61980	FRITCHMAN, CURTIS C	10 MI N OWENTOWN, KY	ALLIANCE, NE
44-12-07-49	43 P-47C	41-6663	FAZEKAS, FRANK	AAB, SCRIBNER, NE	AAB, SCRIBNER, NE
44-12-07-50	43 P-47D	42-22575	BETHES, WILLIAM E	AAB, SCRIBNER, NE	AAB, SCRIBNER, NE
44-12-13-43	43 P-39N	42-4953	STORZ, ROBERT H	LINCOLN AAF, NE	LINCOLN AAF, NE
44-12-14-12	43 B-24J	42-100010	PATE, EDWIN H	OMAHA, NE	FT WORTH AAF, TX
44-12-14-52	43 B-17C	42-31530	HOGG, RICHARD W	AAB, KEARNEY, NE	AAB, KEARNEY, NE
44-12-15-01	43 B-17G	42-31654	ROCKNEY, ARLO D	3 QTR MI N AAB, KEARNEY, NE	GORE FLD, MT
44-12-16-12	43 C-53D	42-68745	OTTOMANN, RAYMOND H	BAER FLD, FT WAYNE, IN	ALLIANCE, NE
44-12-17-63	43 CG-4A	42-77110	LYONS, DOUGLAS W	MONTGOMERY CITY, MO	ALLIANCE, NE
44-12-18-71	43 P-47	42-74767	PADGETT, WALTER F	AINSWORTH AAB	AINSWORTH, NE
44-12-19-72	43 B-17G	42-38040	SANDERSON, MURDO W	NE SW RNWY, AAB, KEARNEY, NE	AAB, KEARNEY, NE
44-12-23-17	43 UC-78B	42-39299	BERRY, WAYNE S	MUN ARPT, OMAHA, NE	FT-ORTH AAF, TX
44-12-29-44	43 B-17G	42-39955	SCHIMMEL, ROBERT C	UNKNOWN	GRAND ISLAND, NE
44-12-30-70	43 AT-23A	42-43456	LA ROQUE, RICHARD W	SCRIBNER AAB	SCRIBNER, NE
44-03-24-43	44 B-17G	42-102685	EPPINGER, THOMAS G	6 MI N BERTRAND, NE	KEARNEY AAF, NE
45-01-09-28	45 B-29	42-63387	EMRICH, DANIEL C	76-059	7616
45-01-10-12	45 B-17F	41-24600	JOHNSON, HERBERT O	76-089	7280
45-01-12-32	45 R-5C	42-39591	AKERSON, GEORGE E	75-021	7652
45-01-15-06	45 B-29	42-24495	ROBERTS, CHARLES H	76-035	7652
45-01-15-503	45 C-47	42-32804	ABNGY, THOMAS M	08-010	7648
45-01-26-20	45 C-64A	43-5326	COMEAUX, EDRIC J	76-157	7601
45-01-26-22	45 B-29A	42-93842	ERWIN, GEORGE P	73-161	7648
45-02-06-01	45 B-29	44-69692	TITSWORTH, JAMES H, JR	76-145	7672
45-02-07-19	45 L-5	42-98249	COLLINS, HERBERT F	76-145	7672
45-02-10-09	45 B-17F	42-5254	GREENE, RODNEY S	76-043	7280
45-02-15-03	45 B-29	42-24617	SOUTHWORTH, BILLY B, JR	23-081	7648
45-03-11-03	45 P-63A	42-68958	ABBITT, CONRAD D	08-010	7648
45-03-13-24	45 B-17F	41-24634	BACON, WILLIAM C	67-007	7672
45-03-14-25	45 AT-6C	41-33069	POWELL, MAX A	76-019	4117
45-03-15-14	45 B-17F	42-5442	TOWNSEND, GUY M	42-095	7616
45-07-01-16	44 RA-24B	42-54605	BIRDSONG, GEORGE P	70-042	7648
45-07-02-05	44 B-24J	42-50748	JENNINGS, DOUGLAS J	76-109	7668
45-07-04-10	44 P-47D	42-23046	RAMIREZ LOSE (NMI)	96-169	7606
45-07-04-45	44 P-47G	42-25269	PESCHKEN, STANLEY F	76-169	7606
45-07-05-30	44 P-47D	42-23062	HEARN, WILLIAM D	76-119	7606
45-07-07-13	44 L-5	42-98681	KENNEDY, BERNICE L	76-145	7672
45-07-07-27	44 P-47G	42-25252	PETERSON, DON M	76-169	7606
45-07-09-05	44 P-47D	42-8022	BOUTWELL, WILLIAM C	76-169	7606
45-07-12-16	44 P-47D	42-23008	JEWETT CHARLES F	76-095	7606
45-07-12-16	44 B-17F	40-30944	SCHMIDT, JACK	76-095	7606
45-07-12-65	44 B-17F	42-6010	MARTIN, NORRIS L	76-035	7652
45-07-13-28	44 CG-4A	43-42483	JOHNSON, ERIC S	76-013	7601
45-07-13-28	44 C-47A	43-15604	REASE, PHILLIP W	76-013	7601
45-07-14-05	44 P-47D	42-23021	JELLEY, CLAYTON R	76-169	7606
45-07-14-07	44 P-47D	42-23015	GEHR, RICHARD O	76-169	7606
45-07-15-27	44 C-47	41-18462	TINSLEY, DONALD H	76-157	7601
45-07-15-57	44 AT-7	42-2434	TALBERT, DENMARK K	78-081	7681
45-07-16-20	44 JC-47A	43-15562	FUCHS, JOHN	76-101	7601
45-07-19-58	44 B-17F	42-3467	RICHARDS JEFFERY (NMI)	76-079	7648
45-07-22-43	44 B-24J	42-78488	SPIETH KENNETH W	76-035	9134
45-07-26-15	44 B-24J	44-10605	KEECH, KENNETH H	73-091	7668
45-07-28-62	44 P-47D	42-8222	KNIGHT, CHARLES E	76-169	7606
45-07-29-25	44 P-47D	42-23001	ERICHSON, GEORGE E	76-095	7606
45-07-29-38	44 C-47A	43-30674	HANKS, KENNETH	76-013	7601
45-07-30-03	44 P-47G	42-25269	KELLER, GERALD C	76-151	7606
45-07-30-18	44 PT-19A	41-14782	MARRS, ROY M	76-055	7380
45-07-31-22	44 P-47D	42-23061	CLARK, THOMAS L	76-095	7606
45-07-31-51	44 UC-78C	43-31930	ENEWOLD RICHARD C	76-145	7672
45-09-01-15	44 L-4B	43-929	STRONG, WILLIAM D	76-013	7601
45-09-03-12	44 B-26	42-43350	REDANS, WILLARD L	23-063	7652
45-09-08-26	44 P-47D	42-74782	MCCARTHY, JOHN T	76-169	7606
45-09-08-26	44 B-17G	42-107159	WASHBURN, WILLIAM F	76-169	7606
45-09-14-14	44 P-47D	42-22577	LEONI, ALBERT G	76-169	7606
45-09-14-15	44 P-47D	42-28253	ROBBINS, GEORGE F	76-159	7606
45-09-14-27	44 P-47D	42-28764	HARRIMAN, DONALD M	76-169	7606
45-09-16-30	44 P-47D	42-74770	MAXSON, JAMES L	76-169	7606
45-09-18-33	44 B-29	42-24511	WHITE, MARVIN L	76-145	7672
45-09-19-06	44 B-25D	41-30415	POWELL, ALBERT R	76-111	7068
45-09-19-39	44 RA-25A	42-80149	LIVINGSTON, JOHN W	91-093	7663
45-09-19-500	44 B-17F	42-30572	GUAY, PHILIP A	67-007	7648
45-09-20-11	44 B-29	42-24607	SPIETH, CHARLES JR	42-091	7663
45-09-21-17	44 B-17F	42-20842	LOCKER, H M	84-109	7663
45-09-22-12	44 P-47D	42-22399	BENNETT, DOEWIN J	76-169	7606
45-09-24-02	44 B-29	42-24602	SEWELL, ROBERT JR	76-099	7663

Plane Crashes --WWII

Nebraska Accident Report List

45-09-24-06	44 L-5	42-98769	MATHERS, MARK J JR	76-159	7616
45-09-25-23	44 P-47D	42-28195	HILDEBRAND, JOHN R	76-169	7606
45-09-26-05	44 B-17F	42-2977	BRIANT, GEORGE H	76-079	9398
45-09-26-47	44 P-47D	42-23002	WILLIAMS, THOMAS A	76-169	7606
45-09-28-04	44 B-29	42-63433	MURRAY, FRANCIS J	78-071	7663
45-09-28-04	44 B-29	42-65215	WHEELER, BILLY J	78-071	7663
45-10-01-18	44 B-17G	43-37578	ARMSTRONG, FRANK A JR	85-141	7648
45-10-07-10	44 CU-78C	43-31930	YAKUMITHIS, KARL E	76-145	7672
45-10-07-37	44 B-29A	42-93843	RICHARDS, JEFFREY	76-079	7648
45-10-10-05	44 B-25J	44-29428	WATSON, JAMES L	76-063	9337
45-10-10-07	44 I-47D	42-22571	HURD, EDGAR W	76-169	7606
45-10-11-41	44 B-17G	42-30743	HICKERSON, PERRY J	85-439	7616
45-10-12-12	44 P-47D	42-28763	BRACE, JOHN L	76-119	7606
45-10-16-09	44 BT-13B	42-90349	DULGARIAN, DICK G	76-023	7606
45-10-22-04	44 P-47D	42-23003	STEINER, JOSEPH R	76-199	7606
45-10-22-20	44 L-5	42-98771	THRESTO, CHARLES F	76-141	7652
45-10-24-04	44 B-29	42-63373	FORBURGER, DEAN C	76-035	7652
45-10-24-05	44 B-29	42-24536	DOWLING, PAUL T	88-015	7652
45-10-26-11	45 B-17F	42-5330	CARLTON, REUBEN W	75-107	7648
45-10-27-15	44 B-29	42-24694	WEISS, ALEX	76-019	7663

Falcon Field Station Box 22049
Mesa, AZ 85277
(480-218-8196)
www.sonic.net/azfuller

AAIR
Aviation Archaeological Investigation and Research

10/30/00
Page 5

SPRING FLIGHT

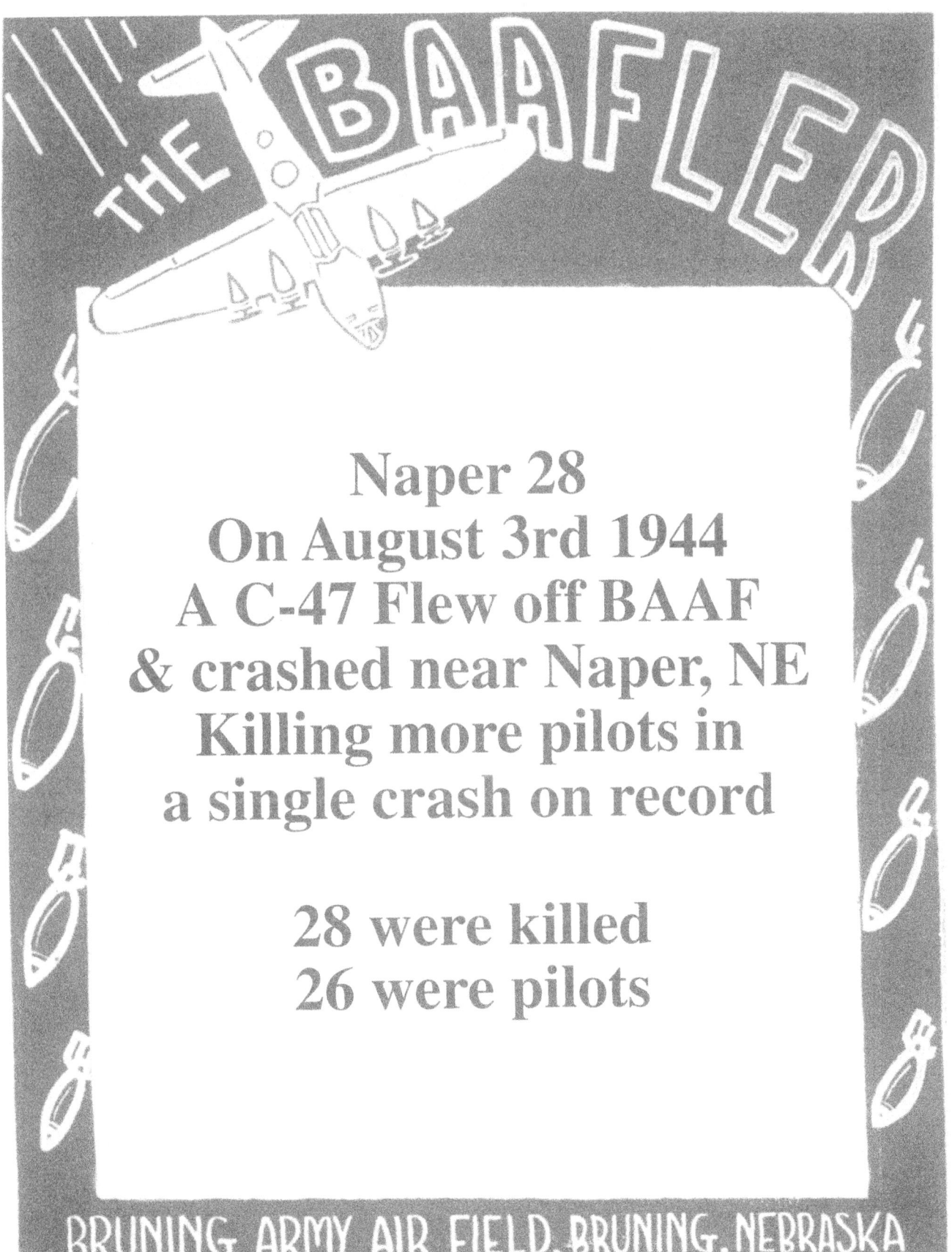

Naper 28
More pilots were killed in this single crash than any other in the US

The Naper 28 investigation was started and was so named by Lt. Col. Dale Hueske, a Korean War fighter pilot who lives in White Cloud, KS. The story that 28 young flyers took off from the Bruning Air Field in 1944 and all were killed haunted Dale. He had hoped it was just a "bar" story and called Frank Bruning of Bruning to see if it were true or not. Frank referred him to Virginia Priefert, Bruning AAF historian, who told him it was definitely so and gave him the information about the crash that was known at that time. This accident is believed to have killed the most pilots in a single plane crash in the U.S.

Dale sent for the Official Aviation Accident report and learned the details: On August 3, 1944, a plane took off from Bruning with 24 pilots who had just gotten their wings and were to be transported to Pierre, S. D. for gunnery training. The plane, a C-47, serial number 42-23852, crashed about six miles southwest of Naper, NE, killing all occupants when it encountered a rain storm. The reason of the crash was listed as 50 percent pilot error (the pilot did not try to avoid flying into the turbulent storm); 25 percent material error (the right wing separated from the rest of the plane at 1000 ft.) and 25 per cent weather information (the storm had not been adequately forecasted)

With the list of the 28 flyers who were killed, Dewaine Erickson of Wilcox, NE who had been stationed at the Base at the time of the crash, went to Lincoln to the Bureau of Statistics and looked up the death certificates of the men. This gave limited information about them but gave the birth dates and home of most of the men.

Larry Carpenter and his wife Vi, of Estes Park, CO, who research plane crashes, became interested in the story and did extensive research to find the relatives of the victims. One of the first found were the Jolley twins, Leonard and Clayton of California. Their pictures were printed on the front page of the Hebron Journal and a dinner was prepared by the Thayer County Historical Society for several relatives of the twins who came back to visit the crash site and the Thayer County Museum in Belvidere. Several members of the Society went to Naper to visit the crash site.

Those Who Flew
Bruning Army Air Field

Naper 28
Those who were killed August 3, 1944
In a C47 crash

The rain from the previous night's thunderstorm caused the ground to be too soft and muddy for the ambulances to drive to the wreckage area. Con Sattler was requisitioned by authorities to use his team of horses and wagon to haul the bodies to the nearest road.

NAMES of Crash Victims

Stanley	J	Meadows	O-431467	Capt	C-47 Pilot
Robert	K	Bohle	O-665166	Capt	C-47 Co-Pilot
Orson	H	Hutslar	15323217	SGT.	C-47 Crew/Chief
Leslie	B	Roberts	O-490591	Capt	Flt/Sgn
William	F	Acree	O-777967	2nd Lt.	Pilot
John	F	Albert	T-126015	F/O	Pilot
William	C	Armstrong	O-721322	2nd Lt.	Pilot
Millard	F	Arnett Jr.	O-695289	2nd Lt.	Pilot
Herbert	A	Blakeslee	O-721327	2nt Lt.	Pilot
George	E	Boeckman	O-721428	2nd Lt.	Pilot
Jack	L	Brown	O-721336	2nd Lt.	Pilot
Richard	E	Brown	O-721338	2nd Lt.	Pilot
James (Jr)	C	Burke	O-731343	2nd Lt.	Pilot
Donald	C	Clarkson	O-721347	2nd Lt.	Pilot
Loyd	L	Hemphill	O-728658	1st Lt.	Pilot
Arthur		Johnson	O-763216	2nd Lt.	Pilot
Clayton	R	Jolley	O-1290431	1st Lt.	Pilot
Leonard	C	Jolley	O-1290432	1st Lt.	Pilot
Gerald	C	Keller	O-774183	2nd Lt.	Pilot
Jack	E	Lytle	O-721462	2nd Lt.	Pilot
Robert (Jr)	E	Nesbitt	O-721498	2nd Lt.	Pilot
Bernard	W	O'Malley	O-721506	2nd Lt.	Pilot
Anthony	J	Paladino	O-721508	2nd Lt.	Pilot
Bruce	S	Patterson	O-1031830	2nd Lt.	Pilot
Lelan	A	Pope	O-721516	2nd Lt.	Pilot
Charles	V	Porter	O-721517	2nd Lt.	Pilot
Pat (Jr)	N	Roberts	O-721525	2nd Lt.	Pilot
LaVon		Sehorn	O-774323	2nd Lt.	Pilot

Naper 28

OFFICIAL ARMY AIR CORP REPORT

Written August 12, 1944

Description of Accident

A crash of C-47A 42-23652, piloted by Stanley J. Meadows, Captain, Air Corps, apparently resulting from extreme turbulence and lightning in a storm cloud, occurred approximately six (6) miles southwest of Naper, Nebraska at 2030 hours on 3 August, 1944.

There were only two witnesses who saw the airplane emerge from the storm cloud. Their statements are attached hereto. All witnesses agreed (except the opinion of Mr. Helenbolt) that the airplane was operating normally prior to entering the storm cloud. The statements of Mr. Windmeyer and Mr. Helenbolt both indicate that; (1) The plane flew into the storm cloud in which there was a great amount of lightning. (2) A very heavy lightning flash occurred and the noise of the motors stopped immediately. (3) A very few moments thereafter, the airplane appeared coming out of the base of the cloud in a very steep dive and continued in this flight path until it disappeared from their sight.

The appearance of the wreck (debris trail), which was seen for a mile along the northwesterly flight path, bear out Mr. Helenbolt's testimony that the pieces flew off of the airplane and that the airplane was descending at an angle of approximately 45 degrees. The pieces on the ground dropped down instead of being knocked off by contact with the ground.

Many pieces were in a field of shocked barley and not a single shock was disturbed even by the right wing which was the largest piece in that field. The remainder of the plane struck on a 30 degree down slope apparently on its back and stopped at the bottom of this down slope in a ravine where it caught fire.

No definite evidence of destruction by lightning was found.

However, Mr. Helenbolt was quite certain that a flaring light was in the front end of the fuselage as the plane descended and Mr. Windmeyer, on the night of the accident, stated that he also saw a fire on the plane.

The edge of the right wing which broke away from the center section indicates a failure of the top surface in tension. The wing tip section of this wing was bent parallel to the span and concave on the underside. This would indicate terrific overloading on the upper surface of the wing, and it is believed that the plane was upside down when inside the cloud and hit a terrific updraft in this position.

The condition of the other pieces, such as the horizontal stabilizer tips and the control surfaces indicate that the plane was broken up due to the turbulence in the storm cloud.

The pilot, Captain Meadows, was considered well qualified in this type of airplane and he had been over the route between Bruning and Pierre many times. The condition of the airplane engines and propellers was considered excellent by maintenance personnel and pilots who had flown it just previous to the accident. The weather was contact, (WWII term for clear weather, no clouds) all along the route with scattered thunderstorms forecast in South Dakota only. The accuracy of this forecast was confirmed by witnesses in Naper and Atkinson (35 miles south of Naper) who stated that the weather at the time of the accident was clear or partly cloudy to the southwest, south, east and northeast.

A Reverend Birmingham of Atkinson stated that his hobby was the study of tornado type of storms and said that the storm cloud into which the plane flew was very definitely of the tornado type, also that tornadoes can often times pass overhead without coming down to the ground.

Those who Flew
Naper 28

Fairbury Journal
Fairbury, Jefferson County Nebraska
Thursday, August 10, 1944

Soldiers Killed in Crash Known Here
Six of 28 killed last-Thursday lived in Fairbury

All of the 28 men who were killed when a C-47 transport plane crashed last Thursday night near Naper, Nebraska near the Nebraska-South Dakota line were known in Fairbury and 6 of them maintained homes here.

The plane which had just left the Bruning field and was headed for Pierre, S.D. hit a severe electrical storm, which might have been the cause of the accident.

Army officials said the wreckage was strewn over a two-mile area. Horses and wagons were borrowed from farmers to haul the bodies.

2nd Lt. Williams Franklin Acree lived with his mother and brother-in-law and sister, Mr. and Mrs. Arlie G. Oglesby at 1224 5th Street.

A military funeral was held Tuesday at 7 p.m at the Christian church for Lt. Acree. Chaplain P.F. Anderson of the Bruning Base conducted the funeral. The base quartet, consisting of Pfc. James Mc Donough, S/Sgt Vernon Bobb, Cpl. Travis Mullins and Pfc. Paul Price, sang. Mrs Charlotte Henney played the pipe organ at the beginning and close of the services. Soldiers acted as pallbearers and burial was in the Fairbury Cemetery.

2nd Lt. Pat N. Roberts Jr. who also lost his life in this crash lived in an apartment belonging to Harry Schenk at 901 D. Street. He was married July 23.

Capt. Robert K. Bohle lived with his wife at the Donna Lee apartment house at 909 C. Street.

2nd Lt. Jack L. Brown, lived with his wife at the E.T. Woods home at 1022 B Street. His home was at Milwaukee near Portland, Oregon. Lt. Brown's mother was here to be with her daughter in-law who expected to be confined soon. His father accompanied by Mrs. Jack Brown's mother, arrived in Fairbury Monday but found Mrs. Jack Brown and her mother-in-law had left for Oregon. They left Tuesday in Lt. Brown's car for Oregon.

Lt. Lloyd L. Hemphill also lived in Fairbury, but his address has been impossible to secure. *(continued on following page)*

Those who Flew
Naper 28

One sad feature of this tragedy was that twin brothers who were popular at the base both lost their lives. They were Lt. Clayton R. Jolley, Del Rey, California and Lt. Leonard C. Jolley, Fresno, California.

Others who lost their lives in this accident included Capt. Stanley J. Meadows, Grimes, Nebr.; Capt. Leslie B. Roberts, Brooklyn, N.Y.: 2nd Lt. Bruce S. Patterson, Cleveland, O; 2nd Lt. Herbert A. Blakeslee, Eddiville, Nebr.: 2nd Lt. Donald J. Clarkson, Kansas City, Mo;; 2nd Lt. Richard E. Brown, San Leandro, Calif.; 2nd Lt. Richard E. Brown, San Leandro, Calif.; 2nd Lt. Jack Lytle, Morton, Texas; 2nd Lt. William O. Armstrong, Mineral, Ill; 2nd Lt. George E. Boeckmann, Charlotte, N.C.; 2nd Lt. James C. Burke, Jr. Milton, Mass; 2nd Lt. Robert E Nesbitt, Chicago, 111; 2nd Lt. Millard F. Arnett Jr, Short Faimont, W.Va; 2nd Lt. Lavon Schorn, Klamath Falls, Ore; 2nd Lt. Arthur Johnson, San Diego, Calif.; 2nd Lt. Gerald C. Keller, Middletown, Md; 2nd Lt. Anthony Paladino, Los Angeles, Calif.; 2nd Lt. Bernard W. O'Malley, Little Rock, Ark.; 2nd Lt. Lelan Al Pope, Oklahoma City, Okla. F/O John F. Albert, Chicago, Ill. and Sgt. Orson Hutslar, Springfield, Ohio.

DOUGLAS C-47D "SKYTRAIN"

Dale Hueske
Haunted by the *"Naper 28"* story

Dale Hueske was born in Hastings, NE in 1929. He learned to fly as a teenager. He became a USAF Combat Jet Fighter Pilot and flew 29 Combat missions in Korea. Flew with the Nebraska National Guard from 1955-1972. Retired in 1975 and on October 24, 1981, be became a recovering alcoholic (He says he had been an alcoholic since the age of 17.) and started a new life thereafter.

Founded the Delmmar Communications in 1987 in White Cloud, Kansas. He built, owned and raced "Formula V" aircraft named the "PHOENIX BIRD 51 "after the bird who raises from the ashes just as he felt he had done after he became sober. He has had several other planes. He retired in 1995 from flying with 8500+ hours and 50 years in the cockpit.

Haunted by the "Naper 28" story which he heard as a "bar story" at the age of 14, he sent for the Official Army Report. With the help of Dewaine Erickson of Wilcox who went to Lincoln and purchased the death certificates for the men who were killed, Dale started his search. Larry Carpenter and his wife, Vi , of Estes Park, CO who investigate crash stories started making telephone calls and investigating. Larry came up with the contacts with the families of the victims and obtained stories and pictures.

Dale has since maintained a web site entitled "Naper 28" and has devoted many hours to the project. He was instrumental in getting a new iron cross to replace the old wooden cross in the Sattler's pasture where the crash occurred. Get complete details on his website — http://v;ww.angelfire.com/ks/phxbrd/

Those Who Flew
Naper 28

Visiting the Crash Site

After Mr. Hueske had revived interest in the 28 men who were killed at the Naper crash site, relatives of the victims as well as several interested and sympathetic people have come to visit the site. Although the Sattlers do not want the site to become just a tourist attraction, they have been most hospitable to those who have a sincere interest in the site.

Mrs. Sattler showed the dog tag that her mother-in-law had found years before. It was the dog tag of Clayton Jolley, one of the Jolley twins who died in the crash. The twins both had nephews who were named after them. The nephew, Clayton Jolley, named after his uncle, visited the site later. Several members of the Jolley family, including the twin's brothers and Judy Pullium, the daughter of Leonard Jolley, who was only 6 weeks old at the time her father was killed. Judy and her sons visited again after the iron cross was erected on August 3, 2001. Delores, the wife of the co-pilot, Capt. Bohle and her daughter, Barbara, who was a baby at the time of the crash also visited the crash site.

John Beckman, his wife, Deb, his sister, Nancy Kirk and her husband visited the site and the Bruning Army Air Field on August 3, 2000. Their brother George Broeckman whom they fondly called "Sonny", was killed in the crash. It was an emotional time for all concerned.

In the picture below are members of the Thayer County Historical Society including Dewaine Erickson who was stationed at the Bruning Base at the time of the crash. Mabel Sattler made iced tea and the most delicious brownies to feed the group.

Visiting the crash site
note the cross between trees
back row, L-R:
Kent Williamson
Jackie Williamson
Virginia Priefert
Dale Hueske
front row:
Stub Priefert
Dewaine Erickson
Gary Hoffman
Mabel Sattler

Jim Sattler showing plane parts

Naper 28

Jim Sattler, Naper, NE. Cross marks crash site.

Naper 28

Lonely White Cross on Nebraska Plain Remembered on Memorial Day

Herald, Omaha, May 31, 1946. **Nebraska News**

Atkinson, Neb. (Special)—Memorial Day found a lonely white cross bearing a freshly placed wreath in a desolate gulley between the Niobrara and Keya Paha Rivers near the South Dakota line.

The cross marks the spot where an Army transport plane crashed in August, 1944, bringing death to 28 passengers and crewmen. It was Nebraska's worst airplane disaster.

The ship was carrying 24 pilots from the Fairmont Army Air Base to Fort Pierre, S. D. It ran into a violent wind and rainstorm, which was believed to have caused the crash.

C. F. Sattler, owner of the land on which the plane fell, reached the scene in less than 10 minutes, battled futilely to stop flames.

The bodies and wreckage of the plane were removed, but people in the vicinity placed a cross to mark the spot where the 28 men died in the service of their country.

Rachel Birmingham, daughter of the Rev. W. C. Birmingham of Atkinson, placed the wreath on the cross to mark the first peace-time observance on the lonely, windswept hill.

Rachel Birmingham... honors memory of 28 fliers with wreath.

The Iron Cross which replaced the 53-year-old wooden cross. Delivered to the Sattlers at Naper July 22, 2001.
Made by Stub Priefert.
Set up by the Sattler Family.

Pictured: Burdette (Stub) Priefert
Mable Sattler
Jim Sattler

Naper 28

Naper is located 5 miles south of the South Dakota line. The plane had crashed in a pasture region of the Sandhills. It is very difficult to reach the site, just as it was at the time of the crash when the bodies had to be carried out with a team of horses and wagon through the mud.

James and Mabel Sattler are the owners of the ranch. Jim's parents lived on the ranch at the time of the crash. They have found several pieces of the wreckage and the dog tag of Clayton Jolley which was given to his namesake, Clayton Jolley, a nephew of the victim. James and Mabel are very hospitable to all of the crash victim's relatives and those interested in the crash.

After the crash, the people of the vicinity erected a wooden cross to mark the place where the plane crashed. This cross had marked the spot for over 50 years but had rotted off at the base. Dale Hueske wished to have a more durable marker placed there and asked Stub (Burdette) Priefert of Hebron to make an iron pipe cross from 4 $^{1/2}$ inch by 12-foot pipe with a 4 foot cross arm. Mary Bruning of Bruning, NE who runs "Feed Lot Fencing" donated the pipe. Stub welded pertinent information on the pipe with nickel welding rod. The Sattlers and their sons and son-in-laws cemented the new cross into the ground. On August 5, 2001 a group of crash victims relatives and interested personnel came to dedicate the new cross.

At Naper
Picture by Burdette Priefert

Naper 28

Loading the iron cross
Stub Priefert & Shep
in Hebron, NE

Putting up the Cross
Naper, NE at Sattler's
Jim Sattler
Monte Calroy
Ryan Vogt
Bryon Vogt

Those Who Flew
The Naper Iron Cross is up

Dewaine Erickson & Dale Hueske
Photo by Jackie Williamson

Chris Sattler, Ryan Vogt, Jim Sattler, Monte
Cahoy, Jenny Sattler, Bryon Vogt
Photo by Sattlers

Last Update 03.18.02...2315 C hrs

"For 55 years my sister and I thought that we were the only people in the whole wide world that remembered a great person, our deceased brother. Then to our joy we became aware of a whole group that "remembered him"..re: John Beckman...Tues evening March 5 2002
(These very touching words make it all worth while, with the help of Virginia, Stub, Dewaine, Larry and Vi)....the webmaster

WELCOME TO THE NAPER 28 HOME PAGE

This website is dedicated to the
28 WW2 Airmen who lost their lives at Naper Nebraska.

This story began about the first of November, 1998 when **DH**, a retired businessman and ex-USAF Korean Jet Fighter pilot, decided to check out a vague story of a terrible WW2 aircraft accident.
This hazy story had been bothering him for now too many years.

After making a call to the the Bank at Bruning Nebraska, the president suggested that DH contact Virginia Priefert, the current Bruning Army Air Field historian. Virginia said it was a true story but due to the War Time news restrictions very few facts were ever known.

DH was hooked!

In viewing the recently released government documents and in retracing the events leading up to this accident **DH** realized that he had a deep emotional connection to those 28 airmen.
He now hopes that publishing the facts of the accident will provide closure for himself and all the others who have now become involved with this tragic event.

Briefly the facts are as follows...

During World War II, a military passenger plane disintegrated in flight near a line of violent thunderstorms in Northern Nebraska, a few miles Southwest of a small town called Naper. There were 28 fatalities representing the crew and all passengers. Hence the name **The Naper 28**

John and Margaret Allison
Please read Margaret's comments at the end..

Please note all persons interviewed by DH on telephone were quite articulate but a lot of "proper grammar" is lost in transcribing from a tape recorder......DH

Lt. John A., then the Base Engineering Officer, was supposed to be on that C-47 flight but was told by Col. McAllister, Base Commander, to stay at the base. For that order John feels quite fortunate today.

DH in reading between the lines got the idea that John was one of the "Old Man's" favorites. The story, of how the Col. M took John A along when to check themselves out in a "spare" B-17 on the ramp, is a hair raising tale all by itself.

After being told of the accident John A was immediately assigned as the Engineering Representative and got to Naper early the next morning.(August 4) With memories now being hazy he thinks that he flew there with Col. A. in a <u>UC78</u> and landed in a cow pasture....DH

John
NARRATIVE
Col. M told me that I originally was supposed to be on that flight. But then he decided not to send me because needed (me)there (At Bruning). I supposed it was for test flights.
(August 4th Morning) I don't know of any other military that was there before us. After flying there we landed at a (pasture landing)site. I'm not sure, but I think it was pretty close to the crash sight. I think they had a little transportation there for us to drive to the crash. It may have been a half a mile away.
Anyway, they took us over and we walked the crash sight, saw bodies and some (that)of them had already been removed, some had not. We made a complete survey of the crash. I recall now the C-47 did flip over on its back. The significant thing for me was that the control surfaces on the C-47 were fabric and they were literally gone and torn off of the structure. Which lead me to believe in the storm that they had, I don't know about hail, we don't know anything about that, but it made me believe that they (the control surfaces) were damaged. We saw fabric down the field from the landing sight. There was some fabric around that point before it hit the ground.

That led me to believe that the actual damage to the control surfaces was **long before it made that flight.** That?s the reason in my opinion. It was the basic cause of the accident. I don't know if that got on the report or not.(It did not..dh)

There were four people in the plane (UC78)with me.

We stayed about ten hours. We didn't go into town, but we stayed there at the scene. I did what I was supposed to do in connection with gathering information of the (aircraft)structures. I didn't have anything to do with the bodies, except they said there were bodies underneath the wing. I did the investigation from the stand point of (the) mechanical. That was my main emphasis.

We (Bruning AAF) were a replacement training unit(262nd FPTS) for P-47 units who had lost pilots. We trained them as much as we could about flying planes and the (flying) characteristics. We did dog fighting and (practice)gunnery (passes). The reason that people were in that plane is that they were going up for a gunnery mission (30 day LIVE gunnery school with Hot Guns). I (also) did that in Pierre South Dakota.

I didn't get into the age (?) of the plane. As I recall they had little lanterns there lining the take off field, located to mark the take off direction. We went back to the direction of the crash. We went back to the last few moments before the crash, and observed structures, and ground clutter and any metals and so forth to see if we could determine anything that failed on it as it came down. We found a few parts, most of them were just before the crash. I do recall that they indicated that there were bodies under the wing. And I didn't know the wing surface. And I did not see those, but I was told that was the case. One of the members of the board.....

Was asked if he remembers any of the other crash site members
I don't remember all the names of the people (Accident Investigation Team)that were there. There were other inspectors that came in. I'm not sure about them coming in from other bases. I believe that the commanding officer probably requested additional help because of the massive destruction. And they wanted to really determine if they could determine much of what happened.
Question Did you have to refuel the UC78 before going back to Bruning AAF that Nite?...DH
The thing that would come up in my mind is just the fact that we, had so much fuel and I don't recall stretching it or not. A long trip. I have a feeling on it that we did not have to get any gas at the point where the crash was. We just used a full tank. DH-How many (total AF Flying)hours did you have at the time?
JA- oh, probably 1000.
I have a history of going around and flying at night in a SBD's, A-24's, Dive bombers. I did that in Florida. Let me think of if there is something else in this connection.
Break in the interview ...DH
John Allison-
I have talked with one person who is a cousin of my wife about the C-47 and I told him about my thought of loss of fabric on the control surface. He said he hadn't heard of that happening, but he did say that C-47 doesn't take much negative G's. That s probably what happened. I'm not convinced.
Those two pilots were experienced pilots even though they had flown most of their time in fighters. They were experienced pilots. I don't know how many hours they had. I would say that they did not fly in the storm cloud. That's my opinion
I would not have done it and I think that they flew below the storm cloud. And that the people that had said that they saw them coming out of the cloud it could be. (Difference in stories can now be explained...dh)I think what happened, is they got underneath it(roll clouds) and actually lost the fabric on the control surface, particularly the elevators. That they would lost have control of the C-47 in very rough weather. And it could have caused them to roll over underneath and cause them to dive right into the ground. If they were going down, and they pulled up on that elevator

that didn't have any covering on it, I believe firmly that they would not have any control to bring the nose of the plane back up. Those pilots were excellent and I hate to see them get the blame for all or any part of that. I think they did a marvelous job in trying to control it but they had nothing to control it with, and there's no chance for them in that situation for ever recovering.
When did you go up there?
I went up the 4th. The next morning. I think that McAllister may have been up there that night.

Margaret's Comments...

While DH was interviewing John about those years Margaret, with her sweet southern Texas accent, would jump on the other phone with some very wonderful memories that she had as a "mature" 18 year old WW2 military bride.

She and John lived in Hebron Nebraska in some apartments. When John would leave in the morning for the base, the German war prisoners (Local PW Camp) working close by, would all smartly salute HER 2nd Lt. She said the PWs liked the cookies that she and the others would make for them.

She also remarked that they and another local couple went to Kansas to a small restaurant for some excellent steaks, supposed to be rationed but they got them anyway...

She said she was considered one of the "old timer" wives as they had some wives that were still 17 years old and she had to show them the "ropes"

Margaret's closing comment was quite telling of the times. She said that before John left that morning to go to the crash site that he was a happy, carefree, happy-go-lucky young husband, but when he came back late that night after 10 hours investigating that terrible accident that John had aged 10 years....*Thank you very much Margaret...DH*

Those Who Flew
Bruning Army Air Field

Naper 28
Those who were killed August 3, 1944
In a C47 crash
Alphabetically listed

	F Name	Int	L Name	Number	Rank	Status	Birth	address
1	William	F.	Acree	0-77067	2nd Lt.	Pilot	12-6-1933	OKlahoma
2	John	F.	Albert	T-12615	2nd Lt.	F/O	6-10-1922	Chicago, IL
3	William	C..	Armstrong	0-721322	2nd Lt.	Pilot	3-7-1923	Mineral, IL
4	William	F.	Arnett Jr.	0-695259	2nd Lt.	Pilot	3-10-1920	Fairmont, W. Va.
5	Herbert	A.	Blakeslee	0-721327	2nd Lt.	Pilot	1-19-1920	Eddyville, NE
6	George	E	Boeckman	0-721328	2nd Lt.	Pilot	1-12-1923	Charolette, NC
7	Robert	K	Bohle	0-665166	2nd Lt.	Pilot	11-1-1918	Chicago, IL
8	Jack	L.	Brown	0-721336	2nd Lt.	Pilot	11-13-1922	Portland, OR
9	Richard	E.	Brown	0-721328	2nd Lt.	Pilot		San Leandro, CA
10	James	C.	Burke Jr.	0-72-1343	2nd Lt.	Pilot	6-11-1923	Milton, MA
11	Donald	J.	Clarkson	0-721347	2nd Lt.	Pilot	6-19-1923	Kansas City, Mo
12	Lloyd	L.	Hemphill	0-728658	2nd Lt.	Pilot		Missouri
13	Orson	I	Hutsler	15323217	2nd Lt.	Crew C	1915	Springfield, OH
14	Arthur		Johnson	0-761316	2nd Lt.	Pilot	2-27-24	San Diego, CA
15	Clayton	R.	Jolley	0-1290431	Capt.	Pilot	9-1-1919	Del Rey, CA
16	Leonard	C.	Jolley	0-1290432	Capt.	Pilot	9-1-1919	Freson, CA
17	Gerald		Keller	0-774183	2nd. Lt.	Pilot	7-28-1925	Middletown, MD
18	Jack	E.	Lytle	0-721462	2nd Lt.	Pilot		Morton, TX
19	Stanley	J.	Meadows	0-431467	Capt.	Pilot	1-13-1919	Sioux Rapids, IA
20	Robert	E.	Nesbitt Jr.	0-721498	2nd Lt.	Pilot	4-28-1924	Chicago, IL
21	Bernard	W	O'Malley	0-721506	2nd Lt.	Pilot	4-28-1923	Little Rock, AK
22	Anthony	J.	Paladino	0-721508	2nd Lt.	Pilot	11-11-1922	
23	Bruce	S.	Patterson	0-1031830	2nd Lt.	Pilot	2-7-1922	Clevland, OH
24	Lelan	A.	Pope	0-721516	2nd. Lt.	Pilot	11-2-1923	Oklahoma City, OK
25	Charles	V	Porter	0-721517	2nd. Lt.	Pilot	3-8-1923	Prosper, TX
26	Leslie	B.	Roberts	0-490591	Capt.	Flt. Sgn.	5-3-1916	New York, NY
27	Pat	N.	Roberts Jr.	0-721525	2nd Lt.	Pilot		McKinney, TX
28	LaVon	H.	Sehorn	0-774323	2nd. Lt.	Pilot	8-17-1921	Oklahoma

Naper 28

The Jolley Twins — Killed at Naper

Naper 28
Those killed at Naper

"For 55 years my sister and I thought that we were the only people in the whole wide world that remembered a great person, our deceased brother. Then to our joy we became aware of a whole group that "remembered him"
… re: John Beckman March 2, 2002

Lt. George "Sonny" Broeckman

Those Who Flew
Bruning Army Air Field

A set of twins together in the Army is rare enough, but when THREE sets find themselves together at Foster Field, taking cadet training--that brother, is no coincidence — that's a miracle. But, sure enough, we do have three pairs here and this is how they look. Left to right: Millington E. (Mickey) and Lelan A. Pope of Oklahoma City, Robert R. (Bob) and Royal W. (Bill) Harris of Kansas City, Mo., and Lts. Clayton R. and Leonard C. Jolley of Del Rey, Calif., who are training in grade after transferring to the AAF from the infantry.

Three Sets of Twins

Of these three sets of twins, the Jolley twins were on the same plane together and both killed at Naper. The Pope twins were separated, however and only Lelan who was called "Alec" was sent on that fatal trip to Naper. Alec's twin brother, Mickey, visited the Thayer County Museum and told how it hit him on August 3, 1944 when the plane went down. He called his mother immediately and told her he could feel that something terrible had just happened to Alec. He was devastated but he knew nothing concrete but had this feeling. In the special bond that twins have, he felt that his brother told him he must carry on without him and this was of such comfort to Mickey.

Bruning Army Air Base
Three Sets of Twins (continued)

Mickey Pope went on to fly transport planes over the China Hump and was given China's highest award by Chiang Kai Shek. They were to fly mules over and drop them down to the Burma road. They would push the mules out but they would be hit by the plane's tail and be killed. With true Yankee resourcefulness, one farm boy from Missouri took an old telephone generator and connected electric wires to it. When the mule was to leave the plane they gave the mule an electrical shock in the rear which would make the mule jump so far out that it was cleared of the tail of the plane and with the static line could safely parachute down to the Burma road.

As those pilots were working for the Chinese, they were also fed merger rations by the Chinese. Each evening a tall stack of bread was brought and placed in the center of the table. The pilots drew lots to see who got the top slice. They went around the table, each man taking a slice until the stack was depleted. They each put a determined amount of money in the center of the table and started picking out large bugs which were in their slices of bread. The pilot who had the most bugs got the jackpot.

The Pope Twins

Lelan "Alex" Pope
Killed at Naper
August 3, 1944

"Mickey" Pope
Decorated by
Chiang Kai Shek

Naper 28
Captain Robert Kenneth Bohle, Co-Pilot of the C-47 transport plane that went down at Naper.
Survived by his wife, DeLores Bohle Henehan and daughter Barbara Bohle Kuska

Lt. Lavon "Bill" and Alice Sehorn, survived by Alice and son Thomas.

Other picture of those who perished at Naper

Lt. Richard E. Brown
Photo thanks to Rick (Richard G.) Brown

Lt. Charles Porter

Lt. Donald Clarkson

Lt. Millard Arnett Jr.

McKinney, Texas
Sept. 30, 1944

Mr. and Mrs. C.F. Sattler
Naper, Nebr.

Dear Friends:

We thank you for your kindness in writing us the particulars of the plane wreck that you saw, and it means much to us to have such information.

We are enclosing a picture and newspaper clippings conerning both our son and Charles Porter, who lived in this same county. We knew most of the boys on the plane, but were very close to four, with whom our son did all his training. They were Porter, Jack Lytle, Lelan Pope and Barney O'Malley. Our son and these four, all of whom were as fine specimens of young American manhood as could be found, were very close.

We were at Fairbury on July 23, when our son was married, and had dinner with the five boys. Our son was all one could ask, as I am sure the others were. He had no bad habits--didn't even swear-- but was all boy. He loved life and people, was charitably inclined, and could overlook another's faults and forgive everything except dishonesty. All his friends say that the outstanding virtues they will always remember in him were honesty and truthfulness.

The class of fighter pilots were finishing their training preparatory to overseas service. Incidentally, that particular class had been cited at three different stations as having been the best class ever to pass through those stations. Our son loved flying and turned down an instructor's assignment in advanced flight in order to go to combat with his close friends.

We hope to be able to come up there next Summer or Fall, conditions permitting, and will be sure to look you up when we do. Again thanking you for your kindness and promptness in writing, we are
  Sincerely,
  Mr and Mrs Pat N. Roberts

Lt. Pat N. Roberts, 0721525

FUNERAL SERVICE HELD WEDNESDAY FOR PAT ROBERTS

Charles Porter

KILLED IN CRASH; MILITARY FUNERAL WEDNESDAY

Military funeral services were held in Morton High School auditorium at 3:00 p.m. Wednesday, with Rev. W.E., Peterson of Levelland, officiating, for 2nd Lt. Jack E. Lytle, 20, son of Mr. and Mrs. Edgar Lytle of Morton. Lt. Lytle was killed Thursday night, August 3, near South Dakota-Nebraska border, when a C-47 Transport plane crashed. The plane was ferrying 24 pilots from

LT. JACK E. LYTLE

Bruning Army Air Field to Pierre, S.D., all of whom were killed, along with 4 other airmen. Eyewitnesses said the plane was caught in a severe electrical storm and appeared to catch fire after a flash of lightning. The scene of the crash was a hilly, rugged section not easily accessible.

Chaplain Sloan of LAAF, was in charge of the graveside rites, in the Morton Cemetery.

Lt. Lytle was born in Lubbock Sept. 14, 1923, moving to Morton with his parents the following year. He attended Morton schools and was a member of the Methodist church. He volunteered in the U.S. Army Air Reserve Nov. 20, 1943. He received his wings and commission at Foster Field, Victoria, Texas, April 15, 1944, and was stationed at Bruning Army Air Field at the time of his death.

Besides his parents, he is survived by four brothers, Sgt. Ray Lytle of Bryan Field, Hugh and Floyd of San Diego, and Maurice Lytle, Gunner's Mate 3/C, U.S. Navy, somewhere in the Pacific; two sisters, Mrs. Lola Mae Stephens, Oakland, Calif., and Mrs. Vernon Brown, Morton.

Lieut. Bruce S. Patterson

Lieut. Bruce S. Patterson was among the 28 men killed in the crash of a C-47 transport plane Thursday night near Bruning (Neb.) Army Airfield.

The son of Mr. and Mrs. Walter K. Patterson and husband of Mrs. Virginia Roane Patterson, the 22-year-old pilot was a graduate of Shaw High School. He had just paid his fees to enter Western Reserve University when he joined the service in March, 1941, as a member of the 107th Cavalry.

He received his commission from Ft. Riley, Kas. In July 1943, he transferred to the Army Air Force, receiving his wings at Victoria Field, San Antonio, Tex., last April.

His wife was with him at his last station, Bruning Airfield. He also is survived by two brothers, Com. Gordon A. of Washington, D.C., and Walter S. a stepbrother, Capt. Charles L. Ebert of Los Angeles, Cal.; four sisters, Mrs. Theodore Mandeville, Miss Ethel A., Mrs. Myron A. King of Richmond, Cal., and Mrs. William Pfahl.

Those who Flew
Naper 28

Name	Orson H Hutslar	Orson was the oldest at 31 years of age
Rank and Serial Number	Sgt 15323217	

The following letter was recieved from Dr Berchem June 11 1999.
Dr (1st Lt)Berchem escorted the Jolley twins bodies home in WW2. His orginal Telphone interview of the escort trip is posted elsewhere. Lt Red Berchem came from the Armored Corp as a Tank Commander hence the Insignia and his rank as 1st Lt J W Berchem.....DH

Julius W Berchem, D.V.M
514 Northwood Drive, Modesto CA 95350
6-7-99

Dear "Colonel."
Please excuse the penmanship. I have arthritis in the thumb of this writing hand and also in the little finger. I always have to apologize in my letters!

You have no idea what a 24 hours I went through after talking to you on the telehone on June 24th. I had always wanted to see the names of my classmates who were on that ill-fated C-47. Time went by and here one half of a century later you lay the whole episode in my lap. Thank you, thank you.

I couldn't sleep all Friday nite due the memories that were aroused in my mind as to what a trauma I was subjected to so long ago. I always condemmed myself for not doing more to try and contact Clayton's little daughter and tell her about the wonderful father who was so tragically taken away from her. (About)the last time we sat in the PX (Post Exchange)

Those Who flew
Naper 28

Charles Rodwell of Fairbury, NE who was in maintenance at the Bruning Army Air Field, stands by the marker of William Acree in the Fairbury Cemetery. On one side there is written ACREE OGLESBY. Oglesby was Lt. Acree's sister. Mr. Rodwell wrote the words carved on the stone:

INTO THE SUN

WILLIAM FRANKLIN ACREE

Second Lieutenant U.S. Army Air Corps. Born Dec. 6. 1922 at Wakita, Oklahoma
awarded his pilots wings, May 23, 1944
at Luke Field, Phoenix, Arizona
Lost his life in the crash of an army
air transport near Atkinson. Nebraska
August 3, 1944
THE GREAT PILOT CALLS AND HEROES ANSWER

THE BAAFLER

Vol. 1 AUGUST 21, 1943 No. 25

FIELD DEDICATION

Bruning Army Air Field, Bruning, Nebraska, will have its formal dedication on Saturday afternoon, August 28, with ceremonies appropriate to a modern and important military establishment. The public has been invited to the event, which will commence at 3:30 p. m. Outstanding military, political and civic leaders will be present.

Among the important guests who have tentatively promised to attend, and some of whom will be keynote speakers, are Governor Dwight Griswold, Congressman Curtis, General Henniger of the State Selective Service Board, General Vanaman, Commanding General of the Air Service Command of Oklahoma City and many other generals.

The program will lead off with a caravan motor tour of the Field, led by Major Frank E. Quindry, Commanding Officer. Sometime during the afternoon a cordon of paratroopers from Alliance Army Air Field will arrive over Bruning Army Air Field in Army transport gliders and descend with their chutes in a mock invasion.

The two heaviest "bruisers" of the Army Air Forces, the 4-engined Flying Fortress and the Liberator bombers, will be on display. Also to be displayed in the south hangar will be a collection of equipment and materiel used by the Army Air Forces. Contributing to this exhibit will be the Ordnance Detachment, Chemical Warfare Service, Signal Corps Medical Detachment, Quartermaster Detachment and the Sub-Depot.

Included will be a display of the complete clothing and gear issued to a soldier, with the price of each item labeled; five types of gas masks, including that used in the last war; weapons and ammunition; a 2,000 lb. "block buster" bomb; flying suits; crash kits; jungle clothing, etc.

The program will be concluded with a formal Regimental Retreat Parade at 5 p. m., with all units on the Field participating. The Topeka Army Air Field Band will supply all music for the afternoon. The program, as announced, is tentative and subject to change.

BRUNING ARMY AIR FIELD, BRUNING, NEBRASKA

Bruning Army Air Field Monument Program
July 19, 1998

Master of Ceremonies ---- Rodney Kirchhoff, Co. Service Officer
Star Spangled Banner -------------------- Tina Hergott, Fairbury, NE

Color Guards --------- Strategic Air Command, Omaha, NE
                    Durham, Mammen, Post# 166, Bruning, NE
                    Saxton Legion Post # 180, Hebron, NE
Invocation ------- Rev. Dr. John Tritenbach, Lt. Commander, USNR

Beginnings ---- Dwaine Erickson, 507th Fighter Group, Wilcox, NE
Building the Base -------- Marlyn F. Huber, Post #166, Bruning, NE
Civilian Personnel --------------------- Dorothy Bunker, Milligan, NE
Dedication Aug 1943-----Bill Phillips, 456th HB, Manhatten, KS
Fighter Group-Don Worthley, 36th Fighter Gp, Monte sano, WN
Introductions:
    Thayer County Commissioner ------ Russ Loontjer, Hebron, NE
    Nebraska Dept. of Roads -------- Supt. Allen Horak, York, NE
    Dedication Facilities & Tours ----- Julius Lentfer, Bruning, NE
                                Larry Hinrichs, Bruning, NE
                                Frank Bruning, Bruning, NE
    State Historical Coordinator ------ John Schleicher, Lincoln, NE

Speaker --------- Keith Fickenscher--NE Director of Veterans Affairs,
                                                      Lincoln, NE
Remarks ----------------- Virginia Priefert, Pres. TCHS Belvidere, NE
Prisoners of War ----------- Lt. Col. John McCormick, Orlando, FL
Unveiling---Lt. Col. Hollie Wilkes, 449th H Bomb Gp. Biloxi, MS

Firing Squad Salute----------Saxton Legion Post #180, Hebron, NE
Benediction---Rev. Tritenbach, Thayer Co. Presbyterian Churches
Taps--------------------------Larry Hergot, Hebron & Fred Bruning

Dinner by reservation following at Belvidere Quonset at 5:00 p.m

Bruning Army Air Field
Historical Monument Dedication

Dinner in Belvidere at 5:00

Dedicated July 10, 1998
BRUNING ARMY AIR FIELD

Bruning Army Air Field, located northeast of here, was one of eleven army airfields in Nebraska during World War II. Construction began in September in 1942 on 1,480 acres of farmland for which the government paid twelve landowners $73,400. The field was activated on March 18, 1943. It eventually included 1,720 acres, 234 buildings, and three 6,800 foot runways. By December 1943 nearly 500 civilians and 3,077 military personnel worked there.

Bruning initially provided training for the 456th, 449th, and 487th Heavy Bombardment Groups, flying B-24 Liberators. The 449th moved directly from Bruning to Italy, where it flew 245 group missions, losing 101 planes, 388 men killed in action and 363 men as prisoners of war. In 1944 the field was home to P-47 pilots from the 23rd Fighter Squadron, later sent to Europe and the 507th and the 509th Fighter Groups which flew in the Pacific. The field was declared surplus by the war Department on November 21, 1945, and transferred to the State of Nebraska in 1947. Bruning was maintained as a state airfield until 1960. The site has reverted to agricultural uses.

Thayer Co. Historical Society

Nebraska State Historical Society

Those Who Flew
Dedication of the BAAF Monument

July 19, 1998

The Rev. Dr. John K. Tritenbach
Pastor : Thayer County Churches:
Alexandria, Deshler, Hebron
(former) Commander & Chaplain
United State Naval Reserve

Invocation

Lord, we invite you to be present within us and among us this afternoon as we dedicate this historical marker, and all it commemorates. Remind us of the many men and women whose time and energy and skills were centered here as they did their part toward the defeat of those who threatened our lives and our freedoms. We are grateful to you for each person who served here, and for their sacrifices, as they gave up individual careers and personal opportunities for the sake of this nation and its citizens.

All went from here to experience fear and separation from those they loved. Some went on from here to experience the pain of wounds, the uncertainty and privations prisoners of war face and too many lost their lives. May we never forget the sacrifices made by all.

Surrounded by these fertile fields so far from the horrors of war, give us the courage and strength to resolve that those sacrifices were not made in vain. All this we pray in the name of the Prince of Peace, Jesus Christ. AMEN

Benediction:

In the name of God who has given us life and demonstrated love, I encourage you to go from here with gratitude for all who served here, and with renewed determination to embrace the challenges and responsibilities our freedoms place on us, as well as the privileges our freedoms provide for us. Go as children of God, in thankfulness, joy and peace. AMEN

Speakers at the Dedication

M. F. Huber

Mr. Huber spoke at the dedication telling about working at the BAAF when he was a teenager. He and his father both worked there helping in the building and he was a driver for officers.

All of the barracks had three coal burning stoves in them. The Hubers went to Alexandria every day and got a truck load of coal from the Union Pacific Railroad. They would then bring it to the base and distribute it in the coal containers in each one of the barracks.

Dorothy Bunker

Dorothy Bunker told of being a secretary at the Base. Her experiences are printed in this book.

Dewaine Erickson

Dewaine was stationed at Bruning with the 507th Fighter Squadron. He also told of the eminent domain and the how the land was acquired and how much was paid for the Base.

Those Who Flew
Bruning Army Air Field

Dedication speech of
Keith Fickenscher, Nebraska Director of Veterans Affairs
for the Bruning Army Air Base Marker
July 19, 1998

This is an historic day for the folks of Thayer, Jefferson, Saline and Fillmore Counties and for all those who served in the development or mission of the Bruning Army Airfield. To be honest, I was intimidated by the prospect of speaking at this dedication because I wasn't sure my remarks could pay proper tribute to the significance of this place in the history of World War II.

So to get myself into the proper frame of mind, I paid a visit to the State Historical Museum in Lincoln. If you've never seen their World War II Exhibit, you're missing a real experience. The displays present a balanced picture of the civilian, industrial and military contributions made by Americans to the allied victory in World War II. Industrial employees worked an average of 90 hours per week and 19 million men and women worked to produce ships, tanks, planes, ammunition and weapons. And, as has been their history, America's farmers performed their own miracles. Despite a 10 percent decrease in farm labor, increases in livestock and crop production yielded a 36 percent in farm productivity during the war! Rationing gasoline, sugar, meat and butter ensured that both civilian and military needs were met.

It was in that remarkable era of national sacrifice and unity of purpose that the Bruning Army Air Field was built. Construction started in September of 1942 and six months later, on March 18, 1943, the field was activated! Nine months later, nearly 500 civilians and 3077 military personnel worked at this field. The activity around that place must have been awesome with its 234 buildings and three, 6800 runways.

It was at this place, Bruning, where the 456th, 449th, 487th heavy bomber groups trained, flying their B-24 liberators. The 449th moved from Bruning to Italy where it flew 254 group missions losing 101 planes, 388 men killed in action and 363 taken prisoner of war. In 1944 the field was home to P-47 pilots from the 23rd fighter squadrons and the 507 and 508th fighter groups which flew in the Pacific.

Those Who Flew
Bruning Army Air Field

Memorial Marker Dedication Speech
by Keith Fickenscher

The intensive training that characterized Bruning, inevitably led to unfortunate accidents and untimely deaths. But remember this ... the patriots who trained here did so NOT FOR THE GLORY OF WAR ... BUT FOR THE PRIZE OF FREEDOM.

The Axis Powers envisioned that after they won the war, this country would become a giant concentration camp! The cause to which the patriots of Bruning Army Air Field dedicated themselves was nothing less than civilization. This isn't sentimentality... this is fact. When Eisenhower ordered the C-47's into the night skies over Normandy on June 6, it remained much in doubt who would prevail in the struggle between democracy and totalitarianism. Hitler THOUGHT he knew ... He thought the Nazi Youth would outfight the Boy Scouts . Hitler was wrong! So it is fitting in our tribute to what occurred here, that we recall the words of the philosopher John Stuart Mill, who wrote:

"War is an ugly thing, but not the ugliest of things. The decayed and degraded state of moral and patriotic feeling that nothing is worth war, is much worse. A man who has nothing for which he is willing to fight, nothing he cares about more than his own personal safety, is a miserable creature who has no chance of being free."

This monument represents more than the memory of the Bruning Army Airfield and the sacrifices and heroics of those who served and trained here. This monument is now a constant reminder to generations to come, of part of the price paid for their Freedom.

This monument commemorates not war, but peace, and not the defeat of evil, but the triumph of good ... and it will forever remind us of the contributions that arose from this place to win that peace and achieve that triumph!

Freedom has never been free ... in 1775 Patrick Henry said, "If we wish to be free; if we mean to preserve ... those inestimable privileges for which we have been so long contending ... we must fight! Is life so dear or peace so sweet as to be purchased at the price of chains and slavery? Forbid it, Almighty God! I know not what course others may take, but as for me, give me liberty or give me death!"

Those Who Flew
Bruning Army Air Field

Memorial Marker Dedication Speech
by Keith Fickenscher,

A year later when Thomas Jefferson wrote our Declaration of Independence, he penned powerful words that have echoed across the centuries in defining our national identity… "We hold these truths to be self evident; that all men are created equal; that they are endowed by their creator with certain inalienable rights; that among these are life, liberty and the pursuit of happiness."

And THAT is why the Bruning Army Air Base existed ... It was part of the price that had to be paid to preserve Freedom for Posterity. This monument recognizes the debt we owe to all those who served the cause of Freedom through Bruning. Our debt to them is eternal, and that is why I am humbled by what we do at the Department of Veteran's Affairs. Each time we give assistance to a veteran or his widow or dependent child, <u>we help pay the debt.</u> Every time we arrange care for a veteran in one of our four state Veterans homes, <u>we help pay the debt.</u> Whenever we see to it that a veteran is buried in a space of honor with the promise of perpetual care, <u>we help pay the debt.</u>

And ladies and gentlemen, by your presence here today to honor the memory of this place and its contribution to our Freedom, <u>you also help pay the debt.</u>

Americans are a kind and generous people... slow to anger and quick to forgive. We are a humanitarian people and in that regard we have fed more people and fed them better, and clothed more people and clothed them better, and provided more military and emergency assistance than any other people in the history of the world, and we can be proud of that! But remember, the Bible says "To whom much is given, much is expected in return."

After learning of the accounts of bravery and heroics by those who trained here I have to believe they knew that much was expected of them.... they knew civilization was at stake. They accepted that responsibility, they endured and they prevailed. They were the sons and daughters of democracy and they saved democracy.

We owe them a debt we can never repay.

Remarks Made at the BAAF Marker Dedication
July 19, 1998 by Virginia Priefert, President of TCHS

History is repeating itself. When the Bruning Army Air Field was dedicated on August 29, 1943 it was unbelievable HOT, but the boiling cars did not have air conditioners then and there were no air conditioned sanctuaries.

It would be impossible to thank everyone who made this marker and dedication possible. As a girl sitting on the steps of our farm house I used to watch the planes from the Bruning AAF take off and land and wonder who was in them and what would be their fate.

I had no concept that we might actually learn about and actually meet some of these noble and heroic men who were stationed here. To learn about them has been a great experience and we of this county were privilegd to be the host to these men.

Thanks to the Bruning schools and Gaylord Johnson for taking school bus or van tours to the base.

When I received the 449 Book III a couple of years ago, I opened up the page to see these headlines:
"BRUNING--A GOD FORSAKEN HOLE" so I wrote the author of these words--Lt. Col. Pat Gentry of Arizona and asked him to tell about these conditions.

His answer reflected the many years of public relations he has been in since he wrote those words printed in the book. He answered that we shouldn't think it was because of Nebraska, the county or the people but it was because the base was so new and ill-equipped. Of course all of the 11 generic bases built in Nebraska so quickly were that way in the beginning of the war. Colonel Gentry died recently and I want to read from one of his last letters:

"Looking back now from my 80 year old vantage point, Bruning served it's purpose very well. We had only a few short weeks to do a critical job. We had to take ten strangers for each crew, put them together as a cohesive unit, give them the basic rudimentary training as a combat team, and convince them that we could survive at least long enough to reach the combat zone.

Had Bruning been other than a quiet, rural station, the problems would have been more severe. The lack of amenities, urban lights and pleasures, and major distractions was a BLESSING in disguise. As first Pilot and A/C commander I put the people assigned to me together as a crew that did its job. Every one of my crew survived a tour in combat in Europe although several were injured seriously. We learned early at Bruning how to work as a team. Bruning served its purpose well. Signed Pat Gentry

Dedication of the State Historical Marker
Bruning Army Air Field
19 July 1998

Those who provided a fly-over during the Dedication were:
Jeff Engels, Bill Stelling, and Randy Trellwitz

Donors to the BAAF Marker:

Bruning, Mary Beth--Bruning, NE
Bruning Motor Service--Bruning, NE
Bruning State Bank--Bruning, NE
Bunker, Dorothy & Jim--Milligan, NE
Callison, Lorraine--Fairbury, NE
Cope, Col. E.A. & Wynola--Oklahoma, OK
Durham, Mammen Auxiliary--Bruning, NE
Durham, Mammen Legion Post--Bruning, NE
Dickman, Mrs. Edmund P.--Menlo, KS,
Erickson, Dewaine--Wolcox, NE, 507th GP
Garland, Allan--Bruning, NE
Gates, Walter--449th FIB
Hume, Linda & Duane-- Bruning, NE
JML Enterprises--John Lentfer--Bruning, NE
Johnson, Mary Beth--Hebron, NE
Kaley, Robert L.--449th HB

Lentfer, Julius and Lillian--Bruning, NE
McCormick, John--Orlando, FL
Metal-Tech Partners--Tom Hawks, Bruning
Morrison, Leila, Denison, IA
Norder Agri Supply Inc.-- Bruning, NE
Norder, Jean & Robert--Bruning, NE
Pierson, David R.--Rolling Hills Est., CA
Priefert, Stub & Virginia --Belvidere, NE
Sass, Edward J.--East China, MI
Shick, Lorene Howard--Lincoln, NE
Swan, Colonel A.D.--USAF
Trope, Brig Gen. Win. A.---Monument, CO
Trogon, Gen. Floyd--Melbourne, FL-- USAF
Wilkes, Hollie & Exie--Biloxi, MS
Young, Anita-memory of Harold-449th HB
Young, Horace. St Charles, IA 507th FG

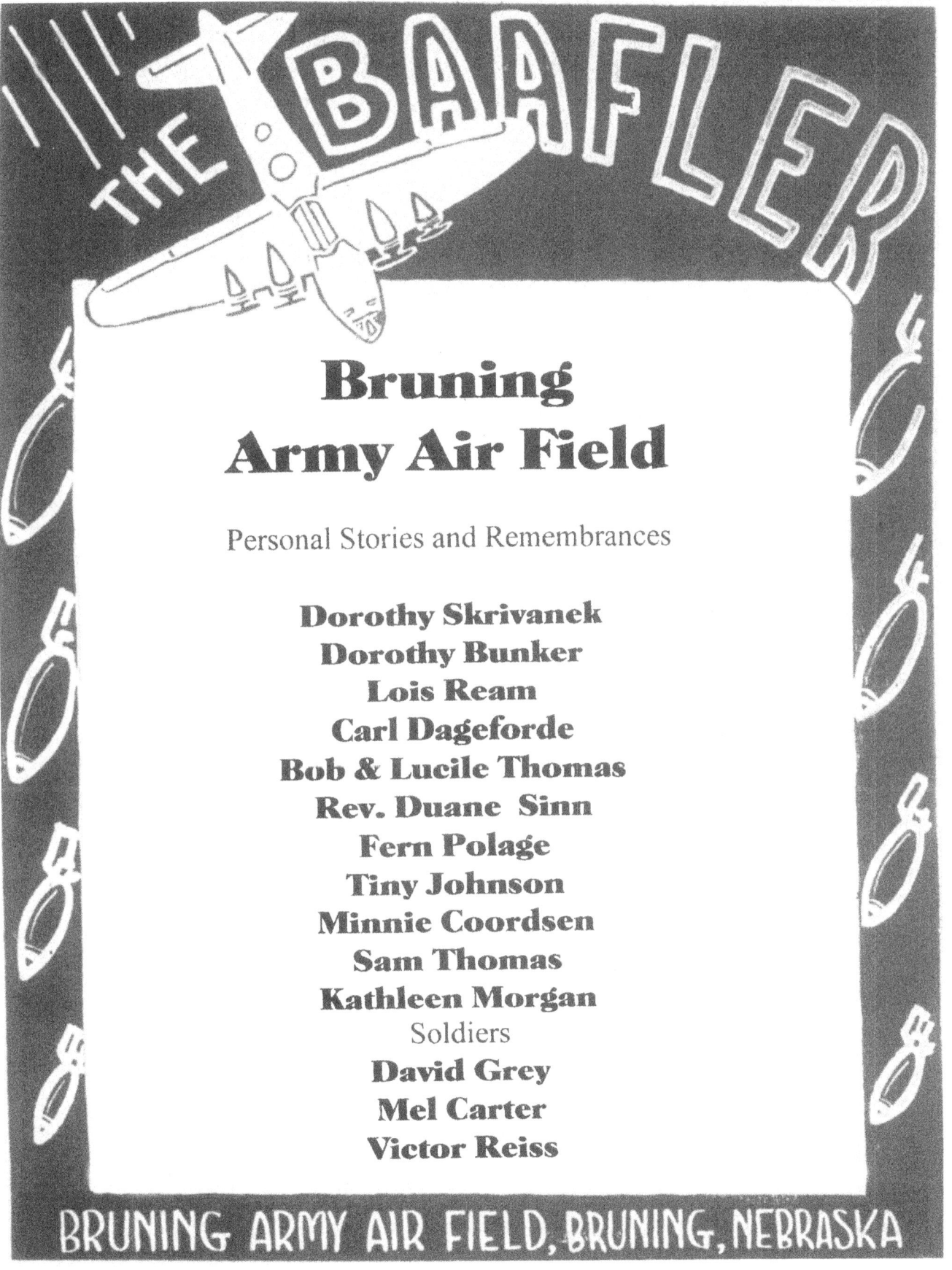

The Bruning Army Air Field

PERSONAL STORIES
By Dorothy Vnoucek Skrivanek
Milligan, NE 68406

I started working for the Area Engineers in November of 1942. I had come home on vacation from business college when Sheriff Frank Steinacher and Harrison Bauchman came to our house on the farm near Friend, NE to ask whether I would want to come work for the Area Engineer, Captain Helge Olson. I decided why go back to college when I am being offered a good job with good pay. Jobs were hard to find at that time.

We had an office in Fairmont, NE on the west side of the street, with desks and typewriters on each side of the room. We typed orders for material and correspondence for Fairmont, Bruning and Harvard. This is where and how they were sent:

For 105's--6 copies
Original and 3 copies signed
    4 to Omaha
    1 to Colonel
    1 for files

Letters of Transmittal
Original and 3 copies signed
    4 to Omaha
    1 to Colonel
    1 for files

Telegrams
    1 original form
    1 Bond
    2 flimsy

        R. W. Leisenring,
        W.O.J.G. Air Corp
        Assistant Base Adjutant

        Division Engineers M.R.D.
        Repairs and Utilities Branch
        Federal Building Omaha 2, Nebr.

        Headquarters 72nd Wing
        Office of the Commanding General
        P.O. Box 1519 Colorado Springs, Colo.

Information Copy
        Headquarters 2nd Air Force
        Office of the Commanding General
        Colorado Springs, Colorado
        Att: Statistical Control Office

        Commanding General
        Headquarters Seventh Service Command
        Attention: Service Command Engineer
        Federal Building Omaha 2, Nebraska

        Headquarters 72 Fighter Wing
        Office of the Commanding Officer
        Colorado Springs, Colorado

        Commanding General
        72nd Fighter Wing
        Petersonfield, Colorado Springs, Colorado

The Bruning Army Air Field

Dorothy Vnoucek Skrivanek (Continued)

I would also be sent out to the farm house near the Fairmont, NE Airbase on the north side (which later became the home of the Colonel) where they had me type and fill out forms on people that came to apply for jobs. They also taught me how to fingerprint so that I could help when they couldn't keep up with the applicants.

Approximately 1,000 workers were employed during the early phases of construction. I rented a room in Geneva at Dr. Carlson's and rode to work with Bud Cumberland. When the Area Engineers finished building the airbase, Capt. Olson asked me to work for him on their next job to build runways overseas. I almost did, then changed my mind. Didn't think I wanted to be shot at.

I was transferred to the Bruning Airbase Post Engineers to work for Captain William A. Grant and Major Switzgable. I never saw so much mud. Seemed like it rained all the time. The G.I.s would come and pick us up at noon to eat with the G.I.s at their mess hall. Our building was at the north end of the base. The Quartermaster buildings were across from the Post Engineers.

We would go to the PX ever so often which was at the south end of the base. I can remember the '40's music always being played by the G.I.s in the Juke box. I remember the center post with a circular seat all inlaid with the most beautiful colors of wood in the Officer's Club.

They would fly in bands to entertain the troops in the big hangar. I remember when Count Basie played in the hangar. I can still see the G.I's as they sat on the planes while the band played this great music--the smiles on their faces as they kept time to the music.

I remember the day when Capt. Darling came to have me make out a work order for him--one of the most handsome officers I had ever seen. Told me they were to fly to a Kansas Airbase with a group of officers. Next day we were told their plane had crashed, all were killed. No one can know the pain we felt for these men.

So many accidents with the P-47s when they were practicing their "dog fights". I remember the one that flew over our Post Engineers Building and over the Quartermaster Building to the north of us. Missed the roof, hit a high line wire. We were told later that the wire had cut his head off.

I would also be sent to the main gate when they needed typing and fingerprinting done--there I worked with Sgt. Joe Curley. I also had to work some weekends when paper work piled up and had to be done. Seems like all we did was get up at dark, go to work, get home, eat supper, go to bed and get up early again for work. Our work days were long. We pooled rides.

The Bruning Army Air Field

Dorothy Vnoucek Skrivanek (Continued)

Dances were held at the Big Theater Building. Once you went in you couldn't leave until the end of the dance. Our problem driving places besides work was we didn't have the gas since we were rationed so many things--gas, tires, coffee & sugar. So many of the G.I.s came to the Milligan, NE Auditorium for the dances. Also had ball games by the High School.

While working at the Bruning Air Base I lived at the Albert Kassik Sr. Home. Pooled rides with Joe Oliva and Evelyn Frycek from Milligan. Went to several weddings at the Base Chapel: Ruby Rischling Belemecich and Dorothy Koca Bunker. They both married G.I.'s.

I remember the Prisoner Of War Camps- the tall fence posts and the barbed wire fence which angled in at the top.

Major Gandrud, the Dental Surgeon, at the Fairmont Air Base Hospital Dental Clinic had lost his secretary. She had shipped out with her husband. Major Gandrud put in a request that I be transferred to the Dental Clinic as his Secretary and Receptionist. It was approved and I ended up back at Fairmont.

Dorothy Remembers the Fairmont Army Air Field

I remember the roar of the bombers as they took off down the runways and then landed. The base was a hustle and bustle from morning 'til night. The bloody bodies brought in to the hospital on stretchers. They are such a vivid memory.

The 350 bed hospital at the Fairmont Base served air bases in Harvard and Bruning as well as Fairmont. It was the largest hospital in Nebraska at that time. Sandra Sattler was the first baby to be born at the hospital on April 3, 1944.

The three large hangars at Fairmont AAF were big enough to enclose the B-17's, B-24's, and the B-29's that once roared down the runways. The 451 Bomb Group arrived in September 1943 for Final Phase training with B-24's.

Behind the hangars is the base water tower, the tallest structure then and now. It over looked the base hospital, barracks, motor pool, PX, movie theater, chapel and many other buildings. There were 1980 acres in the base and every bit of it was very busy. Once it housed almost 6000 officers and enlisted men, some assigned permanently, others making up the groups being trained. The Base Commander's home still sits by itself on the edge of the field.

Harvard and Bruning were being built at the same time each within 30 miles of Fairmont. Construction of Fairmont was scheduled to begin on September 16, 1942, but because of the rain it began the next day.

The Bruning Army Air Field

Dorothy Vnoucek Skrivanek (Continued)

The first military personnel arrived around noon in Fairmont on Nov. 10, 1942, under the Quartermaster Corps Officer, 2nd Lt. William Prince Jr. The small group of six men was an advance party and they would pave the way for the thousands to follow. The first civilian Ted Everts was employed on November 23, 1942. I, Dorothy Vnoucek Skirvanek, was also one of the first to be employed.

We were knee deep in mud. Construction workers came from many surrounding areas and states. They worked around the clock, the field was ready for operation January 1943. The 541st and the 485th would train with B-24's, the 504th and the 16th with B-29's and the 98th, 4678th and 489th were groups returning from Europe for training on B-29's.

The first Bomb group to occupy the Fairmont AAF was the 451st Bomb group with B-24's. The 451st came from Wendover Field, Utah.

I remember these bomb groups that returned from Europe, they had to come in to get their teeth checked as soon as they came into the Dental Clinic, half of them had Trench Mouth. Each one walked out with a bottle of mouth wash especially made for Trench Mouth by the dentists, which I would disperse to them. I learned a lot about dentistry while I worked at the Clinic.

I remember there were 22 airmen killed in all, while training in the skies over Nebraska.

The 451st had the worst air accident when at about 4:30 p.m. on October 25, 1943, two B-24's collided at 20,000 feet. Seventeen men were killed and one survived. The flight was to be one of the last prior to finishing training. Most of the men's wives and girl friends were waiting at the PX.

The 485th Bomb group followed the 451st and began arriving in late October of 1943. The 485th completed training in March of 1944 and moved to the Mediterranean Theatre flying B-24's. The group took additional training in Tunisia prior to going to Italy.

Half of the 831st Squadron, eight officers and 146 men were lost while moving from Africa to Italy. A torpedo attack on their troop ship took a total of 498 lives. The missions and targets were similar to those of the 451st. The 485th won a Distinguished Unit Citation for its attack on an oil refinery at Vienna.

The first group to take B-29 training at Fairmont was the 504th and it began arriving on March of 1944. There were few B-29's available anywhere for training so most of the group's early work was done on reconditioned war weary B-17s. At the time B-29's were considered an elite operation and the pilots had to have considerable flying time prior to being assigned the command of a B-29.

The Bruning Army Air Field

Dorothy Vnoueek Skrivanek Continued)

The last group at Fairmont was the 16th and it began arriving on August 15, 1944, while the 504th was in the process of leaving. The 16th then left in March 1945 and moved to Guam to fly missions over Japan. This group also won a Distinguished Unit Citation.

During the May through July 1945 period three groups returning from combat tours were assigned to Fairmont for training with B-29s. They were the 98th from the 14th Air Force all of which had used the B-24. This is when we became so busy in the Dental Clinic.

TINIAN *12-Crew members of the historic mission were selected by Tibbets (second from right).*
Col. Paul Tibbets came to the Fairmont Air Base and selected his crew for the Historic Mission over Hiroshima in Japan dropping the first nuclear bomb on August 6, 1945. He named the Boeing B-29 "Enola Gay" after his own mother. The P-47 escort for the "Enola Gay" came from the Bruning Army Air Base.

Lt. Col Paul Tibbets--The Enola Gay

In September of 1944 the then Lt. Col. Paul Tibbets visited the Fairmont Airbase in Nebraska and selected the 393rd Bomb Squadron of the 504th Bomb Group to become part of his 509th. The Squadron left for further training at Wendover Field Utah.

Left in the night

While the squadron flew to Utah, the ground personnel secretly left Fairmont on a troop train at night. None of their friends knew what had happened to them. They had simply disappeared--no one had any idea where they had gone. No one suspected that this group was on such a historical mission as to drop the first atomic bomb on Hiroshima.

While working at the Fairmont Airbase Hospital Dental Clinic we received word that my brother, Loren J. Vnoucek was killed in action in the Philippines on Luzon on Feb. 3, 1945. So many young men gave their lives for our country. "They gave us their tomorrows so we might have our todays."

My last day of work was October 15, 1945, so that I could get married on October 23, 1945. Goodbyes are never easy to say to your fellow workers who have become your friends--people you will never forget. We were glad the war was over but for many of us the pain and heartache in the loss of loved ones was not.   DVS

The Bruning Army Air Field

TAS/TBC/pb

WAR DEPARTMENT
UNITED STATES ENGINEER OFFICE
BRUNING, FAIRMONT & HARVARD AIRFIELDS
FAIRMONT, NEBRASKA

ADDRESS REPLY TO THE OFFICE
AND NOT TO ANY INDIVIDUAL

IN REPLY REFER TO:

June 8, 1943

Miss Dorothy Vnoucek
U. S. Engineer Sub-Office
Bruning Army Airfield
Bruning, Nebraska

Dear Madam:

Inclosed you will find two copies of Form PCS-5. Kindly sign both copies and return to this office as soon as possible. Also inclosed are two copies of Form 124b. Answer all questions. Attention is invited to Question No. 8. This includes members of your immediate family only.

An envelope is inclosed for your convenience.

For the Area Engineer:

T. A. SMITH
Administrative Assistant

Incls--
1 Incl: 2 copies of Form PCS-5
2 Incl: 2 copies of Form 124b
3 Incl: Envelope

The Bruning Army Air Field

Form No. 208

APPLICATION FOR ANNUAL LEAVE
OMAHA DISTRICT

Location __Fairmont, Nebraska__

Date __July 10, 1943__

Annual leave with pay is requested for __1__ days, from __July 9__
to __July 9,__ 19__43__, inclusive.

_____
(Address while on leave)

Dorothy E. Unoucek
Dorothy E. Unoucek
Under Clerk-Typist
(Designation)

APPROVAL RECOMMENDED. This employee can be spared for the period of time requested without detriment to the work and without having to employ another person to perform his duties during such absence.

REMARKS:

Taking brother who was home on furlough to train.

Brother of Dorothy Unoucek
Killed in action 3 Feb. 1945

Departed on leave __July 9, 1943__

Returned to duty __July 10, 1943__

Dorothy E. Unoucek
(Applicant)

_____
(Immediate Superior)

APPROVAL RECOMMENDED. _Francis A. McGinley_
(Official Superior)
FRANCIS A. MCGINLEY
Jr. Administrative Assistant
Chief Clerk

APPROVED.

_____
(Date)

_____
(District Engineer)

NOTE: To be submitted in duplicate and leave not entered upon until receipt of approval, except in case of emergency which shall be explained under "REMARKS."

The Bruning Army Air Field

MEMORIES FROM AND ABOUT BRUNING, NE ARMY AIRFIELD

by Dorothy Koca Bunker as given at Historical Society
Bruning Air Field Banquet, April 15, 1996

I started working at Fairmont, Nebraska in September 1942, in a building on Main Street downtown which people said was at one time the Fairmont Creamery, for the US-Corps of Engineers. My job was typing and filing clerk, sometimes operating the telephone switchboard. Our section of the office was called "The Steno Pool," consisting of about 30 girls. Lt. Prince was our boss. I drove a 1929 Model A Ford to work from Milligan, 25 miles away.

The three bases of Bruning, Fairmont and Harvard were just beginning to be constructed. While the runways were being poured, the men were working knee-deep in mud as it rained every day. They would come into town for lunch and sometimes to change into dry clothing before going back to work. About 174 buildings were being erected for the bases. The bases were built with efficiency and speed in approximately 90 days. There were about 8000 military personnel at each base of about 1980 acres. There were 11 bases built in Nebraska. This was like a citadel for defense between the Appalachians to the Rockies, for training purposes of low flying practices. Bases were built in Nebraska because it was away from the coast in case of invasion and because of the low population here.

Family housing was at Hebron, Fairbury and Bruning. Area people housed some of the military men and their wives stationed at the Bruning Army Air Field.

A favorite place for the airmen to go on a pass, was the Marietta Hotel in Fairbury, which is torn down now. The USO in downtown Hebron was best for dancing.

In 1943 on about 20 acres of land the Bruning Housing was built in the southeastern part of town. It was called "Brair Park," with 25 units for 120 families, and it had a community building and other utility buildings. An addition of 24 x 25 feet was added, to the Post Office about this time. After the war 10 of these apartments were given to the village of Bruning and the rest moved away. The American legion bought the community building.

In September 1942, Bruning Army Air Field was started to be built for a cost of $2,000,000.00 and it had 3 paved runways. It was dismantled in 1947, one of the 174 buildings.

An Infirmary and Dental Office were built but any serious illnesses or accidents would be sent to Fairmont AAF to the main hospitals located there.

The firing range was located along the west side of the north and south roads which formed the west boundary of the base. It started at a point at this road, two miles south of

The Bruning Army Air Field

Highway 4 and continued about 2 miles south. Accuracy in handling all types of guns and marksmanship were practiced here.

Lt. William W. Ford headed the Special Service Department at the Base. The enlisted men's service club and a library, a social home for the soldiers of the field, the post theater, which showed the latest Hollywood films seven days a week, the base chapel, a non-sectarian place of worship, a group of day rooms, which were individual social homes for the various squadrons, were created, outfitted and maintained by Special Services. Also entertainment in the form of traveling shows, service club dances, soldier shows, concerts and entertainment from surrounding Nebraska towns were held here. They also published the weekly base newspaper, called "The Baffler."

During the war, there was rationing. An office at the base for issuing the stamp books to purchase gasoline, tires, automobiles, shoes, sugar, meats processed foods, fats and fuel oil was housed at the base. Berneice Koch worked in this office.

Tools were made of brass and shoes were made without nails in them to eliminate sparks in danger areas. Scrap iron and metal of all kinds, waste fat and scrap paper were collected for the war effort. Clothing was collected for the war victims. War Bonds were sold and drives were held in all the surrounding towns around here, to purchase the bonds.

The shell of the bomb I brought today, was from the Bruning Base. When they were dismantling the base and were selling the scrap lumber which the salvaging contractors didn't want, you could buy the scrap for $1.00 per truck or wagon load. My uncle got his load of lumber and threw the shell on also. When his sale was being held after he passed away, I got the shell from a pile of junk from his son.

The airmen at the base wanted a swimming pool, so they dug a hole for it, by hand and the foundation was poured for it. The pool was never finished as the base was getting ready to close. I believe part of the cement foundation is still visible.

I transferred to the Bruning Army Air Field from Fairmont when the base was about to open. I worked at north end of field for Lowe Construction Company near the north gate to the field. Then I transferred to the south end of the base to work for Headquarters as a clerk-typist. I filed Army regulations and other office duties, helping sort mail for personnel stationed already at the base and helped update the men's 201 files, these were their personal files. 1st Lt. Victor F. Pettit and Captain Woodrow R. Wilson were my bosses. I also did typing for the M.P.s. Sgt. John Dyer had charge of the dogs being trained. Cpl. Joseph L. Curley was the postal clerk and we ate our sack lunches together.

After the supplies started arriving at the base, typists were needed at the north end of the field in Sub Depot and Quartermaster (Supply). Ordinance and Motor Pool were buildings near there too. The Corps of Engineers offices were across the road to the north of Quartermaster. In QM offices, general office work was done and requisitions for equipment at the base. Here in supply I worked for Captain Edwin T. Zeitlin. My other boss here was

The Bruning Army Air Field

Lt. Harold D. Paddock, who by the way, was also my husband's supply officer, that he worked for overseas.

The airmen had baseball teams and one of the teams came to play our Milligan local teams. In August, 1944, at the game being played in Milligan, was when I met my future husband. He was the catcher on the base team and the only guy I did not know as he had just recently shipped into Bruning Base from Pocatello, Idaho AAF. I knew all the rest of the players on the team from working at the base. My husband and I were the last wedding at the chapel at Bruning AAF on 2 December. We have been married over 51 years now. We were going to have Chaplain M. Shuler, who my husband was a friend of, marry us but they shipped him on to Dalhart, AAF, Texas and by-passed Bruning where he joined the 507th Fighter Group.

The parachute building was across the road from the hangars. I brought this skirt which I made from the cords of the parachute rigging. While my husband and Wally Busing from Alexandria, were dismantling the parachute building, my husband had an appendix attack while on top of that tall building and had to be brought down and rushed to hospital in Lincoln, Nebraska for an emergency appendectomy.

In July 1944, a P-47 Fighter Plane and a B-17 Bomber from Sioux City Army Base collided east of Bruning AAF and eight men were killed.

In August 1944, a C47 army transport was ferrying 24 pilots to Pierre South Dakota, crashed near Naper, Nebraska after leaving Bruning AAF, killing 28 men. Before they left Bruning, they had come into the Post Exchange (PX) for sandwiches and took them with them to eat on their trip.

A basic trainer pilot and a P47 Fighter pilot from Bruning AAF, collided northwest of Ohiowa, Nebraska in May 1944. Both pilots were killed. One man from the trainer plane, parachuted to safety.

P47 pilots from the Bruning AAF were disciplined for flying too low over Beatrice, Nebraska in July 1944.

Bruning AAF had the following Bomb Groups stationed here: 449th, 456th and 487th which was activated 20 September 1943 and left the base 15 December 1944. These were combat groups training at Nebraska bases, B-24's and B-17's.

The 516th and 517th Fighter Squadrons trained at Bruning AAF from March to April 1944

The 23rd Fighter Squadron was at BAAF from December 1943 to March 1944. I worked in their supply office. They were getting all olive drab clothing and blankets for shipment overseas and could not take anything white or light colored wear, so instead of burning all this, the office in charge, gave it all to me to take home. I still have some of the towels and sheets, that haven't worn out.

The Bruning Army Air Field

The 508th Fighter Group was also stationed at BAAF. There was also a Squadron of black soldiers stationed here.

The 507th Fighter Group was organized in the fall of 1944 at Bruning from the core of manpower originally taken from the 262nd AAF Base Unit, which was a training group teaching combat fighter tactics to newly commissioned pilots in combat units from the European and Pacific Theaters.

The 507th had Headquarters: 463rd, 464th and 465th Squadrons in their Group. On 12 December 1944, the 507th transferred to Dalhart AAF, Texas for intensive training to IeShima, in the Pacific, near Okinawa, arriving there in July 1945. They were in the 220th Air Force but operated with the 8th Air Force based on Okinawa. From 11 July through 15 August 1945, they flew 46 missions. They flew escort to the planes Enola Gay and Bock's Car that dropped the atomic bomb on Japan on Nagasake and Hiroshima. The crews of these planes were chosen from the Fairmont Army Air Field, Nebraska by Colonel Paul Tibbits, trained here before going to Wendover AAF, Utah before going over seas to drop the Atomic bomb to end the big World War II in the Pacific.

All of the 507th Fighter Group personnel lined the runway when the Japanese dignitaries landed their Japanese Betty planes on the IeShima airstrip, when they came to sign the Peace Treaty aboard the battleship U.S.S. Missouri out at sea near Okinawa. The Japanese were put into jeeps and were taken out to a smaller boat to take them to the Missouri, out in Tokyo Bay. One of the Japanese dignitaries did threaten suicide. General Douglas MacArthur signed as the Allies representative, Fleet Admiral Chester Nimitz signed for the United States and Admiral William F. Halsey signed next. Officers from Britain, Canada, China, Australia, Soviet Union, France, New Zealand, the Netherlands, all signed for their countries, on 2 September 1945 with General MacArthur saying that the table bearing the surrender documents, transformed it into "An Altar of Peace." The Japanese were returned to IeShima and boarded their planes for the journey back to Japan, after the signing.

The 507th Fighter Group (our own Bruning AAF personnel) did their part in the Peace Treaty and helping to end World War II. My husband was one man in this Group.

The 507th Fighter Group were awarded the Asiatic-Pacific Ribbon with 3 battle stars: China Offensive, Ryukus Campaign and the Air Offensive Japan Campaign and the Presidential Unit Citation and many of the pilots received the Air Medal.

Ernie Pyle, the war correspondent was killed on Ie Shima, where the 507th Fighter Group was stationed. The monument was left on the island after his remains were reburied in Hawaii.

Propaganda was broadcast to the troops in the Pacific Theater Operations. This was done on the radio of "Tokyo Rose." She said they would never see their families again or return home as the Japanese were winning the war over there.

The Bruning Army Air Field

The 507th has continued as a Unit since the end of WWII with only the 465th Squadron on active status, now based at Tinker AAF, Oklahoma City, Oklahoma but has now been deactivated and the personnel moved to a tanker unit still at Tinker Field.

The P47's were called Thunderbolts with a speed of 470 miles per hour, had drop fuel tanks, 18 machine guns, guns, 4 blades in the propeller and only 1 pilot in each plane.

A Memorial Plaque was dedicated to the 507th Fighter Group on 28 July 1995 at the United States Air Force Academy Cemetery Memorial Wall in Colorado Springs, Colorado. Several of the 507th personnel attended the dedication. The James H. Mosbey's and the Charles E. Clauss' stopped at the James A. Bunker's at Milligan to show them the beautiful plaque to be given to their group. They all had supper with the Bunker's.

                    By: Dorothy R. Bunker
                    wife of James A., who was a
                    Member of 507 Fighter Group
                    stationed at Bruning AAF, Nebr.

I typed this from my notes, about the report about activities at the Bruning Army Air Field, Bruning, Nebraska, that I spoke on at the meeting and banquet supper at Belvidere, Nebraska for the Thayer County Historical Society on 15 April, 1996 at the Belvidere Quonset.

You Are Invited to the

1996 Reunion

of the Fairmont & Bruning Airfields

The Bruning Army Air Field

Personal Stories--Lois Ream
Bruning Airbase Bivouac Area 1942-1944

BRUNING AIRBASE BIVOUAC AREA 1942-1944

The Bruning Airbase Bivouac Area was located along the Big Sandy Creek about six miles south and one mile east of the Airbase. The soldiers would begin marching at the south entrance of the Airbase, then to the southwest corner of the base, across Highway #4, then south 5-1/2 miles, cross Sandy Creek bridge to the next road crossing, then turn east approximately one half mile or so. There were approximately 200 to 300 men marching 8 abreast. The Bivouac Area was about one-half mile east on the north side of the road along the creek in the wooded area. It was all contained in a half mile area. The east bridge was the end of the Bivouac Area and was where the guards were.

J. Lois (Mahaffey) Ream lived directly south across the road from the area. I was about twelve to fourteen years of age at this time, so I was really interested in what was going on. The DeWald family lived just west of the area, up the road a quarter mile. We all have memories of the men marching and the fighter planes going over, very low.

These fighter planes would fly over the area and drop paper sacks containing flour on the men when they were marching to the area. The soldiers were to duck down into make-believe fox holes to escape being hit from the flour bombs. The men would scurry for the grader ditches, which we're sometimes filled with water from rain, and might even be stagnant water. Sometimes they would grab the barb wire fence or even an electric fence, occasionally. Supplies would be dropped from these fighter planes, too, for them to use when they reached the camping area. The area was cleared of trees, bushes, weeds, before the tents could be set up. Once this was done, it was much easier the next time they came to practice Army survival technique. I'm not sure how often they did this, but I'm sure it was at least a couple times a month during the summer and fall months. The mosquitoes were bad because of the standing puddles of water and being near the creek. From our house we could hear the men cursing at the mosquitoes during the night as we had our windows open.

There was a small sandy area just west of the main camping area, where more tents were set up. I thought these were probably the officer's tents. There were guards on each end of the mile road to stop all cars travelling the road to see what business they had in the area. When we were in school we had to walk this road and sometimes would get asked where we were going. We often hurried to get chores done so we could watch out the windows to see what was going on. Our folks didn't like to have us go very close. Once in a while, some men came to the house and wanted to buy eggs or a chicken.

The DeWald children said that they would run out to the road and watch the soldiers marching by. Sometimes they threw candy bars to them. Their parents never wanted the children to be frightened of the soldiers, because they said they were fighting for our country so we could keep our freedom. Ralph DeWald, Jr. was already in the Army, so it just made it more real for them to know and understand what Army life was like for their brother. This Bivouac Area was near their land, as their Dad farmed right up next to the area. Their Dad would go with some of the children to see what was really going on. When the Airbase had Open House one Sunday, they went up to see what the base looked like, to see the runways for the planes and to better understand what all was involved in Army life.

The Bruning Army Air Field

I heard there was a Fuel Depot over by Alexandria. The Government established the fuel depot one mile west of Alexandria, just south of the cemetery, along the railroad tracks on the east side of the road. Some of the local people told them that it was not a good idea to put it there, as it should be on the west side of the road, because the east side would flood. The tanks were in place and the railroad had built a side spur track to the tanks. They had even established a Guard Post there. Before any fuel was put into the tanks, there was a flood. When some officers and soldiers came down to change the Guard, they found him standing in the only dry place available, the middle of the main line railroad track. After this there was never any fuel put into the tanks, they were loaded up and moved to Ohiowa.

There was a Rifle Range area approximately 1 and 3/4 mile south of the Airbase on the same road they traveled to the Bivouac Area. It was south of Highway #4 on the Levi Knigge family farm, I think. Then there was a Bombing Practice Range a mile or so south of the Rifle Range. It was where the P-47 Fighters did their practice dropping make-believe bombs to hit their targets. The farmers who had land adjoining this target area had to do do most of their farming at night. Some of the bombs dropped weighed as much as 100 lbs., others much less. They didn't always hit their targets either. Sometimes I think they were just "horsing" around.

After the Airbase closed and the Bivouac Area was no longer used, we and the neighbors kids would scout around the area and find a number of interesting things, such C and K rations. The area was free of weeds and brush for several summers. They had clothes lines stretched from tree to tree. This is about all that I really remembered. We never had a family member in the Army so this was the part that stood out in my mind which I remembered the most at that age.

--Lois (Mahaffey) Reams.

"Wild raspberries may be in season, Private Buck, but may I remind you there's a war going on?!"

The Bruning Army Air Field

Personal Stories
Extravagant Waste of Time & Money
As Told by Carl Dageforde
Deshler, Nebraska

Carl Dageforde felt it was his patriotic duty to work at the Bruning Air Base during World War II as he had been rejected by the Army because of his health. He filled out sheets of application blanks and was fingerprinted. As he owned a half-ton farm truck, this was just what was needed to haul scrap lumber. He was paid $1.00 an hour and for his truck he got 90 cents an hour.

Then he received a "steel". This was a metal tag that had his name on it and when he started work he had to take the "steel" from a spot on the wall and keep it. When he finished at night the "steel" was put back in place. This was the way the records were kept on the amount of time worked.

There was a mounting pile of scrap lumber. He asked what was to be done with this lumber and was told it would be burned. To Carl and his fellow farmer workers this was unbelievable waste. Men who had been through the drought and depression days of the '30's could not imagine this good useable lumber just being burned and they let their feelings be known.

As a result, a small Caterpillar tractor was brought in and divided the 200 yard long scrap pile into smaller piles. Then they had a "Lumber Day" and anyone who wanted to buy a pile of lumber was welcome to pick up a pile for $5.00.

A lumberman was among the men gathering a pile of lumber and he found a metal box in the middle of his pile. He told the foreman about it and was told that as he had bought that pile, anything in it was his. He could not load it himself and had to have the help of several men to load it. When he opened the box he found a brand new radial arm saw which was worth about $800 at the time and he got it and the lumber for $5.00.

One of the most unbelievable extravagances that Carl saw was one cold Nebraska day some men tried to start a Caterpillar tractor. Farmers know how difficult, if not impossible, it is to start tractors (especially diesel) in a Nebraska winter. Carl and the fellow farmers were shocked to think someone would try to start this tractor in the cold weather. They were appalled when, after about two hours of trying, it was decided the tractor was no good and a back hoe was brought in and the Caterpillar tractor was buried.

As Carl remembers two men from Milligan came down after the base was closed and dug the Caterpillar up and repaired it. In later years it was sold on a farm sale.

While the civilians were so strictly rationed on gas, Carl saw gasoline wasted at the Base when the tank truck would take gasoline to fuel up the planes. If the driver had taken more gas than was needed, the driver could not take it back and he would let it run out onto the ground.

The Bruning Army Air Field

Carl Dageforde (Continued)

Carl remembered a young man from Ohiowa who was was hired as a skilled carpenter. He was given no orders to do anything, and as he was a noted prankster, he took a board about five feet long and six inches wide and walked to sawmill #1, then to sawmill #2 and on to the nail house to collect nails. Then he would repeat that process.

All that time, a man walked about 12 to 15 feet behind him. The man, never said a word so, the prankster repeated his process. By lunch time, he still had not received any instructions so he repeated his sawing rounds again. Once again the man followed him. Finally he thought this man must be an inspector to see what he was doing and as he thought he must really be in trouble so he confessed to the follower that he wasn't really a carpenter and he didn't know what he was supposed to be doing. The man then told him that he had been hired to be his helper and was getting $1.90 to follow him around.

The waste was shameful everywhere according to Carl. Every evening his truck was swept out. There were always nails left in the truck, and they were swept out into a dump site. Finally he told them that he would sweep his truck out when he got home. He soon had recovered a case of nails.

Although there were some very conscientious workers at the base, Carl noted that when the concrete runways were being poured, mud got into the cement and this caused the runways to crack and break up.

Carl related stories of men playing pool while they were supposed to be working and hours wasted waiting for work orders. Carl said he could tell of many more wasteful practices and he feels that all Americans have become very wasteful today.

The Bruning Army Air Field

Personal Stories
as told by Bob & Lucile Thomas

Bob Thomas' father, L.E. Thomas, was an optometrist and also ran THOMAS JEWELERS in Hebron. They remember two young couples coming to the Thomas' home and pleading desperately if they could help them find a place to stay as the soldiers had just been stationed at the Bruning Base. Bob said father looked at mother and feeling their desperation, she nodded and they told them they had two bedrooms upstairs. They grew very fond of their roomers and one couple had a baby while while staying there.

Bob's parents couldn't handle all the business while the Bruning Air Base was in operation. They asked Bob & Lucile to come back to help his dad in the Jewelry store just for the duration. They are still there and the store had its' 75th anniversary.

As people usually buy jewelery for special occasions, it is a happy business. However, during war, it had some very sad occasions. The saddest was when lightening struck a B-17 near Sioux City and it crashed and burned. A soldier brought in several brown envelopes each with a man's name written on it. Inside was the charred and bloody jewelry that was taken off each man's body. They were asked to clean the jewelry so it could be returned to the next of kin. Bob said he and his father worked two days cleaning even burned skin from the watches. They cried all the time as they knew most of the men. When the jewelry was picked up at Thomas's they, said there was no charge. "How could you charge for anything like that?"

A second sad time was when a soldier brought his wife into the store and helped her pick out a string of pearls. When the selection was made the soldier told them he would be back next Saturday to pick the pearls up after pay day. That week, that soldier, a P-47 pilot, came out of the clouds and crashed and burned. The wife came into the store and picked up the pearls on her way back home alone.

"Don't ask me what the idea is. The Lieutenant told me from now on I'm to be an airplane spotter!"

MEMORIES OF BRUNING AIR FORCE BASE

Construction of the base began in late summer, I believe 1942. The word got out that they needed places for the construction crew to stay, and since we were still coming out of the depression, it seemed like a good opportunity to bring in some extra money. We boys changed our sleeping arrangements so that five of the workers could have the two upstairs bedrooms. In one room, where three stayed, there was one double bed and a single bed. The other room had two single beds. My brother Bill and I were moved downstairs to sleep in the sewing room, off the parlor.

My mom, Mabel Sinn, would prepare their breakfast and a sack lunch. Usually they would get up at 5:30 to be at work by 6:30, if they were on the morning shift. But construction was taking place 24 hours per day, so some of them worked the night shift and slept during the day. There was an urgency to get the base built, so the men worked seven days a week and only went home on holidays. Mostly, they were older, single men, but one of the younger ones was named Slim and had a medical condition that kept him from the draft.

Mom didn't provide dinner, so we didn't usually see them too much until their bed time, which was about 9:30. They worked long shifts and were serious about their work, but on Saturday night, they would usually go into town to play pool. On Saturday morning before they left for work, they would line up their shoes for me to polish for their night on the town. They were supposed to give me 25 cents per pair, but often they would give me as much as a dollar.

One of the men staying with us was a supervisor. One night he came home discouraged because some piece of machinery they were using was broken and it would take at least 4 days to fly some experts in to get it fixed. Sid Schmidt was at our house for Sunday dinner with his family and said he could probably fix it (he owned a farm implement shop) and sure enough, he went out to the base and had it fixed by midnight and they were back in business. The base was completed in about 9 months.

Later, when the base opened, they flew mainly P-47s and B-17s. The chimney on the Sinns house was the turning point they used when they headed southeast.

The base was, of course, a place where they could train and we saw many a dog fight in the air, as they prepared to go overseas. One night we woke about 3 a.m. to the sound of sirens and fire trucks and jeeps going right through our stock fence. There had been a plane crash and they thought it was in our fields, but it was further away. Another time, a B-17 crashed and they could not find the body of the pilot who had parachuted out. I helped find him in a corner 8 miles north of Alexandria where he had hit a fence post and was killed. It was days before I could stop thinking about seeing his limp body, all broken there in the field.

We boys found many empty bombs in the fields, leftover from their practice flights. We were proud to be this close to the war effort and did what we could to help; collecting empty cans and milk weed pods to be used for silk in making parachutes.

M Duane Sinn
June 5, 1999

PERSONAL STORIES
Memories of Fern Polage, Alexandria

Fern and Laurence, "Skinny," ran a cafe in Alexandria from 1936 to 1951. While the Bruning Air Base was being constructed we fed over 360 people every day of the week from 3:30 a.m. to 1:30 a.m. the next morning. I had 18 women helping me. We would serve breakfast for those who were going out in the morning and would put up sack lunches for them to take along with them at the base.

Then we fed the night shift--the ones who were getting off work at 4:00 a.m. and were going to go to bed and sleep in the day. We served meals all day and of course had big dinner and supper crews that continued to come in until 1:30 a.m.--the time we closed for 2 hours.

It was difficult as we would not know ahead of time how many were coming in at once or how many would come in during the day. We bought our groceries locally in the day time (this was the time before freezers and even refrigeration was very new so we had to get our groceries as fresh as we could). The Ferd McKenzie Grocery Store in Hebron stayed open at night so we could get groceries from them at night.

We were not the only Cafe in Alexandria. The Towers also ran a cafe during that time also. Both Cafes were really busy. "Skinny" and I were completely devoted to serving meals. We took no other time off. We had a bed in the back of the restaurant and we would take a nap and sleep as long as we could whenever possible.

Our restaurant was located on the west side of Main street across from the post office. The building was torn down sometime ago and the area turned into a little Park. As well as I can remember the women who helped me cook and wait tables were Zelda Carson, Ella Joe, Anna Johnson, Dorothy Boyer, Luetta Boyer, Ida Boyer, Bertha Newell, Mary Hazel Taylor (later Starck), Marneta Thrasher, who married a soldier from the base, Forrest Hudkins, Mildred Wolford, who married a soldier from the base, Grady Morris, Faye Stokes, Wanda Lee and Betty Knigge, Faye Rains and Jessie Woltemath.

Mrs. Laurence (Fern) Polage
P.O. Box 15, Alexandria, NE 68303

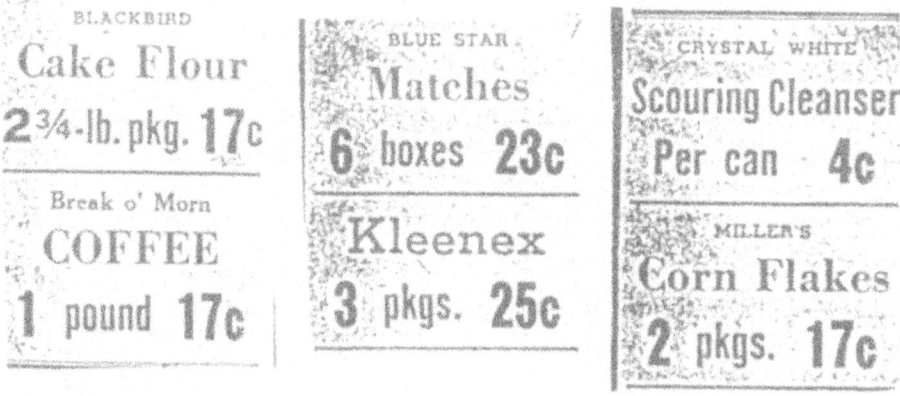

Personal Stories by "Tiny" Hazel Johnson

THINGS ABOUT BAAF WHICH HAVE BEEN TOLD TO ME

Not everyone who had stories to tell of their experiences at the BAAF has jotted down these items for publication. I hope they won't mind that I will relate what they have told me as we have visited.

Daryl Easley, Alexandria, farmed near the base and his pasture was leased to the government to be used for a rifle range. The adjoining fields had to be cultivated so this was done at night. The Easleys figured there wouldn't be any stray bullets coming their way at that time of day.

Bob Frank, Carleton, worked at the base as a 17 year old in the summer prior to his senior year of high school. Taking a noon break one day he climbed into one of the fighter planes on the runway. He pulled the cover over his head and then realized he did not know how to unlatch it. He was afraid to touch anything for fear it would be the wrong button. He had to wait until someone found him before he could leave the plane.

Betty Jo Elliott Bruns, now of Denver, Colorado, worked at BAAF after graduating from Hebron High School. She assisted in fingerprinting workers who were erecting buildings at the base. A naive young girl, she did what her superiors asked her to do. One time they told her to call Lt. Bin Murgatroyd, the Provost Marshal, and ask if he had the keys to the parade ground. Murgatroyd must not have been in a jovial mood that day as he hung up on her.

Another time with similar results, Bruns was instructed to ask him if he had the keys to the latrine.

Earlene Bryan Koves, who is now Mrs. Reiner Andreesen of Beatrice, met her husband, Roy Koves, when he arrived at Bruning. He was from Kensal, North Dakota and had been stationed at Topeka and Utah before coming to Bruning. Earlene was working at the sub-depot, but their romance began at a dance in Hebron. Though he had taken another girl to the dance, he took Earlene home.

Roy was one of the servicemen that came back to Thayer County after the war. Earlene and Roy were married at Belleville, Kansas, on September 12, 1943. The couple resided In Hebron and reared their two children here. He was killed in an accident south of Bruning July 6, 1971.

Other Hebron girls who worked at the sub-depot were Virginia Ramsbottom and Ruth Wellman. Salaries were much better at the base than in most civilian jobs.

Ruth Glaeseman said her husband, Walter, was a member of the fire department at the base. When he went into the service, he was promised his job back when he would return. They kept their word and he returned to duty at the base when he was released from service. Oscar Ireland, another Hebronite, worked as a fireman while Glaeseman was gone.

PERSONAL STORIES
As related by Minnie Coordsen
Hebron, NE

Minnie Coordsen was going to Alexandria high school during the days that the Bruning Air Base was built. She related some of the difficulties being in school during the war. There was an acute teacher shortage as all the men were off to war and only women who weren't working at defense jobs (which paid twice or up to three times as much as teaching jobs which had a lid on them) were left to teach. This meant that the best were not available. Students were forced to take courses by Extension through the University.

Minnie related that the small towns still tried to have football games between each other. As gas and tires were rationed, the high school students put their money together to get enough gas for 1 or 2 gallons; went to some of the elderly women who never drove out of town and asked for one of their ration stamps to get a gallon of gas; and then took the gas can and the ration stamp down to Erle Pletcher's gas station in Alexandria and got the gas.

They gave the gas to Harold Hoppe Senior or Arlo McMillan, who owned cattle trucks (which were used to take the cattle to market) and the truckers would put in new straw, which covered up the cattle manure, and the whole school would pile in the trucks--standing room only and they were off to another school within the county to play ball. If it rained, the truckers covered the truck racks with a tarp. That meant the students could no longer stand upright, but had to crouch or sit on the straw.

Minnie went to the Bruning Base Open House and it was there that she saw her first black person. This made a lasting impression on her. (It would be hard for the youth of today to relate to this as there was no television then and magazines with pictures were limited, so many in this farm country, were not even aware of other races.)

Minnie remembered shoe rationing. Nylon or silk hose were unavailable, so girls bought a paint at the dime store which was made for the purpose of putting on the legs, as you would put on sun lotion today, and this would color your legs so as to give the impression that the wearer had on hose. Hosiery in those days had a black seam down the back and a series of 6 or 8 knots on either side of the seam at the thigh. The girls would take a black eyebrow pencil and draw the line up the back of the legs to simulate the seams and make the little dots on either side of the seam to give the appearance of knots. She also remembered her father diluting gas with tractor fuel, which was easier to get, so as to make the gas go farther.

Her husband, John Wolford, who was also from Alexandria had a sister, Mildred who married a soldier from the Bruning Air Base, Grady Morris.

Those Who Flew
Personal Remembrances

Three Memories of a Nine Year Old
by Sam Thomas, Tacoma, Washington

1. My grandpa Thomas, who owned and operated the Alexandria Lumber yard, was involved with providing materials for the base. One weekend he and I drove over in his 1939 Buick to the construction site. I was very impressed not having ever seen anything like it before. Earth moving equipment had cleared and leveled the site. Huge trucks had dumped cement on the ground. Cement was mixed with sand by graders and tillers and dumped to a thickness of nearly a foot in depth.

Grandpa explained that this was a unique process just invented to expedite the rapid construction of runways. The same method is used today to quickly construct all weather roads in inaccessible locations. Once the soil and cement were mixed and leveled, water trucks were used to dampen the mix and turn it into concrete. As far as I remember no reinforcing steel or rod was used.

2. I lived upstairs in the east bedroom of Grandpa and Grandma's house in Alexandria, NE. During the war they rented the west bedroom to employees of Bruning Air Base. I recall the first couple to occupy the room. Both worked at Bruning and were a very pleasant couple in their early 30s. We shared the upstairs bathroom and I experienced for the first time scents and aromas of cologne, after shave and wintergreen. These cosmetics my austere and puritanical grandparents generally shunned.

3. Once completed, Bruning attracted squadrons and men from all over the country. I remember vividly stopping on my way to school and staring in awe as the sky above would fill, seemingly from horizon to horizon, with countless low-flying B-24 bombers. The din of the engines was a low continual drone which would last for what seemed to me, as a very long time. It was a very impressive display for a nine year old Nebraska boy.

The Bruning Army Air Field

Personal Stories
Earl & Pauline Hawks
Hawks Flying Ranch

Earl Hawk's parents were pioneer settlers three miles west of the Bruning Air Base on highway 4. Earl and Pauline referred to their ranch as Hawksville as the two of them made up a whole village. Pauline had a beauty shop, a grocery store and meat market supplied by the Wilber meat man, on the porch of their big house. Earl raised Hereford cattle, had a large dairy herd, sold gas, had a tire shop, as well as an airport with all facilities. Pauline raised chickens, sold eggs and had a large garden as well as fruit trees. Noted for her cooking skills, Pauline was always ready to prepare a meal for visitors.

On January 26, 1996 both Earl & Pauline were inducted into the Nebraska Aviation Hall of Fame for outstanding contribution to Nebraska aviation. They also received the Hospitality award-- and rightly so, for they have always been noted for their friendly hospitality which they displayed during the days of the Bruning Air Field.

During the Air Base days, the Hawks extended their home and friendship to many at the base. When the construction workers came they asked for a place "just to sleep". Pauline & Earl welcomed the workers, to 2 bedrooms upstairs and put a bed in the living room for another worker. Soon there were up to 7 men staying there.

There was a cook shack at the base and the men were to eat there but they soon complained they had to stand in line so long at the shack that it was time to go to work before they got any breakfast. Would Pauline "just make us coffee before we go to work?" Coffee and toast soon grew into a full all out breakfast with pancakes and fried eggs.

"Would you just make us a couple of sandwiches in a bag to take along for our lunch?" This project grew into lunch pails with thermos bottles which Pauline had to fill every morning. Then the men were so hungry when they got off work they asked for what developed into a entire supper for 10 or more around the dining room table every evening 7 days a a week. Pauline did all the dishes.

Food was rationed and some of the men gave Pauline their ration books; but many of the books had the precious coffee & sugar stamps already removed by wives or mothers back home before they were given to Pauline.

Earl, always accommodating, brought in two trailer houses and built two cabins. When the wives came along with soldiers they had 3 couples staying in their house, 2 couples living in the filling station, 2 couples in the trailer houses and 2 families in the cabins. Pauline particularly remembers Lt. & Mrs. David Edmonds of Salt Lake and The Bill Wilsons of Chicago living in the filling station and Dale and Lottie Simpson in one of the trailer houses.

One of the cooks for the base stayed in the Hawk's Filling Station. The cooks were on for 24 hours then off 24 hours as Pauline remembers it. When a cook went off duty he had to clean out the base refrigerator and dump all the food that was in it.

The Bruning Army Air Field

Earl & Pauline Hawks (Continued)

The cook agreed that this was wasteful and gave some of the food to the Shane boys who lived by the base and eventually brought the rest of the food home with him and distributed it among the other soldiers and their wives.

Pauline remembered one day the cook came over and asked Pauline how to make cream puffs. She told him and he soon came over with the glob of dough in his hands and asked what to do with it next. The cook walked back to the filling station tossing the dough from hand to hand. Suddenly a dog which was following him jumped up and caught the dough in mid air. The cook tried to make cream puffs again but divided the dough into only 4 parts instead of 24 and had enormous cream puffs.

Sgt. Howard and Eleanor Haney stayed in the back bedroom of the Hawk's house. He was the photographer at the base. They kept in touch for many years.

Mrs. Haney, Pauline and Earl Hawks on the Bruning Air Field.

Bruning AAF personal letters
David M. Grey Antonio, Texas

Nov. 11, 1996

Dear Mrs. Priefert:

Today I received my copy of "Late Pass", the periodical of the 449th Bomb grouping which you solicited information on our tour at Bruning.

To begin with, my wife of three months and myself could not find Bruning, but my AAP orders said to report to Bruning Army Air Base. For that matter, the bus company could not locate Bruning but we bought tickets to Lincoln as we learned Bruning was close to Lincoln. But the (Lincoln) ticket agent could not locate Bruning, but a bus driver thought it was close to Geneva so to Geneva we went. No bus to Hebron until the next day, but two men we happened to talk to were going to Hebron and gave us a ride. Our belongings including my personal flying gear overflowed their car.

Living conditions and flying conditions at Bruning was Spartan but nothing compared to my wife's living in Hebron. The only place she could find was a dingy room on the second floor in a large house with many rooms rented to other wives in the 449th. One bathroom in the house and no cooking facilities, but my young wife was determined to stay near me as we both realized the potential of my not coming back.

If I remember correctly there were two eating places in Hebron where she had to eat. The food was so bad and so expensive for the time that I always made sure I ate at the Base before coming to town which was infrequent--about twice a week. Sometimes, my wife along with other wives would come to the Base USO where we could drink cokes and dance to the Juke box.

Hebron was not equipped physically or psychologically to deal with this huge influx of stranger in their midst, which is understandable. What is not understandable is the crude and sometimes lewd remarks leveled at these wives as being camp followers and being married to collect their husband's insurance. I salute my wife and those other wives who had the fortitude to endure.

The training was hard but we had excellent flying conditions. The weather was perfect except for the wind and there were moments of comedy such as coming across a dry corn field in October to about 100 feet above the ground. A farmer shucking corn with a team of horses was bent over backwards trying to control his team, while a small tornado of corn stalks whirled through the field.

At last it was finished and my wife came to the base for a tearful good bye as I and everyone else was restricted to the base. Such a good woman and she followed me all over the world later on as we raised three sons.

Our group received our new B-24 H which we named "Paper Doll" and flew her to South America and then to Africa and to Italy and her final resting place is Rumania-a shattered and burned hulk. Thanks for remembering us after so many years.

Sincerely, David M. Grey

Those Who Flew
Bruning Army Air Field
My Life in the Service
by Victor Reiss of Wilcox, NE

Victor Reiss has written a booklet about his life in the service and has donated a copy to the Thayer County Museum in Belvidere, NE. Here are some of the items he touched on in his book:

"In the early '40s, the United States passed the selective service act. Eligible men of a certain age would be drafted into the armed services. I was of that certain age and very eligible. Before anyone was drafted there was a lottery to determine the order they would be called. Each man was given a number and was to report in the order that these numbers were drawn out of a fish bowl in Washington, DC. I got a high number so I was to be drawn out towards the last. But it didn't work that way because of the deferments, I soon got a letter from President Franklin Roosevelt to join the armed forces of our country."

After going to Fort Leavenworth, I acquired G.I. clothes, got $21 a month and went through much marching at Boot Camp. If anyone had any college they were sent to officers training for 90 days to become a "shave tail" or a second Lieutenant. We called these men "90 day wonders."

After going to Sheppard Field, Texas, Sioux Falls SD, Boca Field Fla., and with two stripes (a corporal) I was sent to Pyote, Texas and finally when I was a sergeant, I was sent to be with the 718th Squadron of the 449th Heavy Bomber Group at Bruning, Nebraska. This was to be my permanent outfit. The 449th was ready to go overseas but they were short on I.F.F. radio men so four of us were transferred there to bring them up to full strength.

Before I could go overseas, there were several things I had to do--I was issued a M-1 carbine and had to memorize the serial number on it. Because I was so close to home I got to go home on weekends and would hitchhike. There was a lot of traffic and someone would always pick me up.

Alkire was our commanding officer. The 449th had a perfect training record in that we never had a plane crash, or anyone killed in training. Don't know if it was just good maintenance, or if we were just lucky.

I was in communications. We had a telephone lineman and a telephone operator. There were probably 20 - 25 in communications. We the 449th, had an engineering department, an ordinance department, a motor pool department, a mess hall, a medical department and operations department. Now we were set to go overseas.

Bruning AAF Personal letters
Mel Carter, Mesa Arizona

Historical Society
Ladies and Gentlemen:

The 449th Bomb Group's "Late Pass" suggests we write and tell you something of our days in Bruning. I arrived there in the fall of 1943 having just been checked out as Pilot in a B-24 in Clovis, New Mexico. Had been in B-26's but volunteered for B-24's and when arriving at Bruning knew so very little about this four (4) engine lumbering air plane. On my check ride at Bruning I failed to line up with the runway properly and was really chewed out. He probably didn't know it was about my fourth time to bring this type plane for a landing.

Each of us got our crew very soon and started flying as a crew immediately thereafter. Got our new plane that we took overseas within days or weeks. While doing our training we buzzed several of the farm houses in the area but out away from the airfield as we didn't want to be caught doing this. Had a engineer gunner from Norfolk so we buzzed the town one day and they had a picture of us doing this in their newspaper.

The description of our plane should have read as follows: #42-07726 to Bruning 15 Oct. '43 and assigned to Carter's crew, tail #25. Received damage from a RAF 2 engine Beaufighter the night they landed in Italy when it lost an engine and in crashing hit our plane and damaged the right wing tip and the top turret, but maintenance corrected the damage and she returned to combat. Salvaged Aug 1, '44.

This was shortly after the Bari Harbor ammunition ship blew up & sunk all the ships in the harbor which included our supplies. So when we landed in Grottaglie our Squadron had no supplies or food. We were all asleep in this plane when it was damaged that night and I was in the waist in a hammock I had purchased in Brazil. Claimed to have jumped from the hammock through the waist window without touching metal. Upon hitting the ground the Beaufighter went up in flames some 200 yards beyond us and its ammunition started going off and zinging across the sky. My only protection was the tire of our plane. At that time I didn't know where this plane came from and I thought "Combat is Hell."

We got to see very little of Bruning during our stay at the airbase. A few week-ends we got off the base and two of us would ride with our engineer to Columbus and stay in a motel while he went on to Norfolk.

Very truly yours,

Mel Carter

Museum Muse

published by the

Thayer County Historical Society

THOSE WITH WINGS
Aviation History of Thayer County, Nebraska

Picture of Frank Kaiser Miller, Hebron Aviator, at the Belleville Fair September 15, 1911

Museum Muse --Those With Wings

The cover of this issue of the Museum Muse shows the Republic County Fair at Belleville, KS. This composite picture taken on glass negatives and printed as a postcard, shows Frank Kaiser Miller, of Hebron, NE flying, his Strobel plane with the Surrey Race in front of the grandstand, while the enormous ferris wheel turns and the flag waves. It was written to Mr. William Miller, RFD 4, Hebron, NE. It is postmarked Oct 12, 1911 and reads, "Hello Will—this is Frank on Friday afternoon at Belleville, the best flight he made here (signed) Clayt."

Thayer County Nebraska

Thayer County Nebraska is 24 miles square and located along the Kansas line in central Nebraska. For a small county in Nebraska, it has had a lot of aviation history and many great flyers have lived here.

During the 1980s, the Thayer County Historical Society printed information regarding the County and called the publications the ***Museum Muse*** printed by Gary's Printing of Hebron, NE. In 1985 a Muse regarding the flyers of Thayer County was printed. This Muse has been copied in this publication.

At Carleton, NE the Morrow brothers, Edward and Everett, made a plane of bicycle wheels, hand carved axles with a wooden fork, with no real radiator and a small make shift gas tank. This is the first totally handmade airplane made in Nebraska and it flew before July 1911, The Savage brothers who claim the title of the first plane built in Nebraska made their plane from "factory parts" and flew in Ewing, NE. On May 7, 1911.

Pauline Hawks of Bruning received an award from Mr. W. T. Piper for the most hours flown in 1957 at the 13th annual "Flying Farmer's" Convention in New York. Pauline did commercial flying and was the first woman spray pilot in Nebraska. She was the National Flying Farmer Queen in 1951 and served as president of the '99ers, a women's flying organization honoring Amelia Earhart. This organization was so named because there were '99 members when they first were organized. Notice the picture, elswhere in this book of Pauline flying with her mink coat, silk hose and high heels. The 99ers required that women flyer's looked and dressed like ladies at all times.

The first picture printed in this Muse is a balloon ascension in Hebron on August 22, 1907. Ballooning history was made at the former Bruning Army base on Oct. 21, 1960 when Ed Yost flew the first modern free flight balloon for 25 miles. From this, the sport of free flight ballooning was begun.

THOSE WITH WINGS

Aviation History of Thayer County
FRANK KAISER [KEISER] MILLER

Frank Miller was Nebraska's first native born aviator and professional pilot. His career as a professional pilot was extremely short lived, however, as he learned to fly on April 20th, 1911 and died in a plane crash September 22nd, 1911 making him the first Nebraska native to be a powered flight fatality. He is buried in Hebron's Rosehill cemetery.

Frank Keiser, who flew under the name of Frank Miller of Hebron, Nebraska, learned to fly just 9 months after Glenn Curtiss and his troop demonstrated the first powered flight in Nebraska on July 23, 1910 in Omaha. The aviation historian, Bill Robie, of Virginia states that Frank Miller was one of the earliest aeroplane pilots in American History, and recognizes him as an "early bird", or pioneer flyer and as an individual of whom the State of Nebraska should be most proud.

Frank R. Miller, Hebron, Nebraska aviator, made 8 successful flights at the Republic Co. Fair in Belleville, Kansas on September 12, 13, 14 and 15 in 1911 according to the Belleville Telescope. The Belleville paper gives the following account of Mr. Miller's flying in Belleville:

"September 1911--F.R. Miller, the aviator is a young man 26 years of age and began to make flights April 20th. He has been very successful. Four flights were made at the Allen County Fair and nine flights in Pratt, Kansas,

He has had one accident, his magneto failing to work and he fell 80 feet, being slightly injured.

Mr. Miller's home is at Hebron, Nebraska. He uses a Strobel bi-plane 32 feet long with a 50 horse-powered engine and the machine weighs 900 pounds. He has two helpers, Wm. Ainsmith of Port Huron, Mich., and C. Conklin of Toledo, Ohio.

He ascends from 500 to 1500 feet in the air and travels at a rate of about 60 miles an hour.

Mr. Miller is a nervy young man and if we are not mistaken will give an exhibition of air flights that will be satisfactory to the patrons of the Republic Co. Fair.

Aviator Miller made his first flight Tuesday about 6:15 p.m. and he rose from the fair grounds and circled several miles to the northwest. On the second flight he came over the town and circles the courthouse and through the resident section. Both flights were perfect and beautiful demonstrations.

Flights will be made twice each day about 10:30 in the morning and about 2:30 in the afternoon. In all he made eight flights ranging from about four miles to about twelve miles at a speed of a mile a minute."

A copy of this newspaper article and sale bill which has hung in Max Linton's shoe repair shop in Hebron for many years was sent to Bill Robie, Aviation Antiquarian Historian, who, after losing hours of sleep over the matter, deducted that the picture on this article is not the actual plane that Frank Miller flew, but is a copy of The Golden Flier with Glenn Curtiss, aviator. Mr. Robie wrote:

"The photo in the news clipping looked, as I mentioned, like the Golden Flier. I said I doubted that it was. as the only time I knew of a plane flying while it was in the possession of the Strobel group was when Sam 'Tickle' Tickell crunched it in Tampa, Fla., right after Strobel bought the plane.

Well, the mountains in the background of the photo looked familiar and out-of-place. The photo even looked familiar, but I couldn't remember it in any connection with the Strobel Co. There are no hills, much less mountains in Toledo. I just now found out why...

The plane in your news clipping is the Golden Flier and the pilot in the picture is Glenn Curtiss. The photo was taken at Hammondsport, N.Y. in 1909 and the original glass plate negative is probably at the Curtiss museum there. It is curious that the 'Bill' for the Republic County Fair claims that 'this is the plane to he flown at the fair. The explanation is most likely one of the following: (a) that was the only aeroplane picture available to the fair officials, or (b) Strobel was too penurious to have a photo made of the planes he flew. I believe the former most likely."

Bill Praises 1911 Hebron Aviator [16]

From Liberty Ridge To Wings

Aviation was in its infancy. Frank Miller was a part of it. He had grown up living with the William Miller family of Liberty Ridge in Thayer County, Nebraska. Liberty Ridge was a farming area 7 miles south and east of Hebron. There was a school and a church called Liberty Ridge. Frank had a great interest in mechanics and was encouraged to pursue this interest by the Millers.

As a young man Frank Miller went to Cleveland, Ohio, to work in an automobile factory. It is believed that it is there that he met Stan Vaughn. Stan Vaughn worked for the White Motor Car Co. of Cleveland, Ohio and then he joined the Stroble Co. Vaughn probably persuaded Miller to join in the Strobel Exhibition Company of Toledo, Ohio. also. It was here Frank Miller learned to fly.

Mrs. Evelyn Martin, great-granddaughter of the Miller's, who raised Frank Keiser, sent this article about Frank:

"TOLEDO, OHIO, MAY 9, 1911, C.J. Strobel, of this place is getting his crew of fliers in good shape for the exhibition season, after training most of them for more than a year. He recently took them to Cuba, where they underwent the finishing touches of their training. Most prominent among them seem Howard Le Van, a 17 year-old boy from Allentown, Pa., who recently made two 30 mile flights over water, and one with a passenger. ANOTHER IS FRANK MILLER, WHO JOINED THE TROUPE A FEW WEEKS AGO AND IS ADVANCING RAPIDLY...Le Van made the other over-water trip, starting at Bay View again and going up to within a mile of Toledo Beach before he began his return flight. The distance between these two points is 17 miles, and so, deducting the two miles the young aviator lost by turning short, the ground covered was this time approximately 32 miles. He returned to the park where MILLER had been making short flights in his absence.

Most of Strobel's men were with him formerly as dirigible operators. He adopted the aeroplane idea only a short time ago, but since then he has been very busy training his team. The young men with him at present are: Van Parker, Stanley Vaughn, Howard Le Van, Jack Dallas, Frank Goodale, Harry Ginter, Frank Gay, Frank Seyfon and Charles D. Brown. Most of these names are familiar to followers of dirigible balloon history during the past few years."

Bill Robie, aviation historian and aircraft researcher from Virginia and North Carolina, provided the following additional information regarding Frank Miller:

"Frank Miller was working for the Strobel Exhibition Company of Toledo, Ohio. This company was headed by Charles J. Strobel who was involved in many crowd-drawing ventures, including marching bands, baseball teams (he owned the team which became known as the Toledo Mudhens-the team 'Klinger' in tile T.V. show M*A*S*H referred to so often) and aerial exhibits. Strobel did not fly and seldom watched his people fly. He was a businessman and put up the cash, hired the people, and arranged the bookings, etc. His aerial exhibition venture started with 'airships' or small dirigibles, then worked into aeroplanes as they became popular and somewhat practical.

As the first exhibition aeroplane tour was in 1909 (by Chas. Willard in the 'Golden Flyer' the first aeroplane designed and built by Glenn Curtiss), you call see that Frank Miller was one of the earliest aeroplane pilots in American history. He had a very short career and is virtually unknown, but we will do all we call to have the Air and Space Museum recognize him as all 'early bird', or pioneer flyer. Your photos and information help a great deal" (this reference is to Mrs. Evelyn A. Martin of Minneapolis, Minn., who is a relative of Robert Thomas of Hebron, and who sent 4 pictures of Frank Miller to the National Air and Space Museum at the Smithsonian.)

"The photos on postcards of' Frank Miller were typical of most exhibition flyers. The ground crew members would sell these during the exhibitions to further generate income. The plane in the photos appears to be one of the Strobel Company 'Red Devils.' These were copies of the

Golden Flyer mentioned above. Strobel bought the Golden Flyer in January, 1910 and made several duplicates of it. Perhaps I should say his employees made the copies. Strobel never made much of anything but money. The planes were actually made by Stanley I. Vaughn. Some of them were constructed at Alexander Black Cloak Company in Toledo and they were tested at Bayview Park in that city.

It was at Bayview Park that Frank Miller learned to fly. He was taught by Stan Vaughn. There was not a great deal to instruct in those days and the planes were fairly flimsy. Accidents were common and fatalities were accepted as part of the game. Vaughn himself built and flew his first aeroplane before he had ever actually seen a plane fly. It was this plane-Vaughn's first-in which Frank Miller was eventually killed. It was an almost identical copy of the same Golden Flyer from which Strobel's Red Devils were derived, but it had a different engine."

Frank H. Miller - Strobel's Aeroplane in Flight, Pratt County Fair, Aug. 17, 1911.
Pratt Co., Kansas

On the back of this Post Card which is owned by Evelyn Martin of Minneapolis, Minn. is the following message in Frank's own handwriting:

On August 22. 1911, Frank Miller sent a Post Card picture of his flight in Pratt Co., Kansas. On it he wrote, "Hello folks better come and take a ride in my flying machine my next stop.

Good Bye Frank

The invitation did not go unheeded. The whole community would turn out to see the local boy in a flying machine. The HEBRON JOURNAL ran a column at that time which was called Liberty Ridge news. At that time a lot of activity was going on in the Miller family: "Will Miller was building a new barn; Fred Miller went to Hastings and purchased a new REO automobile; Will Miller went to Fairbury to get nursery stock and made the trip in only 50 minutes; Fred Miller took his neighbors to meet the train in his new REO; and he took the newlyweds of the community on their wedding trip."

Everyone was busy and happy in their activities and now they would get to go to Belleville to see the young aviator in his local professional debut. The Hebron Journal states: "Quite a number of Hebron folks went to Belleville to the fair and saw the air-ship flight of Mr. Keiser, the operator is known to many Hebron people, having been raised by Mr. Miller out in the Liberty Ridge Community."

In the Liberty Ridge Column: "Mr. and Mrs. Fred Miller, Mr. and Mrs. Will Miller, Mrs. Davis, Mrs. Degenhardt (Max Degenhardt tells us this was his mother, Sarah, Mrs. Robert Degenhardt), Lloyd and Arthur Boyce and Mr. & Mrs. Walker attended the fair at Belleville. Frank Keiser, a former Liberty Ridge boy, made two flights daily in an aeroplane during the fair."

Frank Kaiser Miller and his Strobel Aeroplane
[Nebraska State Historical Society Photograph]

TRAGEDY STRIKES

Aviation was in its infancy just as was the flying career of Frank Miller when he was killed in September of 1911. (Some accounts give the day as Sept. 22 where as others give the day as Sept. 23. His tombstone in the Hebron Rosehill Cemetery gives his death date as Sept. 22, 1912).

In the October issue of AERONAUTICS 1911 on page 133 there is a listing of all those who were killed in aviation and aviation related accidents. There are 19 such accidents listed: 5 in France; 5 in Germany; 1 in South America; and one each in the states of Iowa, Missouri, N.Y., Pennsylvania, Washington and Ohio. The French and German fliers were killed in the military. The most notable was Edouard Nieuport who developed planes in France. He was flying in the presence of military authorities when he was killed at this time. On the same page there is an advertisement with Mr. THOMAS SOPWITH and his Burgess Biplane which had a Gnome motor built by the Burgess Co. and Curtis, Marblehead, Mass. Most readers are familiar today with the plane Sopwith later developed--the Sopwith Camel which "Snoopy" flies as he goes after the Red Baron atop his doghouse in the comic strip PEANUTS.

The Ohio accident on this page reads: "Troy, Ohio September 23, 1911--In making his last flight closing his exhibition at the local fair, Frank H. Miller, flying another Curtiss--copy built by Charles J. Strobel, of airship fame was burned to death in the fire resulting from a headlong dive to the ground, or was killed by the fall itself. He was descending from an altitude of about 200 feet when the plane suddenly turned it's nose directly down and took fire. Miller came from Cleveland. Miller could be seen frantically trying to right the machine. Other witnesses state that the machine was afire before it started its headlong flight."

Frank Killer, taken in the Griffin Studio In Hebron. Taken when he lived with the Wm. Millers. [Photograph Courtesy of Evelyn Martin]

Obituary of FRANK KEISER MILLER
AS PUBLISHED IN THE Hebron Journal

BURNS WHILE IN AIR

"A Former Hebron Boy Meets Tragic End--Oil Tank Explodes Aloft--Impelled to make flight against better judgement by Taunts of Crowd who called him a coward.

Last Saturday a telegram announced the death of Frank Keiser Miller in a burning aeroplane at Troy, Ohio. The young man was well known in Hebron, having lived at Liberty Ridge (a farming community southeast of Hebron), between Hebron and Hubbell.

His original name was Keiser, but he took the name Miller after being raised by Mr. and Mrs. William Miller, both now deceased.

About the age of eighteen he united with the Christian Church at Liberty Ridge. Striking out in the world, at the age of twenty years, he located at flights at Belleville, Kansas, but a few weeks (actually 8 days) ago, were witnessed by a number of friends from this vicinity.

His tragic death at Troy, Ohio, Sept. 22nd, at the age of twenty-seven years, is deeply mourned.

On the day of his last flight the machine had not acted right and he demurred about going up again, until goaded to desperation by the jeers of the crowd calling him a coward,--and they were in effect his real murderers! Courageously he accepted the challenge, and was burned to death in the gasoline explosion in mid air, before the eyes of those who are morally, if not legally, responsible for his sacrifice.

The body was brought to Hebron Monday and the funeral sermon was preached by Rev. W.E. Brandenburg at the Christian Church the following day, in the presence of many sympathetic friends of the deceased.

Frank Miller's tombstone is in the Miller plot near the entrance of the Hebron Rosehill Cemetery. There is a tall grey stone and three smaller stones. The smaller stone north of the large stone is marked "Keiser Sept. 21, 1884--Sept. 22, 1912". The stone is a misprint as it should have been Sept. 22, 1911.

Mrs. Verna Sell (Mrs. John) of Chester who is a granddaughter of the William Millers, wrote to Miss Dale Swank of Toledo, Ohio for some time after Frank K. Miller's death. Miss Swank, who attended Frank's funeral in Hebron was his girl friend.

Jack Miller of Marysville, Kansas sent this report apparently from the Hebron Journal:

A DIFFERENT REPORT

W.R. Miller Receives a New Version of the Aviator's Death:

Wm. R. Miller has received information stating that press dispatches grossly exaggerated conditions at the time of the fatal accident to Aviator Frank Miller who was buried at Hebron, and who was not jeered to his death as reported. Embalmer E.E. Thomson in writing from Troy, Ohio said:

" Mr. Miller had already made a flight at two o'clock of the same afternoon that he met his death. Everybody was satisfied and did not expect another flight. In fact the crowd was surprised when the judges announced that at five o'clock he would make another flight, so you see he was not jeered nor even asked to make the fatal flight. There is a difference of opinion as to when the tank exploded. I think it first hit the ground. His skull was crushed by the engine striking him just as he struck the ground. Had it not been for this and the gasoline, the fall would not have killed him.

Very respectfully,
(signed)
Elmer E. Thomson, Adm."

Mr. Miller also received a letter from one of Frank's helpers, stating that in that last flight he was descending from a height of about 1,000 feet and when about 200 feet from the ground he slacked the engine too slow, and then he opened it up too fast, causing him to lose his balance. This writer stated "that the cause of the death was due to a mistake of the aviator."

Bill Robie, current aviation historian writes:

"The 'new' account of Miller's death was most interesting. It may be true, or it may have been the result of guilty feelings on the part of a community leader (the 'jeered into the air' account was printed in the *Aeronautics* magazine the month--national press about the insensitivity of a town's populace.) It makes me wonder--either story could have been true. The 'helper' seems to describe the makings of a stall/spin situation. This would have put him in the ground nose--first and account for the engine coming in on top of him.

Speaking of the engine, there were two of them built. Thy were designed and constructed for use in dirigibles in 1908 by Lincoln Beachey. Beachey is one of my favorite (if not **The** favorite) people of the barnstormer era preceeding WWI. He started flying his first dirigible in 1905 in his hometown of San Francisco. Beachey was about 15 at the time and he built this first 'airship'. naming it the 'Rubber Cow'. One of his first flights he landed amongst a group of citizens who had never seen anything fly. This group of clods had no appreciation for progress and they reacted by destroying the airship and beating Beachey rather soundly. This was the start of a love/hate relationship that Beachey had for exhibition audiences. Later he joined the Strobel Amusement Company to become the No. 2 attraction (second to Roy Knabenshue). He soon became the top star of the 'aeronauts' and flew the gas bags at fairs and exhibits all over the country. When the airships seemed to be nearing eclipse by 'aeroplanes', Beachey built two. The first didn't fly--it went through a fence. The second was the sister ship to the one in which Miller was killed (I am restoring this one). The engines used on the Beachey plane and the one used by Miller were two dirigible engines converted to water cooling.

Beachey's second plane flew successfully--two or three times, then he had a crash similar to Miller from which he emerged literally knocked out of his shoes.

Stan Vaughn, Frank Miller's instructor, lived until early 1972. He mentioned the crash by Frank in a taped interview made in 1962. NASM, Smithsonian, has my copy of the interview.

I have gotten out a tape recorded interview done with the late Stan Vaughn in 1962. Vaughn had worked at White Motor Car Company in Cleveland, Ohio before becoming a Strobel pilot ... I quote the interview exactly as I can. Unfortunately there was little mention of Miller. Vaughn had built his own plane and five Curtiss #1 copies for Strobel.

INTERVIEWER: Well, in this airplane business that Strobel developed with these five, what did he do with these five, by the way, did he sell them to other people?
VAUGHN: No, he done exhibition work with 'em.
INTERVIEWER: I see.
VAUGHN: The ship that I built was finally cracked up at, uh, I believe it was Coshocton, Ohio.
INTERVIEWER: Uh huh.
VAUGHN: By a fellow name of Miller, ugh, who used to work with me at White Motor Car Company who got interested in aviation and came to Toledo and started off flying--he became one of the best ones we had.
INTERVIEWER: Is that a fact?
VAUGHN- He flew considerable, ugh, quite a few contracts with the airplane--he never flew, dirigibles, though.

This is where they went on to other matters. Please keep in mind that Mr. Vaughn was about 70 years old at the time of the interview. He was exceptionally sharp at that age. but can be forgiven for not remembering the town Miller had died some 50 years earlier."

FRANK KAISER

Although Frank Miller gave his name as Frank Miller and his hometown as Hebron, Nebraska, he was actually born as Frank Kaiser at Humphrey, Nebraska and later from Ainsworth, Nebraska in Brown County. He was the 6th child in a family of eight. A census taken the 29th day of June in 1895 gives the children of Wilhelm Kaiser as being August 18, Will 16, Fred 14, Ed 12, Bertha 12, Frank 10, Henry 7 and Rosa 6.

On page 174 of the Criminal docket of Brown County, Nebraska with James C. Toliver as county judge in a case of the state of Nebraska vs. Eddie Kaiser and Frank Kaiser it reads:

"The complaint of Justine Kaiser filed charging her two sons with on or about Sept. 26 willfully maliciously and purposedly set fire to a certain building located about 1 1/2 miles northeast of the Bone Creek Mills in Brown County, Nebraska and that the sons Eddie and Frank Kaiser did on or about. Sept. 15, 1895 steal numerous articles to the amount of $100 and that said defendents are incouragible and cannot be controlled by their parents.

The following witnesses were called and sworn and duly examined concerning the above charges: Robbie Ferguson, Mrs. J.Y. Ferguson and Justine Kaiser who was the mother of the defendants. After hearing the evidence, the court being finally convinced in the premises. Find that the said Eddie Kaiser and Frank Kaiser are guilty of the charges set out in said complaint and that the said Eddie Kaiser is of the age of 13 years and that Frank Kaiser is of the age of 11 years. It is ordered that said Eddie Kaiser and Frank Kaiser be sent to the Industrial School for Boys at Kearney, Nebraska.

Issued a warrant to convey the said Eddie and Frank Kaiser to the reform school in Kearney, Nebr. and placed the same in the hands of John Murrey, Sheriff of Brown County, Nebraska for service. (signed)
J.C. Toliver, Co. Judge"

Mr. John S. McCarty, Superintendent of the Department of Correctional Services, Kearney, Nebraska stated that the records dating back to 1895 are very limited at this institution, but that he found that Frank Kaiser was committed to the institution on October 3, 1895 from Brown County and that he was paroled to the foster home of William Miller in Hebron, Nebraska. The parole was effective April 5, 1898. They have no way of knowing why or how the Miller home was selected for placement of the young Kaiser boy.

The following account was given in an Ainsworth, Nebraska newspaper:
AVIATOR KILLED IN OHIO ONCE LIVED IN AINSWORTH

AINSWORTH, NEBRASKA, Oct. 16, (1912)

Frank H. Keiser, son of Wm. Keiser of Ainsworth, was instantly killed at Troy, Ohio while making an exhibition flight in an aeroplane at the Miami Fire Grounds. Keiser was known as Frank Miller, having taken that name from the family that he made his home with near Hebron, this state, for many years, although he was never formally adopted by the Miller family.

Although the accident happened on Sept. 22, word has just reached here that Miller was Frank Keiser, formerly of this place.

The records of Brown County show that Keiser, when eleven years of age, was sent to the Industrial School at Kearney, with an older brother. James C. Toliver was County Judge at the time and remembers the circumstances distinctly. The boy remained in the Industrial School for a number of years and then went to make his home with Mr. Miller near Hebron. From that time he became known by the name of Frank Miller. In the home of Mr. Miller he grew to be a man of thrift, industry and of good habits. He was of a mechanical turn of mind and after attaining his majority, worked in the automobile business for a time.

Early last spring he went to Toledo, Ohio where he began the study of aviation and after a short time began to make aerial flights. When the Exposition season opened, he thought to be sufficiently learned in the new science to go out in demonstration work, and was given a number of dates to fill. He had almost successfully completed his list when at Troy his engine exploded when 200 feet in the air, resulting in instant death.

Upon hearing of his death Mr. Miller ordered the body sent to Hebron-and the funeral was, held at that place.

The particulars of the accident sent here are as follows:

"Forced into the air by the jeers of thousands who called him a coward, Frank H. Miller, twenty-three years old, a Toledo aviator, shot into the sky at twilight and when 200 feet up was burned to death before the eyes of the spectators on the Miami County Fair grounds at Troy, north of Dayton, Miller had circled the race track and was just starting into a spiral glide whensomething went wrong. He could be seen making a frantic attempt to get his machine under control, when suddenly the whirring of the propellers ceased. The craft dropped like a shot for fifty feet, a tiny blue flame was emitted from the engine and in an instant the gasoline tank exploded. The machine was wrecked and debris was hurled hundreds of feet in all directions. What remained of the aeroplane and its driver were burned almost to a crisp as they dropped rapidly to earth. It was Miller's second night of the day and fifth and last of the week. In a short flight soon after noon, his machine acted unsteadily and he did not care to go up."

Frank Keiser Miller grew to manhood on a farm between Hebron and Hubbell. NE. The Hubbell Standard newspaper at that time gave no account of his death or of his flying, but on Oct. 6, 1911, (just 2 wks. after his death) T.M. Casad. Publisher of the Hubbell Standard newspaper published at Hubbell, NE printed the following on the editorial page:

SANITY IN AVIATION

"Is it not time that steps were taken by various organizations which are promoting aeronautics meets to secure something akin to 'sane avaition'? Flying, be it followed either as a sport, as was the case with Johnstone, or as a business, after the manner of the Wrights, will by its nature always attract reckless spirits, says the Cleveland Plain-Dealer. But it is noticeable that many of those who have died in the cause have come to grief through attempting some unnecessarily dangerous feat, calculated to hold crowds breathless. The public does not demand thrills which cost human lives and if it did demand them it should be denied. The day of the old Roman holiday, fortunately, has passed. Flying is too important and wonderful a thing to be brought to the level of a trapese performance or a bull fight by permitting everything to become subservient to the spectator. Its possibilities are too wide, and those most concerned in its success owe it to themselves and to the public to take care that they do not allow their profession to fall into disrepute. Automobiling went through a similar process of evolution. Not so very long ago dare deviltry was considered heroic, and scores of lives have been sacrificed to this foolish sentiment. But, generally speaking the pursuit of automobiling among the vast majority has now become eminently sane."

The following week the Hubbell Standard has this remark about flying, "A trip in the air is the quickest way to get underground quickly."

Frank Keiser Miller--Pratt Co. Kansas Fair 1911

This envelope contains a fragment of fabric believed to be from the Vaughn/Curtiss aeroplane in which Frank (Keiser) Miller was killed. It was given to me by Stan Vaughn, Jr. In 1982.

Bill Roble

ONE OF THE FIRST AIRPLANES MANUFACTURED IN NEBRASKA
AIRPLANE MANUFACTURED IN CARLETON, NEBRASKA

Morrow brothers' plane [Photograph courtesy of Carleton Community Club]

The Morrow brothers, Edward and Everett, manufactured an aeroplane in Carleton, Nebraska in 1911. The brothers, the sons of Carleton's Blacksmith, were but 19 and 20 years old when they completed their plane. They built it outside their father's blacksmith shop which was located southeast of Jack Blunk's feed store. The brothers had made an automobile earlier from a buggy frame and using buggy wheels. Their automobile had been successful enough that it made the trip to Hebron, NE, a distance of about 12 miles, on several occasions.

Morrow brothers' plane and auto. [Photograph courtesy of Carleton Community Club]

Mr. Frank had interviewed his uncle, Frank Baker, who had been a witness to the Morrow Brother's first flight. Mr. Baker had reported that the flight, was a huge success, that the brother flying it became scared and brought the plane down to the ground so fast that it broke off the landing gear which was built from bicycle wheels and tires put together with a wooden fork and axle.

As soon as this story came out in the paper in 1967, the controversy began. One of Carleton's older citizens. Cecil Stables, told Frank that he, too, had been an eye witness to the first flight and that the plane barely rose 8 to 10 INCHES, not FEET. A third person entered the debate and said that neither was correct, that the plane never left the ground. The successfulness and date of the Morrow brother's first flight still remains a mystery.

July 4, 1911 was to be the second flight of the plane. It was advertised to be the feature of the Fourth of July Celebration in Carleton. People flocked from all around to see this flight of a homebuilt powered aeroplane. One account said that they believed there were 4000 people in Carleton to see this exciting event. (We have found that the successfulness of all special events in this era was usually filled with hyperbole effecting the competitive spirit between the towns). There was no debate of the successfulness of the Morrow Brother's flight before the multitude of people, however.

The plane absolutely refused to get off the ground. The Morrow Brother's plane was considered to be a total fiasco. The spectators became disgruntled and booed the hometown failure. Today there are children of the Carleton natives who witnessed the flight who still deem the Carleton built plane to be a disaster or a joke. THE DISHEARTENED MORROW BROTHERS NEVER TRIED TO FLY THEIR PLANE IN CARLETON AGAIN. We believed that this was the end of the Morrow brother's plane.

Another phase of the Morrow brother's story began to unfold. There were those who said that then an aviator was brought in to look at the plane and told them it was perfectly well made, but the brothers had no training as pilots and it was their inexperience that had kept the plane from flying. If the brothers would learn more about aerodynamics the plane would fly.

SUCCESS
Everett Morrow flying In Ord, NE., 1912

[Photograph courtesy of Nebraska State Historical Society.]

In the photographic archives of the State Historical Society, we found there is a picture of the Morrow Brother's plane being flown by Everett Morrow and is pictured well above the telephone wires. The picture was taken at Ord, NE. in 1912.

Subsequently the State Historical Society has a series of pictures of the Morrow Brothers' plane taken in the south--one at Sampson, Alabama shows the plane on the ground; Opelika, Alabama is the site for a take off of their plane in 1913.

In the fall of 1914 there is a short notice in the Carleton News that Everett Morrow received a message to come south and accompany an aviator, and departed on Tuesday night. He moved his family back with his parents.

Crashed Morrow Plane. [Photograph Courtesy of Nebraska State Historical Society]

The determination of Everett Morrow is denoted on the back of a picture postcard with the plane, now sporting box-like rudder changes, and labeled 1915. The plane has hit a telephone pole and crashed. On the back is a scrawled note stating that it will be no time at all and this plane will be back in shape and flying. (signed) Everett

As we were unable to document the date of the Morrow brothers' first flight, other than to say it was before July 1911, we cannot claim the Morrow Brothers' plane as the first plane manufactured in Nebraska. Ewing, Nebraska makes this claim, as the seven sons of Mr. and Mrs. Martin Savidge made and flew an airplane on May 7, 1911. The Savidge brothers sent to St. Joseph, MO. for their custom built engine and sent to St. Louis, MO. for some of the other equipment, using "factory parts".

Bill Robie, aviation expert tells us there was a British catalog that advertised parts, engines and plane accessories as early as 1909 and that the June and July issue of the 1910 POPULAR MECHANICS features drawings of the DEMOISELLE (a plane later developed by Santos-Dumont) for the home builder. Several companies jumped on the aeroplane bandwagon as suppliers of aeroplane parts. The later models of the Morrow Brothers' plane also used "factory parts" in their wheels, radiator and fuel tank. Their first plane built in Carleton used bicycle wheels, a handcarved wooden fork, wooden axels, had no real radiator and just a tiny, experimental use, gas tank.

Thayer County can be so proud of this first plane and those farsighted, determined brothers who had the fortitude and persistence to build and fly one of the first, if not the first plane manufactured in Nebraska.

FIRST AIRMAIL FLIGHT INTO HEBRON

The Thursday, May 19, 1938 HEBRON REGISTER has a red and blue border around the front half of the newspaper and a red monoplane printed on the front page. This issue commemorates National Air Week May 15th to 21st, 1938.

The week before the headlines read "Plans complete for first airmail flight." With a picture of the Thayer County Courthouse with a flag flying atop the tower, air mail envelopes had been printed with the wording "Hebron, Nebraska--First Air Mail Flight May 19, 1938." These envelopes were given to all Hebron school children. We wonder if anyone has one of these commemorative envelopes.

The paper goes on to say (fiat the reports reaching the Hebron Post Office indicate a lively interest in Hebron and vicinity in the observance of National Airmail week, May 15 to 21.

"It is the aim of the post office department that every family in the county mail at least one air mail letter during the week. The Hebron off would like to see Hebron well represented by a large mailing of air mail letters. From present indications, it would seem that there will be a large dispatch from this point. The plane which will pick up mail here, will arrive at 12:14 p.m. Thursday, May 19 from Chester and will take the mail to Lincoln via Wilber.

The local office has received from the department, 1000 air mail envelopes which will be distributed free to school children and anyone else who wishes to use them. The Civic Club has had a picture of the courthouse and the date of the first air mail flight from Hebron imprinted on them. They are attractive in blue and red edges.

A shipment of new 6 cent air mail stamps which will be on sale here has also been received, and will be on sale beginning Monday. However, airmail stamps are not nececssary merely place six cents in stamps on an envelope for airmail.

The Alexandria and Gilead mail will be brought to Hebron for pickup by the plane here next Thursday, it was learned today. Other surrounding towns will likely bring their special air mail to Hebron on that (lay to be picked up by Weblemoe, pilot of the plane which will stop here."

The May 19th HEBRON REGISTER headlines AIRMAIL PLANE TO ARRIVE IN HEBRON AT NOON THURSDAY. First air mail pickup service will take place today. Thursday, at 12:13 p.m. A plane piloted by George Weblemoe of Fairbury, will arrive at that time picking up the special air mail pouch and will depart five minutes later at 12:18 for Wilber.

This is part of the state wide special air mail feed flights in observance of National Air Mail Week being celebrated this week May 15 to 21.

The route of the plane picking up mail at Hebron is 150 miles long, the plane starting at Fairbury, stopping at Chester at exactly noon, Hebron at 12:13 then on to Wilber at 12:30 and on into Lincoln at 1:15 where 18 special planes will land in two hours from different routes in southwestern Nebraska.

All air mail on Thursday will be placed in a special government mail pouch and taken by postmaster Albert Nacke to the landing field which the Civic Club selected as the hay meadows three-fourths miles east of the Oregon Trail marker north of Hebron on highway 81. Cars may park on the roadside but no one will be allowed on the landing field.

Postmaster Nacke said the pouch for air mail on Thursday will be closed at 11:40.

Air mail may also be delivered to Hebron on the same flight, as the pilots have been instructed to deliver pouches of air mail on this route. The only way air mail can be delivered to Hebron is from Chester. Should you desire to receive a letter via air on May 19, it will be only necessary that you forward a letter to Chester addressed to yourself at Hebron. Address an envelope and forward it to Postmaster Rhea at Chester. The plane will pick tip the mail at Chester at noon Thursday and deliver it to Hebron in 8 minutes.

Special air mail letters may be obtained at the post office this week free of charge. They are letters trimmed in blue and red, bearing the 'cachet', a beautiful picture of the courthouse at Hebron with an inscription signifying the first air mail flight from Hebron.

There are a total of 59 flights to be made Thursday covering 10,088 miles and picking up airmail in 208 towns and cities in Nebraska.

Gilead, Alexandria and Deshler will deliver air mail to the plane in Hebron.

This air mail pickup service over Nebraska is an experiment on feeder lines to the transcontinental lines. Within a few years it is expected that planes will cover much territory in out-lying territory to pick up air mail and deliver to main transcontinental lines. Postmaster Nacke voiced the opinion that no doubt Hebron may be included on a route within the next few years, should such a service be inaugurated."

Air Mail In Bruning. Fred Bruning and "Tully" Bowman of Bruning.
[Photograph Courtesy of Thayer County Museum]

ANTEDOTES FROM OR ABOUT LOCAL FLYERS

BARNSTORMERS

Barnstormers were early aviators who made their living by flying passengers on irregular flights or joy rides and performing airplane stunts and making flights at fairs, circuses and carnivals.

Most of the people interviewed for this article said that the first aeroplane that they ever saw or rode in was one of an unknown Barnstormer.

Thomas Griffin recalled what a thrilling sight it was for him to see his first plane, a Curtis-Jenny which circled their farm, as well as other farms around Alexandria, drumming up business. He recalled that his little brother who was born in April of 1919 was about a year and a half old and was wearing a red romper suit, and as Tom and his older sister climbed to the top of the pig house roof to get a better view of the plane, they discussed waving their little brother so as to get attention of the Barnstormer.

From atop the pig house roof they watched the plane land and persuaded their father to go to the landing spot on the east side of the road 6 miles north of Alexandria. Other farmers and their families had flocked to see the aircraft and pilot.

This pilot would take anyone up for $12 and Tom recalled how he envied Flora (Mrs. John) Westerhoff as she paid the $12. Mr. Griffin, who was about 8 years old at the time, said he was so thrilled to think he knew someone who had been up in an aeroplane and quered Mrs. Westerhoff at great lengths about her adventure.

Today Mr. Griffin whose private beech-bonanza's identifying number is N9K (being the 9th plane of that series made) has flown from New Mexico to Hawks field regularly for many years and in 1984. 72 year old Griffin still made the trip in his "antique" plane.

August Wind, the son of Alexandria blacksmith was the first man to learn to fly that Mr. Griffin could remember.

Tom Griffin and his Bonanza N9K. [Photograph Courtesy of Tom Griffin.]

Harold Beisner's first plane ride was in a Barnstormer who landed out on what is now the Hebron Golf Course. It was a two place bi-plane. He also remembers a Ford Trimotor landing on the John Eggert farm north of Hebron.

Ralph Hawkins of Hebron remembers a Ford Trimotor landing near Hebron's Golf Course. His mother, Mrs. Jenny Hawkins paid the pilot the $5.00 to fly over Hebron in 1935.

CHARLES LINDBERGH IN HEBRON, NEBRASKA

Several people that were interviewed for this article told us that Charles Lindbergh came into Thayer County on a barnstorming tour.

In the booklet DEVELOPMENT OF AVIATION IN NEBRASKA, Jack V. O'Keefe, Chief of aviation, education and safety with the Department of Aeronautics in Lincoln, tells of Charles A. Lindbergh coming into Lincoln on April 1, 1922 on an old motorcycle to enroll at the Lincoln Aircraft School. His first ride was with Otto Timm on April 16th in a Lincoln Standard plane. After just 7 hours of instruction the teacher, Ira Biffle, said that Lindbergh was ready to solo. Ray Page, the director of the school required a money deposit be put down before a plane could be taken up in case the plane was damaged and as Lindbergh didn't have the money, he was not permitted to solo.

Mr. O'Keefe wrote:

"Lindbergh had no money and did not solo. In order to raise the necessary cash, Charles Lindbergh went on a 'barnstorming' tour with E.G. Bahl over southeastern Nebraska. Lindbergh was a helper and mechanic on these tours. He returned in the fall to take more flying lessons ... That same fall 'Swede' (Lindbergh) also called 'Slim' went 'barnstorming' again."

One of the best sources to verify this report was Mary Carter Beisner of Hebron, who said that she and her girl friend, Evelyn Keith Flynn were in high school when a barnstorming plane landed north of Hebron. Evelyn had her father's car and they drove out to see the plane with the two young men with it. The charge was $3.00 pet person to ride and Mary had no money, but Evelyn worked after school in her dad's store and provided the $6.00. Mary and Evelyn in the back seats and the pilot and Mr. Charles D. Day got in the front seats. As they taxied past the row of automobiles that lined highway 81 watching the plane, they saw Evelyn's mother and she saw them, but it was too late for her to stop them and the plane took off.

Later Mary was told that the man with the plane was Charles Lindbergh, and when she saw pictures of him she thought it was right.

Barnstormer Verlie Hedden and Brothers, Milton and Marion Hedden
[Photographs courtesy of Frank Hedden, Scandia, Kansas]

Verlie, Elvira and son.

Elvira and Verlie Hedden

Hedden's Plane

Verlie with Taylorcraft at float, Tacoma, Washington, July 1947.

Verlie Hedden

Verlie Hedden at Mankato, Kansas Airport.

Verlie Hedden and wife Elvira.

Every New Year's Eve at the stroke of midnight Verlie Hedden and his wife, Elvira, had to be in the air to celebrate the coming of the New Year. Getting a plane started in sub-zero weather, taking off and landing on an ice and snow covered field, lit only with a couple of kerosene lanterns wasn't always easy, but that was the goal the Heddens set for themselves and they usually accomplished their celebration.

Verlie Hedden was a barnstormer pilot well-known in southern Nebraska and northern Kansas. He was an easy going, good natured, carefree man who flew with the gusto characteristic of the early barnstormers. He was a "natural" flyer, one who flew by the seat of his pants and had complete faith in his own ability which compensated for any deficiency in his aircraft.

Earl Hawks, who later became a pilot, tells of a trip he took with Verlie from Bruning to Lincoln, a distance of 80 miles. "We had to make three emergency landings before we got there. One time we had lost a spark plug wire. That didn't bother Verlie. He went over to a near-by barbed wire fence, cut off a piece of barbed wire, put it on the spark plug and we were off again until the next emergency landing. The water sprayed back from the radiator and blew in your face--and that was HOT water, too," remarked Earl.

Verlie Hedden was the fourth child of James and Mary Houch Hedden who lived northeast of Bruning near the Harmony Church. Verlie was born on that farm and continued to live there for a few years after he had married Elvira Hilton of Geneva on Jan. 13, 1919. They moved to Belvidere, Nebr. where they converted the livery stable into a motor car garage and sold gasoline. They moved to Haddam, Kansas and then to Oak, NE. where he had a job running the motor grader for Nuckolls County.

In 1929, Verlie was in Kansas City and there he went for his first plane ride. "He fell in love with flying at that moment," said his nephew Frank Hedden, "He loved the feel of it and he knew that flying just had to be his life from then on. He immediately took 30 minutes of flying instruction and was ready to solo."

Verlie Heddens first plane was a Swallow.

Verlie Hedden delivering the SALINA JOURNAL. He would drop them down to the newspaper boys. [Photograph Courtesy of Frank Hedden]

Verlie stayed at the Belleville Airport for 14 years. During those early Kansas years, Verlie had a paper route. Every day he would fly to Salina to get the Salina Journal. The Journals would be rolled into a roll and Verlie would load them into his plane, drop them off in the surrounding towns for the paper boys to deliver.

One day an irrate father called up and said that Verlie was dropping the papers too far from the house and it was too far to walk to get them. The next day, Verlie made a special effort to get the papers thrown right on the man's porch. He made a direct hit. The trouble was the paper hit the edge of the porch, bounced off and went through a window of the house. Verlie called the man and told him that he would pay for repairing the window. The man told him absolutely not as he was the one who had requested that the papers be dropped closer so they wouldn't have to walk so far--Verlie couldn't get any closer than that.

Hedden Brothers Planes
The American Eagle

He bought a SWALLOW bi-plane and began barnstorming. The Wooden hanger it was kept in burned down and the plane was lost. He bought a PARKS and convinced his brother, Milton, to buy an AMERICAN EAGLE. His younger brother, Marion married Adaline Higel, and took up flying also. The two brothers would barnstorm together- -Verlie in his PARKS and Marion in Milton's EAGLE. It was the depression days of the '30s and Verlie would charge 50¢ to $1.00 for a plane ride. If a person showed up who indicated any sort of interest in flying and didn't have the 50¢ for a plane ride, Verlie made sure that they went for a free ride so that they could experience the joy of flying. "Verlie would go without food hinself so he could buy gas for his plane," Hawks said.

"Verlie was too anxious to fly to spend any time working on his plane," said Nephew Frank Hedden," Whereas Milton would rather tinker on his engine than fly." After Milton's EAGLE beat Verlie's PARKS in a race, Verlie asked to swap engines. After this had been done, Milton again worked on the engine and when they raced again, Milton's EAGLE (with the PARKS engine) still beat Verlie's PARKS (with the EAGLE engine.)

The brothers had to think up stunts to attract a crowd. Besides racing their planes, the brothers raced an automobile against a plane in what they called a sprint race. They would also have one man stand out from the crowd and they would drop raw eggs on him for the entertainment of the crowds. The eggs rarely hit the man, however. Eventually Verlie hired another pilot, Louis Shetler, who would jump from the plane with a parachute and that would draw crowds so they could sell rides. Verlie's next plane was a WACO.

Verlie, Elviria and their children Lillian, Lyle and Lloyd moved to Ruskin, Nebraska and in 1940 Verlie got a job as airport manager and flying instructor at the Beloit, Kansas airport. In 1942 he bought three Aeronca Chiefs and started an airport at Mankato, Kansas on the south side of Highway 36. When a student, Anna Burks, said she would take over the Mankato Airport as manager, Verlie started an airport at Norton, Kansas. Later that year when Anna's sister, Mary Burks, said she would like to be an airport manager, Verlie moved to Belleville where he started the airport and stayed there as flying instructor and manager, plane mechanic, with an A & E rating, and he rebuilt wrecked planes with Elvira's help.

Elvira, who had always embellished Verlie's life style would cut, sew, dope and paint the planes. (Dope was a sort of clear varnish which was painted on a cloth covered plane to make the cloth stronger, waterproof, and airtight.) Elvira refabricated many planes.

It would be impossible to name all the planes that Verlie and Elvira have owned or rebuilt At the time of Verlie's death, he was running Hedden's Flying Service of Scandia, Kansas he died February 25. 1967 from a heart attack. With him died the age of a flying era in southern Nebraska and Northern Kansas.

Verlie Hedden had 3 Aeronicas

HARLEY PRIEFERT

Harley Priefert of Belvidere enrolled in the Lincoln Aircraft School run by Ray Page in 1927. His relatives were dismayed that he had spent so much of his father's inheritance money on something so foolish and pressured him not to persue his flying career beyond the lessons. It is reported that 10 hours of instruction at the school cost $300. In order to solo the student had to make a deposit on the plane to cover any damage. The PAGE TOURABOUT plane was used to solo and was valued at $3,500.

EVELYN SHARP

The niece of Herbron resident. W.G. Carter, Evelyn Sharp of Ord was a frequent visitor to Hebron. At the age of 16 she received her private license and at 18 received her commercial license. The people of the Ord community and Valley County helped her to buy an airplane in 1937 and she completed paying for it by barnstorming. When WWII broke out she joined the Woman's Auxiliary as a service pilot. She was killed in April of 1944 when a twin engine fighter plane crashed near Middletown, Pennsylvania.

MAX LINTON

No one is more enthusiastic about aviation than Max Linton of Hebron. Max Linton learned to fly in a WACO in 1937 at Concordia, Kansas. On the walls of his shoe repair shop hangs a picture of Thayer County's first aviator, Frank Keiser Miller.

Max has flown Charley Blosser's 1928 LINCOLN PAGE, a plane built in Lincoln by Ray Page's Aircraft factory. There is a short paragraph about both of these men at the end of this article. Max Linton has also flown a C3 AERONICA and a HEATH PARASOL.

GWEN [BABE] BARBEE

Babe Barbee got his pilot's license oil September 15, 1940 from Sam Stall, flight instructor at Hebron. Babe financed his flying by working as a mechanic at Ed Schleif's Cafe, Gas Station and Garage on the corner of Lincoln Avenue and Highway 81. After he received his pilot's license he was washing parts in the garage with gasoline and suddenly the fumes exploded. catching spilled gas on the floor from a wood burning stove that was in the garage. Babe's clothing caught on fire and in a panic he ran from the garage. Shorty Helt caught him, knocked him down and put out the fire. Babe was badly burned and was laid up for a long time as his legs were so badly burned he could not put any weight on them.

The Hebron airport was having a spot landing contest and a sheet was placed on the landing strip to represent a fence. Each pilot was to cut his engine at 1000 feet and then come in over the sheet. The pilot landing closest to the sheet won the contest. Although Babe was unable to walk he wanted to enter that contest. His brother, Jack, carried him to his PIPER CUB, put him in the plane and Babe took off and won first place in the spot landing contest.

Gwyn "Babe" Barbee and Piper Cub. [Photograph Courtesy of Babe Barbee]

PAULINE AND EARL HAWKS

Aviation would not be the same in Thayer County without the Hawks'--Earl and Pauline. Fliers from all over the United States have landed on Hawks' Field, the personal field of the Hawks which is opened for all. After World War II, GI Flying School was taught at the Hawks' Field and any WWII veteran could learn to fly on the GI bill. Earl believes that about 80 persons learned to fly at his field, but there are no records available to list them. They came from several of the surrounding counties.

Earl learned to fly in Fairbury and when the war broke out, the Civil Air Patrol was organized, December 1, 1941, and they asked for volunteers. Several Bruning boys signed up for this, including Frank and Willis Shane, Bill Hines, Ronnie Carnell and Earl Hawks; Ed Duncan from Alexandria.

The Civil Air Patrol, or CAP as it was called, was part of the U.S. Civilian Defense. According to the National Headquarters of the CAP in Maxwell AFB in Alabama, the CAP members flew more than 24 million miles of Coastal Patrol; summoned help for 91 ships in distress and 363 survivors of submarine attacks. Patrol crews spotted 173 enemy submarines and dropped depth charges on 57 of them.

Earl Hawks completed the training with the CAP, became a part of the Courier Service. Each man in the Courier Service had to furnish his own plane or use a "drafted" civilian plane. Earl flew a "drafted" AT-16. The government paid them to haul parts from the Courier Headquarters which was called "Smokey Hill" and was located in Salina, Kansas, to the government satellite bases which were beginning to spring up all over the mid-west, such as airfields at Fairmont, Ord, and Bruning.

One of the members of the Courier Service was Phil Brown and he spun out over the Blue River near Hebron and landed atop of the trees. His foot was caught in the wrecked plane, and other than that he was unhurt. The Hebron Fire Department was called out to free Mr. Brown's foot from the wreckage, and get him down from the trees.

Earl Hawks, in a BT13, Commander of CAP Interceptor Squad in Burbank, CA
Photo Courtesy of Earl Hawks

Earl Hawks, Civilian Air Patrol

The CAP asked for volunteers to go to the west coast to help patrol the coast. Hawks volunteered with the stipulation that he be permitted to return to his farm during harvest time.

As the US was unarmed to (to the patrolling of its coast line, every civilian plane was "drafted" on the west coast. The government agreed to return the plane completely overhauled after the war was over to the private owners. The coastal patrol which Mr. Hawks belonged was made tip of a conglomerate of ill-assorted planes having every type imaginable arid in every sort of repair and condition.

Each plane was fixed up with a 10 pound bomb on cacti wing and a 25 pound bomb on the belly and the members of the volunteer Coast Patrol flew these looking for submarines. They were also asked to pull targets for the anti-aircraft gunners to shoot at for experience.

The members of the CAP squadron were trained to fly P-51 and they became known as the Interception Squadron out of Burbank. They were to intercept and shoot down any Japanese planes should the Japanese decide to attack the West Coast. This was a shakey time in the history of the US. Soon the Navy was built up and able to take over the job of defending the West Coast. The P-51s were then needed in Europe and assigned to the US Army. Earl remained in the CAP until 1944.

When the war was over Earl and his wife, Pauline, flew back to the PIPER factory in Lockhaven, Pennsylvania in 1947 arid bought a J-3 Cub right out of the factory for $1650. and flew it back to their farm near cast Bruning on highway 4 which became known as the "Flying Hawks Ranch".

The two of them furnished a private airstrip, airport, grocery store, beauty parlor, cafe, dairy, arid motel and called their place Hawksville. People came, landed and stayed at Hawksville from all over the US. During the 1950's Earl wrote a column in the Bruning Banner which gave an account of all the people who landed and visited their ranch.

Earl and Pauline wanted to get a chapter of the National Flying Farmers started in Nebraska. Jess Quinn of Gothenburg, "Pinky" Schneider of Culbertson, "Rag" R.C. Carleson of Silver Creek, Reed Carson of Hallam, and Earl and Pauline Hawks of Bruning were charter members of the Nebraska Flying Farmers Association. Nearly every pilot, not just farmers, became a member of this organization, which was very active during the '50s and '60s. A "Fly-In" would be scheduled somewhere almost weekly. The pilots, their families would pack up a pot luck dinner and fly to various airports and strips. Breakfast would be served by the host airport and after a morning spent in telling about flying experiences, close calls, weather and flying antedotes the pot luck dinner would be served at 12:00, followed by entertainment put on by the host airport-usually musical numbers. A business meeting would be held and the flyers would head for home. These Flying Farmers Meetings became the main social event in the lives of many pilots.

Pauline Hawks was the 1951 State National Flying Farmer Queen and was runner up in the National Flying Farmers Contest.

She was president of the Nebraska 99ers, an organization of women pilots organized by Amelia Earhart. The group got their name from the fact that there were 99 charter member women pilots in the US at the time the organization was started.

Besides running a GI flying school, the Hawks ran a crop dusting service. They then employed a full time flying instructor and another crop duster. Larkins, McAbe, Eirsman were flying instructors arid T.B. Sherrill and Clyde Eirsman were crop dusters.

Pauline and Dean Osher bought 2 super-cub X crop dusters and with Earl's original cub they had three crop dusting planes. Pauline believes she was the first woman crop duster in the state of Nebraska in 1951.

She also ran a charter air service and flew people into O'Hare in Chicago, Dallas and any

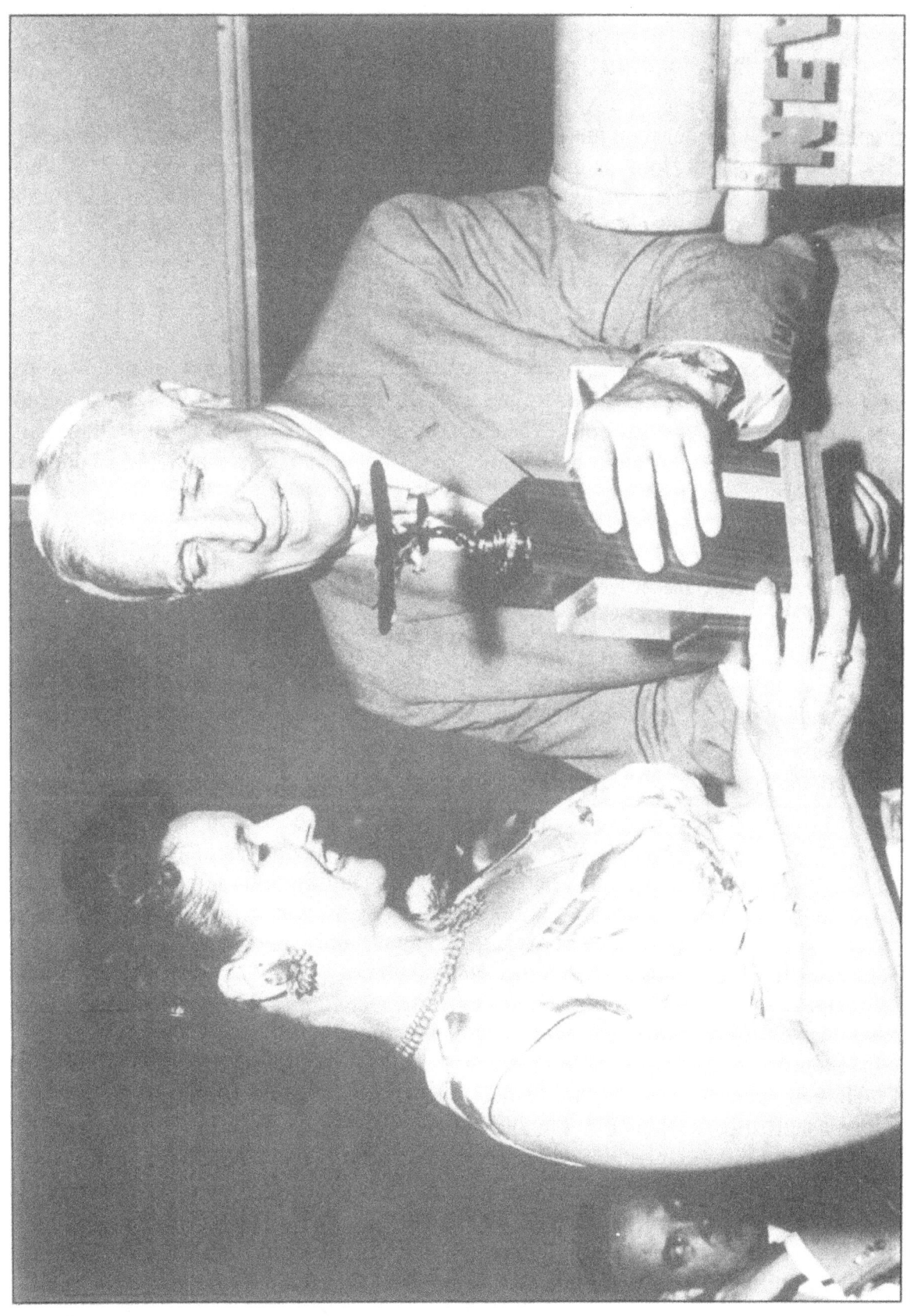

Pauline Hawks receiving the 1958 National Flying Farmer Woman's Flight Achievement Award, being presented by Mr. W.J. Piper at the 14th Flying Farmers Convention in New York City, NY. Mrs. Hawks flew the most hours (140 hours) equivalent of 16,800 miles: from June 15, 1957 to June 15, 1958.

Dallas and any place anyone wanted to go in a hurry. She was given an award by Mr. Piper, of the Piper Manufacturing Company for being the Flying Farmer woman pilot who logged the most number of hours in 1958, a total of 140 hours.

Pauline's talents weren't confined to aeronautics. She was known as an excellent cook and was always ready to cook a feast for anyone who happened to be at the Hawks Ranch at mealtime. Pigeon pie was never better than made by Pauline. She raised chickens, washed the separator (which separated the milk from the cream in their dairy business), ran the motel, fixed hair in her beauty shop, had a large garden and orchard, canned fruits and vegetables, made prize winning quilts and fancy work and was one of the most gracious hostesses anywhere.

In 1955 Pauline was the first woman pilot in Nebraska to be granted a permit for aerial hunting.

DR. R.E. PENRY, M.D.

In 1946 it wasn't easy for a new doctor to get started. Unlike 1984 when a town will go to any lengths to get a doctor and offer all sorts of inducements to get a doctor, in 1946 it was often a struggle to get started. Dr. Penry, out of medical school and the army came to Hebron to visit an old dentist friend, Dr. Baker. When he asked if Dr. Baker knew of a town that needed a doctor, he was told that Hebron could use one.

Dr. Penry opened his office up over the top of the old Thayer County Bank where Things and Stuff is now located. Dr. Penry laughs about the trip up the 20 steep stairs to his office really tested the coronary patients. Thayer County did not have a hospital at that time.

Dr. Penry took up flying after he came to Hebron and got his license in September of 1946 after taking flying lessons at the Hebron Airport. He trained and soloed in an AERONCA Champ. In August of 1947 he bought his first plane, a LUSCOMBE which was used mainly for a hobby and he also used it to make some long distance house calls.

AIR AMBULANCE

In 1950 the Blue River went out of its banks and completely isolated Hebron from surrounding communities. It made Dr. Penry conscience of the town's need for an air ambulance. A patient. injured badly in an automobile accident was hospitalized and was treated for multiple lacerations and shock, but his condition called for immediate attention by bone specialists. Dr. Penry called an Omaha air service and two hours later the patient was flown to Omaha.

Dr. Penry decided to buy a plane and convert it into an air ambulance. He purchased a twin engine Cessna UC-78. It was an army Executive plane with the seating capacity of 7 and powered by 2-350 hp. Jacobs radial engines. He completely recovered and overhauled it, but it proved too expensive for ambulance and commercial flights.

In May of 1956, he traded the twin engined Cessna and the Luscombe both off for a new Cessna 182. He converted it to an air ambulance with an air speed of 160 mph and he flew patients on many short trips, such as Lincoln and Omaha. When this plane was converted from a four place passenger craft to an ambulance plane there was still room enough for an attendant as well as the stretcher, oxygen bottle, and medical equipment. This conversion took just 10 minutes. A commercial pilot, Kenneth Butler served as his first co-pilot. Dr. Penry also flew patients to Mayo Clinic in Minn. and made his plane and pilot available for all doctors in southern Nebraska.

On December 22, 1966 Dr. Penry purchased a new Piper Cherokee 300 at the factory in Vero Beach, Florida. It was a 7 passenger, easily converted to cargo or ambulance, which would accomodate the stetcher and attendants as well as first aid equipment. Dr. Penry, retired in 1984.

Dr. Penry's Piper Cherokee in flight [Photograph Courtesy of Mrs. R.E. Penry]

EDDIE RICKENBACKER WRITES TO MRS. PAYSEN

Mrs. Paysen was the wife of the music professor in the Hebron Academy. April 18, 1943 Hebron Journal:

"Hero of World War was former pupil of Hebron Lady. Several months ago, we published a story regarding the boyhood of Eddie Rickenbacker, who, with his sister were pupils of Miss Zwerner (Mrs. M. Paysen of Hebron) back at Columbus. Ohio. Mrs. Paysen recently received the following letter from her former pupil--an outstanding hero of World War I and II.

EASTERN AIR LINES
Office of the President

April 2, 1943

My dear Mrs. Paysen:

It was like turning back the pages of history to receive yours of Jan. 31st, and altho I have been somewhat delayed in replying to it, I want you to know I appreciate your thought and faith during our sojourn on the broad Pacific.

Yes, I was in your class, many years ago, and little did we think then of the changes that would take place in a few short years.

If ever I happen to be in your vicinity, you may rest assured I will be delighted to look you up, but in the meantime kind regards and best wishes to you and yours.

Sincerely,
Eddie V. Rickenbacker
Pres. and general manager

WORLD WAR II PILOTS

Many Thayer County boys flew during the World War II. Here are bits we found about them in various county newspapers. We found several articles about the same person as they progressed through the war. To anyone we left out, we apologize! It became more of a job than we realized. We started naming only pilots and co-pilots, but added gunners, navigators and bombardiers If they were killed in action. We hope to make a list of all Veterans in the near future. Send us your service record.

FREDERICK C. AHRENS

Frederick C. Ahrens, son of Mr. and Mrs. August Ahrens of Davenport received his wings and was a flight instructor at Sequoia Field, Visalia, California. He was killed in an airplane accident June 21, 1944. Memorial Services for him were held a Christ Evangelical Lutheran Church at Davenport on July 30, 1944.

CHARLES BACKER

Charles Backer, 24 year old son of John and Iona Backer received his wings and commission and is at the AAF Redistribution Station at Santa Anna. He was later stationed at Hunter Field Georgia where he was a B-24 Co-Pilot. He was stationed in England with the 303rd Bomb Group. He flew 12 combat missions and received the air medal, oak leaf cluster, and the European Theatre ribbon with 2 battle stars.

PATRICK BAILEY

Patrick Bailey, son of Mrs. F.J. Maher of Hebron is taking his preflight training at Birmingham, Ala. at Maxwell Field where he is an aviation cadet. In the Deshler High School Library there is a picture of Pat Bailey with the following information: He was killed in action over Japan. His father was James Bailey and his mother was Lois nee Cooperrida. He had been awarded the purple heart and distinguished Service Citation over Nagasaki.

ELLSWORTH "BILL" BILLMAN

E.L. Billman of Bruning got his wings on February 6. 1943 at Luke Field, Phoenix, Arizona. He flew over 50 missions as a pilot with the 15th Army Air Force where he was a B-24 pilot in Italy, Balkians and southern Germany. He was awarded the air medal with 7 oak leaf clusters and the African- European Campaign ribbon with 1 star, Air Medal and the Distinguished Flying Cross. He was killed in an automobile accident in the 1950s.

BILL BERGAN

Bill Bergan, Hebron, son of David Bergan received his commission and wings January 9, 1943 at Tuscon, Arizona and was transferred to Alamogordo, New Mexico. He flew with the American African forces in Sicily where he flew B-24s on the attack on Rome. He received the Oak Leaf Cluster Air Medal and was recommended for the distinguished flying cross. Later on the paper tells that he has received 3 distinguished Flying Medals and 7 Air Medals.

DONALD BRANDT

Lt. Donald Brandt, son of Mr. and Mrs. Charles Brandt of Davenport graduated May 30, 1943 in a class of 43-E pilots at Marfa Army Base.

DALE BRANDT

Lt. Dale Brandt, son of Mr. and Mrs. Charles Brandt of Davenport, Nebraska was the first pilot on a B-17. (That's all the paper says about it. We tried to find out about that statement, but have not). He was born near Carlisle, Nebraska June 10, 1920 and graduated from Davenport High School in 1938. He received his wings and commission from the Army Air Force Pilot School St Stockton Field, California and left for overseas duty August 1, 1944. He was stationed with the 8th Air Force in England, being a member of the 91st Bombing Group 322 Squadron. He was killed while on a mission over Merseburg, Germany. Enemy gunfire damaged his plane. He had given orders to all crew members to bail out and that he would follow: as the radio man bailed out, the plane broke in two making it impossible for Dale to escape.

MERLE BRINEGAR, JR

Merle J. Brinegar, son of Mr. and Mrs. Merle C. Brinegar of Alexandria was inducted into the army February 20, 1943 and received his wings and commission at Altus, Oklahoma. He served with the Eleventh Air Force in the Aleutians for nine months and has participated in bombing missions of the enemy over Paramushiru, Shimushu and Matsuwa Islands of the Northern Kuriles Group. He has been awarded the Air Medal and Bronze Oak Leaf Cluster and the Distinguished Flying Cross. He is a member of the "I Bombed Japan" Club.

GENE BULLER

Gene Buller of Hebron is in the Army Air Forces Control Flying Command at Randolph Field, Texas. He became a pilot on February 16, 1944 and is assigned to Gulf Coast training command as an instructor in navigation. He flew B-24s.

DALE BUTLER

Dale Butler, formerly of Belvidere and nephew of Dail Wills of Belvidere was killed in action on December 3, 1942 in the Canadian Air Corps.

KENNETH BUTLER

Kenneth Butler, son of Mr. and Mrs. O.M. Butler of Hebron was commissioned as a U.S. Naval flier and received his wings of gold on December 31, 1942. He graduated from the air school at Corpus Christie, Texas. His father ran the Hebron Bottling Works at that time. After the war he flew for Dr. Penry.

WILLIAM BRUNING

Lt. William Bruning, son of Mr. and Mrs. Hugh Bruning, formerly of Belvidere, was wounded in action July, 1944. He was a pilot of a Marauder bomber and has been in the European area.

HUGH DeLOSS BRYAN

Hugh Bryan, son of Mr. and Mrs. Harry Bryan, received his golden wings in the United States Navy. He flew at Pensacola, Florida, where they flew close rank--so close their wing tips nearly touched. He felt his eyes going bad and reported this to his commander and after examination they took his wings away from him. He then reenlisted in the navy where he was stationed at the Great Lakes and Florida. He worked with missiles and went in on the third wave at Iwo Jima, where he stayed throughout the rest of the war. (Information from Harry Bryan, Hebron.)

CECIL CANNON

Cecil Cannon, son of Mr. and Mrs. Lloyd Cannon, received his wings and commission in Match of 1942. He flew the AT6--with 650 Hp. and cruised at 180 mph. Its cost was $50,000. Cecil wrote, "Who'd think the government would trust me with anything worth that much?" He was a flight instructor in New Mexico.

DONALD E. CANNON

Donald Cannon, 23, son of Mr. and Mrs. Lloyd Cannon of Hebron, Nebraska and brother to Cecil Cannon, received his wings on December 5, 1943, and was a Mustang fighter pilot. He was later stationed in England where he participated in several escort missions deep within Central and Eastern Germany. The April 25, 1945, Hebron Journal states: (special) "An Eight Air Force Fighter Station, England--Nazi troops will long remember the day First Lt. Donald E. Cannon, 23, Mustang fighter pilot, Hebron, Nebraska, strafed at tree-top level in the vicinity of Nordlingen, Germany."

The stocky, tow-headed graduate of Hebron High School reported these results: "a large troop truck exploded in flames; a military camp was riddled and a radar station was put out of operation."

HARLAND FINTEL

Lt. Harland E. Fintel of Byron was born November 14, 1922. He was the son of Edward Fintel and Bertha nee Fangmeier. He graduated from the Air Force Aviation School, May 30, 1944, and died when his plane was shot down March 27, 1945. (From the Deshler High School Library.)

JAMES W. GRAVES

James W. Graves was killed 12 Sept., 1945, a few minutes after take off when his plane crashed to the ground. The accident occurred in Furth, Germany, about five miles from the airbase. During the take off the right engine of this aircraft failed but Lt. Graves managed to get the plane into the air. He apparently had the ship under control when he suddenly had to lift the wing to avoid hitting a building because of the low aititude. This caused the ship to turn over and crash into the ground.

GERALD GEORGE

Gerald George, son of Mrs. Ida George of Chester, received his wings and commission. He was killed in a plane crash in May, 1943, in Louisiana and was buried June 10, 1943, in Chester. He was 27 years old.

PHIL GREGORY

First Lt. Phil W. Gregory of Deshler was stationed at Rosewell, NM. where he was an instructor and flight commander. A later paper stated he is a navigator, meterologist and bombardier instructor.

LEONARD HOSACK

Leonard Hosack, son of James and Francis Hosack of Alexandria, was reported missing in action March 30, 1944. On March 6, 1944 which was called Bloody Monday because 80 bombers were lost that day, Leonard was in the lead group of 900 bombers. It was to be his 13th mission. His bombardier had been killed on one of his earlier missions. When he was 40 miles from his assigned target, the group was attacked by a group of German fighter planes. The No. 2 and 4 engines were hit as well as the right wing. The entire crew bailed out at 22,000 feet. He spent 3 days and nights hiding out in a forest and tried to hike out at night and hiding by day. He accidently ran into two German soldiers who were as surprised to see him as he was to see them. They put him in the nearby jail and he was later taken to a prison camp in Madgeburg, Germany. He spent from March 25, 1944 to Jan. 28, 1945 in the camp as a POW until he was freed by the Russians.

HAROLD HOPPE

"Bud" Harold O. Hoppe, Jr., son of Mr. and Mrs. Harold O. Hoppe of Alexandria, Nebraska,completed 45 missions with the 13th Air Force and has the record of never losing a plane or a member of his crew. He flew from Guadalcanal to the Philippines. He considered the bombing of Turk as his toughest assignment along with the oil fields and installations in the Dutch East Indies. The Alexandria Argus states that he has had many close contacts with the old man with the sythe. Captain Hoppe returned from the South Pacific, March 6, 1945, where he had been the flight Squadron Commanding Officer. He worked at the Pentagon for awhile but when later wars broke out he reenlisted for active duty, this time as a helicopter pilot, where Major Hoppe flew "his boys". After the " Conflicts" he was stationed at Strategic Air Command at Omaha where he flew superjets on missions worldwide. Col. Hoppe retired from the Air Force and moved to Wichita, Kansas. (Information from his cousin, Vera Mae Powell.)

CHARLES HUGHES

Charles Hughes was a P-47 Thunderbolt fighter pilot and was stationed at Luke Field in Phoenix, AZ., Fort Crook and Bruning, Nebraska. He new air combat in the Balkans, No. Opennines and PO Valley. He flew 52 missions and only three members of this 79th Fighter Group made it through all the missions. He was awarded the Army Occupational Medal, Victory Medal, Air Medal with 1 oak leaf cluster, Distinguished Air Badge with one oakleaf cluster, FAME Campaign Medal with 3 bronze stars and the American Theatre Campaign Medal. He married Virginia McKenzie, Hebron music teacher, and lived in Hebron until 1980 when they moved to Belleville, KS. He died at the age of 58 in Belleville. (Information from Virginia Hughes.)

WALTER HARRIS

Lt. Walter Harris of Hebron was a member of the famed Black Sheep Squadron #214. He participated in an aerial flight attached to the Marine Fighting Squad against the squadron of Japanese Zero's which greatly outnumbered them. He was listed missing in action over the Solomon area in Sept. 1943.

LEONARD KENNEL

Nov. 26, 1942: Ernest Kennel of Chester received word of the death of his son, Leonard J. Kennel, caused by an accident in an airplane. Leonard has been in the Navy for the past fifteen years, and was a flying instructor at San Diego, California where the accident occurred.

LAWRENCE C. KENNEDY

Lt. Lawrence C. Kennedy, the nephew of Mr. and Mrs. Bill Wright, Mrs. Chester Barr of Hebron and Mrs. Jo Cerveny of Reynolds flew a RAF 4 motored plane. He is a commander of a bomber flight squadron at Lakeland, Florida.

LOUIS KERL

Louis Kerl, son of Mr. and Mrs. William Kerl of Bruning is an aviation cadet and has completed his Primary Flight Training at Rankin Aeronautical Academy. He flew a B-17.

VICTOR KUHLMANN

Victor Kuhlmann of Byron is missing in action in the battle of Sicily where he was a radio operator on a plane. Mrs. Kuhlman's parents are Mr. and Mrs. Renz of Byron.

WALLACE LAKE

Wallace Lake of Hebron graduated from the British Flying Training School at Miami, Oklahoma. He received his wings with the Royal Air Force Cadets in this country from the Central Flying Training Command at Randolph Field, Texas and received his wings and commission June 17, 1944 in Miami, OK from both the American and British Royal Air Force.

Lt. Lake received further instruction in instrument flying at Romulus, Detroit. He served overseas with the American Transport Command in China. On Oct. 7, 1944 he was reported missing in night over the Burma Road between Kunming and Chengtu, China. Last contact was made by radio when the pilot was ordered to return to Kunming and searches along the route failed to reveal any trace of the plane and crew. These records, reports and circumstances were considered and after 12 months the War Department must terminate by a presumptive finding of death. His parents were Mr. and Mrs. Frank Lake of Hebron and his brothers were Mirza and Eugene.

WILBER LEFF

Wilber Leff, son of Mr. and Mrs. Thed Leff of Carleton, received his wings and commission on January 7, 1944. He flew in Corsica, Italy and Yugoslavia. He received the "Croix de Guerre" Award from France in his participation in a precision attack. He received the presidential Unit Citation, African-Middle East Theatre Ribbon with 3 battle stars, the American Theatre Ribbon and the Victory Ribbon. Captain Leff was the pilot of an A-26 Invader in combat against the Japanese. He flew B-26 Maurauders and B-25 Mitchells. He participated in 45 bombing and strafing missions against the enemy in both Europe and Pacific Theatres.

WILLIAM LOWREY

March 1, 1944: Air Cadet William R. Lowrey has been transferred from Fort Stockton, Texas to Poster Field, Texas where he is training with the U.S. Air Force. April 19, 1944, Second Lt. William Lowrey, son of Mr. and Mrs. Ray J. Lowrey of Davenport, receives his commission and wings in the U.S. Army Air Corp of Aloe Corps at Victoria, Texas. He was later stationed at Walla Walla, Washington. He became a B-24 Liberator pilot with the 4th Army Air Force.

GILBERT MAPLE

Gilbert Maple, son of Mr. and Mrs. Jay Maple of Hebron received and air medal for participating as a gunner on a B-17.

DONALD McKENZIE

Donald McKenzie, son of Mr. and Mrs. Lloyd McKenzie, earned his wings and commission and flew pursuit planes. He learned to fly at the Hebron Airport and had 85 civilian hours to his credit before entering the Air Force. The April 1942 Hebron Journal states he is learning to do blind flying, just following the beam signals which was a new technique at that time.

DUANE McKENZIE

The *Hebron Journal*, Dec. 25. 1941, has large headlines that read: "Duane McKenzie flew 18,000 miles in 6 days." It goes on to say that most of this flying was done over water in the Pacific. He had been an instructor at Jackson Field, Mississippi. He has been in 10 different organizations or bomb groups. He was in 9 crackups riding the plane down and has parachutedto safety 11 times. On one bail-out a wing folded and caught a gunner across his waist. The gunner, who, knowing he could not jump with the others, calmly removed his signet ring and gave it to Duane.

DOYLE McLAUGHLIN

After Doyle McLaughlin received his wings and commission he was stationed in Brazil for a time. On D-Day, June 6, 1945, Doyle was the pilot of a C-47 transport plane. He wrote the *Hebron Journal* that he was one of the planes which took off at 7 second intervals and lurched into the sky in an seemingly endless stream. He carried paratroopers over and returned with wounded soldiers. Lt. McLaughlin received the Air Medal for his achievements on D-Day.

THOMAS McGOVERN

Thomas McGovern, son of Mrs. Carl McGovern, Hebron, enlisted February, 1943 and received his commission and wings Jan., 1944 at Fredrick, OK. McGovern was a B-25 pilot and was reported missing in action. The War Department later declared him dead.

WILFRED MIESSLER

Ist Lt. Wilfred Eugene Miessler was born June 20, 1922. His father was a minister at St. Peter's Lutheran Church from 1938 until Dec. 29, 1942 when he became and army chaplain. Wilfred graduated from Deshler High School on May 24. 1940 and from the Air Force, March 12, 1944. He served with the 8th Air Corps until March 9, 1945 when he lost his life in an accident in a practice gunnery mission over the North Sea. (information from the Deshler High School Library.)

CHARLES NACKE

Aviation Cadet Charles Nacke, son of Mr. and Mrs. Albert Nacke, was a member of the largest class in Coffeeville, Kansas Army Air Field. He received his wings and commission and was listed as both a P-38 and P-39 Pilot in the *Hebron Journal*. He was transferred to Ontario, California where he piloted P-38s. The Feb. 6, 1946 *Hebron Journal-Register* printed a letter from the War Department: Since your son, Flight Officer Charles C. Nacke, T123776, Air Corps was reported missing in action 29 January 1945, the War Department has entertained the hope that he survived and that information would be revealed dispelling the uncertainty surrounding his absence. However as in many cases, the conditions of warfare deny us such information. The record concerning your son shows that he piloted a P-38 Lightning fighter plane on a patrol to cover a convoy west of Panay Island, Philippine Islands, on 29 January 1945. The last contact with your son occurred on the return flight to Leyte, about 20 miles northwest of Beybey, Leyte, over the Camotes Sea, during adverse weather conditions, when he advised his flight leader by radio, that he was leaving the formations for reasons not determined at this time. Immediately thereafter the control point at Baybay reported seeing a flash on the water believed to be made by a burning plane, at the approximate position where your son was last contacted. No trace of him has been found since this date ... In view of the fact that 12 months have now expired without evidence to support a continued presumption of survival, the War Department must terminate such absence by a presumptive finding of death. Accordingly, and official finding of death has been recorded under provisions of Public Law 490, 77th Congress, approved March 7, 1942 as amended. The finding does not establish an actual or probable date of death; however, as required by law, it includes presumptive date of death for the termination of pay and allowances, settlements of accounts and payment of death gratuities.

WILLIAM NAVIS

1st Lt. William I. Navis, son of Mr. and Mrs. G.H. Navis of Chester, Nebraska was awarded 5 oak leaf clusters to his Air Medals. Lt. Navis was a pilot of the Veteran 60th Troop Carrier Group, which staged the first Allied Airborne Invasion in the war at Oran, Algeria in 1942. His awards have been presented in recognition of his outstanding work in dropping by parachute by night, vital war supplies to Allied partisan forces operating behind enemy lines in the Balkans and in evacuating the wounded who had been forced down behind the lines. He had performed 70 such missions in transport type aircraft. The landings he had made behind the lines at night were on short and rough improvised fields in narrow mountain valleys.

JAMES Z. PAYSEN

1944: 1st Lt. James Z. Paysen, Hebron, Nebr. is a co-pilot in the 461st Bomb group, a 15th AAF B-24 Liberator unit. He has been overseas since last January and has participated in bombing attacks on vital Nazi targets along the Eastern and Italian fronts; giving support to the Russian armies driving in Austria and Germany and to the Allied Forces smashing the German divisions in Italy. Paysen entered the SSF on Sept. 28, 1943 and received training at the army airfield at Victoria, Texas. He graduated from Hebron High School in 1941. His parents are Mr. and Mrs. Magnus Paysen. His father was the music professor at the Hebron Lutheran Academy.

GERALD POWELL

Gerald Powell, son of Mr. and Mrs. John Powell of Alexandria received his commission and wings and was a fighter pilot. He was on a routine training mission flying from Boston to New York when he and his plane mysteriously disappeared. In a telephone interview with his sister, Mrs. Lily Wilson, on March 10, 1985, she said that Gerald is still classified as missing, over 40 years later. Because nothing was ever found of him or his plane and he was not over enemy territory, the War Department says no date for his actual death has ever been established, so they have never paid the usual death gratuities. Mrs. Wilson said that the government eventually paid his mother $24.40 a month missing compensation. Speculation has been that perhaps his instruments failed and he got vertigo and turned towards the sea.

GERALD "JERRY" POWELL

Jerry Powell, son of Mr. and Mrs. Walter Powell of Hebron won his wings March 12, 1944 at Williams Field, Arizona. He was with the 15 Air Force Base and flies a P-38 Lightning. He was awarded the Air Medal for "meritorious achievement" over Italy. He had logged 7 combat missions while flying over Czechslovakia, Germany, Italy, Yugoslavia and Austria, and new as a member of the top scoring American group in the Mediterranean Theatre Operations with 550 aerial victories.

EUGENE A RODENBURG

March 7, 1945: *Hebron Journal* — Credited with a torpedo hit on a Japanese carrier in the waters of the east coast of the Philippines last Oct. 25, Lt. Eugene E. Rodenburg, USNR, son of Mrs. and Mrs. E.A. Rodenburg of Deshler, Nebr. has been awarded the Navy Cross, the Eleventh Naval District announced today. He was one of 80 pilot officers and air crewmen of the Navy's carrier based Air Group 20 who were decorated by Rear Admiral Alfred E. Montgomery. Displaying extraordinary heroism while serving as a pilot of a carrier based torpedo plane, Lt. Rodenburg pressed his attack through intense AA fire to score his hit. The carrier sank as a result of his and other hits. Lt. Rodenburg participated in the aerial defense and occupation of Guadalcanal and also in the New Georgia Campaign.

MARTIN ROTH

Lt. Martin Roth, husband of Barbara Hess, the second daughter of Judge and Mrs. Hess of Hebron, was a navigator on a B-24 Liberator called the "Dixie Belle". He was reported missing in action April 24, 1944, and was later found a prisoner of war in Rumania, May 11th. After several months in prison camp he was released. Lt. Roth remained in the service and retired in 1984 as a Lt. Col. He lives in Kittyhawk, NC.

DEAN AND DALE SANNER

Lt. Dean Sanner entered the aircorp in 1942 and received his wings and commission Sept. 1942. His brother, Dale took his training at a University and received his commission. The two brothers met in England during the war. Dean later received the Distinguished Flying Cross for his participation as a pilot. They were the grandsons of Mr. and Mrs. W. Sanner of Davenport and U. M. Lowery of Davenport.

BENJAMIN STAUBER

Ben Stauber, son of Paula Stauber and Clarence E. Stauber, was born in Hebron, November 21, 1920. He was a student at the Civil Aeronautics School in Hebron and earned his civilian pilots license September 27, 1940. With the completion of a course in Aircraft Mechanics in Kansas City, Missouri, he was employed by Douglas Aircraft in Long Beach, California. He enlisted in the Army Air Corps on August 14, 1942. He entered training at San Antonio, Texas in February 1943 and received his commission in Navigation at Hondo, Texas, Dec. 4, 1943 with additional training at Roswell, New Mexico. He received his wings as bombardier, qualifying as a crew member of the Superfortresses B-29. He participated in the first two strikes over Tokyo, and he took part in the incendiary raids over Nagoya, Osaka and Kobe. He received the Air Medal and Oak Leaf Cluster. He completed more than 20 missions over Japan. He was killed in action over Tokyo on April 2, 1945. His plane was hit by enemy aircraft fire and crashed into the mountainside. (Information from his Memorial Service, Feb. 3, 1946 — Presbyterian Church.)

GEORGE SUCHUKAR

George Suchukar, son of Mr. and Mrs. Frank Suchukar of Byron received his wings and commission and was the pilot of a B-17. He was reported missing in action on June 21, 1944.

LELAND SCHAINOST

Leland Schainost of Gilead was the chief flight director of Lincoln Flying School and was then promoted to Kansas City with the CAA and designated to be the Senior Flight Supervisor of the large cross country program at Des Moines.

PHILLIP W. SLAGLE

Lt. P.W. Slagle of Davenport, the son of Mr. and Mrs. Carl Slagle was commissioned Nov. 1, 1942, and was with the USNR doing patrol duty on the Atlantic.

CLIFFORD THRASHER

Clifford Thrasher, son of Mr. and Mrs. Elza Thrasher of Alexandria, entered the Air Force Sept. 8, 1942. He received his pilot training at Bytheville, Ark. and was assigned to duty as a pilot with a B-24 Liberator heavy bombardment group of the 15th Air Force. He received the Air Medal for meritorious achievement in aerial flight while participating in combat missions against the enemy in the Balkans, Northern Italy and Germany. Lt. Thrasher is a B-24 pilot with the veteran 460th Bombardment Group of the 15th Air Force. In Italy he was entitled to the Distinguished Unit Badge and European African Middle East Campaign Ribbon.

H.H. THOMPSON

Harold H. Thompson of Belvidere was stationed at Ellington Field, Texas, the largest multi-motored training school in this country. Captain Thompson gave pre-flight training for bombardiers and navigators and advanced training for pilots.

HARRY WARTHEN

Harry Warthen, son of Mr. and Mrs. Calvin C. Warthen of Hubbell, was a cadet pilot in 1943, and flew the BT-13.

ERVIN A. WILKENING

Ervin A. Wilkening, formerly of Kiowa, was inducted into the army Febr. 11, 1942. He was the tail gunner of a bomber and was lost in action in Sept. 1943.

JOHN WITTENBERGER

John Wittenberger, son of Herbert B. Wittenberger, has moved to Fort Dix, N.J. He received his commission and wings as a P-47 pilot. He flew with the 65th fighter squadron in Corsica. He was killed in action Sept. 5, 1944 while on a strafing mission near Pavia, Italy. On Oct. 9, 1945 at a special military ceremony held at Lincoln Army Air Field, Mr. Herbert B. Wittenberger of Carleton, NE. was presented with the Distinguished Flying Cross and the Air Medal with three Oakleaf Clusters which were posthumously awarded to his son, 1st Lt. John A. Wittenberger; killed in action. Lt. Wittenberger had served overseas with the 12th Air Force. The citation for DFC was for extraordinary achievement while participating in aerial flight as pilot of a P-47 aircraft. On 20 July 1944, Lt. Wittenberger led a twelve plane formation of fighter bombers in an attack upon a railroad line. Displaying great courage and superior flying ability, he skillfully maneuvered through intense anti-aircraft fire upon the approach to the target. Lt. Wittenberger's precision directed run over the objective enabled his P-47 to score many direct hits cutting the line in 5 places, destroying 15 freight cars and damaging 30 others. The Oak Leaf clusters were'- 'for achievement while participating in aerial flight as a pilot of 2 P-47 on an attack upon enemy a communication lines near Certaldo, Italy, on April 18 and the shipping harbor at Porto Perraio, Elba on May 15, 1944; a railroad bridge near Empoli, Italy and supply and communication lines and military installations in Toulon, France August 19, 1944.

SHERMAN WOLFE

Sherman Wolfe, son of Elmer and Francis Wolfe of Alexandria, got his golden wings at Corpus Christi, Texas. He made 15 combat missions flying the Avenger, Torpedo bomber based on one of the Navy's escort carriers. His combat history included support in Palau, Philippines and Iwo Jima invasions. His skipper was shot down over Iwo Jima and he survived 3 typhoons with winds over 100 knots an hour.

MAYNARD J. WIENS

Lt. Maynard J. Wiens, formerly from Hubbell, was the pilot of a P-38 fighter plane in England, and received a citation and air medal for exceptionally meritorious service.

In 1946, the "Thayer County Servicemen's Directory was printed. We tried to determine how many of the men who were killed in World War 11 were in the air corps or air force. As near as we could determine 18 of them were. Rather than to leave anyone out we decided to print the entire list of those who are gold star men, from World War II (The Museum Muse plans to print an issue on all servicemen in the future. Please send us any information on this subject.)

Frederrick Ahrens, Davenport	Gilbert Maple, Hebron
Clarence Asche, Deshler	Tyndall Marshall, Davenport
Patrick Bailey, Hebron	Tommy McGovern, Hebron
Bert Bailey, Jr., Davenport	Wilfred Miessler, Deshler
Dale Brandt, Davenport	Joseph Miller, Hebron
Donald Cane, Alexandria	Lowell Miller, Davenport
Maurice Clements, Davenport	Richard Mueller, Deshler
La Vonne Doehring, Hubbell	Charles Nacke, Hebron
Freeland Dunker, Hebron	Eldon Philippi, Bruning
Harland Fintel, Byron	Gerald Powell, Alexandria
Rudolph Fischer, Byron	Lester Powell, Alexandria
Lewis Fisher, Davenport	Clarence Rippe, Hebron
Arthur Gallion, Chester	Lester Schussele, Carleton
Gerald George, Chester	Eldred Sedden, Hebron
James Graves, Carleton	Norval Sims, Alexandria
Max Henderson, Carleton	Ben Stauber, Hebron
Duane Hubbert, Alexandria	Anton Stofer, Carleton
Melvin Naiman, Gilead	Rudolph Stofer, Carleton
Marv Knowlton, Belvidere	Kenneth Whale, Carleton
Edward Koci, Hebron	Theodore Wagner, Bruning
Wallace Lake, Hebron	Vernon Welch, Hubbell
Otis Lemke, Bruning	Arnold Werner, Hebron
Bill Lietsch, Carleton	La Vern Werner, Deshler
Hubert Lipker, Deshler	John Wittenberger, Carleton
Lawrence Mammen, Bruning	

DR. LOUIS BUNTING, M.D.

Dr. Bunting learned to fly from a man named Bird in 1952. He and "Chris" M.L. Christensen owned a metal LUSCOMB plane top-ether and it was in this plane that Dr. Bunting soloed.

About a year and a half later Dr. Bunting drove to Colorado in a brand- new Chrysler automobile. The distance seemed so long that when he got to Colorado he traded-the Chrysler for a Cessna-170 and flew back home,

After the Buntings had their Cessna 170, they bought a BONANZA and the last plane he owned was a twin engine PIPER COMANCHE. Dr. Bunting and his wife, Marge (Wittenburger of Carleton) put over 1200 hours on this plane flying all over the U.S., Canada, Newfoundland, and the Bahamas.

At that time the Hebron airport had 3 runways and one wooden hangar. The State gave them a tower if they would go get it. Dr. Bunting, Dean Osher and another man drove Richard Reinke's truck to Kimball and disassembled the tower. They brought it back to Hebron and put it together and put it up. Harold Werner dug the trenches for the air field lights and Dr. Bunting put them in. 71

HENRY KORENSKY

Thayer County's County Judge, Donna Fink sent a copy of her father's private pilot's license and his aircraft registration certificate, along with a picture of her father's Piper J-C3, her father, Henry Korensky, with David Korensky and Ron Verjraska.

Piper J-C 3 owned by Henry Korensky. Pictured In plane are: Henry Korensky, David Korensky & Ron Vejraska.

She gave a brief story about her father. Henry Korensky was a lifelong resident of Thayer County and very much enjoyed flying around this area. He received his private pilot's license on October 15, 1962. Most of his training was under the instruction of Dean Osher. On February 25, 1963, he purchased a 1946 Piper J-3C aircraft, registration #N98344, from Babe Barbee of Hebron, Nebraska.

Henry was killed in this same aircraft, along with Russell "Dusty" Mittan, on September 1, 1963, while flying through a severe thunderstorm.

DEAN OSHER

Dean Osher was born March 30, 1920, and was killed while crop dusting on February 22, 1973. He learned to fly in Estherville, Iowa from a man named Ralph Bryan. He took his Civilian Pilot Training in Des Moines, Iowa and served four years with the United States Air Force during World War II and four years as a Korean war pilot.

He did crop spraying for Dick Matthews after Korea. He became the airport manager of the Hebron Airport and ran a spraying service as well as being a flight instructor there.

COMMERCIAL AIRLINE PILOTS
PAUL OLSON

Paul Olson was born in Hebron in 1925 and grew up east of Belvidere. During World War II he was with the Navy's "SeaBEES" and when he got out of the Navy he learned to fly in 1945. He worked for Everett Kilmer in the Chevrolet Garage and did flying for Mr. Kilmer. He attended the University of Nebraska the next four years. Mr. Kilmer would permit Paul to use his plane to go to and from Lincoln to school.

After he got through school he got a job doing crop spraying along the Republican Valley with the Biggert Brothers of Shickley. Biggert's were noted for having the largest spraying operation in the United States. They took a four engined B-17 flying fortress bomber and converted it over to a spray plane. Paul flew the smaller crop duster planes.

After returning from a crop spraying job Mr. Olson found a tree top on the struts of his plane and decided to get out of crop dusting. In 1951 he started working for Trans World Airlines out working for Trans World Airlines out of Chicago. He worked for TWA until 1984 when he retired. His headquarters were in New York and he flew regular flights to Paris, France and Cairo, Egypt. Sometimes he made flights to Los Angeles, going over the North Pole.

ROBERT BECK

Robert Beck was the son of Bill and Carrie Beck of Hebron and was a pilot for TWA. His run was into Germany and Switzerland.

ALLEN SCHWAB

Allen Schwab, son of Noel and Doris Backer Schwab of Alexandria joined the ROTC when he was a junior at the University of Nebraska. The Vietnam War was on at that time. He was given the opportunity to get his wings at the Reese Air Force Base near Lubbock, Texas. He was given his choice of bases to be stationed and he chose the Colorado Springs Base. He was stationed at Peterson, Colorado where he flew a T-29 and was with the Aero-Space Defense Command where he flew VIP's. After he completed his Air Force hitch he taught in St. Louis, Missouri, where he taught using in assimulated cockpit. He received a call from Pan-American and has been flying for Pan-Am world wide since.

DOUGLAS WILLIAMS

Douglas Williams, son of Lawrence and Pauline Corliss Williams of Belvidere, Nebraska got his preflight training in the Navy at Pensacola, Florida. He was stationed in New Iberia, LA., where he flew a P-30. He served four years in Hawaii flying a 13 man submarine patrol. After the service he got a job with American Airlines where he flew 727s, DC-10s, DC9s and is currently flying the 747 to and from the Mainland to Hawaii.

[Photograph Courtesy of Pauline Williams]

RAY MIETH
40 YEARS ACTIVE PILOT

Date of first flying lesson - 11 February 1945 - Piper J-3 "Cub" - Grand Island, Nebraska as a high school junior.

Present ratings - Commercial, Single and Multi Engine Ratings.

Business - Owner of Great Plains Aviation, Inc. (Used aircraft sales business) in Hebron, Nebraska

Taught Aviation Ground School in Springview, Nelson, Bruning and Hebron, Nebraska to well over 100 would-be pilots. I would estimate that about three out of four active pilots in the Hebron area are products of those classes.

Civic accomplishments - Driving force behind the building of the new airport at Hebron. I

Single-handedly worked with State and Federal officials to build an airport at Springview (Nebraska) which had no airport before.

Represented the Nebraska Department of Aeronautics in 1965 in hearings before the Federal Aviation Administration in Washington supporting Aviation Education in public schools.

Flown 45 different models of aircraft, and owned all but 11 of those, which includes 13 different Cessnas and 15 different models of Pipers.

Family - Mary, soloed in 1972, did not go any further
Douglas - Commercial and Instrument rated (Air traffic controller in Des Moines)

Bruce - Private Pilot

Currently vice chairman of the Hebron Airport Authority.

Actively support the Mission Aviation Fellowship, a world-wide organization that furnishes over 75% of the planes and pilots and support equipment for churches of all denominations, world-wide in the mission fields.

I would imagine my 40 years of flying is about high for active, certified pilots in the county. Certainly, I'm not the oldest, or perhaps the most total years, but for those still flying. (signed) Ray Mieth

Ramon Mieth was the Superintendent of Schools in Hebron for many years and is employed at Reinke Manufacturing.

NEWEL SANDERSON
AIR TRANSPORT RATING

Newell Sanderson learned to fly in Lincoln at the Lincoln Aviation School in a Piper 140. He had about 60 hours flying time before he entered the Air Force. He was in the Advance Air Force Base in Oklahoma and flew a Cessna 172. In 1971 he flew a primary trainer, the small twin T-37 jet, for 50 hours. I Then he flew the advanced Jet T-38 super sonic plane and has broken the sound barrier twice. He graduated in January, 1972, and made operational flight from Norton Air Forge Base in San Bernadeno, California. He flew the C141, Starlifter, the 4 engine jet transport world wide making flights to Germany, England, Australia, Samoa, Japan and Vietnam. After that he flew the small 8 passenger VIP business jet, the T-39. He has a single and multi-commercial instrument jet rating, as well as an Air Transport rating. Sanderson is in sales and flies for Reinke Manufacturing doing the business flying in a Twin Beech and Single Piper.

LAVON BOHLING

Lavon Bohling started flying when the State Department of Aeronautics offered 10 hours of dual, free, to teachers who started an Aviation Class in High School. Mr. Bohling was teaching in Geneva at that time and started a course which eventually became a credit course. He took his flying out of Crete in 1967 and soloed in a Cessna 150 at Fairmont. He then got his commercial rating and moved to Tennessee where there was a college that offered a masters degree in aero space technology. After completing that course, he worked for Cessna in Wichita in marketing and flight school. He is in sales for Reinke Manufacturing and flies in his work

RONALD WERNER

Ronald Werner of Deshler learned to fly under Dean Osher while he was in high school. He became an instructor at Duncan Aviation in Lincoln.

In 1964 he became a pilot for United Air Lines and has flown 8 different types of planes. He is still employed at United at this writing.

CAROLE SUTTON

Carole Kreydle Sutton learned to fly in 1968 in a Piper Sub Cub in Belleville, Kansas and then attended the Salaton Texas Flying Service to master her speciality of crop spraying. In the May 2, 1976 Nebraska MIDLANDS she was featured as being the only woman aerial applicator among the 252 male sprayer pilots in the state of Nebraska. Today there are male and female sprayer pilots.

When her husband, Stuart Sutton, went into aerial spraying, Carole took to the air while her husband did the ground work. They have an air strip east of Chester, Nebraska and fly out of the Belleville Airport in Kansas. Carole flew a 235-horsepower Piper Pawnee. As ''Chester Spray, Inc.'' they hire two other pilots and own 3 Piper Pawnees and 1 Eagle She has 3200 hours of flying time logged.

In January 1978 Carole Sutton was awarded the 99's Amelia Earhart Memorial Career Scholarship award which is awarded annually to help develop the flying talents of women. She used her scholarship to attain her instrument rating. She wanted to obtain her CFI so that she could instruct students who belong to her flying club. She is past president of' the 99er's.

Carole was horn, grew up and attended school in Belvidere and has two children. She is on the board of Nebraska Aviation Trade Assn.

HELICOPTER PILOTS

GENE DAVENPORT

Gene Davenport got his basic aerial experience in the military, where he was crew chief on a UH1 helicopter in Vietnam. After he got out of the army he returned to Vietnam to work as a civilian for about a year.

In 1976 he went to school at York to get his "Fixed Wing rating" and Commercial License. He did aerial spraying from Hawks Field near Bruning and then came to Belvidere, Nebraska where he runs the Davenport Flying Service. His first plane was a Cessna-188B AG Truck and presently is flying a Grumman AG-CAT. The AG-Cat has the capacity of holding 300 gallons of spray but on a hot day. Mr. Davenport said he only, loads 200 to 250 gallons.

WAYNE HENNING

Wayne Henning of Hebron learned to fly in Texas in 1968 in the Army where he flew Bell 47 Helicopters and became a Warrant Officer. He married Rhonda Davidson of Alexandria in March of 1968, and was sent to Vietnam in December of 1968 where he flew the Bell UH1's or "Huey's" and hauled troops and went on combat assaults. After a year in Vietnam he went to Aircraft Mechanic's School in Sidney. He then joined Johnson Flying Service in Hebron and flew the Hiller 12F helicopter for crop spraying. He went on his own and bought a Hughes 269 and does crop spraying.

JOHNSON'S FLYING SERVICE

Tom Johnson and his family moved to Hebron in March of 1973, from Brookings, South Dakota. Tom was hired to be the airport manager at Hebron. In South Dakota. Tom worked as a flight instructor in the ROTC program, through the University of South Dakota at Brookings.

Tom Johnson and Wayne Henning shown with 1973 Ag Truck, owned by Tom Johnson.
[Photograph Courtesy of Tom Johnson]

1965 Hiller Helicopter, owned by Tom Johnson. Bought as Government surplus and rebuilt for use in Tom's aerial spraying business. Tom Johnson on left, Wayne Henning on the right. [Photograph Courtesy of Tom Johnson]

Tom Johnson was the airport manager from April, 1973. until December, 1977. He was the airport fixed base operator at Hebron, from April, 1973, through 1979. Tom operated an aerial spraying service as well as flight instructing, charter and aircraft maintenance, while operating the Hebron Municipal Airport.

In 1974, there were only eight commercial helicopters registered in the State of Nebraska, and two of them were owned by Tom Johnson. He bought, rebuilt, and sold government surplus helicopters.

Tom Johnson sold his aerial spraying business in 1979, and started a new aerial spraying business in Hastings, in 1983, and in Hebron in 1984.

It was in a BELL Helicopter. that Tom Johnson received his commercial license. It was based at Lincoln, NE and cost $105.00 an hour to rent. Other helicopters that he has owned included a 1965 Hiller Helicopter.

Tom Johnson, was the first to seed wheat with an airplane in Thayer County. He used a Grumman Ag-CAT with tanks, which would hold 20-25 bushels of wheat. The wheat would be loaded into the plane by bucketfuls.

The Thayer County Lions Clubs, built a heli-pad, at the Thayer County hospital in Hebron, and Tom Johnson was the project chairman. Helicopter come from Lincoln, bringing in associate doctors and land on this pad. Patients can also be flown to larger hospitals, using the pad.

Heli-pad at Thayer County Hospital, Tom Johnson was project chairman.

Ray Meith, fueling one of his many aircraft, he has bought and sold over the years. Tom Johnson flew this plane from Hebron to Washington, D.C., for the new owner, in 1972.

Pete Brewer's plane after landing in a gusty wind.

[Photogtaphs courtesy of Tom Johnson]

VOTIPKA FLYERS

Ten of the twelve children of Charles and Ferne DeWald Votipka of Alexandria have served in the military. Of these 3 are pilots:

DAVID VOTIPKA - David received an appointment to the United States Air Force Academy as a member of the Class of 1980. He graduated at Laughlin Air Force Base, Del Rio, Texas, June 25, 1981. He had placed 2nd overall in the National College Parachute Championships held at Dayton Beach, Florida.

Using a ran-air canopy parachute which acts as a collapsible glider, David demonstrated his parachuting skills at the Hebron Airport, July 20, 1978 when Clarence McGhghy of Hebron took him tip 7500 feet. David was at that time a member of the "Wings of Blue" a four man parachute team representing the Air Force Academy. David was stationed at Myrtle Beach, South Carolina and is currently a flight instructor at the Holloman Air Force Base in Alamogordo, New Mexico.

FIRST WOMAN AVIATOR IN NEBRASKA'S NATIONAL GUARD

JOANNE VOTIPKA - JoAnne graduated as a warrant officer in the Rotary Wing Course Class of 1983 at Fort Rucker, Alabama. JoAnne became the first woman aviator to join the Nebraska National Guard in December of 1984. She will fly Cobra for the 24th Medics running an Air Ambulance.

BENJAMIN VOTIPKA - graduated from the US Aviation Center in Fort Rucker, Alabama as a warrant officer in the Rotary Wing. on September 21, 1984. He is on duty in Korea.

David Votipka, photo taken from United States Air Force Academy Brochure, which featured David In several photos.

JoAnne Votipka, first woman aviator in Nebraska's National Guard. [Photograph courtesy of Fern Votipka]

Ben Votipka - [Photograph courtesy of Fern Votipka]

THAYER COUNTY AIRMEN AND WOMEN

When we started to gather information for this article in 1976 a letter from Michael Larson, Aviation Services Representative of State Aeronautic Dept. invited us to research the state airman registration list and the annual reports. Since that time the State Dept. of Aeronautics has gone entirely on computer. We were told that no records are kept in Lincoln at all. It is all on the computer at the Federal Aviation Administration in Oklahoma City.

A letter from the Federal Aviation Administration Jan. 28, 1985, Oklahoma City, Oklahoma states that their computer records contain only current data and that no historical data is kept. The computer would not be programmed to compile a list from a particular county.

With no records being available a list of Thayer County current flyers was compiled with the help of Lavon Bohling, Ramon Mieth, and Earl Hawks. Earl named flyers who were former residents which use his field regularly Asterick denotes those who have a students license. All others are private. Addresses may be at the time they learned to fly.

Myron Ammeter, Hebron
Edward Babka, Columbus (Hawksfield)
Leonard Babka, Columbus (Hawksfield)
B.J. Bedford, Carleton
Babe Gwen Barbee, Hebron
Albert Beu, Gilead
Wilbur Beu, Gilead
Roger Bohling, Byron
Lavon Bohling, Hebron
Vaughn Bowen*, Hebron
John Brewer
Peter Brewer, Hebron
Phil Brown, Hebron
Dave Bruning, Bruning
Dr. L.G. Bunting, Hebron
Randy Bumgarner, Bruning
Gene Butler, Hebron
Dr. John Butler, Hebron
Kenneth Butler, Hebron
Marlene Butler*, Hebron
Floyd Christency, Bruning
Bruce Christensen
M.L. Christensen, Hebron
Rollin Collison, Bruning
Gene Davenport, Belvidere
V.J. Deepe, Bruning
Darrel Degner, Deshler
Alan Doll, Bruning
Ed Duncan, Alexandria
Bill Easton, Chester
Gene Ells, Hebron
Gordon Fleming
Clarence Folkerts, Bruning
Robert Folkerts, Davenport
Wessel Folkerts, Davenport
Harry Franz (Hawksfield)
Dolan Frye, Chester
Don Gerdes, Hebron
Tom Griffin, Alexandria (Hawksfield)
Harley Grone, Davenport

Earl Hawks, Bruning
Fieldon Hawks, Bruning
Pauline Hawks, Bruning
Fred Henrichs, Bruning
Joe Hergott*, Gilead
Mark Hergott, Gilead
Bernard Heinrichs, Bruning
Vaughn Heinrichs, Carleton
Wayne Henning, Hebron
Marlowe Huber, Hebron
Charles Hughes, Hebron
Steve Hoffmeyer, Deshler
Wayne Jagels, Davenport
Basil Johnson, Bruning
Gaylord Johnson, Bruning
Tom Johnson, Hebron
Vic Johnson, Deshler
John Jordon, Alexandria
Jan Kenner*, Hebron
Jim Kenner, Hebron
Pat Kenner*, Hebron
Willis Kettlehut, Deshler
Craig Kirchoff, Hardy
Eldon Kirchoff, Byron
Galen Kirchoff, Deshler
Steve Lempke, Bruning
Bill Linton, Hebron
Max Linton, Hebron
Walt Magnus, Hebron
Clarence McGhghy, Hebron
Logan McGinnis*, Hebron
Ruth McGinnis*, Hebron
B.E. Mieth, Hebron
D.R. Mieth, Hebron
Mary Mieth*, Hebron
Ramon Mieth, Hebron
Albert Muehling, Deshler
Mike Ohlrich, Deshler
Robert O'Neal, Hebron
Bill Ortman, Hebron

Dean Osher, Hebron
Rick Osher, Hebron
Ted Paid, Davenport
John Perry, Hebron
Dr. Richard F. Penry, Hebron
Burdette Priefert, Belvidere
Dr. Hal Pumphrey, Hebron
Don Rempe, Hebron
Lester Reinke, Hebron
Dr. Waller Reiss, Belvidere (Hawksfield)
Dr. Eugene Rizek, Hebron
Rev. F.G. Richart, Hebron
Gerald Ross
Newell Sanderson, Hebron
Doug Schardt, Deshler
Ron Schardt, Deshler
Willis Shane, Bruning
Frank Shane, Bruning
Sam Stall, Hebron
Jack Stewart, Hebron
Carole Sutton, Chester
Stuart Sutton, Chester
Dean Swaney, Hebron
Ted Tietjen, Jr., Byron
Lawrence Traudt, Hebron
Deb Vorderstrasse
Duane Vorderstrasse, Hebron
Jim Voigt, Davenport
Darrell Walker
Robert Waring, (Hawksfield)
Dave Wenske, Deshler
Bob Werner, Hebron
Clint Werner, Carleton
Kent Werner, Carleton
Bob Werner, Carleton
Bud Zeuhlsdorf, Hebron

AIRPORTS

Besides the 3 main airports in Thayer County — Bruning State, Hebron Municipal, and Hawks Field at Bruning there were several small grassed runway landing strips in the county during the 1950-60s. These included:

SEIBER — South of Ohiowa, altitude 1572'
STUBS STRIP — Southeast of, Belvidere. altitude 1500'
SWANEY — One mile north of Hebron, altitude 1540'
VORTMAN — south of Carleton, altitude 1600'

Private Strips today in 1985 are:
   Clarence Folkerts, Carleton
   Robert Werner, Carleton
   Robert Folkerts, Davenport
   Harley Grone, Davenport
   Richard Reinke, Deshler
   Stuart Sutton, Chester
   Bill Easton, Chester
   Byron Community Strip

Flying Hawks Ranch Airport [Photograph Courtesy of Earl Hawks]

John Penry - Custom to cut off the shirt tail when soloing accomplished. [Photograph Courtesy of Mrs. R.E. Penry]

JOHN J. PENRY

John Penry was the son of Martha and Dr. Richard E. Penry of Hebron. John enjoyed flying with his father and took formal lessons in a Cessna 150 on April 3, 1966 and made his solo flight May 25, 1966.

It was the custom that whenever a man made his solo flight his shirt tail was cut off and kept as a souvenir of the event. These shirt tails were frequently hung in the airport's lounge.

John received his private pilots license on December 10, 1966 and continued on his commercial and instrumental flight training. He received these licenses December 3, 1968. He flew many commercial flights, taking private passengers and business men to meetings.

He entered law school and during the summer he flew as a crop duster. On June 4, 1969 he was killed in an aerial spraying accident.

An Indian Prayer Garden was placed in the Hebron Rose Hill Cemetery as a memorial to John, 93

THE PRAYER GARDEN

At the west side of the Hebron Cemetery there is an Indian Prayer Garden put there by Dr. and Mrs. Richard E. Penry, whose son, John was killed while spraying crops. It is taken from the Indian teachings of Black Elk.

There is a hedge circle with two sidewalks criss-crossing the circle. One is painted black and the other red. In the center there is a mountain ash tree. Plaques tell the symbolic significants of the garden.

Those Who Flew
"Those With Wings" update

Morrow Brother's Airplane
1911 Carleton, NE

Everett Morrow built the plane and Ed did the flying. The motor mounts were made of wood and were weak and would break loose in a jar. The wing design was bad on their first model. They used bed sheets and did not coat them and it was impossible for that plane to fly.

The Morrow brother's father was a blacksmith and the boys used materials from his shop and nearly kept their father broke. They moved to Burwell and kept working on the plane until they finally got it to fly. This information and the above picture came from Tom Lucht from Lincoln who talked with John Stables of Davenport. John had visited about the plane with Ed Morrow in 1950 in a Hebron Cafe. The State Historical Society had a picture of the Morrow Brothers plane flying above the telephone lines in Ord, NE.

From Tom Lucht

Flying Doctors

Dr. Louis Bunting, MD, Dr. Penry, MD, Dr. John Butler, OD and Dr. Noller, DVN all flew after World War II. Although Dr. Bunting has owned many planes, he does not hold the record in the county as Ramon Mieth holds that record. Ray has owned 119 planes.

Dr. Bunting first bought a Luscomb in 1954, a Cessna 170 in 1955, a C-35 Bonanza in 1957, a twin engined Comanche in 1965, a J35 Bonanza in 1971, a Cherokee Piper with retractable landing gear in 1980 and owned a share of a 150 Cessna in a flying club with Jack Stewart, Dr. John Butler, and James Kenner. Dr. Bunting and his wife, Marge, flew all over the United States, Central America and to the northern tip of Newfoundland. He logged 2500 hours.

Dr. Richard Noller

Doctor Richard Noller was a Thayer County Nebraska veterinarian. When World War II came along all animals, particularly cattle, became a big business to provide food for the army and the nation. Thayer County was a big cattle producing county. The government ordered that all cattle had to be tested for tuberculosis before they could be sold.

Doctor Noller was called to be drafted and sent to Fort Riley, Kansas. It was determined that he was needed more as a veterinarian than as a soldier. There was only one veterinarian, Dr. Leslie of Belvidere, left in the county and all cattle had to be tested for TB, one veterinarian could not do the job.

After the war Dr. Noller went to Oklahoma where he purchased a Stearman bi-plane. Phil Brown flew it back to Hebron and Doc learned to fly. He used the plane in his veterinarian business landing on farms where he could. He and his wife flew all over several states visiting friends and relatives. They kept the plane for about 12 years and then sold it when the law came out there had to be a fire wall installed between the pilot and the motor.

Those Who Flew
Flying "The Hump"

Wallace Wayne Lake

In '42, the Japanese military force severed the Burma Road, China's last link to the Allied world. The situation was desperate unless the Allies could supply the Chinese with military provisions. The only alternative was to airlift supplies directly to China from Allied supply depots in India. The American airmen would have to fly heavily loaded transport planes over the world's tallest and unforgiving mountains, the Himalayas. Wallace Lake was such a transport pilot.

Wallace Lake was born 1-18-1921. He lived near Hebron, NE. On 22 Aug 1941, he got his private pilot license and enlisted on 20 February 1943. He trained at MO and IL. He attended the Spartan School of Aeronautics and became a Royal Air Force Cadet at the British Flying School. He received his Royal Air Force Flying Badge at Randolph Field, TX.

He was commissioned into the American Air Force June 17, 1944, took Instrument, Detroit Michigan. He flew the American Transport command. He was injured and received the Purple Heart. He was with the 134th Army Air Force Transport and flew a transport plane over the Burma Road. His plane was missing 7 October 1944 while flying over Kumming, China. His body was recovered and returned on train #537 UP Railroad and was delivered on November 4, 1947 at 3:45 at Belvidere, NE. He was interned at the Rose Hill cemetery at Hebron, NE. His picture, uniform, Purple Heart, RAF wings, metal RAF flying badge and plane picture were donated to the Thayer County Museum.

Those who flew
"Those With Wings" Updated

Flying Farmers Organization

After World War II, flying was very popular. Returning GI's could learn to fly on the G. I. bill. Small planes like the Piper J3 and 172 Cessna were comparatively inexpensive and very available. Their cost could range from $700 to $3000 in the 1950s. Larger planes such as the Piper Tri-Pacer were $10,000. The Flying Farmers Organization was very popular, not only for farmers, but for business men and anyone who loved to fly. There are 30 families who belong to the Flying Farmers Organization in Nebraska in 2002.

Back in the 1950's, before small planes had radios, throughout the summer there would be a "Fly In" at some airport nearly every Sunday morning. Hawks field would frequently host such a gathering. Flyers would come flying into the sponsoring Airport in the early morning when the weather was usually calm. They would tie down their plane, eat breakfast together, and visit. Sometimes a pot luck dinner would also be held, but the flyers would usually break up before the afternoon heat and winds would prevail.

In 2002, there are 30 families in Nebraska who still belong to the Flying Farmers. Enthusiastic Flying Farmers thought the plane was the wave of the future. They predicted that by the year 2000 everyone would own a plane. This did not happen, however, as the planes became more sophisticated and technical, requirements more stringent and, of course, more expensive.

Those who flew regularly at the Hebron Airport in 2002:
Robert Reinke, Hebron, NE
Larry Norder, Minneapolis-St. Paul
Jeff Engles (Instructor) Fairbury, NE
Bob and Kent Werner, Carleton, NE
Ray Mieth, Hebron, NE

FLYING CLUBS

By the new millenium, Corporations and Flying Clubs were the way that many could have a plane. Several Flying Clubs housed their plane at the Hebron Municipal airport with its new facilities. Marlowe Huber listed these planes which were kept at the Hebron facility in 2002:

Hastings Aviation Crop Spraying
Belleville Kansas Flyers
Blue Valley Flying Club.
Melvin Broman, Fairbury, NE
Tom Buresh, Davenport, NE
Wm. (Bill) Easton, Hebron, NE
Chris J. and Michael Huber, Hebron, NE

Marlowe D. Huber, Hebron, NE
Pat Kenner, Hebron, NE
Galen Kirchhoff, Deshler, NE
Brent Meyer, Ruskin, NE
Clarance McGhghy, Hebron, NE
Michael Schmitz, Geneva, NE
Justin Johnson, Fairbury, NE

Coyote Hunters

"Babe" Barbee, Earl Hawks, Hollis Dittmer and Mac Ayabe with 119 coyote scalps for the month of February 1952. In 1953 a tornado destroyed these planes and buildings at the "Flying Hawks Ranch", Bruning, NE.

Major Benedict Votipka in 2002

Ben Votipka, pilot instructor in Georgia, sits on the wing of the T-6A. The T-6A is a single-engine, two seat primary trainer designed to train the specialized undergraduate student in basic flying skills. It is produced by Raytheon Aircraft and is the military version of the Raytheon's Beech/Pilatus PC-9 MkII.

In the T-6A, the student sits in the front seat and the instructor in the back seat. It has a side opening, one piece canopy. The Pratt & Whitney Canada PT6A-68 turbo-prop engine with 1,100 hp can make an initial climb of 3,300 feet per minute. It is fully aerobic and has a pressurized cockpit with an anti-G system and advanced avionics package with sunlight-readable liquid crystal displays.

Colonel David Votipka

We have no currant picture of David Votipka as a pilot as he now is with the joint Chief of Staff under the Secretary of the Air Force and works in the Pentagon.

Those Who Flew
Update of Those with Wings

Captain Joseph D. Kunkel of Hebron
F-15E Air-craft commander

On 12 June 2000, Captain Kunkel received the Distinguished Flying Cross for heroism while participating in Aerial Flight of 6 April 1999. In the citation which accompanied this award it states

"After entering enemy territory inbound to his target he was engaged by three surface-to-air missiles. He aggressively maneuvered his aircraft, dispensed countermeasures, and defeated the missiles. With complete disregard for his own safety, he elected to continue to his target and proceed closer to the site firing missiles at him. One minute from the target, Captain Kunkel was surrounded by intense anti-aircraft fire. He carefully maneuvered to defeat the deadly threat while still allowing for target acquisition.

Twenty seconds prior to the release of ordnance he identified the target. After a flawless delivery and laser designation, his two weapons scored a direct hit on the tunnel entrance. Destruction of the tunnel entrance insured the enemy MIG-21 fighters were never able to threaten the Kosovar refugees located throughout Kosovar and nearby countries. The outstanding heroism and selfless devotion to duty displayed by Captain Kunkel reflect great credit upon himself and the United States Air Force"

THE BAAFLER

Effects of World War II on the Home Front

- Victory Gardens
- Meat Rationing
- Shoe Rationing
- Canning Applications
- Gasoline Rationing
- Aluminium Pennies
- Red Cross
- Price Control
- Scrap Drives
- "War Time" time
- Sugar Rationing
- Tire Quotas
- Waste Fat
- Red Cross
- Blackouts
- War Bonds

BRUNING ARMY AIR FIELD, BRUNING, NEBRASKA

The Bruning Army Air Field

THERE'S A WAR ON
On the Home Front
THE EFFECT ON EVERYONE'S LIFE
Victory Gardens & Scrap Drives

Browsing through several of the newspapers of the time reveals of the effect that World War II had on everyone's life. Every citizen seemed to give their all. Every one was asked to participate in some way and did so enthusiastically.

"The Home Front" suffered little in comparison to places where the war was actually fought, nevertheless, the daily lives of Americans were affected from the very beginning of the war.

Every family was asked to grow a VICTORY GARDEN to raise food for their families. Women were asked to can in glass fruit jars as tin became scarce as the war wore on. If one didn't have a garden, and try to put up their own food, it was as if they were a traitor to their country.

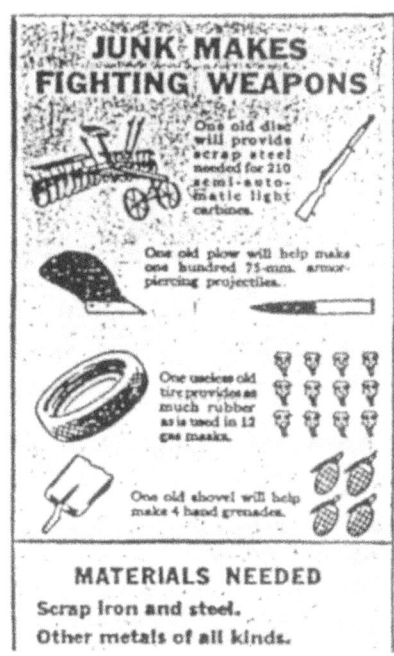

Scrap drives were held at regular intervals. First there were aluminum drives and children were asked to scrounge through dumps to find and bring to school any kind of aluminum. The schools were used to be a collection point. It was the teacher's job take the collections on to a larger collection point. It is hard to believe that at that time there were rural school houses within walking distance of every rural home. Thayer County had 101 such little one room school houses, located about 2 or 3 miles apart. Jefferson County had 103 one room schools at the time.

How hard the children in school worked digging through dumps looking for aluminum, When some arrived at school there was a collection of very rusted tin ware. This was one of the first lessons learned in searching for aluminum--it does not rust and if what was brought to school was rusted, it was not aluminum, and the rusted tin containers had to be carried back to the dump site much to the dismay of the children,

JUNK RALLY
For BRUNING
and vicinity

NATIONAL SCRAP HARVEST

SEPT. 26
at the
Community Scrap Pile

Junk helps make guns, tanks, ships for our fighting men.......
Bring in anything made of metal or rubber...
Get paid for it on the spot

Bring your family
Spend the day
Meet your friends

JUNK MAKES FIGHTING WEAPONS

One old disc will provide scrap steel needed for 210 semi-automatic light carbines.

One old plow will help make one hundred 75-mm. armor-piercing projectiles.

One useless old tire provides as much rubber as is used in 12 gas masks.

One old shovel will help make 4 hand grenades.

Let's Jolt them with Junk from **Bruning**

The Bruning Army Air Field

MORE SCRAP IRON WANTED

The scrap drive in Bruning got off to a good start when nearly three tons of scrap metal was loaded out Monday. More is coming in and we hope to have another load shortly.

To hasten the flow of scrap metal to market from this territory, the Banner has agreed to pay cash upon its delivery to Bruning. The scrap iron should be weighed at the Farmers Grain company office, then unloaded at the community scrap pile between the drug store and cafe. Weight ticket should be brought to the Banner office for payment.

This nation-wide scrap collection is meant to build up stockpiles huge enough to last the mills through the winter months when the weather makes it impossible for most of them to get scrap.

Saturday, Sept. 26, has been set as the date for a Big Junk Rally, both in Bruning and Belvidere, which will wind up the present drive. The success of this effort depends upon every individual. Get in the Scrap!

PLENTY MORE IN THE BARREL

The Bruning Army Air Field

Scrap Drives

Iron piles were cleaned out everywhere. Steam Engines, which had been the workhorse of the farm, running threshing machines and cornshellers were brought in to be "shot to Japan" in the form of war materials. Hebron had a beautiful canon which went into the drive. The Civil War Veterans had always been a patriotic source in Thayer county many of Civil War guns were given up for the drive. Only two of those guns were kept as a momento of another war. One of those is in the Thayer County Historical Society Museum in Belvidere. The other was in a vault in the Court House.

Mrs. Ralph Hill handing over one of the Civil War guns to Mr. Herman L. Boyes while H.E. Shearer holds three of the other Civil War guns which all were donated to the Scrap Drive.

A portion of the scrap metal and tires acquired by the Hebron Community to the scrap drive. The money raised from the drive was led among the five churches.

A nationwide scrap drive and scrap drive contests were held between communities and even between states. Kansas and Nebraska had a big contest and it was pointed they were both winners in helping our nation at war. Each citizen was requested to come up with at least 100 pounds of iron. One boy in the Belvidere schools brought over 1000 pounds of iron to school and another brought 1700 pounds. Scrap iron was weighed and a small amount of money was paid for it. If it rained on the day of a scrap drive, the drive could not take place as most all roads in the county were mud roads and people could not get to town. In that case, it was requested that the iron scrap be brought to the local elevator when the roads dried off.

"WAR TIME" TIME

In an attempt to get longer days "War Time" was instituted. All clocks were to be set back one hour. Editor Cramb of the *Fairbury Journal* wrote an Editorial in the *Fairbury Journal* stating that people who were not connected with defense work shouldn't have to comply to "War Time". He thought that it was particularly hard on school children during the months of November through to March and it required more fuel used for heat and light. He suggested all mayors declare that time of the year to go back to Standard time.

PENNIES AND NICKELS

After October 1942, nickels would not contain nickel as this was needed for the war effort. Copper was also needed for the war effort so a plastic penny was experimented with along with a penny made from a new alloy never before made. The new pennies would have the Philadelphia mint inscription on them. The plastic pennies were not developed, but pennies which were locally called "aluminum pennies" were used.

The Bruning Army Air Field

FOOD RATIONING

Sugar and Coffee were the first to be rationed. What a sacrifice that seemed to be as, Americans had a sweet tooth and were quite addicted to coffee. Ration books first came out with coupons which were worth a specified number of pounds of sugar, coffee, meat, etc. By December of 1942, rationing went to the "Point Rationing System."

"POINT RATIONING SYSTEM"

Each of the coupons or stamps, as they were sometimes called, in the Point Rationing System had a specific point value or a number. These books came in different denominations. They would be for meat, sugar, coffee, tires, gasoline, other fuels (tractor fuel and kerosene), overshoes, and workshoes. Later on all shoes required stamps or coupons. Wooden soled shoes were developed that didn't require a shoe stamp.

In the point rationing system a meat stamp was good for any kind of meat--beef, pork, or lamb, but various meats would have different values. For example steak would have the highest value. It would require more points than hamburger. Chicken required the least number of points. The purchaser tore out the required number of points for what was bought. There were small red tokens which were given in change if the purchaser did not have the specific point stamp. Oh yes, the purchase also required money.

The Bruning Army Air Field

CANNING APPLICATION FORMS

Women had canned fruits for their family in glass fruit jars for years, but with sugar rationing, this presented a problem. Fruit had been canned in "heavy syrup" which was made up of water and sugar. How could they continue their canning? For this the government required a canning application.

In October 1942, 423 Home canning applications were made in Thayer County. The Argus states that of these 310 were approved and 6,134 pounds of canning sugar was made available. To fill out an application housewives had to give the number of jars canned in years before and the number expected to can that year. If the number of jars canned, did not equal the application, this had to be reported. The sugar could be used for household use but the rationing stamps of that amount had to be turned back. (We wonder how many didn't use up all their canning sugar for canning)

Sugar rationing meant that desserts became a missing item from food tables. Recipes were published which used honey and sorghum and even saccharin in the recipes to replace sugar so that cookies and cakes could be made.

Coffee was replaced by tea and "maté". "Maté" was similar to tea but was made from the shoots of a South American holly. It was sold in glass jars and had a consistency similar to the instant coffee of today, but not the taste.

RATION BOOKS AND STAMPS

Nearly every week the newspapers would inform the people about their ration stamps. Rationing information was an important column. For example this was the January 1, 1943 Alexandria Argus ration schedule:

"Coupon #10 is good for 3 pounds of sugar, but it expires January 31.
Coupon #28 would be good for 1 pound of coffee after January 3.
Coupon #3 and the 1st page of gasoline coupons will expire January 21.
Fuel oil coupons #2 and #3 are good now.
Fuel oil coupon #2 is good for 10 gallons of fuel oil.
Fuel oil coupon #3 is good for 11 gallons of fuel oil.
You must have an "E" or a "R" stamp to get "hot tractor fuel" (a fuel that was more readily combustible than regular tractor fuel, but not as much as gasoline)."

TIRES

Tires were such a premium. There were tire inspectors all over the county, but most of them were Filling Station operators. Listings of Tire Inspectors were given in the newspapers. If a person needed a new tire, an old tire had to be brought in and the serial number would be taken off it and the tire inspector would determine if a better tire was deserved.

The Bruning Army Air Field

WASTE FAT

In September of 1942 the plea for waste fat went out. Uncle Sam had asked the women of the mid-west to save one half billion tons of waste fat. This would be enough, the article said, to cripple the German war machine or to make explosives for 1,125,000 anti air craft shells.

The fat from any kind of meat was requested. When hamburger or sausage was fried, any fat left in the skillet was strained into a tin coffee or vegetable shortening can. If a hen was boiled, the fat was skimmed off and added to the collection.

When the can was full and there was at least a pound of waste fat, it was to be taken to the nearest meat salesman and it could either be donated for the war effort or 4 cents was paid for each pound of waste fat donated.

GASOLINE RATIONING

In November of 1942, all persons owning a car, truck, tractor or bus had to register to get their gas classification. This classification was made evident by a sticker which was about 2x3 inches in size and was to be placed on the lower right hand corner of the windshield.

All passenger cars received an "A" classification. These stickers would be black with a large "A" on them. People with an "A" sticker got 4 gallons of gasoline a week. "B" stickers were green and these people got 16 more gas coupons than passenger cars and this gave them approximately 320 additional miles of driving, but they had to have work which required over 150 miles of driving a month. The red stickers with a "C" were issued only to doctors, utility workers, farmers, ministers and government workers.

Non-highway fuels were given an "E" or an "R" classification. This would include tractor fuel and kerosene for your lamps and kerosene stoves. "T" classification was for taxis, buses, government vehicles, ambulances and hearses.

The Bruning Army Air Field

Tire Quotas

Each month the county was given a specific number of tires and those who got them would be determined by the tire inspectors. Tire inspectors were under the OPA, the Office of Price Administration. The September 1942 tire quota for Thayer County was as follows:

30 new Passenger Tires
12 new tubes
43 bus and truck tires
18 retreads for bus and truck

For the month of October 1942 the county received for its' quota:
16 tubes
20 truck and bus tires
10 truck and bus retreads

All tires for passenger cars which had 18 inch rims are now declared obsolete. All rubber boots and overshoes and workshoes are now rationed.

Any family who owned more than 5 tires had to take their extra tires to the Federal Railway Station where they would be purchased from them. Anyone caught with more than 5 tires in their possession were not to be given gas even if they had gas ration stamps.

V Mail

To conserve space and to speed up mail service, V mail was initiated. The sender purchased special sheets of paper which were approximately normal typing paper in size. They were made so that they folded into an envelope. These were sent to an Army Post Office--Each APO number was to go to a specific place overseas.

At the A.P.O. a picture of each letter was taken. It was stored on film about the size of camera film. When a film was filled, it was put on an airplane going to that area. At the destination it was run through a machine which developed it into a small approx 4x5" inch letter.

Prices

A farmer could get 7 cents a bushel to store wheat. Warehouse (stored) corn was worth 80 cents bushel.

The new license plates came out in 1943 and were made of metal as the older plates but the new ones were only 2"X 2" which would fasten over the "42" on the old license plates. The cost of these smaller licenses remained the same--$3.00 for regular cars and $5.00 for cars and vehicles over 280 pounds.

THE VICTORY TAX

On January 1, 1943 the Victory Tax went into effect on all salaries over $12 a week. The first $12 was tax free but 5% was to be witheld from wages above the $12. This tax could be held until after the war was over, or was put into Defense bonds or could be used to pay other taxes. Defense Bond and Defense stamps (which could be bought for as little as 10 cents) Drives were held constantly to promote the buying of Defense (or savings bonds).

The Bruning Army Air Field

BIACKOUTS

The first blackout for the state of Nebraska came Dec 13, 1942. A blackout meant the complete extinguishment or concealment of lights that might be visible to enemy aircraft during an air raid.

The Civilian Defense Coordinator under the supervision of the 7th command announced that Governor Dwight Griswold of Nebraska had authorized a state wide blackout at 10:00 p.m.

All towns had Air Wardens. The Air Warden would assign someone to watch a particular area or a number of blocks in the town. In Alexandria the fire siren blew for one minute and this would be the signal to extinguish all lights. The Air Wardens carried a special flashlight so they could see to check their rounds when they walked around their area to see if any light could be seen. If a crack of light could be seen under a door or window, the Warden would tell the people to extinguish the light or put a covering over it so it could not be seen.

No automobiles could be driven during a blackout. Farms did not have electricity at this time as Rural Electrification did not come to Thayer and Jefferson Counties until after the war in 1947. Some farms were equipped with their own 32 volt generating system such as the Delco light plant and these homes were asked to conceal all lights just as in the cities and towns.

Nebraska boasted of being the "Black Spot" of the nation in National War time activities.

AMERICA CALLS
ENLIST IN THE NAVY

RED CROSS

Every town had a Red Cross Chairman and her job was to unite the women to either knit bandages or cut up very white cotton sheets into about 4 inch strips and then roll them very carefully. These Chairmen were very particular and required that all participants comb their hair before putting on a scarf which completely covered their hair. Then they were required to go through a hand washing ritual and if they passed inspection they were ready to roll bandages. If the bandage was not rolled tight enough, were not be perfectly straight, they would be rejected.

The Bruning Army Air Field

THE HEBRON JOURNAL August 26, 1943:

FURNISHING DAY ROOMS FOR SOLDIERS
LADIES DO GOOD WORK

The south-central Nebraska Camp and Hospital Council met at the Bruning Air Field on Thursday, August 19th with a very good attendance. Hamilton, York, Clay, Webster, Fillmore, Gage, Jefferson, Thayer and Nuckolls counties each had a representation and report of the work they are doing.

Thayer County had 55 representatives, twenty-three of whom were from Hebron. The Day Room our county has furnished was completed and opened to the public. It is well furnished and comfortable.

The Bruning Army Air Field

THE DAY ROOM

The Day Room was a room on the Air Base where the Service men could play the piano, cards, ping pong or checkers, read and just generally relax. A lot of public interest was created about the Day Room. Not only did the surrounding counties become involved in furnishing Day Rooms, but NINE counties became involved.

The following articles appeared in THE HEBRON JOURNAL on July 29, 1943 and August 5, 1943:

JEFFERSON COUNTY TO FURNISH ONE DAY ROOM

At camp and Hospital Council Committee Meeting of the American Red Cross in Fairbury July 23, the Jefferson County chapter voted to furnish one of the day rooms at the Bruning Army Air Field. The Thayer County Chapter had also promised to furnish a room.

PLANS FOR FURNISHING ONE DAY ROOM
PUBLIC EFFORTS FOR BRUNING ARMY AIR FIELD

The first meeting of the Thayer County Camp and Hospital Service Committee was held at the Courthouse last Friday evening. A group of about 40 individuals, representing the various civic and community groups throughout the county attended. Mrs. Perce Rosenbaum, County Chairman, was in charge and outlined the objectives for Thayer County.

Lt. Sidney J. Posner, member of the Bruning Air Field, made a talk concerning the Dayroom's needs at his post and Vernon E. Hungate, Field Director of the American Red Cross at the Bruning Field, spoke on the purposes of the organization of the Camp and Hospital service...

The Camp and Hospital Council serves as a centralized medium for all organizations in the county such as clubs, lodges, churches and schools. Through the Council donations may be made and articles of furniture contributed...

The following items are necessary to furnish one Dayroom (100x20) at the Bruning Air Field: 6 smoking stands, 12 straight backed chairs, 1 pool table, 1 piano, 3 floor lamps, 8 writing desks, 6 davenports, 6 easy chairs, 1 ping pong table, 2000 Victory Books, 3 card tables and 4 to 7 rugs.

Will you please took through your homes for something you would like to give to furnish this room. Call one of these ladies if you have something to give: Mrs. William. J. Hill; phone 336; Mrs. Ferd W. McKenzie, phone 312; or Mrs. Harold Shearer, Phone 197.

Nearly the same article as the above is in the *BRUINING-BANNER* except it states also: "This furniture need not be new but in good usable condition.. Anyone wishing to make a contribution of furniture and other items may notify any one of the committee and the articles will be collected. Donations may be sent to Mrs. R.E. Collison, chairman. The committee is composed of Mrs R.E. Collison, Mrs Virgil Bugbee, Martin H. Philippi and R. J. Liliedoll."

Prisoners of War
POW camp in Hebron, Nebraska

During WW II over 3 million prisoners of war were captured by Allied forces. The United States, at the request of the European Allies, who were holding all the prisoners they could, agreed to transfer them to the United States.

In Nebraska 12,000 German prisoners were held in camps across the state: Scottsbluff, Fort Robinson, and the village Atlanta (outside Holdredge) were the main camps. There were smaller camps at Alma, Boyardee, Bertrand, Bridgeport, Elmwood, Fort Crook, Franklin, Grand Island, Hastings, Hebron, Indiana, Kearney, Lexington, Layman, Mitchell, Moral, Ogallala, Palisade, Sidney and Weeping Water. Altogether there were 23 camps in the state. Hebron was a satellite camp of Atlanta.

During the great depression Franklin Roosevelt started the Civilian Conservation Corps. Hebron was selected for a CCC camp. The CCC camps were run by army officers and followed army discipline and routine. The young men received $30 a month, food, lodging and clothing. $25 was sent home to the men's parents and they were allowed to keep $5.00 a month for themselves according to Richard Beitley who provided these pictures of the CCC camp in Hebron.

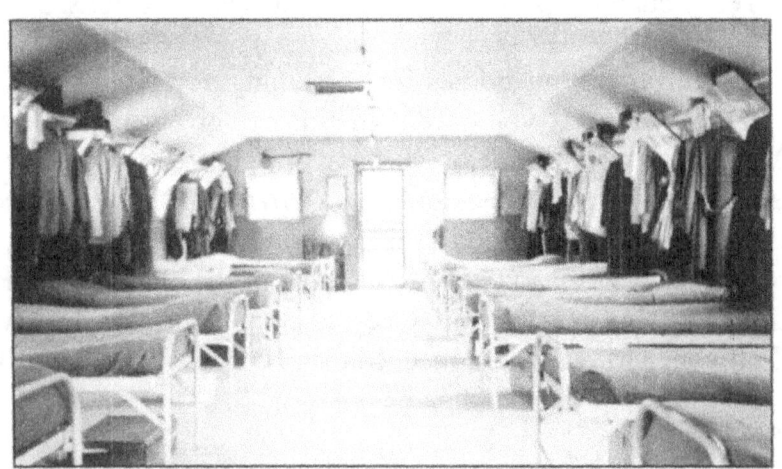

Those Who Flew
Air Bases in Nebraska

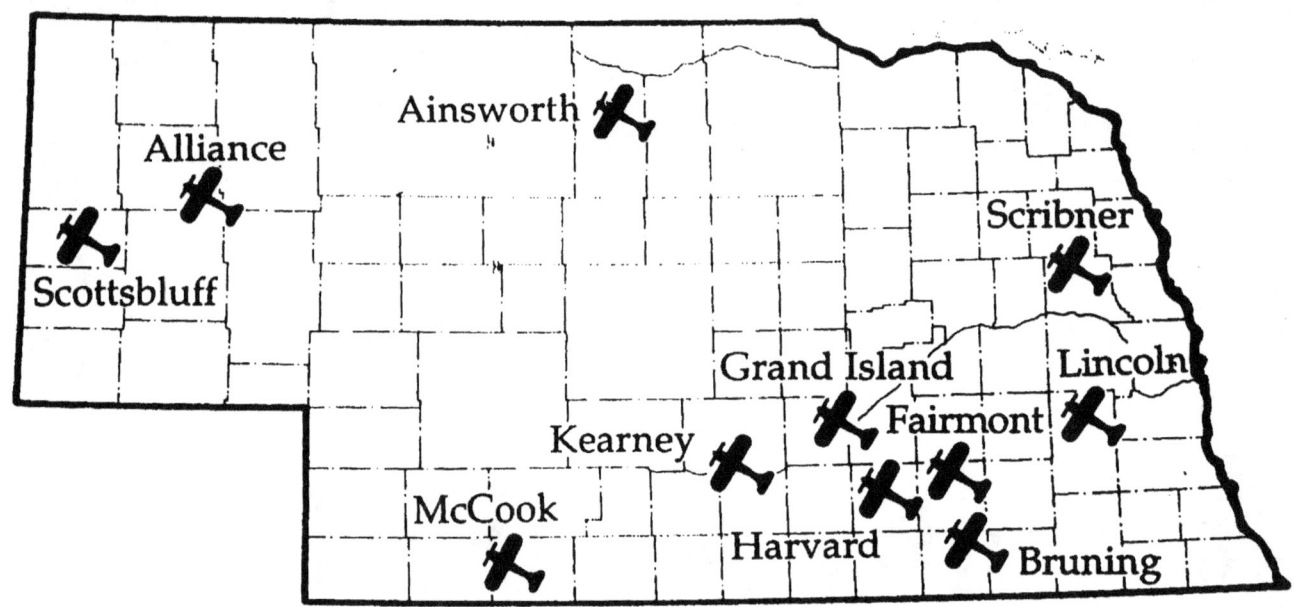

Why Nebraska?

There were 12 Airfields in Nebraska during World War II. Eleven of them were built for WWII and called Satellite Bases. They were located in 1. Ainsworth, 2. Alliance, 3. Bruning, 4. Fairmont, 5. Grand Island, 6. Harvard, 7. Kearney, 8. Lincoln, 9. McCook, 10. Scottsbluff 11. Scribner. Fort Crook later became the Strategic Air Command Base.

Nebraska was equal distance from either coast. It was sparsely populated which made it an ideal location for gunnery, bombing and training ranges. It had a semi-mild climate with an abundance of clear flying weather. Farm land was less expensive. It had reliable public utilities and here were highways and railroads. Most importantly it had a great work pool with people who had hard working ethics.

It seemed a mystery to some why three airfields would be built so close together- -Bruning, Fairmont and Harvard. The rumor went around that originally the order was — Build an air base at Bruning, or Fairmont or Harvard but the order was interpreted to build bases at Bruning, Fairmont and Harvard. In any event this area became part of the "Citadel of Defense". All the bases were built on the same basic generic plan. Several pilots complained that it was hard to differentiate between the air bases from a high altitude when flying.

Nebraska State Historical Markers
McCook Army Air Base

AINSWORTH ARMY AIR FIELD

Ainsworth Army Air Field, completed on November 30, 1942, was a satellite of Rapid City Army Air Field and under command of the Second Air Force. The field was one of eleven Army Air Forces training bases built in Nebraska during World War II.

The 2,496-acre field included three 7,300 x 150 foot concrete runways, a hangar. warehouses, repair and machine shops, link and bomb trainers, Norden bombsight vaults, and barracks for over 600 officers and enlisted men. The base's primary mission was to provide proficiency training for P-39 and P-47 pilots of the 364th and 53rd fighter squadrons, and for B-17 crews of the 540th and 543rd bombardment squadrons before deployment to the European Theater of Operations. Aircraft camouflage experiments were also conducted on the site.

The air field closed in 1945 and the following year the city of Ainsworth received a U.S. Government Revokable License for commercial aircraft operations on the field. In 1948 the War Assets Administration declared the property surplus, and the city of Ainsworth received title to the air field for use as a municipal airport.

Ainsworth Airport Authority   Nebraska State Historical Society

Nebraska State Historical Markers
McCook Army Air Base

McCOOK ARMY AIR BASE

McCook Army Air Base, activated April 1, 1943, was one of eleven Army Air Force training bases in Nebraska during World War II. The base was under command of 2nd Air Force Headquarters, Colorado Springs, Colorado, and provided final training of heavy bomber crews for the B-17 Flying Fortress, B-24 Liberator, and B29 Super Fortress. Some 15,000 servicemen and 500 civilians were stationed here. Among the bomb groups trained at McCook were elements of the 8th, 15th, and 20th Air Forces. These bomb groups saw combat in the European, Mediterranean, and Pacific Theaters.

The 2,100 acre base included three 150 by 7,500-foot concrete runways, five hangars, and barracks for 5,000 men. It operated with three divisions: Base Services (hospital, chapel, theater, band, gymnasium, fire station, post office, photo lab, library, and military police); Maintenance and Supply (air service groups, post engineers, machine shop, warehouses); and Training (celestial navigation, gunnery and bombing, communications, radar, and aircraft maintenance). The base closed December 31, 1945.

Nebraska State Historical Society
McCook Army Air Base Historical Society

Nebraska State Historical Markers
Lincoln Army Air Field
Lincoln Air Force Base

LINCOLN ARMY AIR FIELD
LINCOLN AIR FORCE BASE

Lincoln Army Air Field was constructed in 1942 on the former Lincoln Municipal Airport. The 2,750-acre property was leased to the army by the City of Lincoln. The base provided technical training for aircraft mechanics, basic training for army aviation cadets, and served as an overseas deployment staging area for bombardment groups and fighter squadrons. It was one of eleven U.S. Army Air Forces training centers built in Nebraska during World War II.

At war's end the airfield served as a military separation center for aircrews returning from overseas. It closed in December 1945 and was returned to the City of Lincoln for a municipal airport.

In 1952 the Strategic Air Command activated the airfield as Lincoln Air Force Base under a joint-use lease agreement between the U.S. Air Force and the City of Lincoln. Bomber wings, air refueling squadrons, and an Atlas ICBM squadron were assigned to the base.

In 1966 the base closed and the property was transferred to the City of Lincoln for use as a municipal airport, industrial park, and public housing community.

Lincoln Airport Authority   Nebraska State Historical Society
Preservation Association of Lincoln

(Bowling Lake Park, Lincoln Air Park, NW 44th and Cuming)

Nebraska State Historical Markers
Scottsbluff Army Air Field

SCOTTSBLUFF ARMY AIR FIELD

During World War II, the U.S. Army Air Forces operated a satellite air field at this site. In the fall of 1942 twenty-eight farms were vacated so construction could begin. Some 600,000 cubic yards of concrete for three runways was poured in forty-five days. There were approximately 108 buildings on the grounds including barracks, mess halls, officers' quarters, warehouses, a hangar, a camouflage instruction building, and a bombsight storage building.

The first troops arrived in early December 1942. Initially air and ground crews of B-17 and B-24 bombers of the Second Air Force based in Casper, Wyoming, received final training here. In 1944 the Scottsbluff field became a satellite of the Alliance Army-Air Field and the First Troop Carrier Command, training C47 and glider crews. Aircraft and radio maintenance personnel also trained here.

In 1947 the City of Scottsbluff bought the air field for use as a municipal airport. Most buildings were sold and removed. Since 1970 the property has been operated by Scotts Bluff County.

North Platte Valley Historical Association
Nebraska State Historical Society

Those Who Flew
Air Bases in Nebraska

Byron Behm wrote that the Scribner base was one of two camouflage bases. The other was in Troy, NY. The runways ran east and west and painted the color to match the surrounding crops. Pictures of barns and farm buildings were painted on the side of the hangars. This worked so well that some of the pilots had to ask for a radio beam when coming in to the field for a landing there.

If one had the gas and tires (which were rationed to civilians) to drive through Nebraska from border to border during this time, the air bases rose into view. First the black and orange checkerboard water tank, the blue-green glass of the control tower and hangars housing the big planes with their arched domes across the sky.

Scribner AAF was a satellite of Sioux City (Iowa) AAF, and provided operational training in B-17 and B-24 bombers and P-47 fighters. The air field was also the site on an extensive army camouflage experiment. The entire air field was camouflaged to blend with the surrounding countryside when viewed from the air. An aircraft hangar was painted to give the appearance of a barn and trees. Other buildings were painted to resemble sheds, stacks of hay, or trees. An engineering detachment repainted the buildings to match natural foliage as the seasons changed. *Omaha World-Herald*

Those who Flew
Airbases in Nebraska in WWII

Alliance Air Base
From the Alliance, NE Chamber of Commerce

Alliance played a vital role in the war effort during World War II. In May of 1942, Alliance used 3,264 acres to build an army air base, one of 11 satellite air bases built in Nebraska. On completion the air Base consisted of 775 building plus enlongated runways and taxiways. One of the reasons Alliance was chosen for an airbase was its proximity to the sand hills which were considered excellent for parachute and ammunition training.

Due to the declining war effort, the importance of Alliance Air Base began to lessen. It was redeployed in July of 1945 with the First Troop Carrier command and on 31 October 1945 was finally deactivated in 1953. In 1955, the city of Alliance secured the ownership of the land it is today the site of the Alliance Municipal Airport.

An interesting bit of military history about the air base is that the 507 parachute Infantry Regiment that trained there was later attached to the 82 Airborne Division. This was one of the regiments that landed in France only hours before the D Day landing in Normandy on 6 June 1944. Because of this, many casualties from this battle were known personally to the people of Alliance, NE.

State Historical Marker

B24J Bomber Crash

On June 7, 1944, a B24J bomber -- part of a flight of 15 bombers from the 866th Bombardment Squadron (H), 7th Air Force-- caught fire as it flew over the open western Nebraska prairie. The crew frantically descended to 500 feet, but the aircraft exploded just south of Chappell, Nebraska. This marker was erected to honor the many bomber crews who sacrificed their lives during WWII.

This marker is located just north of the I-80 interchange at Chappell, NE

Nebraska State Historical Markers
Fairmont Army Air Field

Fairmont Army Air Field

Construction began on the Fairmont Army Air Field September 17, 1942. Located east of here, it was one of eleven built in Nebraska during World War II.

The 1,980-acre field began as a satellite of the Topeka Army Air Base. Early in 1943 the name was changed to Fairmont Army Air Field. A short lived training school gave way to the 451st Bombardment Group, which arrived in September 1943. Other groups were the 485th, 504th, 16th, 98th, 467th and 489th.

Hangars of various sizes housed B-24s, B-17s, and B-29s. Extensive concrete runways and other structures were built. The field had barracks for nearly 6,000 officers and enlisted men. Its 350-bed hospital was the largest in Nebraska.

In September 1944 Lt. Col. Paul Tibbets visited Fairmont and selected the 393rd Bomb Squadron of the 504th to join the 509th Composite Group at Wendover Field, Utah. This group dropped both atomic bombs on Japan.

The field was declared surplus in the spring of 1946.

Nebraska State Historical Society   451st Bombardment Group (H) Ltd.
Fillmore County Historical Society   Robert M. Karstensen, Sr., President

Those Who Flew Fairmont Air Field

Fairmont Air Field
written by Ruth Black,
Fairmont, NE Museum Curator

Construction on the Fairmont Army Air Field started Sept. 1942. At first, it was a satellite Air Field with the Topeka Army Air base. However, the name was soon changed to Fairmont Army Air Field. According to research for the historical markers the bombardment Groups stationed there were the 451st, 485th, 504th, 16th, 98th, 467th and the 489th. The planes were B17s, B24 and B29s.

The 451st and 485th flew B-24s and went to Europe from here. Tibbets (who piloted the "Enola Gay" when it dropped the bomb on Hiroshima) selected a squadron of the 504th to go to Wendover for further training with the 509th composite for escort of the "Enola Gay" and then to the Pacific Theater with the Atom bomb. The other 504 went south and then more directly to the Pacific area. They flew B-29s.

The Fairmont Museum has hard backed historical books put out by the three groups as they are well organized and have reunions. Veterans of the 16th said they were a composite group and almost all of them kept in contact with their original group. I do not know of the last three groups mentioned.

The 451st has recently published a new history also: The *Fight'n 451st* Bombardment Group (H) edited by Sedgfield Hill and his son. Wanda Marketer of the public Library is taking orders for the book. This starts with general information and then has personal stories by the veterans of the group.

The 485th has also published a second book that I received last week (Nov. 7, 2000) It, too, starts with general information and history of the group, then goes into a story of each of their 187 missions. *Missions by The Numbers* was edited by their historian Sam Schneider in Littleton, CO.

A member of the 504th group, Fiske Haley is the author of *Accused A* War Criminal. This is a book that gives the history of the group from Fairmont and on to the Pacific where their plane, a B-29 that Mr. Haley was on was shot down when bombing Japan. This book details the terrible treatment and the final rescue. It is an excellent book of that era.

Sincerely,

Ruth Black

Those Who Flew
Story in Honolulu Star-Bulletin

Doris and Martin Deepe were surprised when their daughter, Bev, sent them a front page story from the Honoluly star-Bulletin. It was written by Susan Krifels and Susan has gotten permission for us to reproduce parts of he story.

Those Who Flew
Story in Honolulu Star-Bulletin

Airfield evokes old memories and new bonds

A gray haze over the gray Nebraska flatlands made it even more difficult for the 75-year-old eyes, recovering so slowly from cataract operations. "see anything that looks like a hangar?" my father asked, squinting anxiously along lonely miles of chipped farm houses. Past irrigation pivots, like huge hairless centipedes waiting to crawl atop the endless fields. Only recently had I learned about my father's occasional stops at the old Fairmont Army Air Field along the way to his winter retreat in Texas. How he would make his way to the end of the airstrip, now cracked with weeds and piled with sand, corn and rolls fence wire. How he would step on the gas and roar down the runway in his Chrysler Concord with its B24 license plate, topping 110 mph. and yelling "eeeeeeah" remembering his days as a 19 year old in the bubble top of a B-24 liberator, his gun aimed for German fighters.

I wanted to fly that Concord with him, feel what he felt in the tiny turret, ask all the questions I had asked scored of other World War ii veterans I had interviewed.--American, filipino,Japanese==he was modest about the war avoiding unnecessary talk about it, especially bout fear and death.

"Old guys and their war stories" he often said, tossing me off.

But as the miles ticked off along West Interstate 80 between Omaha and Lincoln, as we pulled off the York exchange down Highway 81, passed McCool Junction, population 372 and Fairmont about twice that size, he started to get excited. Then down a gravel road pasts Boons Auto salvage and sales at the end of a wide abandoned runway. Four hangars now filled with corn and soy beans, stood in the distance.

I think this will be a valuable day," he pronounced, and I pulled out my notepad.

Orville Andrew Kreifels was the lodes of six poor, German Catholic farm kids growing up outside Nebraska City. He enlisted at age 19 at camp Dodge, Iowa in 1943 and considered himself lute to tees high enough for the air crews of the Army Air Force

"God, this was a cold place," Dad remembered about the January 1944 night missions he flew caress the sand hills, and I shuddered at the e cold Nebraska wind whipped us.

Fairmont was one of 11 airfields in Nebraska according to the State Historical Marker. The 1,980 acres had enough barracks for 6,000 airmen who trained in B-24, B17, and B-29s.

...

A 350 bed hospital where casualties from Europe were sent , was the state's largest hospital at the time...

I insisted we look inside each one. "Wouldn't that be something if a B-24 was still in three?" Dad asked wistfully, which brought up a sore point with him. Of 18,479 Liberators built, only seven to nine remain today, said Dad, who has researched the topic. Two of them still fly. A savvy entrjpreneur sold them for scrap metal after the war "before we got smart enough to know it was the end of them..".

But there was no B-24 awaiting us. Only the flap of birds'wings in the rafters. We drove to the end of the runway and hit the

DREAMS:

FROM B-1

gas, took off, racing tumbleweeds and jackrabbits and topping about 80. "Eeeeeah!" he yelled.

Too quickly, we were back at Boons Auto Salvage. Disappointed that he didn't top 110 this time, Dad said, "I'm not quite as gutsy as I used to be."

I wanted to do it again but decided not to push.

We headed back to Highway 81 and stopped at the historical marker. I was surprised to learn that Lt. Col. Paul Tibbets selected his crew here for the Enola Gay, the plane that dropped the atom bomb on Hiroshima. I had reported from Tinian, a tiny Western Pacific island where the Enola Gay took off, as well as from Hiroshima.

In fact, years before, the worst argument my father and I ever had was over that bombing, and we ended in a stony stalemate. That was also years before I had seen the war through the lens of veterans, arguing only from youthful idealism. Dad has since visited the "City of Peace" twice and stayed with my Japanese friend, who bears scars from the bombing. But I never revisited the argument, figuring my dad had his own scars.

WHILE we read, Sarah Reinsch and Rob Roper drove up in their orange state Department of Roads pickup to remind me why I am so thankful for growing up in the Midwest. They gave us a big "Howdy" and offered to take photos. Roper owned a house where World War II airmen used to live. He also explained that the old blue car parked by the small runway, still usable, was left by the Fairmont Lions Club for pilots who wanted to land there, as long as they "keep it in gas."

The two suggested we stop at the Fairmont Museum, which has a room dedicated to the war. It's usually locked, but no problem — stop at the West Brothers Hardware, Lumber and Construction, they told us, and ask them to track down

DREAMS: They didn't think about dying, only living through 50 missions

FROM B-1

gas, took off, racing tumbleweeds and jackrabbits and topping about 80. "Eeeeeah!" he yelled.

Too quickly, we were back at Boons Auto Salvage. Disappointed that he didn't top 110 this time, Dad said, "I'm not quite as gutsy as I used to be."

I wanted to do it again but decided not to push.

We headed back to Highway 81 and stopped at the historical marker. I was surprised to learn that Lt. Col. Paul Tibbets selected his crew here for the Enola Gay, the plane that dropped the atom bomb on Hiroshima. I had reported from Tinian, a tiny Western Pacific island where the Enola Gay took off, as well as from Hiroshima.

In fact, years before, the worst argument my father and I ever had was over that bombing, and we ended in a stony stalemate. That was also years before I had seen the war through the lens of veterans, arguing only from youthful idealism. Dad has since visited the "City of Peace" twice and stayed with my Japanese friend, who bears scars from the bombing. But I never revisited the argument, figuring my dad had his own scars.

WHILE we read, Sarah Reinsch and Rob Roper drove up in their orange state Department of Roads pickup to remind me why I am so thankful for growing up in the Midwest. They gave us a big "Howdy" and offered to take photos. Roper owned a house where World War II airmen used to live. He also explained that the old blue car parked by the small runway, still usable, was left by the Fairmont Lions Club for pilots who wanted to land there, as long as they "keep it in gas."

The two suggested we stop at the Fairmont Museum, which has a room dedicated to the war. It's usually locked, but no problem — stop at the West Brothers Hardware, Lumber and Construction, they told us, and ask them to track down

Curator Ruth Black shows Orville Kreifels around the "war room" at the Fairmont Museum. Honolulu resident Hung Peng Lee's calligraphy hangs on the door.

BY SUSAN KREIFELS, Star-Bulletin

Ruth Black, the 87-year-old curator who would proudly show us around. I grew up in a small Nebraska town of one main street, where everybody knew the whereabouts of everybody.

Dan Kahler at West Brothers called around town until he tracked down Ruth's car. Dad yelled "Thanks a million" to the lumberyard folks, and within 15 minutes Ruth met us with key in hand and head wrapped tightly in a bright scarf against the prairie wind.

Ruth was born in Fairmont, home to Fairmont Foods, which turned out 7,000 pounds of butter a day in 1891 and ended up one of America's 500 largest corporations. Ruth, a former schoolteacher, lived alone in the house where she was born.

It was apparent that she loved to tell the story of how the war room came into being. One day on her way to the post office, she saw an Ohio car parked outside the museum. It belonged to a veteran of the 485th Bombardment Group who was on his way to a reunion. Ruth never thought she would see him again, but a few days later she received $1,000 from the 485th veterans and the man's uniform scarf, now on exhibit.

I asked for the man's name and address. "That's the problem," Ruth said. "I write to them, and the next time I know, they're deceased." It was a theme discussed by my father and Ruth several times that afternoon.

There were glorious photos of the B-24s in action: the "Old Tub," "Big Alice from Dallas," and "Fertile Myrtle," which was lost Aug. 23, 1944. "They weren't the safest planes in the world," Dad told us. "They had a tendency to blow up. But they were the fastest."

When Dad left Fairmont in early 1944, he caught a new B-24 at Lincoln, then flew to Miami, Puerto Rico, British Guiana, Brazil, Dakar, Casablanca, Marrakech, Tunisia, and finally Venosa, Italy, from where he would take off on 50 combat missions between April 1944 and August 1944.

THE bombing raids included Austria, Romania, Italy and Germany, with the most important target the Ploesti oilfields in Romania. The 15th Air Force destroyed half of Germany's oil production, according to books in the museum. For his part, Dad earned the Distinguished Flying Cross and four air medals.

Dad said his greatest concern was flak from the ground, and if you could see it explode, "you knew you were in trouble." The ball gunner had the worst job, hanging from the underbelly of the B-24. "It was horribly uncomfortable and you couldn't get out of the thing. If you were hit and landing, sooner or later you got scraped."

Ruth and I shuddered, and I was glad Dad had sat atop the bomber.

I was hoping to see a photo of Dad's B-24, and like an angel sent from the Red Cross, Ruth pulled out her last copy of "The History of the 485th Bomb Group (H)" by Sammy Schneider. And there among the many photos of B-24 crews stood Staff Sgt. Kreifels of the 831st Bomb Squadron with his buddies in front of the "Valiant Lady." I bought the last copy for my dad, figuring it was the best $35 investment I had ever made.

Also hanging in the museum was a Chinese calligraphy by Hung Peng Lee of Honolulu. A 485th veteran, the calligraphy was in memory of the 50th anniversary of V-J Day.

That reminded Ruth that her friend's husband flew on the Enola Gay. "They even questioned the wives to see how much they knew," she told us furtively. "Everything was so secret."

Then dad raised the issue I had avoided with him for many years. "I've been to Hiroshima twice," he told Ruth. "That was a horrible thing."

Like me, it seemed dad now looked at the day through an extra lens.

Too soon we had to leave, but Dad and Ruth had made a lifelong bond. Ruth's parting advice: "If you want to get in touch with any of these fellows, visit them NOW."

We understood.

Before heading back to Omaha, we stopped at TJz diner for a quick bite among four choices — roast beef fixed three ways plus taco salad — and looked through Dad's new book. I seized the moment to ask those questions that always peeved him: about death and fear.

Did he lose a lot of friends? "Let's put it this way," he said. "Of 13 crews, only three or four whole crews were left. If you didn't get holes in your plane, you didn't really fly."

But still savoring the day, I pushed him more. With some emotion, he told me he lost everyone in his first ground crew on their way to war aboard the liberty ship Paul Hamilton, which exploded and sank in 30 seconds in June 1944, according to Schneider.

Our loss: 154 troops. Dad's buddy, air crew chief Sgt. Michael DeMarco, had chosen to take the ship so he could stop in Rochester, N.Y., to get married. Dad grumbled that the Army never told them much, and when the crew didn't show up, he figured something bad had happened to his friend.

"We didn't even know they went down," Dad said quietly.

AND then I asked, were you scared? "That's a funny question to ask," he growled. "Back then, people didn't ask this stuff."

But being part of the have-to-know-everything generation, I wanted to know how close my father had been to death. Pretty close. A bullet that hit his helmet bounced into his lap. The enemy blew off a rudder and they almost crashed. After a night of repairs, they were back in the air the next day.

Yes, he got scared in the air, he admitted, even though "nobody thinks they're going to get killed." But when crews got down to their last four or five missions, they started thinking they had a chance to make it home.

Many didn't. According to Schneider's book, the final price for the Ploesti raids: 351 bombers, 3,510 crew. Those who survived, and the stories they tell, as Ruth knows all too well, are going fast. I feel so lucky my dad is still here to tell his — and that I asked.

Dad says he doesn't want me spreading his story around. But old guys and their war stories, their kids know, are the best.

Those Who Flew
Closing the Airfields

Air Fields Closed Landing Strips Are Not Usable

According to the April 5th 1969 *Lincoln Journal* the state airfields at Bruning and McCook have been closed permanently for flight operations according to the State Aeronauts director, Howard Vest.

"That means the Federal Aeronautics Administration says we don't have to maintain the runway, but can dedicate the entire property to a revenue function," Vest said.

"However, the state still is compelled by Uncle Sam to maintain fields at Fairmont, Harvard and Scriber as serviceable landing strips."

The five fields were handed over to Nebraska by the federal government at then end of World War II. More recently, the federal government has given the state a quit-claim deed covering the five fields. Senator T.C. Wenzlaff of Sutton has proposed in Legislative Bill 672 that the governor be directed to sell the McCook and Bruning fields to the highest bidder.

At McCook and Bruning the runways had deteriorated to a place where the state would have had to make a repair investment of about $150,000 to live up to its agreement with the federal government.

Those Who Flew
This is what's left of the Bruning Air field Hangars in 2000

Index

A
Aamren 82
Aaron 109, 204
Abbitt 207
Abngy 207
Abraham 109, 205
Acampora 134
Acree 196, 199, 201, 211, 213, 227, 238
Adamo 105
Adams 137, 180, 204
Adcock 109
Adie 180
Ahrens 307, 317
Ainsmith 279
Akerson 134
Albert 196, 199, 201, 211, 214, 227
Albright 105
Aldrich 180
Alexander 135
Alexandria 293
Alkire 101, 102, 103, 104, 105, 110, 125, 134, 135, 275
Allen 105, 109, 134, 139
Allison 105, 190, 224, 225
Allumbaugh 105, 137
Ames 105, 137, 206
Ammeter 326
Anderson 105, 137, 145, 180, 204, 205, 213
Andreesen 269
Andrews 180
Antonakos 137
Arbuthnot 280
Archy 180
Arieff 134
Armoska 206
Armstrong 196, 199, 201, 208, 211, 214, 227
Arnett 196, 199, 201, 211, 214, 227, 234
Arnold 105
Asbury 116
Asche 317
Ashworth 109
Austin 121, 139
Avers 3, 4
Ayabe 333
Ayers 116

B
Babiec 109
Babka 326
Bach 116, 139
Backer 308, 319
Bacon 207
Baden 4
Bago 116
Bahl 294
Bailey 109, 308, 317
Baker 79, 121, 205, 290, 306
Baldwin 139, 180
Ball 134
Ballangee 205
Ballou 134
Bamberg 177
Bamburg 180
Barbee 301, 302, 318, 326, 333
Barber 105, 109
Barbour 109
Barnard 180
Barneson 204
Barnhill 105
Barnski 180
Barns 116
Barr 311
Barrows 206
Bartlett 139
Baruth 151, 155, 157, 158
Bash 116
Bashaw 105, 134
Batdorf 109
Battagliola 139
Batterton 109, 134
Bauchman 250
Bauers 116, 130, 134
Bausch 204
Baxter 121, 204
Bayne 204
Beachey 286
Beam 107, 134, 135, 136
Bean 145
Beatty 121
Beaty 190
Beaver 66
Bechtold 105
Beck 121, 137, 319
Becker 109
Beckley 105
Beckman 216, 223, 229
Bedford 326
Behm 5, 81
Beisner 294
Beitley 350
Belcher 134
Belemecich 252
Bell 26, 116, 134, 139, 205
Belyea 134
Benner 180
Bennet 195, 198, 200, 201
Bennett 109, 116, 207
Berchem 237
Bergan 308
Berkwist 177
Bernard 205
Berry 207
Bethes 207
Betz 137
Betzen 134, 135, 136, 139
Beu 326
Bevans 180
Biffle 294
Biggart 105, 139
Biggert 318
Billman 308
Birbiglia 116
Bird 105, 107
Birdsong 207
Birky 190
Birmingham 212, 219
Birong 205
Bivins 135
Black 180, 360, 363
Blaisdell 116
Blake 105
Blakely 121, 139
Blakesee 196, 199, 201, 211, 214, 227
Blanchard 109
Blankenheim 91
Blankenship 109
Blaugh 105
Bloch 116
Block 134
Blosser 301
Blumberg 180
Blunk 289
Bobb 213
Bobeck 116
Boechman 196, 199, 201
Boeckman 211, 214, 227
Boehnke 139
Bohannon 116
Bohle 196, 199, 201, 211, 213, 216, 227, 232
Bohling 320, 326
Bohrer 105
Boland 180
Bolden 121
Boles 206
Bolon 204
Bolsins 105
Bolt 135
Bolton 105
Bond 204
Bontley 109, 110, 134
Bontly 111
Booth 105, 116
Bordin 105
Boren 116
Bornstein 134
Borton 121
Borucki 116
Bosch 121, 137
Boss 134
Bossom 105
Boudroau 121
Boutwell 196, 198, 201, 207
Bowden 205
Bowen 326
Bowman 109, 293
Boyce 283
Boyer 268
Boyes 341
Boyles 121
Brace 195, 198, 200, 201, 208
Braden 105
Bradley 105, 107, 145
Brady 105, 106, 121, 134
Brandenburg 285
Brandt 308, 317
Braud 116, 137
Brazzale 109
Brethen 195, 198, 201, 205
Brett 206
Brewer 323, 326
Briant 208
Bridgham 105
Brient 180
Briggs 109
Brinegar 64, 308
Brix 134
Broeckman 229
Brogger 134
Brohm 180
Broman 332
Brooks 180
Brouillette 121, 137
Brown 84, 105, 109, 116, 134, 139, 196, 199, 201, 211, 213, 214, 227, 234, 236, 281, 302, 326
Browning 105, 106, 107, 135
Bruce 320
Brunger 105
Bruning 3, 4, 38, 70, 210, 220, 241, 248, 293, 309, 326
Bruns 269
Bryan 121, 269, 309, 318
Bryant 105
Brzostowski 204
Buda 105
Budroe 204
Buehrer 109
Buffington 116
BUFORD 105
Bugbee 73, 349
Buller 109, 309
BULLIS 116
Bumgardner 105
Bumgarner 326
Bunderson 121
Bunger 105
Bunker 5, 156, 159, 161, 241, 243, 248, 249, 252, 257, 261
Bunnell 121
Bunting 317, 326
Buntz 105
Burczak 109
Burke 196, 199, 201, 211, 214, 227
Burks 116, 300
Burnette 134
Burnham 134
Burr 206
Bursio 121, 137
Burt 121
Burton 101
Bush 109
Busing 259
Busonik 121
Butler 109, 306, 309, 326
Butter 137
Button 204
Buttorff 205
Butts 109
Byer 109, 137
Bzan 134

C
Cady 116
Caffey 105
Cahoy 222
Cain 109
Caldwell 109, 121, 134
Callison 248
Calroy 221
Cameron 109
Campbell 109, 134
Cane 317
Caniff 112
Cannon 309
Cappuccilli 105
Carchia 134
Cardie 206
Carey 65
Carleson 304
Carlson 121, 139, 251
Carlton 208
Carnell 302
Carpenter 5, 105, 204, 210, 215
Carroll 205
Carson 268, 304
Carter 105, 116, 118, 138, 249, 276, 301
Casad 288
Cassanova 185, 196, 199, 201
Caswell 116
Cates 105
Cease 121
Celibi 109
Cece 115
Cellilli 109
Cerveny 311
Chadwick 105, 109
Chafin 105
Chalkus 109
Chandler 116, 118, 134
Chapman 109, 205
Chattermole 139
Cheatham 121
Chernak 134
Chonka 109
Christenancy 84
Christency 326
Christensen 109, 206, 317, 326
Christian 105
Christoff 105
Chudyk 116
Clabaugh 134
Clarence 121
Clark 88, 91, 93, 116, 139, 189, 196, 199, 201, 206, 207
Clarkson 196, 199, 201, 211, 214, 227, 234
Clary 121
Clauss 261
Clayton 121
Cleary 138
Clements 105, 185, 187, 196, 199, 203, 317
Cline 109
Cloak 282
Cloud 180
Clough 137
Cobb 121
Cohen 134, 180
Colburn 96
Collins 107, 207
Collison 63, 73, 326, 349
Colson 109, 134
Colwell 134
Comeaux 207
Commers 116
Compson 109
Conarroe 204
Conboy 139
Condon 67
Coniglione 105
Conklin 279
Connally 145
Cook 105, 109
Cooley 121
Coon 105
Cooper 109, 139
Cooperrida 308
Coordsen 249, 270
Cope 109, 248
Copley 109
Cordeira 109, 134
Corliss 134
Corp 205
Corso 121
Council 122, 128
Cover 109
Cowan 205
Cox 134, 195, 198, 201, 205
Crabbe 121
Craig 149
Crain 121
Cramb 342
Creed 109
Crommon 121
Cronin 105
Cross 96
Crossley 135
Crowball 93
Crumpler 109
Crysler 105
Ctapsaddle 139
Cuccia 105
Cumberlan 84
Curley 251, 258
Curr 109
Currey 84
Currier 101, 102, 116, 120, 127
Curry 174, 177, 178
Curtiss 279
Custeau 105
Czerwinsk 109

D
Dacey 105
Dageforde 249, 264, 265
Dallas 281
Daniel 205
Daniels 109
Danison 121
Dannison 115
Darling 251
Darninski 121
Darnley 180
Dassinger 105
Davenport 34, 321, 326
Davidson 109
Davis 70, 105, 116, 134, 180, 205, 283
Dawson 105, 206
Day 69, 294
Daykin 66
Decouncill 121
Deepe 326, 361
Degaugh 121
Degenhardt 283
Degner 326
Dehn 139
Dehoney 204
Delaney 180
Delay 3, 4
DeMarco 363
Dennis 116
Denniston 24
Dentler 91
Deorge 121
DePew 121
Deren 109
Deringer 109
Deshler 293
DesJardina 105
Desmond 105
Devine 109
DeWald 262, 324
Dexter 145
Dickey 197, 200, 201
Dickman 248
Dickson 121
Dietrich 109, 139
Dietz 7, 8, 9, 100, 206
Dill 3
Dillon 121
DiMinno 109
Dittmer 333
Dixon 105, 116, 180, 206
Dobony 195, 198, 201
Dobrick 180
Doehring 317
Doelfel 139
Doelger 206
Doggett 83, 84, 85, 86
Dohass 116
Doll 326
Donavon 137
Dontje 105
Douglas 109, 174
Dowling 208
Downey 5, 100, 104
Doyle 134
Drees 185
Driefke 180
Drinan 105, 106
Druther 121
Ducharme 204
Duff 163, 206
Dulgarian 195, 198, 201, 208
Duncan 63, 302, 326
Dunker 317
Dunlap 178
Dupont 105
Durbin 116
Durham 241, 248
Dyer 258

E
Earhart 278, 304
Easley 64, 269
Easters 121
Easton 326, 327, 332
Eaton 134
Eavenson 116, 134
Eberhart 105
Ebersole 105
Ebert 134, 236
Eck 109, 137
Eckl 109
Edgar 121
Edmonds 272
Ednemano 206
Edwards 109, 204
Edzards 186
Eggert 294
Eggleton 121
Ehert 121
Eirsman 304
Eiselewski 134
Eisenson 85
Eisler 105
Ellefson 109
Elliott 204
Ells 326
Elmore 134
Elsrod 121
Elting 72
Ely 206
Emrich 207
Enewold 207
Engels 248
Engle 134
Englehardt 134, 138
Engles 332
Enyeart 105
Eppinger 207
Erichson 196, 199, 201, 207
Erickson 3, 139, 146, 147, 148, 149, 150, 156, 160, 194, 210, 215, 216, 222, 241, 243, 248
Ericson 5, 180
Erwin 207
Erzar 84
Esper 109
Esposito 105
Euston 204
Evans 116
Eversole 180
Evilsizor 121
Eyler 180

F
Fangmeier 310
Fanslau 204
Farbsten 173
Farish 121
Farnsworth 204
Farrington 134, 135
Fastiggi 109
Fauchenbach 109
Faulhaber 116
Fawcett 206
Fazekas 207
Fechko 116
Fee 113
Feeney 139
Fees 109
Feldman 109
Fenick 206
Fenton 116, 130
Fergus 121, 123
Ferguson 116, 121, 287
Fergusson 204, 205
Ferlberg 116
Ferris 176, 177, 178, 179
Fetting 134, 136
Fickenscher 241, 244, 246
Fields 109
Fiester 109, 139
Filsinger 116
Finch 109, 121
Fink 121, 317
Fintel 310, 317
Firth 134
Fischer 317
Fisher 105
Fitzer 205, 206
Fiumara 177, 180
Fleming 116, 326
Flinn 109
Flory 138
Flowers 116
Floyd 105
Flynn 294
Foley 180
Folkerts 326, 327
Foote 105, 135, 138
Forbes 105, 108, 135
Forburger 208
Ford 258
Forshage 109
Foskett 116
Foster 204
Fowler 109, 110
Fox 121
Fraer 116
Frahlman 180
Frank 269
Franklin 109, 139, 180
Frankovic 138
Franz 139, 326
Frederik 145
French 121
Friedman 204
Friend 180
Frische 109
Fritchman 207
Fritsche 116
Frones 124, 134
Frycek 252
Frye 326
Fuchs 207
Fuller 5

G
Gafarelli 116
Gagnon 109, 139
Gailer 180
Galati 109
Gallagher 134
Gallant 109
Galliher 109
Gallion 317
Galvin 105
Gamet 205, 206
Gandrud 252
Gann 116
Gardtner 116
Garland 84, 248
Garrison 7, 63, 121, 123, 124, 134, 135
Gates 105, 248
Gaunt 180
Gaus 105
Gavalas 116
Gawley 121
Gay 281
Gedrites 180
Gegoulis 116, 134
Gehr 196, 199, 201, 207
Geil 206
Geisel 121, 125
Geisert 136
Geldbaugh 204
Geminder 109, 113, 134
Gent 102
Gentry 5, 98, 99, 104, 121, 125, 247
George 310, 317
Gerdes 326
German 139
Gervasi 121
Gibbo 109, 134
Gibson 121
Gilead 293
Giles 195, 198, 201, 205
Gill 167
Gilson 205, 206
Gima 105
Gimperling 206
Ginter 281
Gittins 204
Glaeseman 269
Glantz 67
Gleason 105
Glenn 173
Godfrey 116
Godiez 109
Godioz 134
Godlewski 204
Goforth 121
Goldberg 121, 137
Golden 93
Goldenberg 116
Good 180
Goodale 281
Goodman 116, 139
Goorlitz 121
Gordon 109
Gorka 109
Gorrell 105, 138
Graci 121
Graffigna 139
Graham 145, 205
Grane 115
Granowski 116

Grant 251
Graves 139, 310, 317
Gray 109, 113, 121, 135
Greehalgh 109
Green 12, 121
Greene 116, 207
Gregory 310
Grey 121, 249, 274
Griffin 105, 138, 293, 294, 326
Grimmer 115, 121, 125
Griswold 347
Grone 326, 327
Grooms 116
Gross 105
Grow 204
Grubaugh 105
Grubb 65
Grueber 93
Grzesik 105
Guay 207
Gudger 105, 135
Guorroro 121
Gurney 109
Guynn 206

H
Hadley 116
Hagan 97
Hagen 88
Hager 116
Haggerty 116
Halcon 185, 187, 196, 199, 203
Hale 137
Haley 360
Hallmark 194
Hallum 105
Halsey 260
Halzel 116
Hambley 121
Hamel 116
Hamilton 105
Haney 273
Hanks 207
Hanley 105
Hanna 105
Hannaford 205
Hannon 93
Hansen 109, 116
Hanson 134, 136
Hargove 204
Harlander 137
Harmon 3, 105
Harper 109, 116, 118
Harrell 137
Harriman 195, 198, 200, 201, 207
Harrington 105, 109, 174
Harris 105, 121, 230
Harrison 109
Hart 10, 20, 24, 25, 26, 35, 40, 45, 51
Hartman 180
Harton 136
Hasselbring 84
Hauser 121
Hawk 273
Hawkins 294
Hawks 248, 272, 273, 278, 298, 302, 303, 304, 305, 326, 327, 333
Hays 121, 124, 135
Hayslett 135

Haywood 136
Headrick 64
Hearn 195, 198, 201, 207
Hebda 135
Hedden 295, 296, 297, 298, 299, 300, 301
Hedrich 64
Hein 180
Heinrichs 326
Heiskell 135
Helenbolt 212
Hemphill 109, 123, 162, 163, 164, 165, 196, 199, 202, 211, 213, 227
Hendershot 85
Henderson 109, 317
Hendricks 12
Hendrickson 109
Henehan 232
Henery 205
Henggeler 135
Henggener 109
Henney 213
Henning 321, 322, 326
Henrichs 326
Henry 105
Henze 116, 139
Hergott 241, 326
Herrington 116
Herwig 116
Herzog 105
Hess 177, 180, 314
Heston 65
Heverle 121
Heyer 139
Hickerson 208
Hidecanage 206
Higel 300
Highsmith 180
Hildebrand 195, 198, 200, 202, 208
Hill 73, 116, 135, 341, 349, 360
Hilton 298
Hines 302
Hinrichs 241
Hinton 205
Hippe 121
Hoavey 116
Hodges 204
Hoeck 180
Hoff 139
Hoffman 216
Hoffmeyer 326
Hogg 207
Hoggatt 116
Hogsed 116
Hohlfeld 85
Holcomb 109
Holcombe 190
Holekamp 177, 180
Holland 121
Hollederer 137
Hollingsworth 115, 121, 135
Holohan 135
Holt 109
Holtgrewe 63, 66
Holyfield 177, 178
Home 135
Hoore 109
Hoover 109
Hoppe 310, 311
Hopponstodt 121
Horak 241
Horan 69

Horn 116
Horne 105
Horner 109
Horres 109
Hosack 310
Hostetler 109
House 121
Howard 105, 206
Howe 116
Howell 105, 135
Hoyle 116
Hrie 116
Hubbard 105, 109, 206
Hubbert 317
Huber 241, 243, 326, 332
Hudkins 268
Hueske 3, 5, 210, 215, 216, 220, 222
Huff 84, 180, 206
Hughes 105, 180, 185, 186, 206, 311, 326
Hume 248
Hungate 73, 349
Hunter 205
Hurd 195, 198, 200, 202, 208
Huskwy 204
Huston 63
Hutslar 196, 199, 202, 211, 214, 237
Hyde 93, 105

I
Ihevinne 109
Inglish 205
Ingram 105
Irwin 121
Isgrigg 105, 108
Ivers 110, 134

J
Jackson 61, 102
Jacobs 204
Jacobsen 109
Jaeger 195, 202
Jagels 326
Jarrard 121
Jarrell 116, 135
Jaworski 6, 33
Jelley 207
Jenner 161
Jennings 207
Jeutter 109, 135, 136
Jewett 185, 186, 196, 199, 202, 207
Joan 105
Jobin 116
Joes 204
Johanas 85
John 116
Johnnsen 109
Johnson 105, 121, 135, 180, 196, 199, 202, 206, 207, 211, 227, 247, 248, 249, 268, 269, 321, 322, 323, 326, 332
Johnstone 139, 288
Jolley 196, 197, 199, 202, 210, 211, 214, 216, 220, 227, 228, 230, 237
Jones 105, 109, 135
Jordon 326
Juetter 110
Julian 139

Julius 105
Junker 57
Junket 85

K
Kaess 105
Kahler 363
Kaiser 286, 287
Kakowski 109
Kalakuka 5, 25, 30, 50
Kaley 248
Kanze 116
Kaplan 204
Kapp 105
Karstensen 359
Kassebaum 37
Kassik 252
Katzoff 116
Kaufman 205
Kautzman 151, 154, 156, 157, 158
Kaylor 145
Kazanowski 121
Keech 207
Keeler 121
Kehm 206
Keil 63
Keilwitz 84
Keiser 279, 281, 283, 287
Keller 196, 197, 199, 200, 202, 207, 211, 214, 227
Kelly 116
Kempson 116, 204
Kendall 105, 106, 116, 117, 135
Kennedy 24, 25, 40, 41, 51, 105, 207, 311
Kennel 190, 311
Kennelly 105
Kenner 4, 326, 332
Kephart 139
Kerl 311
Kerric 63
Kertis 139
Kervin 121
Kerwood 189
Kessler 109, 116
Kesterson 206
Kettlehut 326
Kieskowski 137
Kiewit 67
Killer 284
Killgore 205
Kilmer 318
Kinerd 108
King 105, 116, 236
Kinne 116
Kinord 105
Kirchhoff 241, 332
Kirchoff 326
Kirk 3, 216
Kirkland 120, 135, 136
Kirschler 121
Kita 139
Kithriotis 109
Kittinger 10, 31, 32, 47, 50
Kjera 139
Klein 205
Kline 180
Knabenshue 286
Knaphus 204
Knapp 106, 134, 135, 136
Kneis 116

Knigge 263, 268
Knight 196, 199, 202, 207
Knowlton 317
Knox 140
Knutson 121
Koca 159
Koch 258
Kocher 109
Koci 317
Kohler 116
Kohn 109
Kolezar 121, 140
Kopetchny 116
Korensky 317, 318
Koves 269
Kozekowski 138
Kreifels 362, 363
Krick 105
Krifels 361
Kroll 109
Kruckmeyer 121
Krueger 140, 205
Kruse 116
Kuhlmann 311
Kulasa 206
Kullman 121
Kunkel 335
Kury 109, 110, 111, 112, 113, 134, 138
Kuska 232
Kvaltine 105
Kytle 205

L
LaBrunda 121
Lacastro 109, 135
Lacy 121
LaFountain 180
Lahr 121
Laine 137
Lake 311, 312, 317, 331
Lamarca 116
Lambertz 116
Lamkin 205
Lancaster 88, 96
Lane 173
Lanham 98
Lannin 105, 135
Lannon 121
Lapham 121
Lapierre 135
Lara 121
Larkins 304
LaRouque 207
Larson 116, 180, 206, 326
Lauber 121
Laver 121
Lavergno 116
Lawell 116
Lawhon 145
Lay 85, 95
Lazarus 121
Le Van 281
Leaf 105
LeBlanc 121
Ledbetter 135
Lee 195, 198, 202, 205, 206
Leff 312, 330
Lehmann 24
Leisenring 250
Lemak 105
Lemke 317
Lempke 326
Lentfer 72, 241, 248
Leonard 116
Leoni 195, 198, 200, 202, 207

Leraci 116
LeRoy 121
Leskovar 121
LeVasseur 206
Levenson 105
Lewis 56, 57, 58, 105, 135, 206
Lhevinne 137
Lietsch 317
Light 205
Lightwine 204
Liliedoll 73, 349
Lincoln 105
Lindbergh 294
Lindhorst 121
Linkley 109, 180, 207, 281, 282, 284
Linton 279, 301, 326
Lipker 317
Lipshitz 105
Little 105
Littlejohn 121
Litvinoff 109
Litzinger 105
Livingston 116, 207
Loasia 116
Lobato 109
Locker 207
Lofy 280
Logen 121
Logies 109
Lombardelli 109
Long 26
Loontjer 241
Lopez 109, 135
Lorrilord 109
Loughran 109, 112
Lowe 67, 68
Lowrey 312
Lubin 116, 122, 130
Lucht 329, 330
Lucy 116
Ludtke 113, 135
Luenenborg 24, 51
Luenenbotg 40
Luongo 194
Lutes 204
Lynch 121
Lynn 145
Lyons 207
Lytle 197, 200, 202, 211, 214, 227, 235, 236

M
MacArthur 148, 260
MacDonald 138
MacEacherin 109, 140
Madden 105
Madigan 105, 135
Madsen 105
Magin 204
Magnus 326
Magusson 180
Mahaffey 262, 263
Maher 308
Mahn 116
Mahoney 105, 116, 135
Maich 105
Maiewski 135
Malloy 205, 206
Malone 105
Malrait 121, 135
Mammen 241, 317
Mandeville 236
Manman 121
Mann 116
Manning 105, 116

Manske 116
Maple 312, 317
Maraldo 140
Marcy 206
Marfisi 140
Marketer 360
Marks 62, 63, 65, 66
Marple 140
Marquette 205
Marrs 207
Marsh 64
Marshall 109, 135, 180, 317
Martin 84, 95, 115, 116, 121, 180, 207, 281, 282, 284
Massey 109
Massingill 105
Massino 105
Mastin 195, 198, 202
Mathers 208
Matott 121
Matthews 318
Matya 121
Mawrytko 116
Maxson 195, 198, 200, 202, 207
May 116
Mazlow 105
Mazur 135
Mc Daniel 203
Mc Donough 213
McAbe 304
McAllister 194, 224, 226
McAnally 105, 206
McArthur 121, 168
McBay 116
McCahill 109
McCarthy 109, 195, 198, 200, 202, 207
McCarty 287
McCaslin 137
McClean 206
McClure 64
McColough 109
McCool 135
McCormick 121, 135, 241, 248
McCoy 24
McCubbin 140
McCullough 105
McDaniel 121, 135, 145, 195, 200
McDean 116
McDonald 105, 109, 121, 135
McDonough 201
McEldowney 116, 138
McElroy 181
McFarland 121
McGee 205
McGhghy 324, 326, 332
McGill 105
McGinley 256
McGinnis 145, 326
McGovern 313, 317
McGuire 116
McIlheran 105
McInvale 109, 111, 112, 134
McKeague 105
McKenzie 73, 186, 268, 311, 312, 349
McLaughlin 312, 313

McLay 116
McLean 206
McMillan 270
McMonimon 105
McMullen 116
McNamara 105
McPherson 105
McRaven 206
McSteen 121
McVicars 116
Meade 121, 122
Meadows 197, 200, 202, 211, 212, 214, 227
Mechan 109
Medoiros 121
Meith 323
Melchiarre 109
Menaker 109
Mentemeyer 204
Mercer 195, 198, 202, 205
Merneck 145
Merrifield 139
Merritt 135
Messenger 105, 106
Messing 189
Messingham 204
Meyer 332
Micera 109
Michels 189
Miessler 313, 317
Mieth 42, 320, 326, 332
Mikolajczyk 109, 135
Miles 151, 178, 195, 198, 202, 205
Miller 109, 116, 139, 151, 277, 278, 279, 281, 282, 283, 284, 285, 286, 287, 288, 301, 317
Mills 105, 245
Milnos 105
Mingucci 181
Minor 109
Minow 116
Miser 205
Mitchell 105, 116
Mittan 318
Moen 205
Moininger 105
Molnar 105
Monahan 137
Montagna 105
Montgolfier 29
Montgomery 140, 181, 314
Moore 105, 108, 135, 136, 138, 181
Morello 105
Morey 121
Morgan 249
Moriarty 105
Morris 121, 268, 270
Morrison 116, 121, 204, 248
Morrow 278, 289, 290, 291, 329
Morton 109, 112, 134, 135
Mosbey 161, 261
Moyer 51
Mrenak 195, 198, 201
Muehling 326
Mueller 205, 206

Muller 116, 127
Mullins 213
Mumford 140
Mumper 105
Munley 121
Murgatroyd 269
MURPHY 105
Murphy 116, 206
Murray 115, 121, 135, 205, 208
Murrey 287
Myers 177, 178

N
Nacke 292, 313, 317
Nahigian 105
Nahman 121
Naiman 317
Nairm 105
Nallia 181
Nasser 109
Navis 313
Neary 101
Neel 204
Nehigian 135
Nelms 109
Nelson 105, 109, 116
Nesbitt 197, 200, 202, 211, 214, 227
Nestle 205
Nettekoven 205, 206
Newell 268
Newman 109
Newton 105
Nicholls 194
Nickelhoff 206
Niederklein 154
Nieuport 283
Nixon 135
Noel 105
Nold 105
Norder 248, 332
Norris 137
Nosker 116
Nosse 140
Nugent 105

O
Oates 109
O'Brien 205
O'Donald 205
Oglesby 213
Ogurek 121
Ohlrich 326
Oien 105, 107
O'Keefe 105, 294
Okonieski 140
Oliva 252
Olivette 109
Olson 109, 112, 250, 251, 318
O'Malley 197, 200, 202, 211, 214, 227, 235
O'Neal 326
O'Neil 121
Orchard 140
Orgera 109
Ornstein 135
O'Rourke 121, 135
Orrico 140
Ortgies 63
Ortman 326
Osher 304, 317, 318, 320, 327
Ostrom 121
Ottomann 207

P
Paddock 259
Padgett 204, 207
Page 294, 301
Pagliaro 135

Paid 327
Painter 121
Pair 204
Paladino 197, 200, 202, 211, 214, 227
Paradies 109, 140
Parker 109, 121, 137, 281
Parks 64, 109, 135
Parshall 105, 135
Parsons 105
Patching 205
Pate 205, 207
Pater 109, 181
Paterson 105, 137
Patterson 197, 200, 202, 211, 214, 227, 236
Pavilonis 181
Payne 109, 205, 206
Paysen 307, 314
Payson 116
Pearce 176
Pearlman 204
Peck 135
Pelkey 116
Penry 306, 307, 309, 327, 328
Perkins 95
Perlberg 135
Perri 135
Perrine 140
Perry 327
Peschken 195, 198, 202, 207
Peterson 105, 116, 135, 195, 198, 202, 207, 236
Pettit 258
Petz 116, 117
Pfahl 236
Philippi 73, 317, 349
Phillips 88, 91, 109, 121, 123, 138, 241
Piccard 29
Pick 75
Pickard 116, 120, 134, 135
Pickup 205
Pieh 206
Pieldrszczah 205
Pierson 248
Piland 109
Piper 278, 305
Pitcher 204
Plooger 110
Plourde 109, 138
Pohlo 121
Polage 64, 249, 268
Polink 121, 122, 136
Pollogrino 116, 121
Ponticelli 109
Poole 109
Pope 197, 200, 202, 211, 214, 227, 230, 231
Popken 105
Porter 116, 117, 118, 135, 197, 200, 202, 211, 227, 234, 235, 236
Posner 73, 349
Post 121, 138
Potter 17, 24

Potts 109, 138
Pouliot 181
Powell 109, 207, 311, 314, 317
Powers 105, 106
Prchal 151
Prescher 105
Price 109, 213
Priefert 3, 4, 17, 24, 35, 36, 41, 61, 156, 157, 161, 194, 210, 216, 219, 220, 221, 223, 241, 247, 248, 274, 301, 327
Prince 253, 257
Progar 136
Puff 109
Pullium 216
Pumphrey 327
Putrius 105
Putz 205
Pyle 260

Q
Queen 181
Quinn 304
Quisno 105, 137

R
Radcliff 109, 135
Ragona 206
Raines 206
Rains 268
Ramirez 195, 198, 202, 207
Ramsbottom 269
Randolph 100, 102
Ranger 145
Rapin 205
Rasbach 116
Rasmussen 109
Rawlins 206
Ray 85
Ream 4, 249, 262
Reams 263
Rease 207
Redans 207
Reed 137, 138
Reeves 204
Reinke 317, 327, 332
Reinsch 363
Reisdorf 114, 116
Reiss 249, 327
Remke 185, 196, 199, 201
Rempe 327
Reneau 105, 136
Rensheim 116
Renz 311
Repeta 136
Resnick 109, 116, 140
Reyman 178, 179, 181
Rhodes 115
Rice 5, 162, 163, 164
Rich 121, 136
Richards 116, 207, 208
Richardson 109, 121
Richart 327
Rickels 105
Rickenbacker 307
Rickert 116
Ridgeway 111, 136
Ridgway 109, 134, 135, 136
Riechert 84

Rierson 105
Riley 93
Rim 109
Ring 12
Ringle 121
Rippe 63, 317
Rizek 327
Rizzuti 185, 187, 196, 199, 202
Roach 206
Roades 121
Robason 181
Robbins 195, 198, 200, 203, 207
Roberts 71, 105, 106, 121, 135, 136, 140, 197, 200, 203, 207, 211, 213, 214, 227, 235, 236
Robie 279, 281, 285, 291
Robinson 116, 204
Rocheleau 193
Rockney 207
Rocole 3, 32, 43, 47, 48
Rodenburg 314
Rodwell 238
Roe 140
Roger 118
Rogers 116, 185
Ronsheim 136
Roper 363
Rose 105
Rosefield 116
Rosen 109
Rosenbaum 73, 349
Rosenthal 164
Rositus 204
Ross 109, 121, 204, 327
Rosset 121
Rost 138
Roth 105, 109, 115, 121, 314, 315
Rothenburg 121
Rouse 117, 118
Route 121
Rowan 206
Rowbottom 204
Rowland 206
Ruehlen 181
Runkle 105
Ruppel 121
Rush 121
Rusk 181
Russ 136
Russell 3, 4, 84, 105
Rustad 136, 138
Ruszala 205, 206
Rut 63
Ryan 5, 50

S
Sabinsky 91
Salinsky 109
Salmons 204
Salyer 105
Samson 109, 116, 137, 138
Samuelson 109, 110
San Antonio 136
Sanders 105
Sanderson 207, 320, 327
Sanetta 138
Sanner 315
Sanny 204
Santos-Dumont 10, 13, 14, 51
Sapadin 138
Sass 99, 109,

248
Sattler 216, 217, 218, 219, 220, 221, 222
Sauer 121
Saunders 136
Savidge 291
Sawyer 121
Scarborough 136
Schainost 315
Schaitz 116
Schardt 327
Scharff 105
Schattler 121
Schenk 213
Schierhorst 181
Schievink 138
Schindler 121
Schlaebitz 99
Schleicher 241
Schleif 301
Schlenker 47, 51
Schmidt 185, 196, 199, 203, 207
Schmitt 136
Schmitz 332
Schmmel 207
Schnackenberg 116
Schneider 206, 304, 360
Schneifer 363
Schorn 214
Schran 109
Schreiber 116
Schroer 116
Schulze 138
Schuman 121
Schussele 317
Schwab 319
Schweer 63, 65
Scott 109, 138, 181, 205, 206
Seale 181
Sedden 317
Seeback 109
Sehorn 197, 200, 203, 211, 227, 233
Seiple 206
Sell 285
Senior 270
Sermersheim 116
Sewell 207
Seyfon 281
Shanahan 109
Shane 63, 121, 273, 302, 327
Sharp 301
Shaughnessy 181
Shaw 116, 136, 140, 206
Shearer 73, 181, 341, 349
Shedlock 105
Sheele 185
Sheldon 105
Shepard 109
Shepherd 100, 101, 116
Sheridan 105
Sherland 205
Sherman 115, 121
Sherrill 304
Shestack 140
Shetler 300
Shick 248
Shine 173
Shisler 178
Shoarer 116
Short 181
Shriner 121
Shuler 259
Shumaker 181
Sickley 121, 137

Sies 109, 111
Siewert 109
Sijewic 140
Sildar 116
Silvers 116, 117, 134, 135, 136, 138
Silverstein 105, 181, 185, 196, 199
Simeone 109, 138
Simmermen 105
Simpson 85, 272
Sims 140, 317
Singleton 109
Sinn 249, 267
Sivewright 105
Sjoberg 138
Sjoborg 105
Skalak 116
Skidmore 105, 116
Skrivanek 5, 249, 250, 251, 252, 253
Slagle 315
Slater 206
Slaughter 181
Slusher 139
Small 121
Smilos 105
Smith 84, 105, 109, 116, 136, 137, 139, 154, 195, 198, 203, 205, 255
Snyder 105
Sopwith 284
Southworth 207
Speakman 204
Spence 116, 121
Spencer 206
Spicher 26
Spieth 207
Spinney 116
Spinning 204
Spyres 139
St John 121
Stables 290, 329
Stacup 64
Staghan 121
Stagman 137
Staley 116
Stall 301, 327
Stanley 204
Stanton 204
Starck 268
Stark 84
Starr 109, 111, 112, 113, 121, 135, 136, 204
Stauber 315, 317
Stead 93
Steck 65
Stedman 116
Steed 89, 90
Steele 85, 205
Steinacher 250
Steiner 195, 198, 200, 203, 208
Stelling 248
Stephen 122
Stephens 121, 236
Sterner 116, 139
Stevenson 206
Stewart 93, 116, 140, 151, 327
Stimson 63
Stockwell 5, 25, 30, 50, 51
Stofer 317
Stokes 268
Stoner 121
Storz 207
Stout 105, 138
Strickland 185,

196, 199, 201
Strobel 281, 284
Strom 136
Strong 207
Struve 4
Stull 205
Suchukar 315
Suk 116
Sullivan 108
Sumpter 121
Sunderland 121, 137
Survilla 121
Sutton 206, 320, 327
Swan 109, 248
Swaney 327
Swank 285
Sweebe 140
Sweeney 109, 136
Swift 121
Switzgable 251
Synwolt 181
Syverson 204
Szacum 105, 138
Szymanski 105

T
Tack 121
Talbert 205, 207
Tall 204
Tanner 139
Tarrant 105
Tatnall 193
Taylor 95, 109, 116, 204, 206, 268
Tegtmeier 105
Teicher 116
Temchulla 134
Terkeurst 204
Tharpe 136
Thieme 121, 124, 134, 135, 136
Thietton 121
Thoensen 109
Thomas 3, 72, 181, 198, 249, 266, 271, 281
Thompson 64, 67, 109, 110, 116, 121, 138, 316
Thomson 285
Thornton 105, 136
Thrailkill 135, 137
Thrasher 268, 315
Thresto 208
Thurston 195, 198, 205
Tibbets 254, 359, 360, 363
Tibbetts 116, 136
Tibbits 260
Tickell 279
Tietjen 327
Timm 294
Tinder 136
Tinsley 207
Tippin 204
Titsworth 207
Tjaden 64, 69, 72
Todt 95
Tolisano 109
Toliver 287
Tom 109
Tombro 116
Tomey 105
Tompkins 116
Toney 136
Tosti 105
Toups 181
Townsend 207

Trailkill 134
Trapp 140
Traudt 327
Treadway 105
Trecek 204
Treichak 206
Trellwitz 248
Tripaldi 109
Tripp 109
Tritenbach 241, 243
Trogon 248
Trope 248
Truemper 121
Trumbower 194, 195, 198, 203, 205
Trumbull 136
Tucker 204
Tuis 205
Turekian 116, 137
Turkiowicz 121
Turley 140
Turner 100, 116, 117
Turpin 136
Twitchell 206
Tyler 113, 135, 136
Tyrell 136

U
Uhlman 181
Ullman 116
Umperovitch 109
Urbanek 116

V
Vaagen 121
Vadez 136
Valder 121
Valdes 204
Vallero 105
Value 159
Van Arkel 121
Van Cleve 181
Van Kouren 116
Van Lier 121
Van Sickle 116
Van Syclke 206
Vannater 116
Vaughn 281, 282, 286
Vejraska 318
Velker 138
Venable 105
Vennell 116
Verjraska 317
Verret 109, 136
Vest 364
Viaforo 109
Vian 105
Vickery 116
Visciglia 136
Vital 116, 136
Vitek 105
Vitrano 121
Vnoucek 254, 255, 256
Voegtlin, 181
Vogel 25, 26, 27, 45
Vogt 221, 222
Voigt 327
Vonderhaar 166
Voogd 105
Vorderstrasse 327
Vose 137
Vostrez 63, 65
Votava 67
Votaw 205
Votipka 324, 325, 334

W
Waack 51
Wade 121

Wagner 64, 109, 136, 190, 193, 197, 200, 203, 317
Walasley 174
Walborn 206
Walker 121, 283, 327
Wall 181
Walsh 121, 204
Walter 109
Walther 116
Ward 116
Waring 327
Warner 65, 105, 116, 135, 136, 139
Warsa 136
Warthen 316
Washburn 181, 195, 198, 200, 203, 207
Waterman 190
Watkins 105, 181
Watson 134, 136, 208
Way 138
Wayne 204
Weaver 116
Webb 116
Weber 65, 116
Weblemoe 292
Webster 105
Weddell 185, 196, 199, 201
Wedeking 63
Weihe 205
Weinstein 136
Weir 193
Weisbrod 136
Weiss 105, 134, 208
Weisz 105
Welch 4, 109, 317
Wellman 269
Wells 116
Wench 109
Wenske 327
Wenzlaff 364
Werner 317, 320, 327, 332
Werts, 181
West 72
Westbrook 134, 136, 140
Westerhoff 293
Westlake 105
Westrom 205
Whale 317
Whaley 156, 157, 161
Wheeler 116, 135, 136, 138, 208
Whidden 116, 138
White 134, 136, 207
Whitlock 109, 138
Whitson 138
Wickman 85
Widenhofer 136
Wieland 185, 196, 199, 201
Wiens 316
Wilde 105
Wilder 206
Wildern 105
Wiles 109
Wiley 121
Wilken 67
Wilkening 316
Wilkerson 181
Wilkes 5, 7, 9, 88, 100, 101, 103, 104, 110, 241, 248

Wilkos 105
Willard 70, 281
Willding 136
Williams 116, 121, 136, 195, 198, 203, 204, 208, 319
Williamson 3, 4, 5, 25, 36, 41, 63, 205, 216, 222
Willner 105
Willocks 109
Wills 309
Wilson 116, 121, 136, 181, 258, 314
Wilsons 272
Wiltse 121
Winand 204
Windmeyer 212
Wineinger 121
Wingfield 116, 120
Winkler 10, 17, 28, 45, 49, 50, 51
Winter 116, 136
Wite 116
Witt 136
Wittenberger 316, 317
Wolfe 316
Wolford 268, 270
Woltemath 268
Woltkamp 122, 136, 138
Wood 105, 109, 116, 120, 136, 137, 138
Woodle 121, 124
Woodrick 204
Woods 138, 213
Woodward 67
Wooldridge 140
Woozinski 205
Worrell 181
Worthington 116
Worthley 172, 173, 174, 181, 241
Wright 105, 134, 138, 140, 181, 311
Wunderlich 105

Y
Yaksh 136
Yakumithis 208
Yano 105
Yarian 109
Yorg 109
Yost 10, 12, 14, 16, 17, 19, 24, 25, 29, 30, 31, 41, 45, 46, 50, 51, 52, 53
Young 105, 109, 167, 248
Youngclaus 109
Yuhas 121

Z
Zabinsky 91
Zachary 109
Zathren 205
Zeitlin 258
Zetts 84
Zeuhlsdorf 327
Zickler 109
Zieman 136
Zierowicz 105
Zimmerman 125, 121, 137
Zingler 68
Zoeller 105
Zucker 204
Zuzzola 109
Zwerner 307

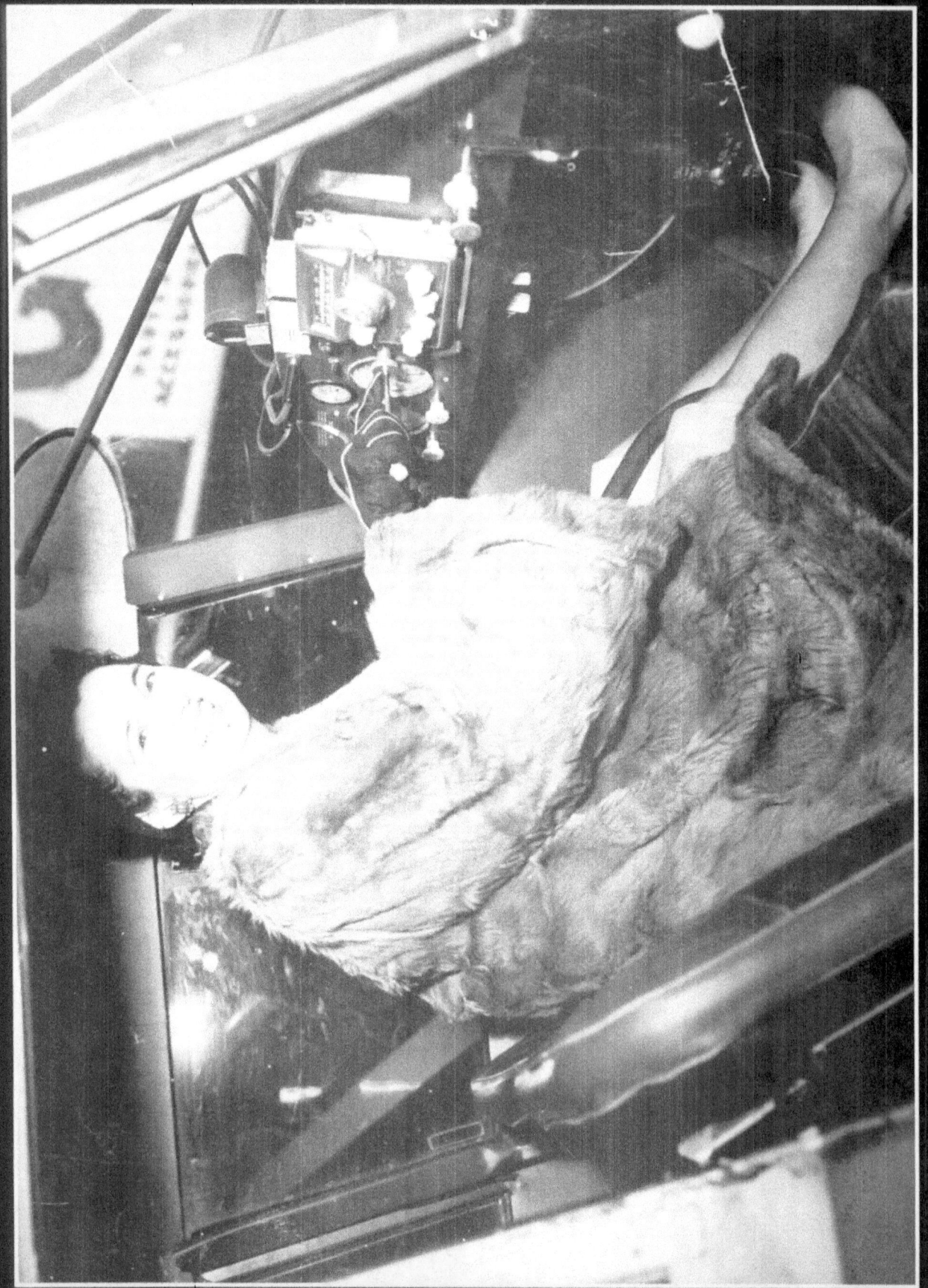

Pauline Hawks, Nebraska 99's President

The 99's, an organization of Women Pilots organizated by Amelia Earhart and named because there were only 99 women pilots in America at that time, required that all women pilots wear nylons and high heels while flying.

www.ingramcontent.com/pod-product-compliance
Lightning Source LLC
Chambersburg PA
CBHW060230240426
43671CB00016B/2897